D1776060

Hampshire Record Series Volume XIII

Parson and Parish in Eighteenth-Century Hampshire: Replies to Bishops' Visitations

Micheldever Vicarage in the {Archdeaconry of Winchester / Deanry of Somborne

John Imber Vicar. 1725

1. The Parish of Micheldever is computed to be more than 30 Miles in Compass.

2. The Vicarage of Micheldever consists of seven Tythings viz: Micheldever als Southbrook: Northbrook: Weston: West-Stratton: East-Stratton: Popham: and Northington. The Inhabitants of the four first Tythings do resort to the Church of Micheldever. The Inhabitants of

	Males		Females	
Micheldever,	70 years old & upwards	= 13	70 years old & upwards	= 17
	from 14 years old to 70	= 174	from 14 years old to 70	= 127
	under ye age of 14	= 73	under ye age of 14 years	= 84
		260		228
East-Stratton,	70 years old & upwards	= 5	70 years old & upwards	= 4
	from 14 years old to 70	= 66	from 14 years to 70	= 66
	under the age of 14	= 36	under the age of 14	= 32
		107		102
Popham,	70 years old & upwards	= 2	70 years old and upwards	= 1
	from 14 years old to 70	= 19	from 14 years old to 70	= 15
	under the age of 14	= 6	under the age of 14	= 4
		27		20
Northington,	70 years old & upwards	= 4	70 years old and upwards	= 4
	from 14 years old to 70	= 55	from 14 years old to 70	= 45
	under the age of 14	= 29	under the age of 14	= 29
		88		78
In the whole parish of Micheldever,	70 years old & upward	= 24	70 years old and upwards	= 26
	from 14 years to 70	= 314	from 14 to 70	= 253
	under ye age of 14	= 144	under ye age of 14	= 149
		482		428

in all 910

3. Micheldever,

Year	Marriages	Births	Burials
1721	1	12	12
1722	2	14	5
1723	7	13	11
1724	2	14	7

since July 1721	Marriages	Births	Burials
Stratton	8.	21.	13.
Popham	1.	4.	3.
Northington	8.	25.	15.

N.B. Those who die within the Chapelries of Stratton and Popham are buried at Micheldever: the Register of those Burials is kept in each Chapel. The Dead at Northington are buried there.

4. The most Noble Wriothesly Duke of Bedford is Patron.

Extract from the reply for Micheldever, 1725 (139).
(Hampshire Record Office, 21M65/B4/1/2 fo. 238)

Hampshire Record Series Volume XIII

Parson and Parish in Eighteenth-Century Hampshire: Replies to Bishops' Visitations

Edited with an introduction
by
W. R. Ward

Hampshire County Council
Winchester
1995

Hampshire Record Series

Published in 1995 by Hampshire County Council
The Castle, Winchester, SO23 8UJ

Printed by Hobbs the Printers of Southampton

ISSN 0 267 9930
ISBN 1 85975 031 1

Contents

List of Illustrations

Acknowledgements

I am very grateful to the editorial board of the Hampshire Record Series for the invitation to edit this volume, and for kind and cheerful assistance altogether beyond the call of duty from the County Archivist Rosemary Dunhill and her colleagues, especially Sarah Lewin, without whom the book could not have been produced at all, let alone expeditiously. Chris Woolgar is a canny lad at giving good editorial advice graciously. To all I am greatly indebted; and no less so to my wife who as usual has put up with the whole project.

W.R.W.

Introduction

Episcopal Visitations and their History

In the eighteenth century the Bishops of Winchester bowed to what was really a rather new fashion by conducting primary visitations of their see three times, Richard Willis in 1725, John Thomas in 1765, and Brownlow North in 1788. Anglican canons enjoined bishops to observe the medieval custom of a visitation every three years, but the special character of more recent visitations derived from contemporary circumstances. Some of the information they sought, especially on population and the number of dissenters had been collected nationally in the Compton census of 1676, as part of Danby's drive to convince Charles II that the established church was politically worth supporting,[1] and early eighteenth-century politics left their mark on diocesan visitation. For the great reconstruction of the English church after the Restoration had not been completed when the whole setting of the establishment was changed by the Glorious Revolution and the limited toleration of nonconformity it made possible. Canon law with its aspirations to unity of faith and moral conduct was then markedly out of line with recent statute law, notwithstanding that (as Blackstone caustically maintained half a century later) religious nonconformity remained a crime of which only the penalties were removed by the Toleration Act of 1689. Moreover the danger from Catholicism was transformed from that of a Popish and Stuart court influence to that of armed insurrection with the prospective backing of aggressive Catholic powers on the Continent. Bishops needed to know what they would find when they first arrived in their sees. Richard Willis, indeed, publicly complained of 'how little of this I have been able to find among the papers left me by my predecessors';[2] and, in company with other eighteenth-century bishops, he turned from the largely formal material which archdeacons had been extracting from churchwardens to seek information from incumbents.

The Winchester visitations fall into the general pattern of the visitations of their period which had been created by two of the most celebrated of contemporary bishops, Wake and Gibson, during their time at Lincoln, and especially in their primary visitations of 1706 and 1718;[3] a tradition energetically continued into the middle of the century by Thomas Secker. Secker was a former dissenter who tried to push the church along according to the rules,[4] and who, in his time at both Oxford and Canterbury, worked up the information yielded by the visitation returns into a *speculum* of his see.[5] Secker's inquiries embodied the general lines of the Winchester visitations below,[6] but displayed a clarity and a rigour in detail which was lacking in the Winchester visitations. Later visitations in other sees made concessions to the anxieties of their day, probing clerical non-residence in detail, inquiring after the state of the parish-church fabric, the recording of its property, the value of the livings.[7] Gradually the questions about the social notabilities resident in the parish, crucial in an age when the church was seeking to make its way on a basis of combining privileged establishment with private enterprise, dropped out.[8]

Willis's complaint of the negligence of his predecessors might have been the prelude to the operation of a new broom in the diocese.[9] Of very humble origins, he got himself on a fast track of promotion by obtaining a fellowship at All Souls immediately upon graduation, winning instant celebrity as a London preacher, and, less than ten years from matriculation, going off to Holland with William III in 1694 as his personal chaplain. A series of prebendal appointments followed, and, becoming Dean of Lincoln in 1701, Willis served in that see during Wake's great years as bishop. In pulpit and out Willis supported the right Whig causes, and in 1714 he was elevated to the see of Gloucester, the very first of George I's bishops, keeping his deanery *in commendam*. Continued political services brought Willis new appointments at court, in the administrative organs of the church, and finally, in 1721, the see of Salisbury. Willis, however, was now more of a meteor than a new broom, and had no defence against the criticism of one of his clergy, barbed though it was by political hostility:[10]

> My diocesan, Willis, was to have held his primary visitation this week. The days were fixed, and public notice given to all clergy to bring their children to be confirmed. Upon the death of Winchester, his lordship appears not, but sends his chancellor. Many poor clergy, who can have no notice, may bring their children with them and find no bishop to confirm them. No doubt his lordship is employed on that which will be of more use to the church of God, the getting a better bishopric for himself.

Sure enough, Willis landed the senior see of Winchester a bare two years after arriving in Salisbury, but his administrative achievement showed no improvement. A loose contemporary note inserted in the disorderly act book of his successor Benjamin Hoadly in the mid-1740s declared that no proper records had been kept since the death of Bishop Morley in 1684, and (galling as it is to the modern editor to have to admit) so far as bishops' act books were concerned this was true.

More immediately to our concern, Willis established a tradition of ineptness in episcopal visitation from which the Winchester diocese did not escape in the eighteenth century. One result of this is that to obtain a picture of church life in Surrey the modern student is much better advised to go to the returns of the Primate's dozen peculiars in the county which are preserved complete at Lambeth, than to the returns from the parishes comprised in the archdeaconry of Surrey which are preserved at

Winchester with an incompleteness which matched the inadequacy of their original drafting. He cannot but regret that the Primate had no peculiars in Hampshire or the Isle of Wight. The visitation inquiries of the Bishops of Winchester suffered defects both of commission and omission. Two important questions in the visitation of 1725 were very opaque to the clergy who had to answer them. The very first asked 'What compass of ground do you suppose to be in your parish?' Many clergy supposed that this was a question to do with beating the bounds, and endeavoured to estimate the circumference of the parish; others as we shall see tried square measures. But it was in any case a question inappropriate to those parishes of which there were a few in Surrey and a good many in Hampshire which had substantial detached portions intermingled with other parishes, or to parishes like Hayling Island (North) the curate of which (when the question was revived in 1788) gently put his Ordinary in his place with the answer 'between 7 and 8 miles exclusive [of] the mud that surrounds the greatest part of it'.[11] If there was no way in which the bounds of North Hayling could be beaten on the mud flats of Chichester Harbour, there was also no way this question could elicit the parochial problems created by two huge blocks of the New Forest, 50 square miles or so, extra-parochial but bordering on a score of parishes. The other obscure question, which Brownlow North in modelling his 1788 inquiries upon those of 1725 actually made worse, was a question about schools. The clergy were always uncertain whether this was a question simply about endowed schools, or about schools of any kind. The result was that their replies told the bishop no more than they tell us about the resources of church and parish for the education of the nation. What may be inferred from their replies is that in Surrey the proportion of parishes in which there was no educational provision at all was rather more than a third (a fraction better than Yorkshire at the time of Archbishop Herring's visitation in 1743) and changed little during the century; Hampshire and the Isle of Wight were noticeably worse off. Of 250 parishes replying in 1725 probably 117 had no educational provision at all; in 1788 the number was about 76 out of 185 respondents, and at neither date did Hampshire boast a parish like St Olave's, Southwark, where generous public endowment was supplemented by private enterprise to a quite remarkable degree. Given the uncertainties in the minds of the clergy replying to these questions, these estimates must be allowed a fair margin of error; but they leave no doubt that the diocese of Winchester was sadly impoverished compared with the elaborate network of parish schools sustained by the church in northern France. Without a specialized study it is indeed impossible to be sure whether the church reinforced such educational provision as there was by providing curacies for so many teachers, or undermined it by syphoning the energies of teachers into the support of clerical non-residence. Certainly the energies of Bryan Robinson who in 1788 combined the village school at Holybourne with the perpetual curacy of West Worldham and the curacy of Hartley Mauditt, James Cookson who combined a mastership at Churcher's College, Petersfield, with the (small) livings of Colemore and Priors Dean, and John Evans who in 1765 came out from a school at

Romsey at weekends to serve East Dean and Lockerley, two small curacies attached to Mottisfont, were spreading their energies rather thinly.[12] And in the schools as in the church, pluralities benefited the grandees rather than the proletariat of the profession.

The questions the Bishops of Winchester did not ask are in their way as surprising as those they did ask. The mainstream of visitations from Wake onwards included a question at the end inviting the respondent to bring any matter to the bishop's intention which he thought fit. The Bishops of Winchester eschewed a slot which might be thought likely to encourage complaints, and so the only complaints which turn up are those of perpetual curates mortified at the contrast between their beggarly stipends and the sums which lay rectors took out of their parishes. Other bishops inquired whether such legislative protection as there was for the interests of curates generally was locally implemented; the Bishops of Winchester did not. Other bishops inquired what services the clergy put on for the people, and in particular whether communion was administered often enough to give parishioners a reasonable chance to fulfil their obligation to communicate three times a year; the Bishops of Winchester did not. Still more striking, it was normal for bishops to inquire of their incumbents whether they resided, and if not, why not; except in John Thomas's visitation in the 'sixties the Bishops of Winchester did not. Thomas's visitation is indeed unlike the others; preoccupied with questions of property, it was a more like an archdeacon's than a bishop's visitation. As will transpire later, there may have been good reasons for this, and the new emphasis upon the church's housekeeping coincided with a welcome and successful effort to restore some order into the diocesan record-keeping. It is therefore all the more regrettable that Thomas's visitation seems to have been treated with some contempt by the clergy. Many returns were not completed; many were not signed; many were left to curates. The result leaves no doubt that the eighteenth-century Bishops of Winchester never knew how many clergy they had in their see, nor who they were; and when at the end of the century an attempt was made to keep track of curates, it was made in a pocket notebook beside the muddle of which the average undergraduate's personal timetable is a model of business organisation.

The fact that in 1788 Brownlow North went back in the main to the pattern of visitation adopted by Richard Willis in 1725 means that in this see the main development of the process was in form rather than substance. Willis sent a printed request for replies 'upon one or more sheets of folio paper' with a broad margin to permit of satisfactory binding-up. The visitations of 1764-5 and 1788 were handled by issuing a standard printed questionnaire. This format reduced the verbosity of many clerical replies, but made many of them less informative; and as Thomas and North, not having taken appropriate precautions with the margins, did not proceed to binding-up, many fewer have survived. There are thus fewer parishes than the student might have hoped for which a complete series of visitation returns mirror developments across two generations. And although compensation for the reluctance of the diocesans to inquire into the important questions of non-residence and pluralism can be found by exploiting extraneous sources, the results are too approximate to permit ready comparison with what is known of other parts.

Parish and Parson

If the Bishops of Winchester conducted their inquiries much less rigourously than other bishops, and the responses they evoked are less informative about church life in Hampshire than one might wish, question and answer together reveal a good deal about clerical mentality in Hampshire. The visitation of 1725 wound up by requiring incumbents to state the nearest post-town by which the ordinary might get in touch with them, and questions of geography, ecclesiastical and human, occupied first place in the visitations both of 1725 and 1788. The bishop's vision of his see was thus to derive from his subalterns' vision of their parishes. The question about the 'compass' of the parish was, as we have noted, a somewhat foolish one, but it set in laborious motion the wheels of clerical imaginations which had mostly been trained on Oxford classics rather than Cambridge mathematics. There were at the outset a number of attempts to get the bishop to see the impossibility or uselessness of what he was asking. The rector of Brighstone in the Isle of Wight put it plainly:[13]

> If by compass of ground is meant the ambitus or circumference of the parish, that cannot easily be determined, because in some parts of it other parishes intervene, but by the best judgment I can make it may be about 10 or 12 miles round. But if, as I conceive, the content or number of acres be intended, it contains about 2,000 acres.

In another bizarre parish in the Isle of Wight, Wootton, 'compass' was even less informative:[14]

> The compass of ground belonging to the parish of Wootton is about 2 miles, consisting only of 2 farms which are at 7 miles distance. The tenant of the farm contiguous to the church conforms to the Church of England as by law established, the other is an Independent,

in the eyes of the respondents almost the only Independent in the county; detached farms, however, were a common awkwardness of parish life in Hampshire.[15]

Like the incumbents of Brighstone and Wootton, most of the parish clergy determined that if 'compass' was what the bishop wanted, 'compass' was what he should have, could they but think how to produce it. There appear to have been only two parishes in the county where the bounds were beaten. Early in the century it was done at Andover every two years, took three days, and (perhaps for that reason) yielded no more precise result than 'between 20 and 30 miles'.[16] At Ashe the bounds were not merely perambulated but measured in 1788; this process produced the neat result of 'rather more than 15 miles', but appeared to the rector seriously to underestimate the area of the parish.[17] The rector of Newnham in 1725 actually paid for a survey to be done, but like a wise man he had his survey conducted in a square measure, acres.[18] Rowner too was surveyed in the early 'twenties with the same result, and with linear measures in furlongs.[19] What the clergy knew was that a really satisfactory answer to this question turned on having a monopolistic landlord in the parish who would go to the trouble of having proper estate maps made. This was still very unusual in the eighteenth century, and so far as the responses to the visitation inquiries tell, obtained in only one parish in the whole diocese, Farleigh in Surrey, where Merton College had its estates professionally mapped. The next best thing was what was known as 'computation'. Where care was taken in a parish with clearly defined bounds (such as Alverstoke, for example)[20] a useful result might be obtained; but in time it came to be admitted that there was such a thing as 'very lax computation',[21] and this was all the clergy generally could provide in 1725. There seem in fact to have been only two models to fire the clerical imagination. Much the commonest was to assume that the parish was rectangular,[22] and to present the bishop with a 'compass', based on the estimated length and breadth of the parish (or leave him to work it out for himself); the rector of Farringdon in 1725 assumed that his parish was circular, and in a homespun recollection of Greek mathematics calculated the compass 'at 3 mean diameters' to arrive at a result roughly half of that which his successor in 1788 attained by beating the bounds.[23]

These statistical gropings by the clergy have a double interest. To the parish historian the figures matters less than the impressionistic information with which they were frequently accompanied about the amount of forest, heath and common, which in Hampshire greatly magnified the problem of calculating the extent of parish. The point of the bishop's question about 'compass', so far as there was one, was that a parish still retained its ancient significance as a device for paying a parson, the bounds signifying the geographical limits within which tithe was due to him; but in so many Hampshire parishes the actively farmed, tithe-producing area was much less than the whole. To the ecclesiastical historian these answers have the second and greater interest of offering an insight into clerical *mentalité*. The fanciful legend that the Church of England once upon a time put a man of learning into every parish will not survive a reading of these returns; but the clergy were supposed to be a learned profession at a time when all professions were changing steadily in response to important changes in the intellectual ambience. Among these the growth of numeracy was as important as the spread of literacy. How did the Hampshire clergy fare in this respect?

The returns of 1788 make it clear that in important respects the Hampshire clergy had moved with the times at their own pace. In Surrey it is quite clear that more sophisticated statistical awareness convinced the clergy that their parishes were smaller than their predecessors had supposed, much as measuring the bounds suggested to the rector of Newnham that something must be wrong with his conception of the parish. He was by no means alone in finding his parish appearing to shrink about him.[24] In Hampshire cases where a direct comparison is possible, however, especially in country parishes, the parish appeared more often to have grown in the interim.[25] That this result was not simply the consequence of substituting one system of random guesswork for another, is evidenced by the fact that it was part of a general revolt against giving the bishop what he wanted, viz. 'compass'. The answers now came in overwhelmingly in acres, a more rational scheme of measurement and one more useful to the clergy in making agreements over tithe. What lay behind the new estimates in acreage comes clearly to light in the returns for Winnall and Wonston which were derived from the sum of all the acreages of the farms in the parish,[26] and in that from Soberton where the curate was frustrated in his attempts to make a similar return by the suspicions of the farmers in the parish that his inquiries were really intended to increase the financial burden upon them.[27] The fine fruit of this frame of mind, however menacing to tithe-payers, was exemplified in the precision of the return for Headley in 1788:[28]

> 14 miles square, or 8,960 acres square, at 640 statute-acres to the mile, of which are 2,434¾ acres arable, 242½ pasture, 285¼ meadow, 85½ woodland, and 5,913 of heathy common.

It is not surprising that the same incumbent reported on the other statistical conundrum set to the clergy, that of population, that 'in October last past, I took an account of the number of houses and persons in this parish; that of houses was 137, and that of persons, 720'.

It is noteworthy that when asked for statistics of the rites of passage, baptisms (curiously referred to by the bishops as 'births'), marriages and burials, most of the clergy went back to their registers and did their arithmetic; but they seem never to have used this demographic material to calculate answers to the question about the 'number of souls' in the parish. The phrase 'number of souls', however, had its effect. When replying to the Compton census in 1676 clergy had often returned numbers of communicants rather than a total of population; now they aimed to produce a head count, often distinguishing the number of children and servants. In this matter the clergy could be extraordinarily vague in even the smallest parishes; 'one family ... who may reside here about 4 months in the year',[29] 'one family, which consists of Farmer Hill and about 5 or 6 servants',[30] 'about 30',[31] 'not above 40',[32] 'near 4 score',[33] being typical offerings even in cases where the result is not offered as a guess. The clergy clearly knew that there were systems of computation for the purpose,[34] and the question, as with the compass of the parish, was what they were, and how to deploy them. In Alverstoke (including Gosport) and the Portsmouth parishes, the problem was at its worst owing to wild swings of business between war and peace; naval mobilisation might treble the number of marriages, and lead to steep increases in the number of baptisms and burials.[35] The rector of Alverstoke in 1725 conceived an ingenious, if imprecise, method of dividing this problem into two:[36]

> Parishioners or inhabitants in families which pay to the rates of church and poor &c. may be reckoned at 3,000. The poor, inmates and strangers [are] a flux body, and not to be ascertained, [but] may be guessed at 1,500.

As those in receipt of poor rate could be reckoned as readily as those assessed to it, the 'guess' at the remainder was probably a good one.

In most parishes the problem was of course easier to grasp. In 1725 the curate of Fawley (standing in for the non-resident incumbent, William Bradshaw, Bishop of Bristol) conveyed the impression that he had conducted a private census:[37]

> According to the strictest examination and inquiry I could make, it [the population] consists of men, women and children, 692;

and in a number of small parishes phrases such as 'upon the strictest calculation', '370 souls, neither more nor less', and confident statements of population to the last digit, suggest that something similar had taken place.[38] The vicar of Micheldever had no scruple in analysing the population of his parish and three chapelries by sex and age.[39] In populous parishes, however, this was less easily arranged, and precision of response could not be expected as a by-product of familiar pastoral oversight. The clergy knew that the professional enumerators of population were given to reckoning households and then applying a multiplier; but which multiplier? What is disconcerting about the parish population returns (which before the census of 1801 are the chief evidence we have) is their clear demonstration that the clergy applied multipliers of 3,[40] 3½,[41] 4,[42] 5,[43] 5½,[44] 6,[45] 6½,[46] and even 7.[47] Some variation was of course essential. Fashionable parishes would carry more servants per household than unfashionable ones; it may be that in urban parishes people were packed in more tightly per house than elsewhere, and the figures carry the plausible suggestion that the size of families increased as the eighteenth century proceeded. However it is clear enough that in the early eighteenth century the diocese of Winchester was entirely innocent of that close cooperation between doctors and clergy which a generation or more before had produced in Breslau the best of all vital statistics, and had got them to London to the delight of the English actuaries.[48] Even here, however, there was progress to report. In 1788 the incumbent of Otterbourne, Samuel Gauntlett, later Warden of New College, Oxford, was able to report that in 1781, i.e. not long after his own entry into the parish, he had conducted an enumeration, and established a population of 357;[49] and the estimates of other incumbents were not wildly out of range of the totals produced by the census of 1801.

Gaps in the evidence and special circumstances make the demographic evidence of the Hampshire returns more difficult to assess than that of Surrey. Surrey was a classic illustration of the way the eighteenth-century increase in population was achieved by a triumph of rural fertility over urban mortality. The country parishes had a consistent surplus of births over burials, a surplus in part balanced and in part consumed by the great surplus of deaths (many of them of immigrants) over births in metropolitan parishes. Even country towns of modest size had difficulty in maintaining level-pegging between births and deaths. This pattern was repeated in Hampshire in a less clear-cut fashion. The rural parishes everywhere had the expected surplus of births. At the beginning of the century Andover had a small surplus of deaths, Alton a small surplus of births, Basingstoke broke even, and Winchester, perhaps more creditably than some cathedral towns, also just about held its own. The crude figures for Portsmouth report political and administrative rather than demographic facts; it was normal for there to be a net surplus of births in peacetime and of burials in wartime, until 1719 when military burials began in St Mary's and produced a level of peacetime burials twice as high as the births. The reporting for Portsmouth for 1788 is less good than for 1725, but if Portsmouth and Portsea are taken together, and an attempt is made to strip out the political accidentals, it looks as if the town normally had a surplus of births. This was actually the case throughout the century with Southampton, and it may be that the port-towns recruited for business purposes a younger population which stood them in good demographic stead. If so they did much better than Surrey port-parishes on the lower Thames like Rotherhithe and Bermondsey. Meanwhile Basingstoke had progressed from breaking-even to a surplus of births, and Winchester held its own by the skin of its teeth.

Parson and Parish

The clergy's route to the parish was via the patron, and the advowson, or right to present, was a marketable commodity. This last state of affairs made the clerical career more of a gamble than it need have been, because, at least in the Winchester diocese, the trade in advowsons was a good deal more brisk than the modern student is given to expect. Over the diocese as a whole, though more in Surrey than in Hampshire, a surprising number of clergy were unsure where the patronage of their parish was located, presumably because it had changed since they were appointed.[50] The result of this lively speculation in advowsons was that it was very unusual for patronage to remain in the same lay families right down the century, and that some very curious and complicated arrangements arose from the willingness of even clerical and academic landlords (such as St Cross Hospital near Winchester, or Winchester College) to lease property for three lives, including the advowson.[51] Speculation in advowsons certainly implies willingness to buy; but the readiness of Hampshire gentry families to sell raises questions about the extent of their commitment to the church. On the evidence of the replies below the presentation to only 29 parishes remained in the hands of the same family from 1725 to 1788, and of these six were clerical families in which the patron presented himself to the living and no less than nine were in the Isle of Wight. What gave stability to (or imposed a deadweight upon) Hampshire patronage was the fact that practically half of it was in institutional hands which did not sell; a quarter of the half belonged to Oxford and Cambridge colleges (with Queen's College, Oxford in the lead), a handful, including several in Winchester, were in the gift of the King or Lord Chancellor, a few belonged to the chapters of Winchester, Salisbury or Chichester, and the lion's share, a goodly patrimony indeed, was held by the bishop himself. When efforts to sway the political opinions of the clergy were of first-rate political concern, possession of the see of Winchester was of more than prestigious or symbolic importance; it carried with it ample inducements to party loyalty in others, and it is not surprising that the first three Hanoverian bishops, Charles Trimnell (1721-3), Richard Willis (1723-34), and Benjamin Hoadly (1734-61), were all strenuous defenders of the new political system.

Winchester was not one of the sees in which the bishop refused to ordain non-graduates or admit them to benefices. Nevertheless, here as elsewhere, the university degree was the badge of the professional guild of the beneficed clergy, more of whom sported letters behind their names than can be traced with certainty in the lists of university alumni or of the Lambeth degrees conferred by the primate. A few had matriculated but never graduated. But in so far as the underworld of the curates comes to light in these papers, it reveals as in the Archdeaconry of Richmond,[52] and in Wesley's encounters with the clerical subalterns, a sizeable body of men who lacked the professional badge, and must limit their ambitions accordingly. A peculiarly heroic effort to pay the Oxford MA fees was made by William Hailes, curate of Titchfield in 1725. He served with Admiral Byng at Messina 'where by his share of the Spanish plunder he was enabled to take the degree of MA'. Alas! even the MA seems not to have qualified him for a benefice any nearer home than Jamaica. The only certain route to a living was to accumulate capital not for a degree, but for an advowson, the route taken by Griffith Richards, curate of Bedhampton in 1788, but finally in 1819 patron and rector of Farlington. This achievement could not have been common, and, unknown both to their ordinary and to posterity, the Hampshire curates, with their fellows in Surrey, remain a ghostly army in both senses of the word.

Yet there was nothing incompatible between curacy and benefice. For the Hampshire clergy were notorious non-residers. Dr Virgin has lately calculated that in the early part of the century the proportion of the clergy who were pluralists varied a little from see to see, usually in the region of 16-20%, and that it was always unusual for incumbents to hold preferments in more than one diocese.[53] My own count based on rather different principles in a see where the bishops only once asked the clergy whether they resided, and which, depending on information about pluralities derived from outside sources, is bound to be an underestimate, is less encouraging. Of the 250 parishes responding to the inquiry of 1725, 137 had incumbents who at some time during their tenure held other preferment (i.e. incumbents whose other preferments were in the Hampshire archdeaconries are counted more than once; there was almost no overlap with the archdeaconry of Surrey, though it was in the same diocese); these pluralities seem to have given rise to 65 cases of non-residence. A good many of these were clergy living well outside the diocese. By contrast there were 107 parishes which were held by men of a single living (and there was one vacancy).[54] In 1765 the question about residence was asked direct, the main effect of which was to reveal other reasons for non-residence than pluralities. In that year of 184 parishes whose replies survive 103 were held by men with other preferments and 54 without. The very large total of 87 cases of non-residence was only partly due to pluralities. There were now ten cases where the incumbent pleaded inability to reside on the ground that there was no house, or no house thought suitable. In two cases the squire was at fault. At Wickham 'my patron, Mr Rashleigh, wanted the parsonage for himself and family, till he had repaired his own house', while at Widley 'though a rectory, I have neither house, out-house, or any other building whatever, or place even to putt a horse in, though where and what they were is sufficiently plain, and swallowed up by the squire, [I] should be glad to know by what means, power or authority'.[55] Cases of this sort do not appear in 1788, though two cases of non-residence due to illness and old age respectively do. 188 responses then yield a count of 131 parishes where the incumbent held additional preferment, 44 where he appears not to have done so, and 96 cases of non-residence. Thus it seems reasonable to infer that pluralism and non-residence, always high in the Winchester diocese, increased somewhat as the century progressed, without ever challenging the levels attained in the see of London, where, according to the calculations of Professor Viviane Barrie-Curien, 71% of the clergy were non-resident by 1790.[56]

In Hampshire as elsewhere various factors could be pleaded in extenuation or aggravation of this result. It is quite clear that parishes were rarely left without pastoral assistance of any kind. A curate would be hired or assistance sought from a neighbouring incumbent, sometimes on a long-term basis, as the rector of Bramdean helped out the rector of Hinton Ampner in his old age.[57] It is also true that some parishes in Hampshire must have involved so little work that it was less anomalous to hold them in tandem with another appointment, than to hold them solo, and that some parishes in the city of Winchester (as in the city of London) were so tiny that it was difficult for the parson not to be non-resident, even if he lived nearby and did the duty. J. M. Newbolt who was rector of both St Mary Kalendar and St Maurice parishes in Winchester in 1788 sized up the one as 1,335 feet by 450, and the other as 1,170 feet by 1,365.[58] He may well have felt that by the time the churches had been taken from the parishes there was hardly room to reside; though this does not explain why he left both to the same curate, any more than the fact that the rector of another tiny Winchester parish, St Michael in the Soke, had no house there in 1765 explains why he lived in Minorca.[59] There is a certain sense in which the argument about pluralities as it raged in the early nineteenth century and as it has continued in the historiographical tradition established by Norman Sykes is a very artificial one. The eighteenth-century church inherited an ancient administrative structure which had escaped the upheavals created on the Continent by the Reformation, Counter-Reformation, the reforms inspired by the *Aufklarung* and the changes enforced by foreign conquest, and operated it partly by doubling up and partly by an impenetrable system of subcontracting for labour. Parsons and curates were not mutually exclusive categories. Of the clergy who appear in the return to the visitation of 1788, James Cookson was vicar of the two parishes of Colemore and Priors Dean, and curate of East Tisted as well as a master at Churcher's College.[60] Gabriel Tahourdin was vicar of Hannington, curate of Bentley and of sundry other parishes in Surrey.[61] Griffith Richards was vicar of Empshott, curate of Bedhampton, and curate also of Farlington, the advowson of which he subsequently bought and used to obtain the living.[62] Curates also multiplied curacies. John Woodburne was curate of three parishes in Winchester.[63] Thomas Trodd was curate of Petersfield and Liss.[64] To multiply curacies or to add them to a living was in principle open to the same objections as holding a plurality of livings, but as curacies were not benefices they never attracted the same political attention.[65] Very occasionally Anglican concessions to dignitarianism did. In this diocese they were chiefly represented by the cathedral and other endowments of Winchester itself. Whatever the case for cathedral appointments *sine cura animarum*, there was less to be said for the way prebendaries and others laid hands on parishes all round Winchester and ran them vicariously by curate.

In due course pluralities came to be defended by two kinds of argument. One was based on the rights of property, the title a man had to do what he would with his own. This argument creaked under the consideration that parish endowments were like trust funds which, in the case of absentee pluralists, were being diverted from at any rate the personal performance of the objects of the trust. It was also held that many benefices were below the bread-line, and could not be held at all without supplementation from elsewhere. No one was blind to the force of this view, though it too was severely weakened by two considerations. Early in the nineteenth century polemical writers established £150 p.a. as the minimum on which a clergyman could survive. This sum was not merely twice what a Wesleyan preacher was paid; it implied in an hierarchical social pyramid which was as steep in terms of range of incomes as it was flat in terms of human numbers above the base, that the lowest acceptable place for clergy was in the top 7 or 8% of earners. This was a view which the spokesmen of the clergy failed to establish then, and which seems breath-taking now. It had also two severe practical flaws. On the eve of the Revolutionary and Napoleonic wars which exacerbated a rise in food prices which evoked a chorus of complaint from the clergy, the system of subcontracting for labour amongst them makes it impossible to calculate now, and made it impossible to guess then, what the actual take-home pay of the clergy was. But for very many it was more than the stipend of a single parish or a single curacy. The second flaw in the defence of pluralities as a stop-gap alleviation of clerical poverty, is that there seems no doubt that the system did much more for the grandees of the profession than for the proletariat. As it happens the Winchester diocese has a spectacular (rather than typical) example of the way the system could work. John Hoadly, the son of Benjamin Hoadly, began his education at the Middle Temple before going up to Cambridge, and looked as though he was proceeding on the law line. A year after his father became Bishop of Winchester, however, he was ordained and immediately appointed Chancellor of the diocese, a post he held till his death in 1776. His entry in the Cambridge *Alumni* tells the rest of the story with a concentrated eloquence:

> Chaplain to the Prince of Wales. R. of Michelmersh, Hants., 1737. R. of Alresford, 1737. R. of Wroughton, Wilts., 1737-60. Preb. of Winchester

1737-60. R. of St Mary, Southampton, 1743-76. R. of Overton, Hants., 1746-76. Master of St Cross, Winchester, 1760-76.

And for what intellectual services to the church is his memory cherished? 'Poet and dramatist'.

The fact that so many incumbents did not reside upon one or more of their charges did not mean that nothing ever happened about the parish churches of Hampshire. Even so friendly a critic of the eighteenth-century church as the late Dean Sykes, wrung his hands over its poor performance in church building.[66] In fact more churches were built where they were needed in the period than Sykes appreciated, as in Hampshire Trinity Chapel at Gosport was built in 1696,[67] and it was in fact to the credit of churchmen that, unencumbered by the delusions which in the next century led to competitive church-building by establishmentarian and anti-establishmentarian forces, they did not pour good money after bad in building where churches were not needed. Moreover it is becoming clear that a good deal of energy was expended in the eighteenth century in enlarging (or making more comfortable) the accommodation in existing churches. Most of the information about this in the returns which follow is provided by Bishop Thomas's visitation of 1765 which enquired whether the church was in good repair, and whether 'the fabrick of the church [had] been altered in any respect, and [whether] ... any pews [had] been erected, galleries built, vaults dug, or dead bodies removed without a licence or faculty from your ordinary'. The way in which the two questions were phrased opens the possibility that the returns might underestimate both the ravages of time upon the church building, and also the amount of contemporary improvement which might have gone on without a faculty.

Taken at their face value, however, the returns support allegations of torpor in neither their nineteenth nor their twentieth century forms. Few incumbents were prepared to say that their church buildings were in poor repair. The vicar of Catherington reported that 'the chancel which belongs to Mr John Brett, a minor, is greatly out of repair. We have everything else that is necessary in good order.'[68] At Bentley 'the great rains and violent winds which we had last year have made some repairs necessary, which the churchwardens and parishioners have promised shall be done this summer.'[69] At Sydmonton 'the chancel is repairing, all besides [is] in good order.'[70] At Widley and Wymering 'both are in as good repair as the generality of churches are, and going to be made better.'[71] The worst case was that of Popham, a chapelry of Micheldever, which may cast some light on the lost churches shortly to be discussed. 'Popham chapel is in so ruinous a condition that divine service cannot be performed there.'[72] But set against these the following. In 1744 the church at Cheriton 'was burnt and rebuilt much after the same manner as before,'[73] At Old Alresford (one of the parishes of the notorious John Hoadly) 'the church was rebuilt AD1753.'[74] At Blendworth 'the church has been entirely rebuilt within about 7 years.'[75] At Stratfield Saye 'the church [was] lately rebuilt.'[76] At Worting 'the chancell [was] rebuilt on the old foundation, and the pews repaired'.[77] Farlington church 'hath been no otherwise altered than from a ruinous condition to a good and decent repair.'[78] At Buriton 'our church was entirely new pewed and a gallery built 30 years ago. The north side of it was handsomely rebuilt last summer.'[79] Lymington chapel had been enlarged ten years previously,[80] while at Whitsbury the 'late Mr Delafaye erected the spire, and built the vestibule and vestry room at his own expence.'[81] There were major refurbishments at East Dean and Rowner, while Houghton boasted that 'the fabrick of our church and chancel have not been at all altered, but have been lately very handsomely repaired and beautified.'[82] Twenty-five years before Kings Worthy had added a gallery by subscription, and there were new galleries at Mottisfont, Lockerley, and Botley.[83] Additional seating at Whitchurch and Bedhampton catered for both public and private convenience,[84] while in places larger windows made prudent concession to theological enlightenment. In view of the fact that in the generation before the inquiry of 1765 a huge proportion of the disposable capital of the nation had gone into the national debt to finance two tremendous wars, this enthusiasm for the utility and beauty of the sanctuary (whether the parson was at home or away) must be regarded as notable.

There was, it must be confessed, a darker side to this story, darker both in its implications, and in the fact that the clergy generally seemed unable to cast any light upon its history. While the Hampshire archdeaconries were improving the capital stock they had inherited from earlier generations, they were also losing track of part of the patrimony. The only parson able even to date the process was William Griffin, vicar of Arreton (Isle of Wight) from 1690 to 1732. He relates that:

> there were at the beginning of the reign of James I 2 free chapels in the parish. One called St Martin's of Britilisford appointed for ever, of whose foundation I can give no account, the incumbent whereof then was one Thomas Cowdray, a scholar of Oxford, having no other living. The other was the chapel of Standen appointed for ever, of the foundation of Richard Cowvert, the incumbent whereof was John Roo, clerk. But now of these chapels there are scarce any remains to be seen.[85]

Sometimes the event was more recent. The curate of Breamore recorded in 1725 that the Duke of Manchester had:

> the nomination to the tythes of Southcharford and the chapel there annext by will to the rectory of Breamore. But that chapel (which within my own memory was a very fair strong stone building) has been taken down and the enclosures thrown open, and a barn, or part of a barn, built across where the chapel stood.[86]

Micheldever, where by the 'sixties, Popham chapel was unused and ruinous, had by 1725 lost other properties altogether:

> There was formerly a chapel at West Stratton. Besides thes[e] in a large tract of land called Norrington ... heretofore stood a chapel. The spot of

> ground whereon it stood, with some adjacent parts is known by the name of Stanchester, now ploughed by husbandmen, as far as the foundations will permit.[87]

A chapel was also lost at Odiham, the very recollection of the site of the Cowderoy chapel at Sherborne St John had gone, and the Godsfield chapel in Swarraton parish, not endowed or served, looked as though it might be bound for the same fate.[88] At Petersfield, 'we learn from tradition that there was formerly a chapel dedicated to St Andrew, but there are now no vestiges thereof remaining, nor have been from time immemorial'. But there was comfort there in the spectacle of 'a dissenting meeting-house in ruins which has not been used these 50 years.'[89] Beside these losses (which almost all seem to have occurred in what are conventionally regarded as ages of faith) Thomas Rogers's encroachment of twelve inches upon North Hayling churchyard, and the ravages of Thomas Archer's hogs in North Waltham graveyard, the worst that the 'age of negligence' could produce, seem very small beer indeed.[90]

Unwillingly to Church?

If the behaviour of Hampshire Anglicans as informal trustees of church property gives pointers, none of them unequivocal, to the strength of their spiritual affiliation, their bishops never asked the direct questions which in other sees cast light on the matter, and in the whole century only one parson, the rector of Farlington in 1765, permitted himself the aside: 'we have no professed dissenters, and consequently no meeting-house in the parish; and yet alas we have more absentees from the church than I could wish'.[91] The bishops asked the inevitable questions about the obvious rivals to the church, the Papists and the Dissenters, and went on doing so in such a way as to discourage their clergy from perceiving that by the end of the century the denominational system those questions presupposed had changed substantially. It must be said, however, that the Hampshire clergy answered these rather limited questions with much less intelligence and perception than their colleagues in Surrey who contrived to tell their ordinary a good deal more than he asked. Part of the trouble was that so many incumbents were non-resident; part was that they came through a highly institutionalised and establishmentarian patronage system; and part was that organised religious deviance in Hampshire was always so weak as to encourage a contemptuous rather than an observant attitude. Phrases like 'there are no meetings of protestant dissenters of any kind (I thank God)', or 'I have the pleasure to say we have no Papists nor protestant dissenters', or 'there are 6 Quakers, 1 of which is a man of weak understanding, and but one degree above an idiot. 2 of the other 5 are an old day-labourer and his wife, and the remaining 3 are a thatcher and his wife, and son', abound.[92] Expansive satisfaction with this state of affairs encouraged the rector of Quarley perhaps to give away more than he intended:

> We have no meeting and not one dissenter. My Lord, I have 2 more parishes in Wiltshire, one as bigg again as Quarly, and the other 5 or 6 times as bigg, and but 1 dissenter in 'em both.[93]

If the Baptists did well at Milford it could hardly be on merit. 'Anabaptists in number 79, edified by Simon the thatcher and John the cooper.'[94] Still, as the last remark shows, reporting from all round the county is bound to cast some light on the fate of religious life outside the church of England, provided that it did not escape the institutional framework to which the episcopal information network was tied.

The fate of the Roman Catholics is not quite simple. Over much of Hampshire as of Surrey the organised Catholic cause collapsed with the total desertion of the propertied classes, leaving behind a sad and tiny unshepherded diaspora who could certainly be of little use to any attempt to overthrow the Protestant succession by force. There were a few cases where men of property might be able to provide pastoral assistance for themselves and their brethren in the faith. Hence the comment of the vicar of Twyford in 1725 about his Catholics:

> 10 families consisting of about 90 souls. The only landed man among them is Henry Wills Esq, who is supposed to have in several counties about £1,000 p.a.[95]

In the middle of the century similar support was provided by the Tichborne family near Cheriton, and by Lord Fingall at Newtown.[96] The Compton census in 1686 had noted numbers of Catholics, in absolute terms not great, but relative to most of the country considerable, and certainly large enough to permit a sense of group solidarity, in Winchester and in the Droxford deanery stretching into the south-east of the county. These areas of strength persisted into the eighteenth century, Winchester being one of the early areas where the Catholic cause regained an organisation. Winchester had been a special case since Charles II had fled there from the plague in London, and commissioned Wren to build him a palace. The Queen and her chaplains and the Duke of York (the future James II) came, and the penal laws were to a great extent locally ignored. A Catholic gentleman, Roger Corham, then went beyond the usual gentry assistance to the faithful by keeping a private chaplain, by appointing a resident priest and giving a house for resident priests to live in. The growth to which this led was reported briefly and uninformatively by the Winchester clergy, but Thomas Brereton, a minor canon, who had the parishes of St John and St Peter Chesil, was thoroughly nettled. 'There are 3 distinct large families who are profest Papists of no considerable note nor substance, and some more poor people who have been seduced by rich Roman Catholicks in the city and, maintained by their allowances, embrace their communion and go to their mass, as I am informed.' In St Peter's 'there are about 8 profest Papists of no considerable note nor substance who go to gentlemen's houses in town where mass is said; and some others who do not openly own the irreligion receive weekly or monthly contributions from them. I find a predominant spirit of Popery among many of my parishioners which urges me the more strenuously to confute their errors among many of my parishioners in almost all discourses. But though I preach with as discreet zeal and moderation as I can, yet I am abused, insulted and persecuted by the prevailing party of rich Papists and their correspondents who instigate the common people to revile me in the street.'[97] Brereton moved off to the quieter pastures of Preston Candover but they were no more trouble-free; his notice in the *Alumni* concludes with the quotation, 'when or where he will be hanged is not yet known'. But that strong-arm tactics against the Winchester Papists were under consideration is implied in the report from St Thomas's:

> Papists or reputed Papists, about 40 or 50, the chief of whom were William Sheldon Esq., George Bolney Esq., Rowland Bellasis Esq., Mrs Smith. These have considerable estates, but not in this parish. The houses Mr Bolney and Mrs Smith inhabit are their own.[98]

By 1765 the Catholics had a chapel of their own in the parish of St Mary Kalendar, and by 1788, so far as the visitations show, were accepted as as part of the parish life and growing only slowly.[99]

The other main area of Catholic strength in the late seventeenth century, the extreme south-east of the county, around Havant, Warblington, Bedhampton and points immediately north and west, also survived and became organized. At Havant there was already a regular Catholic congregation meeting in 1725, and by 1765 they had a 'mass-house'. By 1788 the local congregation was supposed to have doubled over the century and they were still attracting worshippers from the entire neighbourhood.[100] They, in short, exemplified what is known of the Catholic community as a whole in the second half of the eighteenth century, viz. a period of steady growth, a growth all the more curious because it took place at the very gates of Portsmouth, where a peculiarly militant form of Protestantism afforded shelter for every variety of Protestant dissent and kept Popery firmly at bay. After the end of the Dutch wars, the principal function of Portsmouth was to hammer foreign Papists hard.

The dissenting enterprise in Hampshire in this period was clearly on a much bigger scale than that of Roman Catholicism, but the returns are not very informative about it. Two things, however, emerge. Nonconformity in 1725 was distributed on much the same lines as in the previous century had been revealed by the registration of meeting-houses when the penal laws were suspended and by the Compton census. Dissent was almost exclusively an affair of the towns (Winchester excepted) from Andover and Basingstoke down to Portsmouth and Southampton, though it also survived notably in small communities fringing the New Forest, Fordingbridge, Ringwood, Lyndhurst, Fawley, Lymington and Christchurch. What is suspect in the reporting is that Independency which had been the dominant force in Hampshire dissent in the seventeenth century, and which nourished its most distinguished nonconformist son in the eighteenth, Isaac Watts, receives hardly a mention, and attention is concentrated on Presbyterians, Baptists, and Quakers, the latter no doubt because of their prospective threat to clerical income from tithe.[101] The second salient feature of the reporting is the evidence it provides of the decline of nonconformity, and here it is accurate enough. Even in 1725 the

Baptist meeting-house in Alverstoke was 'rarely frequented, and by a very few persons', while the Presbyterian meeting-house was occupied by a congregation of mixed denominational background, here perhaps the result of necessity rather than principle.[102] At Kingsclere there was still a Presbyterian congregation 'but at present in a very declining way. Their number may be about 3 score'.[103] And there were the other tell-tale signs; isolated dissenting families started coming to church, or at any rate sending their children.[104] It was much the same story with the Quakers. In 1725 they were reduced to 3 families at New Alresford and rarely met; by 1765 their meeting-house had long been abandoned and was in ruins.[105] In 1788 this fate was to be expected at Baughurst where the 'Quakers' meeting-house [was] seldom attended except by the male part of only one family'.[106] The returns, however, are alive to the fact that for Reformed congregations and for Quakers there was a possible intermediate stage between organisational collapse and final extinction, the house meeting. These existed in 1725 in Chalton and Whippingham (Isle of Wight).[107] This device, equally useful to dissenters without a ministry and religious seekers weary of institutional Christianity, was a target of revivalists all over Protestant Europe;[108] English Methodists also got their movement off the ground quickly by absorbing many groups of this kind. But this sort of uninstitutional or anti-institutional religious practice was beyond the ken of the Bishops of Winchester and also of the Hampshire clergy who made a much worse job of detecting and reporting it than their colleagues in Surrey.

Methodism was, however, reported as having a meeting-house in Winchester as early as 1765, when Wesley first began his regular visits to that town,[109] and it was characteristic of a movement which would not fit the framework of perception the bishops asked the clergy to employ, that it would establish itself here (as in Ireland) under the wing of the Church, as dissent had not, that it would very considerably precede the arrival of Wesley in the milieu of the armed services where the normal social disciplines were replaced by others of a quite different kind, and that it would also thrive in the liberty of industrial towns like Whitchurch, which had already been well exploited by the dissenters. It is indeed to the credit of the vicar of Whitchurch that in 1788 while classifying Methodists (as the bishop's scheme required) as dissenters, he pointed out more clearly than any other parson in the diocese the inadequacy of the tag: 'The Methodists of Mr John Wesley's persuation [sic] are very numerous, yet attend the church constantly and communicate regularly'.[110] By this time Methodists had a chapel and a good congregation in Basingstoke, Crondall, Eling, Portsea, and, of course, Portsmouth.[111] Its progress in the country and the Isle of Wight is barely mentioned.

But in 1788 Hampshire Christianity was still overwhelmingly that of the Church of England, a Church uncommonly difficult for the historian whose professional equipment does not include a God's-eye view, to assess. It is no use inquiring how successful organisations were at fulfilling purposes which they did not set themselves; indeed the problem with the religious establishments of the *ancien régime* is that they set out not so much to do things as to be things, and one of the sources of strain in the eighteenth century was that states everywhere started to find things for their establishments to do, on terms which those establishments began to find unpalatable. And the familiar rhetoric that the church should be permitted to be the church is employed as often in favour of bad causes as of good. If the church was to *be* rather than to *do*, what kind of body was it? Clearly the church was a highly clericalised corporation, though not as highly clericalised as it is now. If therefore the diocese of Winchester was alive and well it ought at least to have been producing sufficient clergy to provide for its own succession; and in a worldly point it was well equipped to do so not merely because the bishop was well endowed with patronage, but because of the intimate connection between the great foundations at Winchester and those at New College and Magdalen, Oxford. In fact the number of clergy employed in the Winchester diocese who were born in it was infinitesimally small, and the effect of the Winchester foundations was to increase the number of pluralists, many of whom resided outside the see, though of course there were always plenty of clergy about in Winchester itself. Moreover because the honeypot of Winchester patronage was so large the new Hanoverian government had no option but to get hold of it, which they did in the persons of Willis and Hoadly. This meant in turn that Winchester patronage became embroiled in the political faction-fight in Oxford, since Wardens of New College loved nothing better than to move on to the Wardenship of Winchester at a much higher salary. But in spite of endless interference by the government, New College never became an absolutely reliable ally of the Court, and one of Hoadly's last notorious acts as Bishop of Winchester was to quash the election of the seventh Warden of New College in succession as Warden of Winchester in favour of Christopher Golding, a fellow of New College, 'a friend to King George [who] no more dreamt of this advancement than he did of being Pope [and] was frightened out of his wits'.[112] Meanwhile Magdalen developed into a solidly Tory and high-church society as far removed from the political and theological position of Hoadly as the political order could tolerate. In short the national standing of the Winchester foundations and their Oxford connections trapped them in a web of continuous conspiracy which led to no decisive result and was fruitless from the standpoint of the see of Winchester.

There are speculative reasons for suspecting that Winchester (like London) was a net consumer rather than a net producer of clergy, reasons which harmonize conveniently with the imaginative statistical arguments which have convinced Dr Virgin that there was a steady decline in clerical recruitment in the middle quarters of the eighteenth century.[113] There had always been a noticeable minority of Winchester clergy with Welsh names, a minority paralleled by a steady trickle of clergy from the English mountain fringe, the Lake District, who had their education and often their preferment from Queen's College, Oxford. This was no doubt a natural function of the fact that educational provision outstripped the possibilities of professional employment in both areas. What is disconcerting is the steady increase in the number of Welsh names among Hampshire clergy in the course of the century. It is no injustice to the Celtic fringe in that period to doubt whether Winchester would have imported so many of its sons had it produced enough local talent. The labyrinthine patronage system could hardly have accelerated a brain-drain out of the Winchester diocese in the middle of the eighteenth century. It clearly was a serious matter for the church as a whole if so much of the Anglican heartland was not generating its own succession.

But there was one thing worse. The great task which the state had for the Church in the eighteenth century was to assimilate Welsh Wales to English Christianity as the Church of Scotland actually assimilated most of the Gaelic-speaking highlands. This task the church undertook with a good deal of energy but it all went disastrously wrong. The attempt to create an English and Anglican Wales evoked in riposte a tremendous revival which was Welsh, evangelical and dissenting. The degree of this failure becomes easier to understand if the successes of assimilation, those Welsh who were Anglicized and Anglicanized, were being drawn off into sees like Winchester where the clerical reproduction rate was below par. If this hypothesis is correct, then the highly endowed dignitarianism of the Anglican heartlands has a great deal to answer for.

Parochial Charities

A bulky item in many of the returns (though generally much less bulky than for the Surrey parishes) consisted of replies to questions about charities. In 1725 and 1788 the bishops inquired what parish charities there were, what hospitals (or residential charities) and under whose authority. In 1765 the question was whether there had been any losses of benefactions, or whether the churchwardens or other officers were guilty of abuse in distributing their revenues. In short the bishops regarded parochial charities in much the same way as church property, and sought to preserve them from encroachments of various kinds. Indeed down to 1700 much of the inspiration of philanthropy was directly religious (though not confined to any particular religious party) and had religious objects in the narrow sense of the words in view. A well-balanced charity at Hartley Mauditt, for example, paid 20*s*. to the incumbent for preaching a sermon on 'death, resur[r]ection or jud[g]ment' each Michaelmas Day, and 30*s*. 'to such poor people' as came to hear it![114] There was an endowment at Penton Mewsey for a November 5th sermon (though none for the congregation),[115] one at Wymering for the dissemination of religious tracts,[116] and there were endowments for church repairs.[117] Bequests of this sort and also the number of residential charities for the poor (the 'hospitals' of these documents) which often had pastoral objects then began to diminish. Eighteenth-century humanitarians, no less generous than their predecessors, also began to devote themselves to specialised causes such as the relief of debtors in prison or hospitals (in the modern sense) for the treatment of particular groups of diseases or patients, which did not lend themselves to endowment on a parochial basis,[118] and were in any case more appropriate in the Winchester diocese to metropolitan Surrey, than to the rural areas and small towns of Hampshire. One such semi-privatized institution did exist at Alverstoke, 'the hospital for sick and wounded seamen, maintained at the charge of the government and managed by contractors'.[119]

It nevertheless remained the case that especially after the long European recession of the later seventeenth century a huge amount of the national endowment for the needy was parochially based, often administered by the incumbent and churchwardens, and sometimes involving a kind of social Christianity now forgotten. Endowments for distributing bread after Sunday morning service 'for ever', or annually, though much rarer than in Surrey, existed in a handful of Hampshire parishes.[120] And besides the educational charities and the quite numerous almshouses, there were innumerable other parochial charities for providing the poor (and especially those who did not receive poor relief) with work,[121] with shoes, clothing and various gifts in kind,[122] for assisting parents with too many children born in wedlock,[123] orphans with too few parents,[124] and children, apparently of both sexes, with apprenticeships they would not otherwise have.[125] And at least at Andover and Kingsclere a board listing the parish charities was displayed in church so that the poor might know what relief was available to them.[126]

Yet, in terms of endowment for the poor, Hampshire remained sadly impoverished compared with Surrey, and parish after rural parish had never received any charities at all. For this there were two main reasons. One was that perhaps the most notable success of the church in educating the public conscience was to establish it as the done thing for those who made money in trade to bequeath a charitable endowment; this of course favoured commercial towns and London most of all, though there was nothing to stop the successful favouring their native heath. In Hampshire this produced a clear result in the lengthy lists of charities in Alton, Andover, Odiham, Southampton and Winchester. Micheldever was the only small place which scored highly in this field; while Basingstoke with relatively little endowment for poverty, compensated with better than average endowments for education. But in huge numbers of country parishes the poor rate was all that stood between the needy and disaster. The second reason for the clear superiority of Surrey was good fortune in benefiting largely from the philanthropy of one of the most famous of all benefactors, Alderman Henry Smith, known for reasons now impenetrable as 'Dog' Smith.[127] Smith, a London salter, of the early-seventeenth century, turned charity into policy, aspiring to assist the poor on a national scale and actually assisting 219 communities, including every parish in Surrey. He managed the landed property he acquired through an efficient estate office in Great Russell Street, which made available to the churchwardens of each of the benefiting parishes their annual endowment after tax at very little trouble to themselves. As a great deal of Smith's money was laid out in property in Kensington and Chelsea his assets increased wonderfully in value.[128] At least five Hampshire parishes also benefited from Smith's munificence, two of them, Broughton and Longstock,[129] exemplars of the otherwise unendowed communities which Smith benefited right through Surrey, but, for reasons unknown, three, Andover, Odiham and Winchester St John's, relatively well provided for by other benefactors.[130]

The three great problems with charitable endowments (which were doubtless universal) were acquiring them, investing and retaining them, and seeing to their honest distribution. The last matter was specifically inquired into in the visitation of 1765 and seems to have given little trouble in Hampshire, though the vicar of Odiham believed that the town churchwarden had quartered dissenters and maidens on charities intended exclusively for Anglican males.[131] But all three visitations were concerned with the other problems, as if the charitable endowments were church property. Even after benefactions had been legally made it was not always easy for a parish to lay hands on them. Executors might be slow to deliver,[132] might find that no proper arrangements for a continuing charge on an estate had been made,[133] be unable to prevent the estate they must administer getting into Chancery,[134] or discover that the claims of the government against their assets made a bequest impossible to fulfil.[135] But incompetence,[136] embezzlement,[137] the ill-will, dishonesty or mortality of trustees,[138] or simple forgetfulness[139] resulted in a steady loss of endowments, even where the bequest itself—unlike the 20 sheep per annum promised to the church at Preston Candover[140]—presented no difficulties. With many of these troubles the bishop could hardly help at all. He might discipline refractory churchwardens (who seem to have been uncommon in Hampshire), and the documents themselves show direct appeals to him for legal advice,[141] and for intercession with a livery company to pay up.[142] The worst problem, however, was the actual investment of funds received, and here Hampshire country parishes were at a disadvantage compared with the City skills frequently available in Surrey. Land was thought to be the safest investment, but so much real property was tied up in strict settlements that it could often not be bought in convenient places. The next option was to invest in local businesses, and to take it was to enter on the route by which probably the largest number of parish endowments were lost.[143] There was in the eighteenth century no list of trustee securities, but there was a growing gilt-edged market, and it is impressive to see country parishes finally coming to the conclusion that the way to invest what money they had was in a mixture of consols, South Sea stock and mortgages upon turnpike tolls.[144]

One further comment may be justified by the prominence of references in the 1788 visitation to the inquiries made of incumbents under Thomas Gilbert's Act of 1786. It is clear that even an energetic bishop could do little to protect parochial charities beyond extracting assurances that the minister and churchwardens were doing what was expected of them, and exercising their memories at intervals about endowments which were lost or in danger of being lost. Even this minimal oversight had some significance at a time when the public protection provided by the issue of special commissions under the statute of charitable uses to investigate the administration of charities led to such quagmires in Chancery and common law proceedings as to fall into almost total disuse after the middle of the eighteenth century. Not only, however, was episcopal oversight hardly even a palliative, it could not meet the needs of those who were beginning to think about poverty in terms of policy. Gilbert's Act requiring ministers and churchwardens to furnish data on charities for the benefit of the poor, and his previous act requiring overseers to report statistics on poor law expenditure, indicated a new frame of mind. Both sources of income must figure in any national estimate of resources for the care of the poor, and the fact that there were those in Parliament conceiving policy in these terms gave notice of the day, not far distant, when charity commissioners would be appointed not merely to vet new charities, but to reorganise the old. Policy for the relief of poverty like policy for the relief of sickness was beginning to look beyond the parish.

Editorial Policy

The editing of these visitation returns presents problems no solution to which can satisfy every taste. It is in fact impossible to produce a verbatim transcript in book form, for the incumbents of 1788 frequently (though more frequently in Surrey than in Hampshire parishes) accepted the invitation of their ordinary to include a copy of the account of the parish charities they had lately sent to Parliament under the Gilbert Act of 1786. These returns were made on huge spread-sheets which will not satisfactorily reduce to page-size. The information they contain has therefore been extracted and presented in continuous prose. Other changes, though not compelled, are strongly invited in the transformation of MS replies to printed book form. Like their contemporaries, the eighteenth-century clergy employed a bewildering variety of spellings and abbreviations, and indulged a happy individualism in punctuation and the use of capitals. To achieve the standardization without which a printed book becomes hardly readable, while preserving the individuality which is a feature of the responses, the aim has been to produce a lightly modernized text. Punctuation and the use of capitals have been modernized, all statistical information presented in arabic numerals, and abbreviations (which frequently do not shorten very much) expanded. On the other hand the original spelling which offers clues to the literacy of the speller has been retained, even where this affords a contrast between the spelling of a place-name in the heading of a parish and its spelling in the course of the document that follows. Where the editor has been presented by the orthography with the dilemma whether a particular solecism was one of spelling or abbreviation he has opted boldly according to his lights, and left the word or expanded it as seemed best. Square brackets are used for words not in the text but desirable for the sense, for some variations on standard spellings and for editorial additions and notes. In cases where documents have suffered damage, angle brackets are used to supply words now missing, though conjecture has been kept within bounds.

Mention of the place-names introduces another problem. The replies of 1725 were arranged by the bishop's staff alphabetically within deaneries, and bound up. The later visitations were left unbound and those that survive have been arranged in the Hampshire Record Office for 1765 by deaneries, and for 1788 alphabetically. It seemed that the most user-friendly device for both readers and for students who wished to proceed from the text to the manuscript original (references to which introduce every item) would be alphabetical arrangement. The alphabetical arrangement adopted has been that used by Hampshire Record Office, and to make this effective the current conventions in the spelling of place-names have also been employed. It is hoped that that both the arrangement and the text which is not a calendar, but not quite a transcript will prove eminently usable.

It is useful for many purposes to have the dates in which incumbents held their parishes, and at the cost of considerable labour among the lacunae and confusion of the diocesan records the overwhelming bulk of these have been provided. Some gaps, however, remain and a few probably always will remain. Students should bear in mind that the terminal date of an incumbency is normally derived from that of the next presentation, and there is usually no means of knowing how long the vacancy in the parish lasted. Hampshire, however, has lacked the tables of successions provided for Surrey by Manning and Bray, and it is hoped that the material will prove of value.

Notes

1. Anne Whiteman *The Compton Census of 1676. A Critical Edition* (London, 1986) p. xxiv.
2. HRO 21M65/B4/1/1 Visitation 1725 (below p. 3).
3. *Speculum Dioceseos Lincolniensis sub episcopis Gul. Wake et Edm. Gibson, 1705-23* ed. R. E. G. Cole (Lincoln Record Society, 4; 1913).
4. *The Correspondence of Bishop Secker* ed. A. P. Jenkins (Oxfordshire Record Society, 57; 1991) and reviewed by W. R. Ward in *Oxoniensia*.
5. For Secker's Oxford visitation, see *Articles of Enquiry addressed to the clergy of the diocese of Oxford at the Primary Visitation of Dr Thomas Secker, 1738* ed. H. A. Lloyd Jukes (Oxfordshire Record Society, 38; 1957). The returns to Secker's Canterbury Visitation, and his MS Speculum are preserved in the Palace Library at Lambeth. The latter is in course of publication by the Church of England Record Society.
6. The inquiries to which his Canterbury see was subjected were used again in the visitations of his peculiars. Those used for the Surrey peculiars are reproduced in W. R. Ward *Parson and Parish in Eighteenth-century Surrey* (Surrey Record Society, 34; 1994) Appendix 2.
7. See e.g. *Wiltshire Returns to the Bishop's Visitation Queries, 1783* ed. Mary Ransome (Wiltshire Record Society, 27; 1972); *The State of the Bishopric of Worcester, 1782-1808* ed. Mary Ransome (Worcestershire Historical Society, 6; 1968); *The Archdeaconry of Richmond in the Eighteenth Century. Bishop Gastrell's 'Notitia'. The Yorkshire Parishes* ed. L. A. S. Butler (Yorkshire Archaeological Society Record Series, 146; 1990); *Archbishop Herring's Visitation Returns, 1743* ed. S. L. Ollard and P. C. Walker (Yorkshire Archaeological Society, 5 vols., 1928-31); *The Diocese of Llandaff in 1763* ed. John R. Guy (South Wales Record Society, 1991).
8. Cf. M. R. Austin *The Church in Derbyshire, 1823-4* (Derbyshire Archaeological Society, 5; 1972); *Visitations of the Archdeaconry of*

Stafford, 1829-41 ed. D. Robinson (Staffordshire Record Society, 4th Series 10; 1980).

9. There were indeed kindly comments from (not specially obsequious) clergy who saw in the visitation a pastoral willingness to hear the views of his clergy which they had not found in their ordinaries for a long time. See Fawley no. 88; Longparish no. 133.
10. *HMC Report on the Manuscripts of His Grace the Duke of Portland K.G.* vol. 7, p. 65 quoted in N. Sykes, *Church and State in England in the Eighteenth Century* (Cambridge, 1934) pp. 129-30.
11. Hayling North no. 519.
12. Hartley Mauditt no. 515, Holybourne no. 526, West Worldham no. 602; Petersfield no. 570, Priors Dean no. 575, Colemore no. 479; East Dean no. 295, Lockerley no. 344.
13. Brightstone no. 32; cf. Easton no. 67; Eastrop no. 68; Godshill no. 94.
14. Wootton, St Helens and Binstead no. 244.
15. Cf. Monk Sherborne no. 145.
16. Andover no. 7.
17. Ashe no. 440.
18. Newnham no. 153.
19. Rowner no. 178.
20. Alverstoke nos. 5, 436.
21. Crawley no. 483.
22. One parish was indeed described as 'an exact paralellogram'. Stoke Charity no. 199.
23. Farringdon nos. 87, 499.
24. Cf. Bishopstoke nos. 20, 452; Broughton nos. 34, 462; Chalton nos. 42, 471; Petersfield nos. 168, 570.
25. Cf. Amport nos. 6, 437; Boldre nos. 23, 454; Chawton nos. 43, 473; Longparish nos. 133, 544.
26. Winnall no. 614; Wonston no. 615.
27. Soberton no. 584.
28. Headley no. 522. It is worth comparing this return with the one for 1725, no. 107. In each case the incumbent was of above average intellectual distinction, the former a fellow of Queen's College, Oxford, the latter a fellow of St John's.
29. Lainston no. 125.
30. Eldon no. 73.
31. Chilcomb no. 46.
32. Crux Easton no. 59.
33. Farley Chamberlayne no. 84.
34. See Brading no. 26; Fareham no. 83.
35. See e.g. Portsmouth no. 171; Gosport no. 508.
36. Alverstoke no. 5.
37. Fawley no. 88.
38. Ashe no. 9; Crondall no. 58; Ellingham no. 75.
39. Micheldever no. 139.
40. Newnham no. 153.
41. Ringwood no. 174.

42. Old Alresford no. 161; Petersfield no. 168; Southampton St Michael no. 193; Stoke Charity no. 199; Twyford no. 207.
43. Longstock no. 134; Michelmersh no. 140.
44. Alverstoke no. 436.
45. Clanfield no. 51.
46. Chalton no. 42.
47. Southampton Holy Rood no. 585.
48. Hildegard Zimmerman *Caspar Neumann und die Entstehung der Frühaufklärung. Ein Beitrag zur schlesischen Theologie und Geistesgeschichte im Zeitalter des Pietismus* (Witten, 1969) pp. 27-9, 60-62.
49. Otterbourne no. 566.
50. Even Hampshire yielded answers like 'Mr Souch is supposed to be patron'. Grateley no. 96.
51. Long Sutton no. 135; Widley no. 227.
52. *Archdeaconry of Richmond* p. 22.
53. P. Virgin *The Church in an Age of Negligence* (Cambridge, 1989) pp. 192-3.
54. The responses reported here are less than the 250 recorded, as I have tried to exclude from the reckoning chapelries not run as independent parishes, and have treated benefices normally held together (like Hursley and Otterbourne) as single benefices not pluralities.
55. Wickham no. 419; Widley no. 420.
56. *Clergé et Pastorale en Angleterre au XVIIIme siècle. Le Diocèse de Londres* (Paris, 1992) p. 254 *seq*.
57. Hinton Ampner no. 325.
58. Winchester St Mary Kalendar no. 609; Winchester St Maurice no. 610.
59. Winchester St Michael in the Soke no. 425.
60. Colemore and Priors Dean no. 479 and East Tisted no. 489.
61. Bentley no. 448 and Hannington no. 514.
62. Empshott no. 493, Bedhampton no. 447 and Farlington no. 498.
63. Winchester St Mary Kalendar, St Maurice and St Thomas nos. 609, 610 and 613.
64. Liss no. 540 and Petersfield no. 570.
65. By the same token an unknown proportion of the clergy listed above as 'men of a single parish' were in fact curates of others. The rather shrill protests very occasionally to be encountered in some returns by clergy insisting that they had devoted themselves exclusively and single-handed to the service of their parish were warranted by the fact that very few Hampshire clergy in the eighteenth century had a financial interest in only one parish.
66. Sykes *Church and Parish in England* pp. 405-6.
67. Alverstoke no. 5. For other examples see Mark Smith, 'The reception of Richard Podmore: Anglicanism in Saddleworth, 1700-1830' in *The Church of England c.1689-c.1833. From Toleration to Tractarianism* ed. J. Walsh, C. Haydon, and S. Taylor (Cambridge, 1993) pp. 110-23.

68. Catherington no. 276.
69. Bentley no. 259.
70. Sydmonton no. 401.
71. Widley and Wymering no. 420.
72. Micheldever no. 352.
73. Cheriton no. 279.
74. Old Alresford no. 367.
75. Blendworth no. 265.
76. Stratfield Saye no. 398.
77. Worting no. 432.
78. Farlington no. 309.
79. Buriton no. 274.
80. Lymington no. 346.
81. Whitsbury no. 418.
82. East Dean no. 295; Rowner no. 381; Houghton no. 327.
83. Kings Worthy no. 338; Mottisfont no. 358; Botley no. 267.
84. Whitchurch no. 417; Bedhampton no. 258.
85. Arreton no. 8.
86. Breamore no. 31.
87. Micheldever no. 139.
88. Odiham no. 160; Sherborne St John no. 384; Swarraton no. 202.
89. Petersfield no. 570. Another chapel at Nursted had also been lost, no. 465. There were the ruins of a chapel in Brighstone parish, no. 32, and at Calbourne, no. 38, both Isle of Wight.
90. Hayling no. 321; North Waltham no. 365.
91. Farlington no. 309.
92. Catherington no. 40; Rowner no. 578; Sherfield on Loddon no. 184.
93. Quarley no. 173.
94. Milford no. 141.
95. Twyford no. 207. 10 families represented one-eighth of the vicar's reckoning of families in the parish; 90 souls one-third of the population. In 1788 there was still said to be a Catholic gentleman with a priest in his house, but only 20 other Papists were then reported. Twyford no. 596.
96. *Hampshire Registers I. The registers and records of Winchester* ed. R. E. Scantlebury (Catholic Record Society, 42; 1948); Cheriton no. 279; Newtown chapelry no. 363.
97. Winchester St John no. 231; Winchester St Peter Chesil no. 235.
98. Winchester St Thomas no. 237.
99. Winchester united parishes of SS Maurice, George, Vade, Mary Kalendar, Peter Colebrook no. 424; Winchester St Michael no. 611; Winchester St Thomas no. 613.
100. Havant nos. 104, 319, 517; Warblington nos. 411, 598. The returns for many other parishes cast a fitful light on this process.
101. And other church dues, Basingstoke no. 13.
102. Alverstoke no. 5.
103. Kingsclere no. 120.
104. Wherwell no. 416; South Warnborough no. 395; Hordle no. 326; Elvetham no. 77; Weyhill no. 603.

105. New Alresford nos. 161, 360.
106. Baughurst no. 445.
107. Chalton no. 42; Whippingham no. 223.
108. This is one of the themes of my *Protestant Evangelical Awakening* (Cambridge, 1992).
109. Winchester St Peter and St John both in the Soke, no. 426.
110. Whitchurch no. 606.
111. Basingstoke no. 444; Crondall no. 484; Eling no. 492; Portsea no. 572; Portsmouth no. 574.
112. For the politics of all this and references, see my *Georgian Oxford* (Oxford, 1958) pp. 110-12, 185 n. 38.
113. Virgin *The Church in an Age of Negligence* p. 259.
114. Hartley Mauditt no. 101.
115. Penton Mewsey no. 569.
116. Wymering no. 618.
117. Overton no. 162; Ovington no. 164.
118. On this subject see David Owen *English Philanthropy, 1660-1960* (2nd ed. Cambridge, Mass., 1965) esp. pp. 52-3.
119. Alverstoke no. 5.
120. *ibid.*; Andover no. 7; Crawley no. 57.
121. Thruxton no. 204; Titchfield no. 594.
122. Old Alresford no. 161; Kingsclere no. 120; Hartley Wintney no. 103.
123. Broughton no. 34; Nether Wallop no. 151.
124. Arreton no. 8.
125. Buriton no. 37; Cliddesden no. 52; Freshwater no. 90.
126. Andover no. 7; Kingsclere no. 120.
127. For a fuller account of the Smith charities see the introduction to my *Parson and Parish in Eighteenth-century Surrey* (Surrey Record Society, 34; 1994), and also Owen *English Philanthropy* pp. 309-11; W. K. Jordan *The Charities of London, 1480-1660* (London, 1960) pp. 117-22.
128. In 1992 the Smith trustees distributed £12,000,000 (*The Times* 9 March 1993, p. 19).
129. Broughton no. 34; Longstock no. 134.
130. Andover no. 7; Odiham no. 160; Winchester St John no. 231.
131. Odiham no. 160.
132. Appleshaw no. 253.
133. Hartley Mauditt no. 515.
134. Chilbolton no. 280.
135. Portsmouth no. 171.
136. Over Wallop no. 369; Hambledon no. 98.
137. Whitchurch no. 417.
138. Broughton no. 271; West Tytherley no. 413; Odiham no. 160.
139. Bishops Sutton no. 19.
140. Preston Candover no. 172.
141. Fawley no. 88.
142. Weyhill no. 221.
143. Newton Valence nos. 154 and 557; Headley no. 522.
144. East Tisted no. 489; Weyhill no. 603; Winchester St Michael no. 611; Wonston no. 615; Hurstbourne Priors no. 530.

The Visitation of 1725
Hampshire and Isle of Wight

REVEREND BROTHER

OU cannot but be ſenſible, of how great Importance it is, that a Biſhop ſhould be well informed of the State of his Dioceſe; and have ſuch Memorials ready by him, as may enable him without delay to reſolve and act according to the Variety of Occaſions, that ſhall happen. I am ſorry to ſay, how little of this I have been able to find among the Papers left me by my Predeceſſors; and therefore have judged it neceſſary to ſend a Paper of Queries to every Pariſh in my Dioceſe, to which I deſire, that Yourſelf in particular would at my next Viſitation, which I deſign (God willing) this Summer, ſend me an Anſwer, if either ill Health, or other urgent Reaſon ſhall hinder, that you cannot bring it Yourſelf. I deſire, that the Anſwer may be diſtinct to all the Queries, that You would write it upon one or more Sheets of *Folio* Paper, and that You would leave the Margin of each ſide of the Leaf ſo large, that it may conveniently be bound up with the reſt, to be ready for the Uſe of Myſelf and Succeſſors. I deſire alſo, that You would at the top of the firſt Page put your own Name, the Name of your Pariſh, and of the Archdeaconry and Deanery, under which it is, that the whole may more eaſily be digeſted into order.

1. What Compaſs of Ground do you ſuppoſe to be in your Pariſh?

2. About what Number of Souls according to the beſt Information, that you can reaſonably get, do you ſuppoſe to be therein?

3. What Number of Marriages, Births and Burials may you have at a Medium one Year with another?

4. Who is the Patron of your Living?

5. Have you any Chapel or Chapels in your Pariſh; How are they called, or what Names do they go by; By whom are they ſerved; How maintained and ſupported; and Who has the Right of Nomination to them?

6. Have you any Lecturer or Curate in your Pariſh, and Who are they?

7. What Number of Papiſts are there in your Pariſh, and Of what Conſequence and Eſtates do you ſuppoſe them to be?

8. Are there any Meetings of Proteſtant Diſſenters in the Pariſh, Of what Kind; and About what Number of ſuch Diſſenters may there be?

9. What Noblemen, Gentlemen or Perſons of Note of each Sex live in your Pariſh?

10. What Schools are there; How are they endowed; Who are the Maſters or Miſtreſſes; In what Condition are they as to the Number of Scholars; and Who have the Nomination of thoſe Maſters or Miſtreſſes?

Extract from the printed inquiry issued in 1725 by Richard Willis, Bishop of Winchester.
(Hampshire Record Office, 21M65/B4/1/1)

Episcopal Visitation, 1725

Printed Inquiry 21M65/B4/1/1

You cannot but be sensible, of how great importance it is, that a bishop should be well informed of the state of his diocese; and have such memorials ready by him, as may enable him without delay to resolve and act according to the variety of occasions that shall happen. I am sorry to say how little of this I have been able to find among the papers left me by my predecessors; and therefore have judged it necessary to send a paper of queries to every parish in my diocese, to which I desire that yourself in particular would at my next visitation, which I design (God willing) this summer, send me an answer, if either ill health or other urgent reason shall hinder you, that you cannot bring it yourself. I desire that the answer may be distinct to all the queries, that you would write it on one or more sheets of folio paper, and that you would leave the margin of each side of the leaf so large, that it may be conveniently bound up with the rest, to be ready for the use of myself and successors. I desire also that you would at the top of the first page put your own name, the name of your parish, and of the archdeaconry and deanery, under which it is, that the whole may more easily be digested into order.

1 What compass of ground do you suppose to be in your parish?

2 About what number of souls according to the best information that you can reasonably get, do you suppose to be therein?

3 What number of marriages, births and burials may you have at a medium, one year with another?

4 Who is the patron of your living?

5 Have you any chapel or chapels in your parish; how are they called, or what names do they go by; by whom are they served; how maintained and supported; and who has the right of nomination to them?

6 Have you any lecturer or curate in your parish, and who are they?

7 What number of Papists are there in your parish, and of what consequence and estates do you suppose them to be?

8 Are there any meetings of protestant dissenters in the parish, of what kind; and about what number of such dissenters may there be?

9 What noblemen, gentlemen or persons of note of each sex live in your parish?

10 What schools are there; how are they endowed; who are the masters or mistresses; in what condition are they as to the number of scholars; and who have the nomination of those masters or mistresses?

11 What charities have been given to the parish, and how are they distributed; what hospitals are there; for what purposes, and who have the right to look after them?
12 That I may be able the more readily to write to you, as occasion shall require, I desire also, that you would put down, which is the next post-town to you; and likewise that when you have any affairs that require my advice or interposition, you would write directly to myself.

I am

Your affectionate brother,
R[ichard Willis] Winchester

Chelsea, March 4, 1724/5.

1 Abbotstone and Itchen Stoke 21M65/B4/1/1 fo.1
Edward Griffith, rector and vicar 1721–7 3 September 1725

1 Area The parish of Abberston is about 2 miles in length and about 1¼ miles in breadth. Icthin-Stoke is about 2 miles in length and about 1½ miles in breadth. There is in the parish of Icthin Stoke a farm called Hampage surrounded entirely by other parishes which is about a mile in length and about half a mile in breadth.
2 Population There are in the 2 parishes about 125 souls.
3 Marriages &c. We have about 2 or 3 births, 2 or 3 burials and 1 marriage *communibus annis*.
4 Patron The patron is His Grace the Duke of Bolton, but I have a grant of the next vacancy from the duke to me and my heirs.
5 Chapels There is but one church at Stoke; at Abberston there are not soe much as the remains of a church.
6 Lecturer The present curate's name is Hicthins [Thomas Hitchens].
7 Papists There are in Icthinstoke 2 farmers [who are] Papists, having each of them 3 children to be brought up in that way. In Abberston there is a labourer, his wife and 1 child Papists.
8 Dissenters We have no protestant dissenters.
9 Gentry &c. Abberston is a seat of His Grace the Duke of Bolton which he is seldom at.
10 Schools No schools.
11 Charities There has been given to the parish of Icthinstoke £10 the interest of which is yearly distributed among the poor, but when it was given, or by whom, I cannot learn upon the best enquiry I have been capable of making hitherto. As soon as I am better informed Your Lordship shall have a more exact answer to this querie.
12 Post-town Alresford is the next post-town.

2 Abbotts Ann 21M65/B4/1/1 fo.107
Robert Willis, rector 1718–1726/7

1 Area Our compass of ground (according to the best information that I could gett) is 10 miles in circumference.
2 Population The number of souls are 270.

3 Marriages &c. Marriages not above 1 in a year, births about 7, burials at a medium 6 one year with another.
4 Patron The patron is Robert Pitt Esq.
5 Chapels There is no chapel in this parish.
6 Lecturer I have no lecturer nor curate.
7 Papists There is no Papist.
8 Dissenters We have no meetings of protestant dissenters, nor of any other kind as I know of.
9 Gentry &c. Here is no nobleman, or person of note but General Evans.
10 Schools We have no school endowed.
11 Charities There have been no charities given here.
12 Post-town The next post-town to us is Andover.

3 Aldershot 21M65/B4/1/1 fo.201
James Forde, curate 1722–43
1 Area About 10 miles.
2 Population 6 score and 15.
3 Marriages &c. 4 marriages, 6 births, 4 burials.
4 Patron Mr Richard Dean of Crondal.
5 Chapels No.
6 Lecturer No.
7 Papists None.
8 Dissenters Meetings none; 1 Presbyterian; Quakers 4.
9 Gentry &c. German Pole Esq; Mr Charles Viner.
10 Schools None.
11 Charities One alms-house for 4 poor people, without any endowment, but the yearly interest of £12.
12 Post-town Farnham.

4 Alton 21M65/B4/1/1 fo.57
Thomas Mathew, vicar 1697–1727
1 Area The vicaridge of Alton is really supposed to be in length east and west 4 miles; north and south in breadth about 3 miles.
2 Population The number of souls in the same [is] about 3,000.
3 Marriages &c. The number of marriages in the same every year about 20, births about 80, burials about 60.
4 Patron Patron of the same [is] the [cathedral] church of Winchester.
5 Chapels 3 chapels belonging to the mother-church of Alton—their names, Hallybourn, Bensted and Kingsley; [they are] served by myself and curate.
6 Lecturer No lecturer, nor curate in the said vicaridge, saving the for-named.
7 Papists No Papists in all the parishes of the said vicaridge, as ever I heard.
8 Dissenters There are in the town of Alton 2 meetings of dissenters; one of Presbyterians, the other of Quakers; the first consists of about 12

families, the latter of about 20, which, multiplied by 3 or 4 at the most, makes the whole number of dissenters, excepting some strangers belonging to the clothing trade, always uncertain by reason of their oft changing.
9 Gentry &c. No quality belonging to any of the parishes in the same vicaridge, excepting Madam How, and her family, and one Justice of the Peace at Alton, Robert Kricher Esq.
10 Schools 2 schools in Alton, a grammar school and a charity school. The first [is] endowed with £30 p.a., a house, and a close joyning to the same, about 2 acres. [It is] governed by 15 feoffees, the master to be chose by the majority of them. The other hath had hitherto £30 p.a. continued by yearly subscriptions, for the teaching 40 boys and 20 girls. The master and mistress of the same are Isaac Leach and his wife, and have ever been so, since the first erecting of the same. Maintainers of the same at present are your lordship (for which we stand highly indebted to your lordship, and myself returns you many thanks) Esq. Lewis, Madam Knight of Chawton, Mr Colston deceased, lately of Mortlake in Surry, Esq. Kercher, Mr Goodier of Alton, Madam Fisher lately of Chawton, now of Farnham, and myself. The government is in 2 curators chosen by the subscribers, and the contributors to the same school.
11 Charities There be 3 old charities given and continued to Alton, uncertain in the sum by the reason of the variation of the taxes and the price of corn, which one depends upon. One large house given to widows, with little allowances to the same yearly; given by one Mr Geale, formerly of Alton, or now under the pretended right and care of Mr Geale, descendent of the donor: who with Mr Butler claims the nomination of those persons that are to live therein. And at Hallybourn, another parish in the same vicaridge, is lately given by one Mr Andrews, lately citizen of London £150 p.a. and upwards for a free charitie-school for all the youth of Hallybourn and 12 of Alton, 5 of Bensted, and 5 of Froyl, under 5 trustees, 3 of the benefactor's nomination and 2 chosen since by the parish. 20 children are to be clothed yearly at the discretion of the trustees for the time being. Which charitie hath been stopt by the Court of Chancery this 4 years, and humbly begs now the utmost of your lordship's charitable assistance.
12 Post-town From Alton, a post-town in the road from London to Winchester.

5 Alverstoke 21M65/B4/1/2 fo.1

Charles Monckton, rector 1715–40
1 Area A neck of land, open to the Northwest, in length about 4 miles, of an unequal breadth, [it] contains 2,586 acres of land, exclusive of the ground whereon the town of Gosport is built, which may be computed at 35 acres.
2 Population Parishioners or inhabitants in families which pay to the rates of church and poor &c. may be reckoned at 3,000. The poor, inmates and strangers [are] a flux body, and not to be ascertained, [but] may be guessed at 1,500.

3 Marriages &c. Number of baptisms at the parish church:

From October 6th 1715 to October 6th 1716		70
From October 6th 1716 to October 6th 1717		84
From August 1st 1724 to August 1st 1725		84
	Total 3 years	238
	Medium	79
Marriages in the parish church:		
From October 6th 1715 to October 6th 1716		26
From October 6th 1716 to October 6th 1717		24
From Augus[t] 1st 1724 to August 1st 1725		34
	Total 3 years	84
	Medium	28
Burials at the parish church:		
From October 6th 1715 to October 6th 1716		77
From October 6th 1716 to October 6th 1717		97
From August 1st 1724 to August 1st 1725		78
	Total 3 years	252
	Medium	84
Baptisms at Gosport chapel:		
From October 6th 1715 to October 6th 1716		102
From October 6th 1716 to October 6th 1717		97
From August 1st 1724 to August 1st 1725		75
	Total 3 years	274
	Medium	91
Marriages in Gosport chapel:		
From October 6th 1715 to October 6th 1716		35
From October 6th 1716 to October 6th 1717		50
From August 1st 1724 to August 1st 1725		25
	Total 3 years	110
	Medium	36
Burials at Gosport chapel:		
From October 6th 1715 to October 6th 1716		52
From October 6th 1716 to October 6th 1717		72
From August 1st 1724 to August 1st 1725		35
	Total 3 years	159
	Medium	53

4 Patron The Right Revd Father in God Richard Lord Bishop of Winton.

5 Chapels Trinity Chapel in Gosport, erected in the year 1696 and then consecrated by the Right Revd Father in God, Peter [Mews], Lord Bishop of Winton.

6 Lecturer Curate [is] Charles Monckton AM in priest's holy orders, maintained and supported by the voluntary subscriptions of the inhabitants, whose contributions are very precarious, and doe not amount to more than £35 p.a. The duty is very great, viz. 2 sermons on every Sunday, prayers on every Wednesday, Friday and Holy Day, monthly sacraments (the number of communicants about 200) and preparation sermons—a case, with submission, to be commended to the Most and Right Revd and Honourable the Commissioners of Queen Anne's Bounty for an endowment. All perquisites by an instrument at the chapel's consecration are

reserved to the rector, and, by a clause in the same instrument, the chapel doors are to be shut up, and the inhabitants obliged to repair to the parish mother-church of Alverstoake when they neglect or refuse to maintain their curate. Nomination [is] in the rector of Alverstoake, subject to the visitation of the Right Revd Father in God the Lord Bishop of Winton. Upon the rector's neglect to nominate a curate within 6 months after a vacancy, the nomination for that turn is to be by the Right Revd Father in God the Lord Bishop of Winton.
7 Papists None convicted.
8 Dissenters 1 meeting-house for dissenters under the denomination of Presbyterians, but frequented by diverse sects of dissenter and occasional conformists, whose numbers are not great if compared with the members of the Church of England, but can not be ascertained. 1 meeting-house for dissenters under the denomination of Anabaptists, rarely frequented, and by a very few persons
9 Gentry &c. Mrs Oakes of Weovil.
10 Schools 1 school-house endowed with a dwelling-house; master, Mr Young; Mr Dorage, writing-master. Nomination: the schoolmaster [is] chosen by Mrs Oakes who built the school and dwelling-house at her own charge. 12 children are to be taught to read and write gratis, nominated by Mrs Oakes. After the decease of Mrs Oakes, the schoolmaster and 12 scholars to be appointed by the parish officers.
11 Charities £5 p.a. given by Captain Mark.
£2 p.a. given by Widow Holms.
£1 p.a. given by Abraham Hewlett.
These sums received annually by the churchwardens and overseers for the poor, are in part laid out upon bread brought every Sunday morning to the said church and there distributed, the remainder given to poor families. Mr Allen lately deceased gave £4 p.a. to the poor, not yet to be paid.
40*s*. p.a. given by Mr Humphrys deceased to the curate of Gosport for preaching a commemoration sermon on the Sunday after Michaelmas day. Some houses given by the said Mr Humphrys deceased to be inhabited by poor widows placed in them by the executors of the said Mr Humphrys. Some houses given to be inhabited by poor widows that are placed in them by the donors yet living.
1 hospital for sick and wounded seamen maintained at the charge of the government and managed by contractors.
12 Post-town [No reply.]

6 Amport 21M65/B4/1/1 fo.110
Thomas Hayley DD, vicar 1723–39 4 March 1724/5
1 Area Near 2,000 acres.
2 Population 5 or 600.
3 Marriages &c. 2 or 3 marriages, 6 or 7 births, 6 or 7 burials.
4 Patron The Dean and Chapter of Chichester.
5 Chapels 1 chapel at Appleshaw, served by myself and curate alternately.
6 Lecturer 1 curate, the Revd Mr Sheppard.

7 Papists 1 old woman.
8 Dissenters None.
9 Gentry &c. Mr Norton Pawlet, and Mr John Duke, gentlemen.
10 Schools 1 charity school for the instruction of the children of the poor, as they will come; supported by contribution. An old decayd man is the master.
11 Charities None that I know of.
12 Post-town Andover in Hampshire.

7 Andover 21M65/B4/1/1 fo.112

Harry Penton, vicar 1712–28
1 Area There are in the parish of Andover 7,016 acres of ground, the parish being reckoned between 20 and 30 miles in compass. The procession, being once in two years, and lasting part of 3 days.
2 Population The number of souls, as near as I can learn, is about 6,000 in the town and villages.
3 Marriages &c. It appears by the register for 7 years last past, that there have been one year with another about 90 baptisms, 96 burials, 26 marriages.
4 Patron The Warden and Scholars and Fellows of Winchester Colledge are patrons of the vicaridge.
5 Chapels There is one chappel in the parish, called Foscot chappel, served by the vicar of Andover, or his curate maintained by him. Served only the last Sunday in the month in the afternoon, with one sacrament, in the morning, the first Sunday after Easter Day.
6 Lecturer There is no parish lecturer, I with my curates having supplyed it so long as I have been vicar. My late curate Mr Smith being some time since dead, I have no licensed curate, but intend by Your Lordship's leave, to make Mr Thomas as soon as he can gett into priest's orders, my curate.
7 Papists I know not of one Papist in the parish.
8 Dissenters There are 2 meetings of protestant dissenters, and one of Quakers. The 2 former I suppose to be Presbyterians or Independents.
9 Gentry &c. There is no nobleman, and but one gentleman of note in the parish.
10 Schools There are 3 pu[b]lick schools in the parish: 1st the Free School taught by Mr Colter, who hath about 30 scholars and is nominated by the corporation, the salary about £20 p.a. and an house. The 2nd is a charity school of 40 boys, the master Mr Innis, and charges paid by private benefactors, except that by Mr Smith, being about £7 p.a. The 3rd is a charity school created by Mr John Pollen, father of the present Mr John Pollen, for teaching 24 poor children, in the gift of his family, the mistress's name [is] Yates. The next sheets contain the names of the benefactors and benefactions and to what purposes given and to whome the right of looking after them belongs.
11 Charities The names of the benefactors to the parish of Andover, with their gifts when, and for what uses, given, are, as appears by a scheme hanging in the church, and drawn out as I suppose, by order of Edward

Wareham, gentleman, he being either bayliff of the town, or churchwarden of the parish AD 1692.

Anno 1560 John Hanson of this town, gentleman, gave £200, out of the profit of which money is to be paid yearly for the founding and towards the maintenance of a free school in this town, to the schoolmaster thereof £6 p.a.

Anno 1570 Katherine Hanson, spinster, gave the ground called Common Acre for the recreation of the inhabitants of this town.

Anno 1598 Richard Venables, citizen and merchant taylor of London, gave £100 to provide 13 2*d*. loaves of bread for 13 poor people of this town, in the church of Andover every Sunday forever.

Anno 1600 the corporation of Andover added 2 2*d*. loaves to be forever weekly delivered with the 13 loaves given by Mr Venables.

Anno 1611 Richard Keymys of this town, gentleman, gave £400, to purchase £20 p.a. to be disposed of in manner following, viz. £5 yearly to provide 12 2*d*. loaves of bread weekly, 50 weekes in the year, for the poor, on Sunday morning in the church. Another £5 yearly to be distributed to the poor in money on Good Friday. Another £5 yearly to be paid to the schoolmaster of the Free School in Andover. Another £5 to be yearly given to a lecturer besides the minister. And when there is no lecture, those £5 to be yearly given to the poor in money on Ash Wednesday. He gave likewise £40 to buy ornaments for Andover Church, and £10 to buy a fair c[h]alice of silver guilt [sic] for the communion. He likewise gave £100 to pave and repair the High Street and other streets in Andover.

Anno 1622 Thomas Westcombe, citizen and leatherseller of London, gave a little piece of ground wheron a barn formerly stood, to provide 18 penny loaves of bread every quarter day, or Sunday next following, to be given to 18 poor people quarterly, and the sexton of Andover to have the advantage of the said bread.

Anno 1628 Richard Blake of this town, gentleman, gave £30, the interest of it to be paied for ever to the poor on Good Friday. He likewise gave to this town the land whereon the Free School is built.

Anno 1624 Peter Blake, of the Inner Temple of London, Esq., gave a rent charge of £6 p.a. issuing out of his tenements in Andover, to be paid to the poor of Andover, and two other parishes of which Andover is to have the greatest part.

Anno 1631 Joan Blake, widow and relict of Richard Blake, mentioned in the year 1628, gave £10 to be disposed of in like manner as her late husband's £30.

Anno 1610 Thomas Cornelius, of London, merchant, gave by will to the poor of this town £20, the interest of it to be given yearly on Good Friday in money.

Anno 1633 Mary Venables of Basingstoake, spinster, gave by will to the poor of this town £5.

Anno 1633 Michael Peasly, of this town, apothecary, by his will, after his debts and legacys and funeral discharged, gave the residue of his goods and chattels to the poor of this town, which amounted to and was received £35, and disposed of by the corporation.

Anno 1634 George Pemberton, one of the aldermen of the city of Winchester, gave to this town £100 to pay to the poor £6 13*s*. 4*d*. p.a. for ever on St Thomas day, and St George Martyr by equal portions.
Anno 1625 Walter Waite of this town, gent, gave 20*s*. p.a. to the poor of this town, to be paid out of Brown's tenement in Andover.
Anno 1650 Richard Jay, of Reading, gentleman, gave to the poor of this town £100, the produce to be yearly distributed among the poor.
Anno 1658 Nicholas Fishborne alias Beale of this town, gave to the poor £10.
Anno 1642 Henry Smith of London, Esq., gave to the poor of this town £10 p.a. for ever, to be yearly received out of lands in Stoughton *in comitatu* Leicester, by the churchwardens and overseers of Andover.
Anno 1679 the Hon. Francis Powlet Esq. gave to the poor of this place £100.
Anno 1686 John Pollen Esq. erected, founded and endowed an hospital in this town for 6 poor aged men, in the gift of his family, so long as there remains any of it, afterwards in the gift of the Warden of Winchester Colledge, the baylif of Andover and the vicar for the time being. I have seen this last clause in a writing engrossed.
Anno 1690 Mrs Christian Hinxman, widdow, gave by deed to the poor of this town £5 p.a., to be paid by Mr Joseph Hinxman her son, or his heirs, on Twelfth Day for ever.
Anno 1690 Mr Joseph Hinxman gave by will to the poor of this town £5 p.a. to be paid by his son Joseph Hinxman or his heirs for ever, on St Thomas Day.
The yearly charities stand thus:

By Mr John Hanson £200 for paying to the schoolmaster of the Free School yearly	£ 16	
By Mr Keymys yearly	5	
	£ 21	

In weekly bread every Sunday in the church:		
By Mr Richard Venables for 13 2*d*. loaves weekly	£ 5	4*s*.
By the Corporation of Andover 2 2*d*. loaves weekly for ever		17*s*. 4*d*.
By Mr Richard Keymys for 12 2*d*. loaves weekly every Sunday in the year except 2 weeks in the harvest for ever	£ 5	
	£ 11	1*s*. 4*d*

Quarterly bread:		
By Mr Thomas Westcombe 18 1*d*. loaves to 18 poor people on Sunday next after Christmas Day, Our Lady Day, Midsummer Day, and Michaelmas Day		6*s*. 0*d*.

To be given yearly in money on Good Friday:	
By Mr Richard Keymys	£ 5
By Mr Thomas Cornelius	£ 1
	£ 6

By Mr Richard Keymys on Ash Wednesday	£ 5

By Mr Richard Blake and wife on St Thomas Day the interest of	£ 40		
By Mr George Pemberton	£ 3	6*s*.	8*d*.
By Peter Blake Esq.	£ 3		
By Nicholas Fis[h]borne alias Beele on St George the Martyr		12*s*.	
	£ 8	18*s*.	8*d*.

By Mr George Pemberton	£ 3	6*s*.	8*d*.
By Mr Walter Waite on the day of his death, viz. September 9	£ 1		
	£ 4	6*s*.	8*d*.

For apprenticing poor children:			
Mr Henry Smith gave £10 p.a. for that or the like purpose	£ 10		
The Hon. Francis Powlet Esq. gave £100 for that or the like purpose	£ 5		
The Spittle house and land provides habitations for 4 poor people and 10*s*. p.a. for each of them	£ 2		
The 4 tenements in Common Acre are habitations for 4 poor people.			

Purchases made by the Corporation for the use of the poor to support the charitys given by the benefactors:			
Anno 1612 the Corporation purchased the Town Mills and Mead Plott by it, now lett to Francis Grey at p.a.	£ 24		
Anno 1616 was purchased Bordon Gate Mead now lett to John Overton for p.a.	£ 10		
Anno 1617 they purchased 51 acres of arable land, 10 acres of it in Woolvers Dean and 41 on Bear Hill now lett to John Pollen Esqr and John Froud, with 2½ acres called Spittle lands at p.a.	£ 10	11*s*.	
Anno 1663 they built the shambles called The Poor's Shambles in the market place now lett for p.a.	£ 6		
Anno 1642 they purchased the tenements lying next to the 3 Choffs in Andover, and a barn and a tenement on the other side of the street now in lease to Rowland Smith, Scullard Diaper, and Francis Cornelius at p.a.	£ 9	16*s*.	8*d*.
Anno 1653 they let out at interest on a mortgage £40 which to this day brings in p.a.	£ 2	8*s*.	
They formerly built the school and schoolhouse which cost them	£186	13*s*.	4*d*.
Anno 1687 they new built the Town Mills which cost, besides workmanship which the tenant found, of which money they borrowed and stil owe unto the Town Chamber £37	£127	11*s*.	1*d*.

They formerly new-built the Spittle House and 4 tenements in Common Acre, and still repair them with the school and mills.

Pole money was at 8% when part of these sums were given.
As to the distribution of these charitys I know very little, not having of late seen or heard of any distribution of bread, or money, except 20 loaves weekly after Sunday morning service.
There is a benefaction of £10 p.a. for a sermon on St John's day, performed and paid constantly since his death—the donor's name, Williams.

8 Arreton [IoW] 21M65/B4/1/2 fo.149

William Griffin, vicar 1690–1732

1 Area The parish of Arreton is in extent from north to south about 7 miles, and from east to west about 4 miles.
2 Population The number of souls in it I guess to be between 7 and 800.
3 Marriages &c. We have had at a medium for these 7 years last past, 6 marriages, 19 christenings and 18 burials.
4 Patron The patron of the living is Richard Fleming Esq. of North Stoneham.
5 Chapels There were at the beginning of the reign of James I 2 free chapels in the parish. One called St Martin's of Britilsford appointed for ever, of whose foundation I can give no account, the incumbent whereof then was one Thomas Cowdray, a scholar in Oxford, having no other living. The other was the chapel of Standen appointed for ever, of the foundation of Richard Cowvert, the incumbent whereof was John Roo clerk. But now of these chapels there are scarce any remains to be seen.
6 Lecturer We have no lecturer or curate.
7 Papists No Papists.
8 Dissenters No meetings of protestant dissenters.
9 Gentry &c. No persons of any great note.
10 Schools No school endowed.
11 Charities In the year 1595 £100 was given by William Serle. With this money some land with an house belonging to it was purchased. With the rent of this land the churchwardens keep the house in repair for poor people to live in it and the overplus they distribute among the poor according to their discretion.
They receive likewise rent for 2 acres of land given a long time since by Walter Gorman adjoining to a farm called Hollingford and dispose of it in like manner.
There is 10*s*. p.a. bequeathed to our poor by one Richard Gard, and 20*s*., as I remember, by one John Pope.
And since the death of Catherine, Queen Dowager, there have come to us by the donation of John Man Esq., £46 p.a. to be received by the minister and parish officers, and by them with the rest of the inhabitants, land-owners, to be applied towards the maintaining, educating and setting up in the world of orphan children; and after that of other poor children, and after that, towards the relief of poor impotent aged and decrepid people and an yearly account of the disposal of this money is to be laid before our Justice of the Peace in the moneth of April.
12 Post-town Our nearest post-town is Newport.

9 Ashe 21M65/B4/1/1 fo.203

Charles Goldsmith, rector 1713–29 30 July 1725

1 Area This parish of Ash is in lenght about 5 miles, and in breadth above ½ mile.

2 Population Upon the strictest calculation at present [it] hath in it 50 souls.

3 Marriages &c. Births, burials and marriages uncertain and very few.

4 Patron Charles Wither Esq. of Hall in the parish of Dean is patron of the living.

5 Chapels No chappell in the parish.

6 Lecturer No lecturer or curate in the parish.

7 Papists No Papist here.

8 Dissenters No dissenters, nor meetings of any such here.

9 Gentry &c. No noblemen here. Gentlemen 2, Robert Reynolds, and the Revd Mr Jones, rector of Briston [Brighstone] in the Isle of Wight.

10 Schools No endowed school here.

11 Charities No charity money.

12 Post-town I shall be glad to receive and obey your lordship's command at any time, but if by letter I presume to acquaint Your Lordship that my letters are directed for me at Dean near Basingstoke.

10 Ashley 21M65/B4/1/2 fo.209

Francis Cox, rector 1680–1728 19 August 1725

1 Area The compass of ground in longitude 2 miles, in latitude 1 mile.

2 Population 72 souls.

3 Marriages &c. Marriges 1; birth 2; *communibus annis.*

4 Patron Thomas Hobbs Weekes.

5 Chapels One parish church served by the minister, maintained by the parish; the right of nomination [in] Hobs Wieks.

6 Lecturer No lecturer or curate in the parish.

7 Papists No Papists, no dissentor.

8 Dissenters No meeting-house or dissentor.

9 Gentry &c. No gentlemen or persons of note.

10 Schools No schools.

11 Charities 3 acres of land belong to the church.

12 Post-town The next post-town is Winchester.

11 Avington 21M65/B4/1/1 fo.15

John Newey, rector 1722–35

1 Area The said parish is about 1 mile in breadth and 3 miles in length.

2 Population The number of souls in it [is] about 103.

3 Marriages &c. The number of marriages, births and burials at a medium, one year with another, is 1 of the first, and 2 of the two last.

4 Patron Your Lordship is patron.

5 Chapels No chapel.

6 Lecturer Mr William Avery, rector of Hartley, is curate.

7 Papists 2 families of Papists of no consequence; 4 in number.
8 Dissenters No meetings of any sort.
9 Gentry &c. Persons of note and quality, Mr Bridges and his lady.
10 Schools No school endowed.
11 Charities No charities.
12 Post-town Winton is the next post-town.

12 Barton Stacey 21M65/B4/1/2 fo.214
Walter Garrett, vicar 1713–37
1 Area This parish is supposed to be about 5 miles long and 4½ broad; about 12 in compass.
2 Population There are in it about 300 souls.
3 Marriages &c. There are at a medium yearly 7 or 8 christenings; 7 or 8 burials; 2 or 3 marriges.
4 Patron The Dean and Chapter of Winchester are the patrons.
5 Chapels There is no chappel in the parish.
6 Lecturer There is a resident curate.
7 Papists There is one Papist, a farmer, who has no estate in the parish.
8 Dissenters There is no meeting of protestant dissenters, nor is there one dissenter in the parish.
9 Gentry &c. There is no person of any note, but the Revd Mr Woodroffe, prebendary of Worcester.
10 Schools There is no endowed school in the parish.
11 Charities There are no public charities nor hospitals.
12 Post-town The nearest post-town is Andover.

13 Basingstoke, Old Basing and Up Nately 21M65/B4/1/1 fo.205
Thomas Warton MA, vicar 1723–45 29 July 1725
As the vicarage of Basingstoke consists of these 3 parishes the following account includes them all, viz:
1 Area The parish of Basingstoke is generally computed to be 26 miles round, Basing 28, and Up Nately 16.
2 Population The number of souls in Basingstoke are not fewer than 1,000, Basing 350, and Up Nately 100.
3 Marriages &c. Births and burials in Basingstoke are, one year with another, 30 of each, according to the register, and not including the births of the children of dissenters. Marriages are near 20 in a year, but not all of parishioners. In Basing there are *communibus annis* about 12 births and burials and 3 or 4 marriages. In Up Nately seldom above 2 burials or births in a year, and it may be 1 marriage in 3 years.
4 Patron The patron of the vicarage (including these 3 parishes) is Magdalene College, Oxford, who have also the impropriation of them all.
5 Chapels No chapel in either of these parishes.
6 Lecturer The present lecturer of Basingstoke (for there is no lecture at either of the other 2 parishes) is John James MA and rector of Stratfield Turges. The curate (who is John Hoyle BA) assists the vicar in all 3 parishes. There is no house for a minister either at Basing or Up Nately.

7 Papists There is no Papist either convict or reputed in Basingstoke, nor in Up Nately. But in the parish of Basing are 2 farmers Papists whose names are Kemp and Payse. In the same parish is the mansion house of Cufaud Esq., a Papist, but he never resides there. His estate is said to be about £300 p.a.
8 Dissenters As to protestant dissenters, 70 familys of Presbyterians live in Basingstoke, who have also a large meeting-house there, as have likewise the Quakers, but these last do not exceed 10 familys; they never pay church-rates nor any dues to the vicar. The number of Anabaptists are not above 2 familys. I know of no other protestant dissenters in Basingstoke. In Basing there are about 4 families of Presbyterians and 2 of Quakers, but no Anabaptist. In Up Nately is 1 family of Anabaptists, but no Presbyterian nor Quaker.
9 Gentry &c. His Grace the Duke of Bolton has a house at Basing but never resides there. Neither of the other 2 parishes have any person of distinction in them or belonging to them.
10 Schools Schools there are none at Basing or Nately (excepting that Her Grace the present Dutchess of Bolton teaches and cloaths 20 girls in Basing parish). But at Basingstoke are 3 schools endowed, one of £60 p.a., the master of which is Mr James above-written, in which school are more than 20 scholars, one other of £13 6*s*. 8*d*. p.a., the master of which is usually the parish clerk (now Richard Woodroff) and has more than 10 scholars. The third is called the Blue-Coat School where 8 children are cloathed, fed and taught. The master of this school is John Drudge. All these schools are under the government of the mayor and aldermen of Basingstoke, who have the nomination of the masters of the same. Her Grace the present Dutchess of Bolton hath also a charity school at Basingstoke for 20 girls cloathed and taught but not as yet endowed.
11 Charities At Up Nately is only 1 acre of land given to the poor. At Basing about £1 p.a. At Basingstoke the following charitys have been given to the poor, which are distributed by the Mayor and Aldermen aforesaid, viz. Charles, 1st Duke of Bolton £102 p.a. to be divided among 5 parishes of which Basingstoke and Basing are 2; Sir James Dean £86 8*s*. 6*d*.; Richard Aldworth Esq. £200; John Hall £5 14*s*.; Mr Payne £100; Mr Smith £4. These are all distributed yearly (i.e. the interest of the money) and Sir James Lancaster has given an estate of £116 16*s*. 8*d*. p.a. In Basingstoke is also an hospital for 4 men and 4 women, but none at Basing nor Up Nately.
12 Post-town Basingstoke is a post town.

14 Baughurst 21M65/B4/1/1 fo.209
George Prince, rector 1716–43
1 Area I answer that according to the best information I can get, it consists of about 1,300 acres, all commons included.
2 Population I answer that, of men, women and children that are actual parishioners, we have much about an 108.
3 Marriages &c. I answer that, since my time, and for several years before, as it appears by the register book, we have had one year with another, much about 7 births, 7 burials and 2 marriages.

4 Patron I answer that it is in the gift of Your Lordship, as Lord Bishop of Winchester.
5 Chapels I answer that we have none belonging to our parish.
6 Lecturer I answer that we have neither lecturer [n]or curate.
7 Papists I answer that we have the happiness not to have any. No person in the whole parish suspected to be in the least inclined to Popery.
8 Dissenters I answer that, to my great concern, we have 5 dissenting families, 2 of which being Presbyterians, frequent some neighbouring meeting-houses. The other 3 being Quakers, have their meetings sometimes in this parish at a place built about the year 1697, and since left to 'em for that purpose by one James Potter of this parish.
9 Gentry &c. I answer that we have no persons of note, and that our parishioners consist chiefly of husbandmen and day-labourers.
10 Schools I answer that we have none.
11 Charities I answer that we have no hospitals and but 3 smal[l] charities left to our parish, one of which is 50*s*. p.a. payable out of an estate in the parish and to be disposed of among the poor by the minister for the time being in the presence of the church wardens, one half on St Thomas the Apostle, and the other on Thomas à Becket. This charity was left us by Thomas Sympson of the parish of Sherborne St John in this county in the year 1674. Another is 10*s*. p.a., the gift of Robert Green of this parish in the year 1713, payable likewise out of an estate in the parish, and to be distributed among the poor by the minister and the churchwardens on or about Xtmas Day. The other is the interest of £5 to be divided among the poor by the minister and the church wardens. This is said to be the gift of one Smart, long before the memory of any person now living in the parish.
12 Post-town Basingstoke [is] the nearest post-town.

15 Beaulieu 21M65/B4/1/2 fo.270
Philip Sone AM, minister 1725–30
'Bewley [is a] donative[1] in the county of Southampton, exempt from all episcopal jurisdiction.'
1 Area 8,100 acres in the parish.
2 Population 650 souls.
3 Marriages &c. 20 births, 17 burialls, 6 marriages, one year with another.
4 Patron His Grace the Duke of Montagu, patron of the living.
5 Chapels No chapel.
6 Lecturer No lecturer, no curate.
7 Papists No Papist.
8 Dissenters No meeting of dissenters. About 5 Presbyterians and 6 Anabaptists.
9 Gentry &c. No person of note lives here, but the Duke of Montagu hath a seat and resides here some part of the summer.
10 Schools 2 schools, one for poor boys, the other for girls. The boys' school endowed with £10 p.a. by the Duke of Montagu who puts in the master. John Pursar [is the] present master. At the other school 6 poor girls are taught to read and work, towards the charge of which the offertory is applied. Amey Martin [is] mistress. About 20 girls at this school.

11 Charities £90 left long since by — Kemp Esq. The interest to be distributed yearly to poor housekeepers that receive no alms from the parish.
12 Post-town Southampton [is] the next post-town.

16 Bedhampton 21M65/B4/1/2 fo.9
William Lamerton AM, rector 1713–32
1 Area Glebe 30 acres[2]. Parish containes 1,092 acres, a great extent of ground in the forest, and a disparked parke[3] not tythable.
2 Population Number of souls 161.
3 Marriages &c. Marriages 2; births 4; burialls 4.
4 Patron Frederick Fra[n]klin Esqr.
5 Chapels Chapell none.
6 Lecturer Lecturer none.
7 Papists 69 farmers and others, but of little or noe account.
8 Dissenters Meeting of protestant dissenters, none.
9 Gentry &c. Noblemen, gentlemen &c., none.
10 Schools None.
11 Charities None.
12 Post-town To the rector of Bedhampton near Havant, Hants. by Midhurst bagg.

17 Bentworth 21M65/B4/1/1 fo.59
Edward Acton LLB, rector 1719–62
1 Area My parish is about 7 miles in compass.
2 Population About 15 or 16 score souls.
3 Marriages &c. 1 marriage, 7 births, 5 burials.
4 Patron The advowson is my own.
5 Chapels I have no chapel.
6 Lecturer No lecturer nor curate.
7 Papists No Papists.
8 Dissenters No dissenters.
9 Gentry &c. No person of note.
10 Schools None but ABC schools.
11 Charities 40*s*. p.a. which are distributed at a vestry to those poor inhabitants who receive no collection.
12 Post-town Alton in Hants.

18 Bighton 21M65/B4/1/1 fo.17
John Mitchell, rector 1708–32 3 September 1725
William Phillips AM, curate
1 Area The parish is very near 3 miles long, 1¼ miles broad, contains about 1,500 acres of ground.
2 Population The number of souls are about 150.
3 Marriages &c. Births are about 4, burials 3, at a medium. Marriages hardly 1 in 2 years.

4 Patron Sir Robert Worsley is the patron.
5 Chapels There is no chapel.
6 Lecturer There is no lecturer.
7 Papists There is no Papist.
8 Dissenters Here is neither meeting nor protestant dissenter.
9 Gentry &c. Nor nobleman, gentleman, nor person of note.
10 Schools Here is no school endowed.
11 Charities Here is a charity of £50 called by the name of Batchelour's money, at present in the hands of Sir Robert Worsley, who is pleased to allow after the rate of 6% for it, and the interest being payd every half year is distributed among the poor according to the discretion of the minister and overseers. Here is also a gift of 3 acres or thereabout, let for 15*s*. p.a., bequeathed (by whom [is] not known) for the repairs of the church and layed out accordingly. Here is no hospital.
12 Post-town Alresford is the next post town.

19 Bishops Sutton and Ropley 21M65/B4/1/1 fo.40
Henry Cooper AB, vicar 1724–46 3 September 1725
1 Area The compass of the ground of the parish of Bishop's Sutton and its hamlet Ropley is about 20 miles round, according to the best information I can get at present.
2 Population The number of souls therein are I suppose about 620.
3 Marriages &c. Marriages about 4; births about 20; burials about 15.
4 Patron The patroness of the living is Mrs Anne Alexander.
5 Chapels There is a chapel in the parish, viz. in the hamlet of Ropley, called St Peter's (as I find it recorded in an ancient register, now in the parish, in the year of our Lord 1544, in these words, 'William Oliver, sepultus fuit infra cemitoriu parochiae Sancti Petri de Ropley'). It is served by the vicar. The body of it is maintained and supported by the inhabitants of the said hamlet, and the chancel thereof by the impropriator of that part of the parish. The vicar has the right of nomination to it, if, at any time, a curate be admitted.
6 Lecturer I have no lecturer or curate in my parish.
7 Papists There are 2 poor families in the parish reputed Papists, each family consisting of about [number wanting] persons, of no consequence, and of no estate, as far as I can find.
8 Dissenters There is neither any meeting, or protestant dissenter in the parish.
9 Gentry &c. There is no nobleman, gentleman or person of note of either sex (more than the patroness above mentioned) living in the parish.
10 Schools There are 3 schools in the parish that teach small children to read, and one that teaches to write; but no endowed school.
11 Charities There is a charity of £10 given to the parish by one Applegarth. And one other charity of £10 given to the parish by one Corderoy. The interest only of £10 is now distributed to poor housekeepers, the other £10 being said to be now lost. And there is one other charity (as I understand) of £200 given to the parish by the last will and testament of one

William Andrews who died in the year 1714, the interest of which was (as I am informed) disposed of for the apprenticing of poor children during the life of his widow, Jane Andrews, who died in the year 1717. But how or where the said £200 is now placed, or how the interest thereof is disposed of, is at present so kept as a secret, that I cannot, as yet, dive thereinto. There is no hospital in the parish.
12 Post-town New Alresford is the next post-town to my parish.

20 Bishopstoke 21M65/B4/1/2 fo.358
John Chirrieholme, rector 1699–1732 3 September 1725
[The parish is] a peculiar[25] in the deanery of Winton.
1 Area The compass is about 7 or 8 miles round.
2 Population 350.
3 Marriages &c. Marriages 2; births 12; burials 10.
4 Patron The patron is the Bishop of Winton.
5 Chapels Noe chappels.
6 Lecturer Noe curate.
7 Papists 14 [of whom] 1 has £30 p.a., 1 has £20 p.a., 2 has [sic] £5 each. The rest are children and labourers.
8 Dissenters Noe dissenters.
9 Gentry &c. Noe noblemen or gentlemen.
10 Schools Noe schools endowed.
11 Charities Given in the 18th year of King James by Thomas Dummer, 2½ acres of land by surrender for the payment of 40*s*. yearly for the use of the poor at Easter and Christmas. And also by Richard Dummer in the 7th year of King Charles the first [who] did surrender a close called Five Acres for the payment of 40*s*. p.a. at Michaelmas and Lady Day. And also Joan Basset, widow, in or about the year of our Lord 1630, in her last will and testament, did give unto the poor £20 the interest to be paid yearly at Easter, all which sums are constantly received by the churchwardens and distributed accordingly.
12 Post-town The next post-town is Winton.

21 Bishops Waltham 21M65/B4/1/2 fo.86
John Cooke, rector 1717–44
A peculiar exempted from archidiaconal jurisdiction.
1 Area The parish of Bishop's Waltham is by common estimation about 6 miles long and 2 miles broad.
2 Population There are in it about 1,400 souls.
3 Marriages &c. At a medium, one year with another, there are about 5 marriages, and between 30 and 40 births, and as many burials in the said parish.
4 Patron The Lord Bishop of Winton is patron.
5 Chapels There is no chapel in the parish.
6 Lecturer There is no lecturer, but Mr William Pearse is the curate.
7 Papists There are 4 or 5 reputed Papists in the parish, but of mean condition.

8 Dissenters There is no meeting of protestant dissenters, nor indeed one such dissenter in the parish.
9 Gentry &c. There is not any nobleman nor gentleman of note or distinction that lives in the parish.
10 Schools There is 1 school endowed with £10 p.a. by Bishop Morley for the instruction of 10 poor boys in reading and writing; to which hath been added by Mr Robert Kerby, lately deceased, £6 p.a. for teaching 6 poor boys. Mr Richard Gibson is the present master, and the right of nomination of the master is in the rector and churchwardens of the said parish. The said Mr Kerby hath likewise given £7 p.a. to teach poor children, both boys and girls, to read; but hath not determined them to any school, any otherwise, than that the boys are appointed to succeed the other 6 boys above-mentioned (as they go off) into Mr Gibson's school. Both these charities are under the direction of trustees, appointed by Mr Kerby in his last will.
11 Charities There was formerly given to the parish for charitable uses, at several times, the sum of £150 or thereabout; of which sum £100 were laid out by the trustees, appointed from time to time for the management of the said charity, in purchasing a part of the site of the bishop's palace, within the said parish, and the remainder of the said sum in purchasing a small house or tenement. The income of both which purchases is yearly distributed among such poor people of the parish as do not receive the monthly collection. There is also given by the afore-mentioned Mr Kerby the sum of £3 p.a. to be distributed among such poor people of the parish as shall receive the sacrament on the 3 great festivals of the year.
12 Post-town The town of Bishop's Waltham is a post-town.

22 Blendworth 21M65/B4/1/2 fo.11

Thomas Hughes, rector 1711–40
1 Area The parish of Blendworth is supposed to be about 5 miles in compass.
2 Population There are in the said parish about 120 souls.
3 Marriages &c. Marriages, one year with another, 2 or 3; births about 3 or 4 in a year; burials about 2 one year with another.
4 Patron His Grace the thrice noble Henry, Duke of Beaufort is patron of the living.
5 Chapels There is no chapel in the parish.
6 Lecturer There is neither lecturer nor curate; I doe the duty myselfe.
7 Papists There is but 1 Popish family in the parish, and that of no consequence.
8 Dissenters There is not any meeting of protestant dissenters of any denomination whatsoever in the parish.
9 Gentry &c. There is neither gentleman nor person of any note of either sex living in the parish.
10 Schools There have been given to the parish £200 in money by one William Appleford (late porter to the college of Winchester) to purchase lands therewith for the maintenance of a free schoole in the said parish to teach young children of each sex to read, and to buy them books. Which

said moneys (as by the order of the said William Appleford's will) have since been laid out upon lands lying and being in the parish of Catherington to the yearly income of about £8 p.a. The school is taught by women. And it is managed both as to the nomination of those who teach and the number of schoolchildren to be taught by 2 or 3 trustees (inhabitant of the parish) impowered by a deed of trust from both the heir and executour of the donor William Appleford aforesaid.
11 Charities There have no other charities been given to the parish.
12 Post-town The next post-town to us is Petersfield.
Blendworth and Catherington are contiguous parishes.
[The above responses are renumbered to correspond with the order of the bishop's questions]

23 Boldre 21M65/B4/1/2 fo.105
Thomas Jenner BD, vicar 1724–30
1 Area [Boldre] is about 5 miles in length from east to west, and about 4 miles in breadth from north to south; and may be supposed to contain
2 Population About 6 or 700 souls.
3 Marriages &c. About 20 births, as many burials, and 8 or 10 marriages yearly.
4 Patron Mr John Howell, patron.
5 Chapels It hath 2 chapels: 1. Brockenhurst, a small parish lying between Bolder and the New Forrest, and served by a licensed curate, maintained by allowance from the vicar of Bolder himself. 2. Lymington, a borough-town, served by a licensed curate, maintained by allowance from the vicar of Bolder, which allowance is also encreased by the voluntary contributions of the inhabitants. The right of nomination is in the vicar of Bolder.
6 Lecturer The present curate of Lymington, the Revd Mr Francklyn Powell, to whose more particular account of that town your lordship is referred.
7 Papists In Bolder and Brockenhurst only 2 or 3 Papists, and those of mean condition.
8 Dissenters No dissenting meeting-houses. In Bolder some few Independants, and in Brockenhurst some few Independants, and some Anabaptists.
9 Gentry &c. Gentlemen of note are: in Bolder, James Worseley, Paul Burrard, Henry Drax, William Forbes, John Bromfield, [all] Esqs.; in Brockenhurst, Captain Hardy, William Samber, gent.
10 Schools No schools settled or endowed.
11 Charities No hospital. One charity £4 p.a. which is regularly distributed every year by the vicar, churchwardens and other trustees.
12 Post-town The next post-town [is] Lymington.

24 Bonchurch [IoW] 21M65/B4/1/2 fo.151
William Downes AM, rector 1720–1763 25 August 1725
A small parish situate on the east part of the island.
1 Area The parish contains in circumference about 2½ miles.

2 Population [The] number of souls, men, women and children about 50.
3 Marriages &c. Marriages, births and burials, 1 or 2 of each in a year.
4 Patron, 5 Chapels John Popham Esq., living at Newport in the Isle of Wight, who also have a manour seat at Shankling, where is a chappel annexed to the rectory of Bonchourch, maintained at the charge of the patron, and endowed by his ancestours, with 3 score acres of glebe land, and the tythe of 3 small coppyhold estates, the manour farm paying £3 a year modus.[4] The parish in circumference 2 miles, containing about 40 souls. Marriages, births and burials one of each in year.
6 Lecturer [No reply.]
7 Papists, 8 Dissenters No papist or protestant dissenter in either parish.
9 Gentry &c. [No reply.]
10 Schools, 11 Charities No school or charities have been given in either parish.
12 Post-town Newport [is] the next post-town.

25 Botley 21M65/B4/1/2 fo.272
Joseph Walton, rector 1715–33 23 August 1725
1 Area Its length from north to south is about 3½ miles; and its breadth from east to west about 1.
2 Population About 330.
3 Marriages &c. About 3 or 4 marriages, 12 or 13 births, and about as many burials as births.
4 Patron The Dukes of Rutland and Beaufort, who present alternately.
5 Chapels There is only a parish church; no chapel or chapels.
6 Lecturer There is no lecturer or curate in the parish, but the rector constantly resides and does all [the] duty himselfe.
7 Papists There is not one Papist in my parish.
8 Dissenters There are no meetings of protestant dissenters in the parish of any kind; nor one protestant dissenter of either sex.
9 Gentry &c. None.
10 Schools There are no schools endowed.
11 Charities The summe of £35 hath been formerly given to the poor of the parish; which has been customarily put out to interest, and called in, and put out again (as occasion required) by the churchwardens for the time being; and whatever interest has been made has been yearly distributed among the poor widows that did not receive alms of the parish; which (it is said) is agreeable to the design of that charity, but no writings are to be found to direct, nor is it now known who left or gave the same. There is likewise the summe of 10*s*. p.a., with the payment of which a certain estate about 8 miles distant is charged; which is to be paid in Durly church porch (a contiguous parish) on the feast of All Saints yearly for ever, for the same use as the other. The time and place has not been observed in anyone's memory. But the mony has been yearly paid and distributed. There are no hospitals.
12 Post-town The next post-town is Bishop's Waltham.

26 Brading [IoW] 21M65/B4/1/2 fo.153
Richard Palmer, vicar 1725–63
1 Area The parish is computed to be about 16 miles in circumference.

2 Population The number of the inhabitants is computed to be about 1,200.
3 Marriages &c. About 6 marriages, 25 births, 20 burials, at a medium, one year with another.
4 Patron The right of presentation to the vicarage is in the Master, Fellows and Scholars of Trinity College, Cambridge.
5 Chapels We have no chapels, unless Yaverland and Shanklin be such.
6 Lecturer We have no lecturer or curate.
7 Papists There are no Papists.
8 Dissenters There are no dissenters.
9 Gentry &c. The person of greatest note in the parish is Sir William Oglander Bt.
10 Schools There are no endowed schools.
11 Charities No hospitals. But there are £6 p.a. for ever given by Sir William Oglander for the benefit of 6 poor widows paid out of an estate called Pennifeather in St Helen's parish. Colonel Knight gave £12 p.a. for ever to the poor of the parish, and £1 1*s.* 6*d.* to the minister to preach a sermon yearly on the first Sunday in October. The money is paid out of an estate called Lee Farm in the parish of Brading. Mr Gard gave 10*s.* yearly for ever to the poor who do not receive collection, paid out of an estate called Westbrook in the parish of St Helen's.
12 Post-town The nearest post-town is Newport.

27 Bradley 21M65/B4/1/1 fo.20
Thomas Winder, rector 1719–1725/6
1 Area The said parish is upwards of 3 miles in compass, comon and wast included.
2 Population The number of souls therein is 73.
3 Marriages &c. There are 3 births and burials, one year with another, and about 1 marriage in 2 years.
4 Patron Anthony Henley Esq. is patron.
5 Chapels There is no chapel.
6 Lecturer I officiate myself.
7 Papists There is no Papist in the parish.
8 Dissenters No dissenter, and consequently no meeting.
9 Gentry &c. There is no person of any note.
10 Schools No school with any endowment.
11 Charities No charity has been given to the parish, that I could ever learn.
12 Post-town Alresford is the nearest post-town.

28 Bramdean 21M65/B4/1/1 fo.22
Robert Knapp AM, rector 1719–41
1 Area The parish of Bramdean is supposed to be about 4 miles in compass.
2 Population 130 is supposed to be the number of souls therein.

3 Marriages &c. There is, one year with another, 1 marriage, 3 christenings, and 2 burials.
4 Patron The patron of the living is the Lord Bishop of Winton.
5 Chapels There is no chapel in the parish.
6 Lecturer There is no lecturer or curate in the parish.
7 Papists There are 9 Papists in the parish but of no consequence or estate.
8 Dissenters There are no protestant dissenters in the parish.
9 Gentry &c. James Venables Esq. is the only person of note in the parish.
10 Schools There is no endowed school in the parish.
11 Charities There is no hospital nor any charitable donation whatsoever.
12 Post-town The next post-town is Alresford.

29 Bramley 21M65/B4/1/1 fo.213
Stephen Green, vicar 1724–42
1 Area The parish is in compass of ground about 6 miles.
2 Population There are about 230 persons in the parish.
3 Marriages &c. There are about 6 births, 2 marriages and 5 burials (reckoning at a medium) in the year.
4 Patron Queen's College in Oxford is the patron of the living.
5 Chapels There is no chapell in the parish.
6 Lecturer There is no lecturer or curate.
7 Papists There is but one Roman Catholick, and he a day-labourer.
8 Dissenters There is no meeting, nor any protestant dissenter.
9 Gentry &c. No nobleman, gentleman, or person of note lives in the parish.
10 Schools No publick school.
11 Charities £50 given to the parish by William Lord St Johns in the year 1632 to be applied for apprentising out poor boys and girls. The principal money having been lent out upon bond to Mr John Cuffold, no interest has been paid these 20 years. £6 formerly left by two old maiden sisters for the relief of the poor widows of the parish.
12 Post-town Basingstoke is the nearest post-town.

30 Bramshott 21M65/B4/1/1 fo.61
Joseph Jackson, rector 1702–30
1 Area The compass of the parish is about 10 miles; a larg tract of barren heath-ground and some hundred acres of forrest land (in the Crown) being included in itts boundaries.
2 Population By the best information that can reasonably be gott, 'tis supposed there may be about 300 souls in the parish.
3 Marriages &c. One year with another, for the last 20 years, there have been in the said parish 10 births, 2 marriages, and 9 burials.
4 Patron The Provost and Fellows of Queen's College, Oxford, patrons of the liveing.
5 Chapels No chapel in the parish.

6 Lecturer No lecturer or curate.
7 Papists No Papists in the parish.
8 Dissenters No dissenters in the parish except a family of Quakers, of about 4 or 5 in number.
9 Gentry &c. No noblemen in the parish or gentlemen of distinction.
10 Schools No endowed schools in the parish.
11 Charities No charities given to the parish, or hospitall in itt.
12 Post-town The next post-town to the parish is Haslemere in Surry.

31 Breamore 21M65/B4/1/2 fos.115–17
John Crabb, curate 1711–49 23 August 1725
The rectory impropriate, within the Archdeaconry of Winton and Deanery of Fordingbridge, held by lease for a certain term of years.

A fee farm rent of £4 17*s.* p.a. payable out of it to the Crown, and also a yearly pension of 23*s.* to King's Colledg in Cambridg.

The tythes thereof great and small (as I conceive) were before the suppression of the monasterys swallowed down by the Priory here, as also were the tythes of Southcharford, Hale, Rockburn and Whitsbury (except the small tythes of Whitsbury (where there still is a presentative vicarage) [)], as also were the tythes of Quedgly in Glostershire. All which were restored to the church by Sir William Doddington Kt., AD1638. All that I have seen in print relating to is to be found in Mr Boreman's *Plea for Tythes* printed in quarto, AD1652,[5] where 'tis said [p. 31] 'Sir William Doddington, knight of Hampshire, a religious gentleman, restored no less than 6 impropriations out of his own estate to the value of £600 yearly and more.' But the yearly value of 'em *now* is no less than £700 and upwards.
In answer to the queries proposed:
1 Area Breamore with Southcharford annext is in circumference 11 miles, 3 furlongs and 24 lugg.
2 Population The number of souls 422.
3 Marriages &c. Marriages about 2; births and burials about 9, one year with another, for about 50 years last past.
4 Patron His Grace William, Duke of Manchester has the nomination to it, which is to be confirmed by 4 trustees (who have been lately chosen in the room of 4 others deceased according to the appointment of the said Sir William Doddington[)].
5 Chapels His Grace has also the nomination to the tythes of Southcharford and the chapel there annext by will to the rectory of Breamore. But that chapel (which within my own memory was a very fair strong stone building) has been taken down and the enclosures thrown open, and a barn, or part of a barn built across where the chapel stood.
6 Lecturer No lecturer or curate here (but myself).
7 Papists 5 Papists, but of no consequence, or visible estates.
8 Dissenters No meeting of protestant dissenters.
9 Gentry &c. William Grevil, Lord Brooke, the only nobleman; no gentleman or person of note of either sex besides.
10 Schools No school here endowed.

11 Charities One alms-house, but not endowed, and in it there are 6 poor people supported by the parish.
Item, £5 every fourth year given by John Doddington Esq. for the apprentising a poor child of Breamore, being a rent charge issuing out of the profits of an estate called Sandy Balls, now belonging to the aforesaid Lord Brooke.
Item, Henry Johnson, gentleman, gave and bequeathed to the minister, churchwardens and overseers for the time being, and their successors for ever, £100 to be laid out in some lands of inheritance in fee simple for the apprentising poor children of the inhabitants of Braemore or Woodgreen (extra-parochial in the New Forest) which £100 with £20 more since added thereto were lately laid out in the purchase of one moitie of one yearly farm rent or summ of £12 0*s*. 11*d*. charged on all *that* the manour of *Worthesly* with the appurtenences within the parish of Ringwood and Harbridg in the county of Southampton now in the possession of Sir Thomas Hoby aforesaid, which legacy before my admission to this curacy was very much abused and misapplyed, but has since been applyed according to the intention of the donor's will.
Item, one close[6] and half, called *Philpot's close*, let at present for £1 p.a.
Item, one mead called *Church mead* being one close which with a close called *Charford close*. is let for £5 p.a.
Item, half an acre of land within *Durstal Gate* let for 11s. p.a., all which 4 parcels of lands were formerly given by [blank] towards the support of the parish church of Breamore, and the rest of them, has been from time to time employed accordingly.
12 Post-town The next post-town is Fordingbridge.

32 Brighstone or Brixton [IoW] 21M65/B4/1/2 fo.159
Reginald Jones, rector 1719–30 25 August 1725
1 Area If by compass of ground is meant the ambitus or circumference of the parish, that cannot easily be determined, because in some parts of it other parishes intervene, but by the best judgment I can make, it may be about 10 or 12 miles round. But if, as I conceive, the content or number of acres be intended, it contains about 2,000 acres.
2 Population The number of souls are about 250 or near 300.
3 Marriages &c. *Communibus annis* for 7 years past marriages are 2, births 14, burials 6.
4 Patron Patron, Lord Bishop of Winton.
5 Chapels No chapel now standing, but there are ruins of one, which belonged formerly to the mannor-house of Limerston in the said parish.
6 Lecturer No lecturer, nor at present any curate.
7 Papists No Papist.
8 Dissenters Nor protestant dissenter.
9 Gentry &c. No nobleman nor other person of note lives in the parish, above the degree of a farmer.
10 Schools No school endowed, nor any other but for teaching children to read.

11 Charities No hospitall, nor do I find any settled charity.
12 Post-town Newport [is] the next post-town.

33 Brook [IoW] 21M65/B4/1/2 fo.157
John Woodford, rector 1723–60 25 August 1725
1 Area The compass of the ground in my parish is about one mile in length and the same in breadth.
2 Population The number of souls therein is about 70.
3 Marriages &c. The number of marriages at a medium one year with another is 1, births 4, burials 2.
4 Patron The patron of my living is William Bowreman Esq.
5 Chapels There is no chappel therein.
6 Lecturer No lecturer or curate.
7 Papists No Papist.
8 Dissenters No protestant dissenting meetings, nor dissenters of any denomination whatever.
9 Gentry &c. The only persons of note in my parish of each sex are William Bowreman Esq. and his lady and family.
10 Schools There is no school therein.
11 Charities No charity nor hospital.
12 Post-town The next post town to my parish is Newport.

34 Broughton 21M65/B4/1/2 fo.212
Samuel Eyre, rector 1722–42 20 August 1725
1 Area I answer, 2,000 acres.
2 Population I answer 480 souls.
3 Marriages &c. I answer of marriages 3; of christenings 18; and of burials 14.
4 Patron I answer His Grace Evelyn, Duke of Kingston.
5 Chapels I answer that I have one chapel in my parish named Bosington, served by the Revd Mr Lamplugh, maintained by me and my nomination.
6 Lecturer I answer that I have one curate, the Revd Mr Braithwaite.
7 Papists I answer that I have none.
8 Dissenters I answer that there is a meeting of Anabaptists, about 120 in number.
9 Gentry &c. I answer Thomas Edmonds of Bosington Esq.
10 Schools I answer that I have one school in my parish, the salary of which is £25 p.a.; the master Mr Jeane, the number of scholars 30, and the school is in the gift of several farmers in the parish who were left trustees by the donour Thomas Dowse, late of New Sarum, gent.
11 Charities I answer that a legacy of £5 p.a. has been given by Mr Smith to such inhabitants of this place who are not upon the parish book and have more children begotten in lawful wedlock than they can maintain by their labour. I have no hospital in my parish.
12 Post-town Andover is the next post-town to me.

35 Brown Candover 21M65/B4/1/1 fo.24
Richard Burleigh, rector 1709–34
1 Area The parish is about 3 miles in length, 1½ in breadth.

2 Population According to the best information about 8 score.
3 Marriages &c. Marriages at a medium 1, births and burials 3.
4 Patron The Hon. Sir Robert Worsley.
5 Chapels Woodmancott [is] a chapel of ease, depending on the mother church of Brown-Candover.
6 Lecturer A curate, my son Robert Burleigh.
7 Papists Papists none.
8 Dissenters Dissenters of no kind.
9 Gentry &c. None.
10 Schools No schools endowed.
11 Charities None.
12 Post-town Alresford.

36 Burghclere 21M65/B4/1/1 fo.122
Richard Eyre, rector 1690–1745
1 Area I suppose the parish to be about 13 miles in compass.
2 Population I judge there may be about 500 souls in my parish.
3 Marriages &c. At a medium one year with another there may be 2 or 3 marriages; 9 or 10 births; and 7 or 8 burials.
4 Patron The patron of my living is the Hon. Robert Herbert.
5 Chapels I have one chapel belonging to my parish at Newtown, where a curate hath usually been placed on the nomination of the rector of Burghclear; the present curate is Mr Seth Eyre, to whom the tithes of Newtown are allowed as hath been usual.
6 Lecturer There is a lecture at the chapel at Newtown founded by one of the family of the Lucys, for the support of which £20 p.a. is paid out of a farm at Colingbourn in Wiltshire. Sir Berkly Lucy, as heir of that family, hath the nomination of the lecturer, and the present lecturer is Mr Seth Eyre. I have a curate in Mr William Dawes to assist me at Burghclear and to supply for me during my residence at Sarum.
7 Papists There is no Papist in the parish.
8 Dissenters There is no meeting of dissenters in the parish, but in the remotest part of it which lyes near Newbery there are about half a dozen families of Presbyterians, [and] 1 family of Quakers.
9 Gentry &c. There is no person of note in my parish.
10 Schools There is no school in the parish, unless for teaching children to read and without any endowment.
11 Charities There is no hospital in my parish, nor any charity given to it.
12 Post-town Newbery in Berkshire is our nearest post-town.

37 Buriton 21M65/B4/1/2 fo.15
William Lowth, rector 1699–1732
These answers relate to that part of the parish whose inhabitants resort to the mother church, the same queries being sent to the curate of Petersfield, a chappel belonging to the said parish.
1 Area That part of the parish of Buriton which belongs to the mother church, is about 3 miles in length and 2 in breadth.

2 Population There are about 250 souls in that part of the parish.
3 Marriages &c. The number of births and burialls is about 10 of each, *communibus annis*. That of marriages is uncertain, because those that procure licenses are usually married where they take their license.
4 Patron The patron of the living is the Lord Bishop of Winchester.
5 Chapels There is a chapple belonging to the parish at Petersfield, and the curate is named by the rector.
6 Lecturer The curate's name is Mr George Aylmer.
7 Papists A farmer's son whose mother is still living, has bin lately perverted to Popery by some persons living in the neighbouring parish of Harting in the diocese of Chichester, where mass is publicly resorted to every Sunday, and there is a mason's wife of the same persuasion, whose husband suffers her to breed her children that way.
8 Dissenters There is a meeting of dissenters lately set up at Petersfield, of which the curate of the place will give Your Lordship information.
9 Gentry &c. There are 2 gentlemen's families in this part of the parish, the one where a gentleman lives who is Justice of the Peace, the other where an ancient lady lives.
10 Schools There is no school here, but of poor children that learn to read.
11 Charities The only charity belonging to the parish consists of a small estate about £6 p.a., given by Dr Laney, late Bishop of Ely, and formerly rector of this parish; the clear profits arising out of it are laid out every year to apprentice a poor child at Buriton and Petersfield by turns. The rector and the gentleman or lady that enjoys one of the chief estates of the parish dispose of the charity by direction of the benefactor.
12 Post-town The burrough of Petersfield, lying in the parish, is a post-town.

38 Calbourne [IoW] 21M65/B4/1/2 fo.161
Thomas Terrell, rector 1721/2–after 1744 but before 1766
1 Area The parish is judged to be about 12 miles in compass, and to contain upwards of 4,000 acres.
2 Population There are computed to be upwards of 300 souls in the parish.
3 Marriages &c. We have usually in a year about 12 births, 7 or 8 burials, seldom above 2 or 3 marriages.
4 Patron The living is a peculiar in the gift of the Lord Bishop of Winton.
5 Chapels There is 1 chapel in the parish called Newtown chapel, being denominated from the place where it stands, which was anciently a flourishing town, but is now reduced to a few cottages, for which reason the chapel being supported at the charge of the inhabitants, has been out of repair for many years, so that no divine service could be performed in it. Before its decay 'twas served, once a month by the rector of this parish.
6 Lecturer There is no lecturer or curate in the parish.
7 Papists There are no Papists in the parish.
8 Dissenters There are no meetings of protestant dissenters in the parish; there are 2 or 3 Presbiterians and as many Anabaptists.

9 Gentry &c. There is no nobleman or gentleman or person of note of either sex dwelling in our parish. Sir John Barrington has a considerable estate in it.
10 Schools We have no endowed school.
11 Charities Neither have we any hospital. Nor have any publick charities been given to the parish.
12 Post-town The next post-town is Newport.

39 Carisbrooke [IoW] 21M65/B4/1/2 fo.163
Thomas Troughear, vicar 1722–62
1 Area 'Tis in compass about 16 miles.
2 Population In Carisbrook taken separately there are about 800. In Newport about 1,600. In Northwood about 150. In West Cowes about 1,250. In the whole parish there are in all about 3,800 inhabitants.
3 Marriages &c. At Carisbrook church about 10 marriages, 16 baptized, and 18 buryed. At Newport about 6 marriages, about 50 baptized and 40 buryed. At Northwood about 4 marriages, 6 baptized and 6 buryed. At West Cowes chapel, about 40 baptized and 30 buryed. There should be there no marriages, but I am told there are about 6 a year there.
4 Patron The Provost and Fellows of Queen's College, Oxford.
5 Chapels There are 3 chapels in it, Newport and Northwood of ancient erection, and mentioned expresly in every presentation, institution and induction instruments. The chapel of West Cowes is of late erection, endowed by Bishop Morley with £20 p.a. upon condition that the inhabitants raise by subscriptions £40 more for the curate, who is at present John King MA of Queen's College, Oxford. All rights tithes dues &c. being still reserved to the patron and vicar of Carisbrook. Newport is and has been all along maintained and supported by the inhabitants' subscriptions, and is served at present by Cadwallader Williams AB of Christ Church, Oxford. Both these are nominated by the vicar of Carisbrook. *Marginal note*: The nomination to West Cowes is in the parishioners, the bishop's approbation and licence being necessary. He appointed Mr Williams at the nomination of the parish, and not of the vicar of Carisbrooke. Since this paper &c. and since [sic], another nomination by the parishioners has been licensed.
The great tythes of Carisbrook are in the hands of lay impropriators with the tythes of wool and lamb; so that the vicarial tythes there are very small, but the vicar has also the great tythes of Northwood, and has always supplyed the chapel there and the mother church himself, but when hindered by age &c.
6 Lecturer 2 curates, Mr King and Mr Williams.
7 Papists None.
8 Dissenters 3 [meetings] in Newport, one for Presbyterians, one for Anabaptists, and one for Quakers. In Carisbrook there are in all about 170 dissenters, in Newport 260, in West Cowes and Northwood, about 18.
9 Gentry &c. In Carisbrook Lady Miller, Mrs Leigh and David Worsley Esq. In Newport John Popham Esq.
10 Schools 1 free grammar-school at Newport, endowed with a house and garden and lands to the value of £40 p.a. The master is Thomas Dickonson

AB of Queens' College, Cambridge. The right of nomination is at present contested by the corporation of Newport and the gentlemen whose ancestors were chief contributors to the endowment of the said school.
11 Charities To the poor of Carisbrook is given £3 p.a. charged upon Sir Thomas Miller's estate in the parish. To Newport is given by Eustace [*amended*: John] Mann Esq. £43 15*s.* p.a. to put poor children out apprentices with, or for the better support and maintenance of poor impotent persons in the said town.
To Northwood including Cowes is given by the said John Mann Esq. £20 15*s.* for the same uses. To Northwood including also West Cowes is given by Richard Smith Esq., my predecessor's son, to the minister of Carisbrook for ever, his estate in Northwood to the value of about £22 p.a., upon condition that the said minister pay £10 p.a. to the parish of St Mary Woolnoth in London for the officers of the said parish to put out a poor boy apprentice every other year with, which boy is to be born in Northwood or Cowes and nominated by the vicar and 10 of the most substantial inhabitants of Northwood and Cowes. There are no hospitals in the parish.
12 Post-town Newport in the Isle of Wight.
Appended: In the town of Newport, from April 1st 1724 to April 1st 1725, baptized 27 males 28 females [total] 55; buried 19 males, 20 females [total] 39; married 46.
Copy of the clause in Bishop Morley's benefactions relating to West Cowes in the Isle of Wight
And as to the said clear yearly sum of £40 p.a. upon trust and confidence that the said Francis Morley, Walter Darrell, William Harrison, Will Hawkins and John Nicholas, their heirs and assigns, shall from time to time for ever hereafter yearly pay and allow out of the same, to Thomas Gubbs, clerk, lecturer of and in the church or chapel of West Cowes in the Isle of Wight, and coadjutor to the vicar of Carisbrook in the same so long as he shall continue under that character and in that capacity there, viz. of lecturer and coadjutor therein, and to all and every such person and persons as shall successively after him be in like manner lecturers and coadjutors there, so long as the inhabitants of West Cowes aforesaid shall according to a contract and agreement made between the said Lord Bishop on the one part and divers of the present inhabitants there on the other other part, in and by an indenture bearing even [sic] date herewith and made between the same partys recited, specifyed and declared, pay £40 p.a. to the said Thomas Gubbs and unto such person and persons as shall after him be lecturers and coadjutors there as aforesaid, with neglect or default of payment of the said £40 by the year for more than the space of one year, the yearly sum of £20, parcel of the said £4, part of the said fee-farm rent for such lecturers and coadjutors' reading of divine service and preaching and administering the sacraments in the church or chapel of West Cowes aforesaid and to perform such other offices there as belong to the cure of souls. Provided that no person or persons shall at any time hereafter be admitted to be lecturer or coadjutor of or in the said church or chapel or to be taken or reputed to be such who are not respec<tively> and successively approved and licensed by the bishop of the <diocese> for the time being to

be so and do at the receipt of the first payment of the exhibition or stipend hereby and hereafter granted and allowed them for being so, produce such their licences to the person appointed to pay the same, who is hereby required, unless the same be done, not to make any such payment as is herein hereby directed and appointed. And in case that failure shall be made by the said inhabitants for the time being of payment of the said £40 p.a. for more than the space of a year, then upon trust and confidence that the said £20 p.a. shall be no longer paid to any lecturer or coadjutor of West Cowes, but shall be disposed of as followeth for ever, that is to say, the sum of £10 part thereof to be paid to the minister of the parish church of the Holy Trinity in Guildford for the time being in augmentation of his maintenance and the sum of £10 other part thereof to be paid to the minister of the parish of Ewell in the county of Surrey for the time being in augmentation of his maintenance.
By the deed the mony is to be paid by the *housekeeper* of Wolvesey.

40 Catherington 21M65/B4/1/2 fo.12
Thomas Hughes, vicar 1690–1740
Catherington is a vicarage impropriate.[7]
1 Area The parish of Catherington is supposed to be about 9 miles in compass.
2 Population The number of souls in it are about 322.
3 Marriages &c. Marriages are, one year with another, 3 or 4; births about 6 or 7 in a year; burials about 7 or 8 in a year.
4 Patron The patron and impropriator of the living is one Mr John Brett, and lives in the parish.
5 Chapels There is no chapel in the parish.
6 Lecturer There is neither lecturer nor curate in the parish, but I serve the church myselfe.
7 Papists There are 2 or 3 popish families in the parish, and those not of any consequence.
8 Dissenters There are no meetings of protestant dissenters of any kind (I thank God) in the parish. There is only 1 Anabaptist, an old woman.
9 Gentry &c. There are 2 gentlemen and their families in the parish.
10 Schools There is a free schoole in the parish to teach young children of each sex to read, and they are taught by women. It was given by one William Appleford (late porter to the college of Winchester) and he endowed it with an estate of the value of £10 p.a. lying and being in the parish of Barton Stacy near Winchester. It is in the management of 2 trustees (inhabitants of the parish) authorised by a deed of trust from both the heir and the executor of the aforesaid William Appleford, donor. The said trustees nominate who shall teach, as also the number of children to be taught. They likewise buy the children bookes.
11 Charities No more charities have been given to the parish.
12 Post-town The next post-town to us is Petersfield.

41 Chale [IoW] 21M65/B4/1/2 fo.169
Richard Burleigh, rector 1708/9–1734 25 August 1725
1 Area The parish of Chale is about 10 miles in circumference, viz. about 3 miles long and 2 broad.

2 Population The number of souls is about 200.
3 Marriages &c. The number of marriages in one year at a medium is about 3; births 8; burials 4.
4 Patron The patron of the living is Sir Robert Worsley.
5 Chapels There is no chapel in the parish.
6 Lecturer There is no lecturer or curate in the parish.
7 Papists There is no Papist in the parish.
8 Dissenters There is no meeting of dissenters in the parish, and only one Presbiterian in it.
9 Gentry &c. There is no nobleman, gentleman or person of note in the parish.
10 Schools There is no school endowed in the parish.
11 Charities No charities have been given to the parish.
12 Post-town The next post-town is Newport.

42 Chalton 21M65/B4/1/2 fo.23

Thomas Yalden DD, rector 1711–36
1 Area The parish of Chalton from north to south is about 4 miles, and from east to west about 3 miles, the whole compass about 14 miles.
2 Population It contains about 60 familys and 400 souls.
3 Marriages &c. I compute about 4 marriages, 10 births and 6 burials generaly in a year.
4 Patron The presentation to this church was formerly in the lady abbess of Nuneaton, Warwickshire. At the dissolution of abbys it devolved to the Crown. The advowsons [sic] was granted by King Charles the 2nd to the Duke of Beaufort, who presented to it in 1671. Queen Ann[e] in right of the Crown presented one of her chaplains Dr Reeves to it, 1710; but when I produced His Grace's title under the broad seal, the Lord Chancellor Harcourt allowed it good, and I had institution upon it. The present duke is the patron.
5 Chapels There is a chapel at Idsworth in this parish. It was founded by Sir Edward Banister, then lord of the mannor, who endowed it with the tithes of that place about the year 1390. As appears by his composition made for serving the cure of it by the rectors of Chalton for ever. It is supplied every Sunday by my curate Mr Newlin.
6 Lecturer I have no lecturer. Mr John Newlin is my curate who resides in the parsonage house with his family, and has served 13 years.
7 Papists The Lord Dormer and his whole family, being about 21 persons. There are Papists in that tithing besides, about 12 men and women and 6 children. But none of any estate or consequence but his lordship, who lives at, and is lord of, Idsworth mannor.
8 Dissenters Only one Anabaptist, who formerly often had, but of late years very rarely, a meeting at his house. I could never hear that anyone of my parish went amongst them, and those from other parts seldom making up above half a dozen.
9 Gentry &c. The Lord Dormer and his lady, but no other person of estate or distinction lives.

10 Schools There is no school, nor any endowment for one, but a poor woman for children, or an accidental writing-master when he can have business.
11 Charities No charitable benefaction ever given here that I could hear of.
12 Post-town Petersfield is the next post-town, our letters are directed to it, to be left at Horndean, about a mile distant.

43 Chawton 21M65/B4/1/1 fo.63
John Baker, rector 1718/19–1742
1 Area The parish is about 5 miles in compass.
2 Population The number of souls here is about 176.
3 Marriages &c. The number of marriages here are 2, births 4, burial[s] 3, one year with another.
4 Patron Bulstrode Knight Esq. is patron.
5 Chapels Here is no chapel.
6 Lecturer Here is no lecturer nor curate.
7 Papists Here is no Papist.
8 Dissenters Here is no protestant dissenter.
9 Gentry &c. Here are no noblemen, gentlemen or persons of note.
10 Schools Here are no schools.
11 Charities The charities here are £4 13*s.* 4*d.* p.a., distributed by the rector and churchwardens to poor housekeepers.
12 Post-town Alton is the next post-town.

44 Cheriton 21M65/B4/1/1 fo.26
William Trimnell DD, rector 1721–9
Cheriton [is] a peculiar in the Deanry of Alresford.
1 Area The parish of Cheriton with the 2 chappelries annext is supposed to be about 15 miles in compass.
2 Population The number of souls in the sayd parish with the 2 chappelries annext is supposed to be about 600.
3 Marriages &c. The number of marriages in the sayd parish (the chappels included) may be about 5; of births about 18, and of burials about 14 at a medium one year with another.
4 Patron The patron of the rectory of Cheriton is the Bishop of Winchester.
5 Chapels There are 2 chappels annext to the rectory of Cheriton, one of which is called Tichbourne, and the other Kilmiston *alias* Kimston. They are served by 2 curates, viz. the former by John Barrett MA and the latter by Jenkin Williams MA. They are maintaind and supported by the rector of Cheriton, who has also the right of nomination to them.
6 Lecturer There is no lecturer or curate in the parish besides the two curates before mentioned.
7 Papists The number of Papists in this parish (the chappels included) may be about 50; all of them day-labourers or tradesmen, and of little or no

consequence and estates, excepting Sir Harry Tichbourne Bt., who has an estate of about £200 a year within the chappelry of Tichbourne; but how much more elsewhere I am not informed. And Mr Augustine Fisher, who has an estate of about £50 p.a. within the chappelry of Kimston.
8 Dissenters There are no meetings of any protestant dissenters of any kind in this parish, there being only one such dissenter, and he a Presbyterian in Kimston.
9 Gentry &c. There are no noblemen liveing in this parish, nor gentlemen or persons of note of either sex; excepting Sir Harry Tichbourne Bt., in Tichbourne, and Thomas Ridge Esq. in Kimston.
10 Schools There is no endowed school in this parish.
11 Charities About 14 years agoe, the Lady Sadler in the county of Kent did by her last will and testament bequeath the sume of £100 to the intent that the yearly rent or interest of the same should be layd out for ever in paying for the teaching of some poor children within the chapelry of Kimston to read and write. And about 5 years agoe the Revd Mr Morgan Jones, later rector of Cheriton, did by his last will and testament bequeath to the poor of the parish of Cheriton the like sume of £100 for the same use. Both which sumes are applyed to their intended uses. There is no hospital in this parish.
12 Post-town The next post-town to Cheriton is the town of Alresford.

45 Chilbolton 21M65/B4/1/2 fo.216
Alured Clarke MA, rector 1723–42
A peculiar of the Bishop's
1 Area The compass of ground in the parish is about 8 miles.
2 Population There are about 200 souls in the parish.
3 Marriages &c. At a mean computation there are 6 births, 6 burials and 1 marriage yearly.
4 Patron The bishop of the diocese is patron of the living.
5 Chapels There is no chapel in the parish.
6 Lecturer Mr Coulter now master of the free school at Andover was the resident curate, and is to be succeeded at Michaelmas by John Osborne AB.
7 Papists There are no Papists in the parish.
8 Dissenters There are no dissenters of any kind.
9 Gentry &c. The Hon. W. Powlett Esq., eldest son of the Lord William, lives in the parsonage house.
10 Schools There is no endowed school or charity school in the parish, but — Eyre, a foreigner, comes to teach the children of the parish to read and write as often as occasion serves.
11 Charities There is no hospital in the parish; Dr Layfield, late rector of this parish and prebendary of Winchester, who died in May 1715 left by will the fourth part of the residue of his estate after the payment of his debts and legacies to the poor of 5 parishes whereof this is one, but this parish has not yet received its proportion or any moiety of it from his executor, the Revd Mr Benjamin Culme.

12 Post-town The nearest post-town to the parish is Andover.

46 Chilcomb 21M65/B4/1/2 fo.328
John Price, rector 1723–33 3 September 1725
1 Area The compass of ground in the parish, I suppose to be 7 miles.
2 Population The number of souls I suppose to be about 30.
3 Marriages &c. 1 marriage, 1 birth, and 2 burials is as much as I have one year with another.
4 Patron The Bishop of Winton is patron.
5 Chapels There is no chappel.
6 Lecturer There is no lecturer or curate. I serve the cure myself.
7 Papists There are no Papists.
8 Dissenters There are no meetings of protestant dissenters, only 2 women that are called Presbyterians dissent from the church.
9 Gentry &c. There are no noblemen.
10 Schools There are no schools or school.
11 Charities I can hear of no charities given to the parish, nor hospitals erected.
12 Post-town The parish is within a mile of Winchester, the next post-town.

47 Chilton Candover 21M65/B4/1/2 fo.28
John Mitchell, rector 1678/9–1732
1 Area About 3 miles in length and half a mile in breadth.
2 Population 50.
3 Marriages &c. Of each [i.e. of births, marriages and burials] 1.
4 Patron Sir Robert Worseley Bt.
5 Chapels None.
6 Lecturer None.
7 Papists None.
8 Dissenters None.
9 Gentry &c. None.
10 Schools None.
11 Charities None.
12 Post-town Alresford.

48 Chilworth 21M65/B4/1/2 fo.274
Richard Speed, curate 1720–after 1736
1 Area I suppose this parish to be about 3 miles in circumference.
2 Population [I suppose] the number of souls to be about 60.
3 Marriages &c. Marriages at a medium one year with another 1; births at a medium, one year with another 2; burials at a medium one year with another 1.
4 Patron Mrs Serle the donor.
5 Chapels No chapel.

6 Lecturer Myself curate. No lecturer.
7 Papists No Papists.
8 Dissenters No meeting of protestant dissenters.
9 Gentry &c. No nobility or gentry.
10 Schools No schools.
11 Charities No publick charitys, nor hospitals.
12 Post-town The next post-town [is] Southampton.
[Answers renumbered to match the Bishop's questions.]

49 Christchurch 21M65/B4/1/2 fo.111
Edward Bowen, vicar 1689–1749
1 Area The circumference of the parish of Christ Church is about 20 miles.
2 Population The number of inhabitan[t]s therein are about 4,000.
3 Marriages &c. The number of marriages in the year 1724, 20; of births, 59; of burials, 62; and in preceding years much the same.
4 Patron The Dean and Chapter of Winchester are my patrons.
5 Chapels There is one chappel belonging to Christ Church called Holdenhurst, supplyed by Mr Gabriel Ayscough, and maintained, as the vicarige also is, by the church of Winchester.
6 Lecturer No lecturer or curate besides Mr Ayscough.
7 Papists There are but 4 popish families in the parish, and those of no great consequence or estates.
8 Dissenters There is a meeting of Priestbiterian dissenters in the town of Christ Church, and the number [is] about 150 and sometimes more. There is another meeting of Anabaptists near the town, about half as numerous as the Priestbiterians.
9 Gentry &c. The chief persons in the parish are Sir Peter Mews Kt., Edward Hooper, James Perkins, and Joseph Hinxman, Esqs.
10 Schools There is a free school in Christ Church, the salary £25 p.a. paid out of the Exchequer. Francis Gavin Esq. nominates the master and his name is Mr Gabriel Ayscough.
11 Charities There is a small hospital in Christ Church, the income about £8 p.a.
12 Post-town Christ Church is a post-town.

50 Church Oakley 21M65/B4/1/1 fo.280
Samuel Read, rector 1721–41 2 August 1725
1 Area According to the best inform[a]cion, the compass is about 8 miles.
2 Population About 140.
3 Marriages &c. About 1 of each [i.e. of births, marriages and burials] p.a.
4 Patron The Provost and Fellows of Queen's College, Oxford.
5 Chapels None in the parish.
6 Lecturer Mr Richard White, curate. ['No lecturer' obliterated.]
7 Papists None.
8 Dissenters None in the said parish.

9 Gentry &c. One gentleman and his wife, viz. Charles Withers Esq. and his lady.
10 Schools One school to which is annually paid £8 by Charles Wither[s] Esq. who has the nomination of a master to the said school. 8 schollars.
11 Charities Church Acre and £5 in money [given] by Lady Wareham. 2*s*. p.a. for Church Meadow. 1*s*. for Well Lane.
12 Post-town Bazingstoke.

51 Clanfield 21M65/B4/1/2 fo.27
Thomas Yalden DD, rector 1712–36
1 Area The parish of Clanville is about 6 miles in compass, from east to west about 2 miles, from north to south about a mile.
2 Population It contains about 22 familys and about 130 souls.
3 Marriages &c. One year with another I compute in it, marriages 2, births 4, burials 3.
4 Patron His Grace the Duke of Beaufort is the patron and lord of the mannor and place.
5 Chapels There is no chapel belonging to it.
6 Lecturer There is no lecturer belonging to it.
7 Papists I have no Papist, nor reputed Papist dwelling in my parish.
8 Dissenters I have no meeting of any kind in it and but one dissenter, a North Britain accidentally settled here, but the rest of his family keep to the church.
9 Gentry &c. No nobleman, gentleman nor person of any distinction in my parish.
10 Schools No school nor any endowment for one, but a poor woman who teaches young children to read and work.
11 Charities Only one charity of £15 principal. The interest of it is given to such poor inhabitants as receive no allowance from the parish; the money is out upon bond security.
12 Post-town The next post-town is Petersfield, where our letters are directed to be left at Horndean about a mile distant from this place.

52 Cliddesden and Farleigh Wallop 21M65/B4/1/1 fo.217
William Dobson DD, rector 1674–1731 16 August 1725
1 Area The parish of Cliddesden-cum-Farly is in compass about 9 or 10 miles.
2 Population In our parish aforesaid the number of souls is about 170.
3 Marriages &c. The number, *communibus annis*, of marriages [is] about 2, births 4, burials 4, yearly.
4 Patron The patron of Cliddesden-cum-Farly is the Right Hon. the Lord Viscount Lymington.
5 Chapels We have no chapel, but the church of Farly united to Cliddesden in the year 1579 by the ordinary with the consent of the patron and the archdeacon and at the request of the parishioners of both parishes.
6 Lecturer We have no lecturer, but a curate Mr Robert Buswell M of Arts.

7 Papists We have no Papist.
8 Dissenters We have no protestant dissenters of any kind.
9 Gentry &c. We have no nobleman or person of note in our parish.
10 Schools We have one school built and endowed with £10 p.a. by Anne Dodington, widow. The present master is William Lock. The number of scholars is indefinite, it being for the benefit of orphans and other poor children of Cliddesden-cum-Farly. The nomination of the master is in the lord of the mannor with the minister and churchwardens.
11 Charities We have no hospital and only one charity, viz. £100 left by Mrs Theodosia Wallop, the interest whereof is to bind children apprentices.
12 Post-town The nearest post-town is Basingstoke.

53 Colemore and Priors Dean 21M65/B4/1/1 fo.65
William Purbeck, rector 1719–27
1 Area Colmer with Priorsdean included is about 2 measured miles long and ¾ miles over.
2 Population There are in the whole parish about 6 score souls, servants and children included.
3 Marriages &c. Seldom any marriages, 3 or 4 are born in a year, and perhaps 1 or 2 dy.
4 Patron Sir Harry Tichbourne of Tichbourne near Alresford, Hampshire, is supposed the patron.
5 Chapels There is a chapel a mile distant from the church of Colmer called the chapel of Priorsdean, the curate of which with your lordship's approbation is nominated and maintained by the rector.
6 Lecturer Mr Newlyn is the present curate.
7 Papists, 8 Dissenters, 9 Gentry &c., 10 Schools None.
11 Charities Captain Newlyn of Goley gave by will to the poor of Priorsdean £10, the interest of which to be distributed among them at the discretion of the minister and churchwarden every Good Friday. His executor has settled a litle estate near the parish for the due payment of it.
12 Post-town Alton is the most convenient post-town. But chiefly I reside at my other living of All Saints in Southampton. At either place [I] shall be always glad to receive your lordship's commands.

54 Combe 21M65/B4/1/1 fo.125
Richard Westmacott, vicar 1697–1735/6
1 Area The compass of ground in my parish (according to the best information I can get) is between 8 and 9 miles.
2 Population The number of souls in my parish exceeds not 110.
3 Marriages &c. The number of marriages, births and burials, one year with another, rarely exeeds 2.
4 Patron The Dean and Canons of Windsor are my patrons.
5 Chapels I have no chapel in my parish.
6 Lecturer No lecturer or curate.
7 Papists Not one Papist in my parish.

8 Dissenters No meeting of protestant dissenter[s].
9 Gentry &c. Not a nobleman, gentleman or person of note living in my parish.
10 Schools No endowed school in my parish.
11 Charities No settled charities belong to my parish.
12 Post-town Newbury in the county of Berkshire is the chief post-town I make use of.

55 Compton 21M65/B4/1/2 fo.331

Charles Scott, rector 1724–63
1 Area The parish is about 2½ miles in length and 1½ in breadth.
2 Population About 130 souls.
3 Marriages &c. Marriage about 1 p.a.; births about 3; burials about 2.
4 Patron The Right Revd Father in God, the Lord Bishop of Winton.
5 Chapels No chapel.
6 Lecturer The Revd Mr Harvey, curate.
7 Papists None.
8 Dissenters No meeting, 2 protestant dissenters.
9 Gentry &c. None.
10 Schools None.
11 Charities £3 p.a., distributed to the poor by the churchwardens.
12 Post-town Winchester [is] the next post-town.

56 Corhampton 21M65/B4/1/2 fo.31

Michael Ainsworth, curate 1715–28
1 Area The parish of Corhampton is about 6 or 7 miles in compass.
2 Population In this parish, according to the best information I can get, there are 130 souls.
3 Marriages &c. There are at a medium one year with another 1 marriage, 4 births, and 2 burials.
4 Patron The living is impropriate in the possession of Henry Collins Esq., who presents a curate to be licensed by the bishop.
5 Chapels There is no chapel in this parish.
6 Lecturer There is no lecturer in the parish, but only the curate.
7 Papists There is no Papist in this parish.
8 Dissenters There are no meetings of protestant dissenters of any kind in the parish.
9 Gentry &c. There is no nobleman. Henry Collins Esq. is the only gentleman living in this parish.
10 Schools There is a free school in this parish endowed with £22 p.a. and a mansion-house[8] for the master, who is the curate of the parish, nominated by Henry Collins Esq., and obliged to teach 8 boys to read and write and arithmetick. At present there are upwards of 30 scholars in the school 18 of which board with the master in his house.
11 Charities I know of no charities given to this parish. There is no hospital.

12 Post-town The next post-town is Bishop's Waltham, but letters are directed by Fareham bag.

57 Crawley 21M65/B4/1/2 fo.333
Robert Wiseman, rector 1702–55
1 Area The parish of Crawley contains 33 yardlands,[9] with a farm held from the Bishop of Winton about £180 p.a., and a farm called Rookley, about £140.
2 Population It contains about 8 score souls.
3 Marriages &c. 1 marriage, 2 christenings, 1 burial, one year with another.
4 Patron The Bishop of Winton is the patron.
5 Chapels There is a chappel called Hunton annexed to it, supplied by Mr Reginald Jones. The rector has the right of nominating of him with the approbation of the bishop.
6 Lecturer Crawley has no lecturer nor curate.
7 Papists Has no Papists or estate held from them.
8 Dissenters Has no dissenter.
9 Gentry &c. The Right Hon. Lord Tankerville and his lady, the Hon. Dodington Grevile are parishioners.
10 Schools There is no school endowed, but some poor children [are] maintained by the Hon. D. Grevile and the rector.
11 Charities There is £20 left to the parish, the interest of which is annually distributed in bread, called dole-bread money. There is no hospital or any other charity.
12 Post-town Winchester is the nearest post-town about 5 miles from Crawley.

58 Crondall 21M65/B4/1/2 fo.219
Thomas Sone, vicar 1713–50 16 August 1725
1 Area The parish of Crondall is 15 or 16 miles in compass; within this compass there are some thousands of acres of heath.
2 Population The number of souls according to the best information I can get, is 1,059.
3 Marriages &c. At a medium, one year with another, the marriages are 5 or 6, births 32, burials 15.
4 Patron The Master of St Cross Hospital near Winchester.
5 Chapels None.
6 Lecturer No.
7 Papists No Papists live in the parish.
8 Dissenters There are 2 meetings of protestant dissenters, one of Presbyterians, their number about 76; the other a monthly meeting of Quakers, about 12 of these live in the parish.
9 Gentry &c. No noblemen live in the parish. Persons of note of each sex are these that follow, viz. Mrs Mary Bathurst widow, Edward Bathurst Esq., Mr John Bathurst, Mr Anthony Bathurst, Mrs Frances Stacy widow, Mrs

Anne Wyatt, Mrs Elizabeth Terry widow, Mr Robert Deane, Mr Richard Deane, Mr Richard Terry, Mrs Margarett Harding widow, Mrs Elizabeth Harding widow, Mrs Newman widow.
10 Schools There are no schools endowed in the parish.
11 Charities No charities have been given to, nor are there any hospitals in, the parish.
12 Post-town Farnham is the next post-town.

59 Crux Easton 21M65/B4/1/2 fo.123
Seth Eyre, rector 1715–42
1 Area The parish is about 4 miles round.
2 Population The number of souls is not above 40.
3 Marriages &c. Marriages, births and burials, hardly 1 in a year.
4 Patron The patron is Edward Lisle Esq.
5 Chapels We have no chapel.
6 Lecturer No lecturer or curate.
7 Papists No Papists.
8 Dissenters Not one dissenter of any kind.
9 Gentry &c. Here lives Mrs Lisle and 9 daughters.
10 Schools We have no school.
11 Charities Nor charities of any sort.
12 Post-town [Address to] Seth Eyre, Rector of Crux Easton, near Newbury.

60 Deane 21M65/B4/1/1 fo.223
Charles Goldsmith, rector 1713–29 30 July 1725
1 Area This parish of Dean is in length about 4 miles, and near half a mile in breadth.
2 Population Upon the strictest calculation [Deane] at present hath in it 130 souls.
3 Marriages &c. At a medium here, births are yearly 3, burialls 1, and marriages 1.
4 Patron Charles Wither Esq. of Hall in the parish is patron of the living.
5 Chapels No chappell is in the parish.
6 Lecturer No lecturer nor curate in the parish.
7 Papists No Papist here.
8 Dissenters No dissenter, nor meeting of any such here.
9 Gentry &c. No nobleman here. Gentlemen 2, viz. Charles Wither Esq. of Hall and John Harwood Esq.
10 Schools No school endowed here.
11 Charities No charity money.
12 Post-town I shall be glad to receive and obey Your Lordship's commands at any time; but if by letter I pray to acquaint Your Lordship that all my letters are directed for me to Dean near Basingstoke.

61 Dibden 21M65/B4/1/2 fo.276
Nicholas Bennet, rector 1707–43
1 Area 2,000 acres including marsh and common.

2 Population 220 souls.
3 Marriages &c. 9 births and burials; about 3 marriages.
4 Patron James Harris Esq., patron.
5 Chapels No chapel.
6 Lecturer No lecturer, no curate.
7 Papists No Papist.
8 Dissenters No meeting, no dissenter.
9 Gentry &c. No nobleman, no person of distinction.
10 Schools All the poor children in the parish are taught to read and write at the charge of Mr Harris and myself. Mr Harris pays the schoolmaster yearly £4 and I give £2. The master's name is John Doubt of Dibden parish, but his school is at Heith [Hythe] in Fawley parish. 40 scholars. No mistress. Mr Harris nominates the master.
11 Charities No charities given to the parish, no hospital.
12 Post-town The next post-town is Southampton.

62 Dogmersfield 21M65/B4/1/2 fo.225
Richard Rogers, rector 1709–36 15 August 1725
William Allen, curate
1 Area We suppose the parish of Dogmersfield to consist of about 6 miles in circumference.
2 Population According to the best information that can reasonably be got, we suppose 200 souls to be therein.
3 Marriages &c. We suppose 3 marriages, 6 births and burials, one year with another.
4 Patron Ellis St John Esq. is patron of the living.
5 Chapels We have no chapell in our parish.
6 Lecturer We have no lecturer, but a curate.
7 Papists We have no Papist, nor estates belonging to Papists in our parish.
8 Dissenters We have 5 Presbyterians, no other dissenter.
9 Gentry &c. Ellis St John Esq. lives in our parish, and no other gentleman or person of note.
10 Schools We have no school therein, save only a reading school.
11 Charities We have no charity, or hospital belonging to our parish.
12 Post-town Odiham is our next post-town.

63 Droxford 21M65/B4/1/2 fo.35
Lewis Stephens, rector 1722–47
1 Area The parish of Droxford is about 14 miles in compass.
2 Population The number of souls, according to the best information, is about 568.
3 Marriages &c. The number of marriages is 5, births 12, burials 8, one year with another.
4 Patron The Bishop of Winchester is patron of the living.
5 Chapels There is no chapel in the parish.

6 Lecturer There is no lecturer, but a curate, John Shergold.
7 Papists There are no Papists in the parish.
8 Dissenters There are no meetings of protestant dissenters, nor no dissenters of any kind in the parish.
9 Gentry &c. The gentlemen of note in the parish are Charles Morley Esq. and Christopher Myngs Esq.
10 Schools There is no settled school in the parish.
11 Charities There are no publick charities given to the parish, or any hospitals therein.
12 Post-town The next post-town is Fareham.

64 Dummer 21M65/B4/1/1 fo.227

John Dobson DD, rector 1721–30
1 Area This parish is about 5 miles in compass, including 2 large commons, the remainder consisting for the greatest part of common fields.
2 Population The number of souls amounts to 162 *circiter*.
3 Marriages &c. On the parish register are found, *communibus annis*, 7 or 8 births and burials, with 1 marriage, and some years not one.
4 Patron Mr Michael Terry, near 18 years of age, is patron.
5 Chapels There is no chapel belonging to Dummer.
6 Lecturer The Revd Mr Thomas Winder is the present curate.
7 Papists There is no Papist.
8 Dissenters Nor dissenters of any denomination in this parish, consequently no meeting.
9 Gentry &c. No person of any note but the said Mr Michael Terry.
10 Schools There is a school for 6 poor boys endowed with £4 p.a. in the nomination of the said Mr Terry, lord of the manor, the present master of which is Benjamin Pointer.
11 Charities There is a charity of 20s. p.a. charged on lands in the parish, which is distributed to the poor every 20th of March by the lord of the manor. There is allso another charity of £20, the interest whereof is applied annually to the buying of 3 bibles to be given to 3 poor parishioners' children by the lord of the manor, the minister and the churchwardens. What remains after the purchase of these bibles (if any surplus there be) is by order of the benefactor given to the schoolmaster. There is allso another charity of £5, the interest whereof is annually given to the poor.
12 Post-town The nearest post-town is Basingstoke.

65 Durley 21M65/B4/1/2 fo.82

John White, rector of Upham after 1719-1746 30 August 1725
John Rogers, curate
1 Area It is in length from north to south about 2 miles or somewhat more; in breadth from east to west near the same.
2 Population About 300.
3 Marriages &c. About 5 or 6 of each.
4 Patron My Lord Bishop of Winchester.

5 Chapels There is one parochial chapel and no other church, always belonging to the rector of Upham for the time being (though the parishes are distinct). The said chapel goes by no other name that we can learne but the name of the parish. It is served alwayes by a curate, nominated by the said rector of Upham, and paid by him who has the whole tythes, great and small; the whole fabrick which is repaired as well as the chancel as the body of the chapel by the parishioners.
6 Lecturer There is only a curate, at present myself.
7 Papists There is one family only; a man and his wife and 3 children; the man is only a rackrenter.[10]
8 Dissenters There is not one meeting of protestant dissenters, and but one protestant dissenter, who is of the Presbyterian perswasion.
9 Gentry &c. Not one.
10 Schools There are no schools endowed, nor any other but such as a poor woman keeps to teach poore children for a small matter as the parties can agree.
11 Charities The sum of 10*s*. p.a. only hath been given (with the payment of which an estate called Foxholes in the parish of Bishopstoake is charged) to be paid to the churchwardens on the feast of All Saints yearly in Durley church porch, and by them to be distributed among such of the poore that receive no alms of the parish and are most necessitous and according to their severall necessities, at the discretion of the said churchwardens.
12 Post-town The next post-town is Bishop's Waltham.

66 East Meon with Froxfield and Steep

John Downes, vicar 1708–32 21M65/B4/1/2 fo.39

1 Area The circumference of ground in the parrish of Eastmeon is by computation 12 miles. In Froxfield 6 miles. In Steep 4 miles.
2 Population The number of souls in Eastmeon parish are 962. The number of souls in Froxfield and Steep 475.
3 Marriages &c. The number of marriages one year with the other in Eastmeon are 3. Christenings 28. Burials 18. The number of marriages in Froxfield and Steep one year with the other are 5. Christenings 16. Burials 14.
4 Patron The patron of this living is the Bishopp of Winchester.
5 Chapels There are belonging to Eastmeon 2 chapels, viz. Froxfield and Steep, supplied by James Downes, in the nomination of the vicar of Eastmeon.
6 Lecturer No lecturer or curate in Eastmeon.
7 Papists No Papist in the parish of Eastmeon; in Froxfield 1, George Bruning.
8 Dissenters No meeting of protestant dissenters in Eastmeon, nor Froxfield, nor Steep.
9 Gentry &c. 2 gentlemen of distinction in Eastmeon, viz. Lewis Buckle Esq. and Philip Cavendish Esq. In Froxfield 1, Mr Love.
10 Schools No publick school endowed in the parish of Eastmeon. In Froxfield £1,000 left for the endowment of a charity school by Robert Love of Basing Esq. late deceased but not yet put in a method.

11 Charities In the parish of Eastmeon there are no charityes or hospitals of any kind.
12 Post-town The nearest post-town to the parish of Eastmeon is the town of Petersfield.

67 Easton 21M65/B4/1/1 fo.32
Thomas Rivers LLD, rector 1713–31
1 Area The parish is divided into two distinct parts, separated from one another, each part between 5 and 6 miles in compass.
2 Population About 170 souls.
3 Marriages &c. Marriages yearly about 1 or 2; births and burials about 4 or 5.
4 Patron The patron is the Lord Bishop of Winton.
5 Chapels No chapel.
6 Lecturer No lecturer or curate.
7 Papists No Papist.
8 Dissenters No meeting of protestant dissenters.
9 Gentry &c. No nobleman. 2 gentlemen, Edward Hooker Esq. Justice of the Peace and Receiver-General [of land tax], and Mr William Yalden.
10 Schools No school.
11 Charities No stated or annual charities. We support our own poor by yearly assessments.
12 Post-town The next post-town [is] Winchester.

68 Eastrop 21M65/B4/1/1 fo.236
Alexander Litton AB, rector of 'Estropp' 1723/4–1747 13 August 1725
1 Area This parish contains about 700 acres, lying very irregularly.
2 Population It consists of 40 souls.
3 Marriages &c. Marriages about 2 p.a.; births about 2 p.a.; burials about 1 in 3 years.
4 Patron Peter Serle Esq.
5 Chapels No chapel.
6 Lecturer No lecturer.
7 Papists No Papist.
8 Dissenters No meeting-house. One family of dissenters, consisting of 4 souls.
9 Gentry &c. Some part of Hackwood House, the Duke of Bolton's seat, stands in this parish.
10 Schools No school.
11 Charities No charity.
12 Post-town [No reply.]
This is the true state of the parish. [Answers renumbered to correspond with the bishop's enquiry.]

69 East Tisted 21M65/B4/1/1 fo.101
Benjamin Blissett, rector 1725–30
1 Area The compass of ground in this parish I suppose to be about 6 miles.

2 Population I suppose, according to the best information I can get, there are about 120 souls in this parish.
3 Marriages &c. The number of marriages, births and burials, at a medium for 10 years last past, stand thus: 1 marriage, 3 births, 2 burials.
4 Patron Norton Powlett Esq. is patron of the living.
5 Chapels There is no chapel in this parish.
6 Lecturer There is no lecturer nor curate in this parish.
7 Papists There are no Papists in this parish.
8 Dissenters There are no meetings of protestant dissenters in this parish.
9 Gentry &c. There is only one gentleman in this parish, Norton Powlett Esq. There are no noblemen nor persons of note beside.
10 Schools There are no schools in this parish.
11 Charities There have no charities been given, nor hospitals erected in this parish.
12 Post-town Alton is the nearest market-town to this parish.

70 East Tytherley 21M65/B4/1/2 fo.220
Thomas Mundy, curate of 'East Tuderly' 20 August 1725
1 Area I answer 1,500 acres.
2 Population I answer 156.
3 Marriages &c. I answer, marriages 1; births 7; burials 5.
4 Patron I answer that John Rolle Esq. is the impropriator and patron.
5 Chapels I answer that I have none.
6 Lecturer I answer that I am at present the curate.
7 Papists I answer there are none.
8 Dissenters I answer there are none.
9 Gentry &c. I answer John Rolle Esq.
10 Schools I answer that there is one charity school founded by Sarah Rolle, spinster, who is now living. The school is unendowed. The master is Peter Barber, who has at present £35 p.a. paid to him by the said Sarah Rolle. The scholars are about 40 in number. Sarah Rolle has the nomination of the schoolmaster.
11 Charities I answer that no charities have been given to the parish, and hospitals there are none.
12 Post-town Andover is the next post-town to me.

71 East Woodhay and Ashmansworth 21M65/B4/1/1 fo.127
Joshua Wakefield, rector –1753 20 August 1725
1 Area The parish is large, the number of acres above 5,000, but I hope to have an opportunity of informing myselfe particularly of this matter, and to make a return thereof to Your Lordship.
2 Population The number of houses in Woodhay is about 190, in the chappelry of Ashmansworth about 34. Upon calculation I find the number of souls will scarce amount to 5 for each family, but more than 4, being in all about 1,000 souls.
3 Marriages &c. The number of marriages, one year with another, [is] near 7; births 35; burials 24.

4 Patron The Lord Bishop of the diocese is the patron of the living.
5 Chapels One chapel in the parish at Ashmansworth, served by the rector of the parish or his assistant. It is parochial, but has no endowment. I cannot learn whether it was returned in order to be intituled to Queen Anne's Bounty, but it stands in need of it.
6 Lecturer I have an assistant, Mr Philip Morgan.
7 Papists, 8 Dissenters We have no Papists in our parish and not above 3 families of protestant dissenters, all inconsiderable. One man of consequence occasionally goes to the meetings, nevertheless but seldom.
9 Gentry &c. We have no noblemen resident in our parish. The Lord Bishop of the diocese is lord thereof. We have an ancient gentleman's family, viz. of the Goddards. Edward Goddard Esq. is lately dead and his widow is living. In the parish allso lives another gentleman, Mr Thomas Cowslade, who acts as a justice of the peace for Berkshire.
10 Schools We have no schools endowed.
11 Charities, 12 Post-town [No reply.]
Ashmansworth, a chapel in the parish of East Woodhay.
An answer returned to all these queries in the article, East Woodhay.

72 East Worldham 21M65/B4/1/1 fo.97
John Turton, vicar –1727/8
1 Area The parish is about 2 miles in length, and a little above a mile in breadth.
2 Population About 4 score.
3 Marriages &c. Of each [i.e. of marriages, births and burials] 1 or 2 at the most.
4 Patron The President and Fellows of Magdalen College in Oxford.
5 Chapels None.
6 Lecturer No.
7 Papists None.
8 Dissenters No.
9 Gentry &c. None.
10 Schools None.
11 Charities None.
12 Post-town Alton.

73 Eldon 21M65/B4/1/2 fo.224
John Webb, rector of 'Elden' 1679–1739
1 Area I suppose the compass of ground in my parish to be about an hundred acres.
2 Population But one family, which consists of Farmer Hill and about 5 or 6 servants.
3 Marriages &c. Seldom or never any marriages, births or burials.
4 Patron Farmer Hill is the present patron.
5 Chapels No chapel besides the parish church.
6 Lecturer One curate, Nicholas Webb.

7 Papists No Papist.
8 Dissenters No meetings of protestant dissenters.
9 Gentry &c. No noblemen, gentlemen or persons of note of either sex.
10 Schools No schools.
11 Charities No charities nor hospitals.
12 Post-town Winchester is the next post-town.

74 Eling 21M65/B4/1/2 fo.278
Richard Speed, vicar 1714-57
1 Area I suppose my parish to be nearly 30 miles in circumference; but a great part of it, I believe near two-thirds, is common, and part of the New Forest.
2 Population I suppose the number of souls in my parish to be near about 2,000.
3 Marriages &c. At a medium one year with another, marriages 10; births about 50; burials about 40.
4 Patron John Speed MD [is] the patron of my living.
5 Chapels No chapel.
6 Lecturer No lecturer or curate.
7 Papists No Papists.
8 Dissenters No meeting of protestant dissenters.
9 Gentry &c. William Stanley and Richard Pawlett Esqs., gentlemen of estates.
10 Schools No schools of any consequence.
11 Charities No publick charities, no hospitals.
12 Post-town The nearest post-town is Southampton.

75 Ellingham 21M65/B4/1/2 fo.123
John Torbuck, vicar 1696–1738 21 August 1725
1 Area I and others of this parish do suppose the said parish to be 10 miles in compass.
2 Population There are 370 souls, neither more nor less, in the said parish.
3 Marriages &c. I find there are about 24 marriages, 8 births, and 7 burials, one year with another in this parish.
4 Patron The college of Eton are patrons of this vicarage.
5 Chapels I have no chapel in my parish.
6 Lecturer I have no lecturer nor curate in my parish.
7 Papists There is no Papist in my parish.
8 Dissenters There is no meeting of protestant dissenters in my parish; but there are 8 Presbyterians, and 22 Anabaptists in my parish.
9 Gentry &c. The Lord and Lady Windsor and 2 daughters, and John Browne Esq. and his daughter, live in my parish.
10 Schools There is no school endowed in my parish,
11 Charities The Lady Elizabeth Tipping (wife of Sir Thomas Tipping of Wheatfield, in the county of Oxford, Kt.) gave by deed of gift (dated the 30th day of July, in the year of Our Lord 1687) a piece of meadow-ground,

containing (I suppose) about 2 acres, for ever, to be distributed discretionarily to 8 poor persons of the said parish (not receiving weekly or monthly collection) by the vicar and churchwardens of the said parish yearly, on St Thomas-Day; I mean the profits thereof then yearly to be distributed among 8 poor persons; which said profits are uncertain, according to the price and quantity of hay; and I guess the said price of meadow-ground may yeild about 35*s.* p.a. one year with another. We have no hospital in the parish.
12 Post-town Ringwood is the next market- and post-town to us.

76 Ellisfield 21M65/B4/1/1 fo.234
Ezekiel Lion, rector 1703–32
1 Area The compass of ground in the parish of Ellisfield is supposed to be 6 miles about.
2 Population The number of souls in the said parish may be about 6 score.
3 Marriages &c. The number of marriages is uncertain, some time 1 or 2 in a year, and sometimes none in some years. As for births and burials about 3 one year with another.
4 Patron There are 2 patrons of that living who present alternatively. The one is Thomas Brocas Esq. The right of the other presentation is lodged in Mistress Saltmash and Mr Tery copartners of the mannor of Ellisfield.
5 Chapels There were 2 advowsons in Ellisfield *alias* Illesfield, viz. St Martin's appendant to the mannor of Illesfield and All Saints which was an advowson in gross;[11] and the churches by the consents of the ordinaries and patrons were united; and it was agreed betwixt the parties, that the patrons of the advowson in gross should have the first presentation, and so they should present *alternis vicibus* [by turns]. Hughes in the *Parsons law* Chap. 8 p. 62, and in the register at Winchester.
6 Lecturer There is no lecturer in the parish of Illesfield, and there is a neighbouring clergyman that assists me in performing my duty there. Sometimes I have had a curate to do it.
7 Papists There is no popish family in the said parish.
8 Dissenters Neyther is there any meeting of protestant dissenters of any kind.
9 Gentry &c. There is a gentleman, Mr Tery, that has a good seat near the church, but is seldom there.
10 Schools There is no endowed school in the parish.
11 Charities I dont hear of any charity that ever was given to the parish and there is no hospital there.
12 Post-town The next post-town to Illesfield is Basingstoke.

77 Elvetham 21M65/B4/1/1 fo.229
Edward Aspin, rector 1717–30
1 Area Compass of ground, 8 miles.
2 Population Number of souls 400.
3 Marriages &c. Marriages 3; births 10; burials 5; [all] yearly.

4 Patron Hon. — Calthorpe Esq.
5 Chapels None.
6 Lecturer None.
7 Papists None.
8 Dissenters Dissenting meeting, none; dissenting persons 4 (2 Anabaptists and 2 Presbyterians whose children come to church).
9 Gentry &c. Hon. Capel Moore Esq.
10 Schools None.
11 Charities Cottage [worth] £5 p.a. and £100 in money for the use of the poor, given by Reynolds Calthorpe Esq., in the hands of trustees.
12 Post-town [No reply.]

78 Empshott 21M65/B4/1/1 fo.67
William Dalgress, vicar 1721–1728/9
1 Area Empshott is a very small parish, which according to the best accounts I could make, containeth between 5 and 600 acres.
2 Population The number of souls in the parish of Empshott, according to the best information I could get, is some few above 100.
3 Marriages &c. There is scarce one marriage, about 4 births, and 1 burial, at a medium, one year with another, in our parish of Empshott.
4 Patron The patron of our living is Norton Powlett Esq., Member of Parliament for Petersfield, and [who] dwels mostly at Rotherfield in the parish of East Tysted.
5 Chapels We have no chapel in our parish.
6 Lecturer We have no lecturer or curate in our parish.
7 Papists We have never a Papist in our parish.
8 Dissenters There are no meetings of protestant dissenters of any sort in our parish; and not one who goeth to such a meeting elsewhere.
9 Gentry &c. There is not a man or woman living in Empshot that is worth £100 p.a.
10 Schools We have no charity school in our parish, but some few woomen do teach children to read, for 2*d.* a week, payed by the fathers of such children.
11 Charities There hath been £12 given to the parish of Empshot for charitable purposes; and the money hath been put out by the churchwardens and overseers of our parish. It is now, as I have been informed £40 and the churchwardens have land security for the same. But I know no more of it, neither can I be further informed concerning the same.
12 Post-town The next post-town to the parish of Empshott is Alton in the county of Hampshire.

79 Eversley 21M65/B4/1/1 fo.230
Edward Aspin, rector 1707/8–1730
1 Area Compass of ground, 12 miles.
2 Population Souls, 700.
3 Marriages &c. Yearly: marriages 2, births 14, burials 10.

4 Patron Sir John Cope.
5 Chapels Chappels, none.
6 Lecturer Lecturer or curate, none.
7 Papists None.
8 Dissenters Meetings and dissenters, none.
9 Gentry &c. Persons of note, Sir John Cope and family.
10 Schools None.
11 Charities Sir Robert Henly gave £100, the interest thereof to apprentice poor children. Mr Nicholas Parvis gave 6*s*. 8*d*. p.a. to the poor. Mr Thomas Atwood gave a cottage of about 40*s*. p.a. to buy ornaments and necessaries for the church. In the hands of trustees.
12 Post-town [No reply.]

80 Exbury 21M65/B4/1/2 fo.284
William Bradshaw, rector of Fawley 1722–7 23 August 1725
James Price, curate
1 Area Our parish is 3 miles in length and 1½ miles in breadth.
2 Population The number of souls in our parish is 205.
3 Marriages &c. The number of births may be about 8, burials 5 or 6, and marriages 3 or 4, more or less.
4 Patron The patron is the rector of Fawley.
5 Chapels Our chapel is called by the name of Exbury Chapel served by James Price by the nomination of the said rector of Fawley.
6 Lecturer We have no lecturer but the curate.
7 Papists We have but one Popish family, one Mackerell, a renter of about 4 score pounds p.a.
8 Dissenters We have no meeting of dissenters of any sort.
9 Gentry &c. We have no noblemen, gentlemen &c; but one William Mitford Esq., lord of our mannour.
10 Schools We have no school in our parish, but small children are taught by a dame.
11 Charities We have no charity given to our parish.
12 Post-town The next post-town to us is the town of Southampton.

81 Exton 21M65/B4/1/2 fo.41
John Newlin, rector 1716–26
1 Area The compass of ground in our parish I suppose to be about 10 miles.
2 Population The number of souls (men, women and children) is about 180.
3 Marriages &c. The number of marriages is 1, births 4, burials 5, at a medium one year with another.
4 Patron The patron of our living is the Lord Bishop of Winchester.
5 Chapels No chapel.
6 Lecturer No lecturer nor curate.
7 Papists No Papist.

8 Dissenters No protestant dissenter.
9 Gentry &c. Only one person of note, viz. Richard Chandler Young Esqr.
10 Schools No schools.
11 Charities No charities, no hospitals.
12 Post-town Our post-town is Fareham.

82 Faccombe and Tangley 21M65/B4/1/1 fo.135
Francis Eyre, rector of 'Faccombe cum Tangley' 1706–39
1 Area As to the compass of ground, upon the best enquiry I am capable of making, I can give noe manner of estimate that can be depended on.
2 Population As to the number of souls, we are about 120.
3 Marriages &c. As to the marriages, births and burials, we have very few; 1 or 2 in a year.
4 Patron Sir Berkley Lucy is the patron.
5 Chapels Tangley is the only chappel served by a curate.
6 Lecturer The curate of Tangley is Mr White.
7 Papists There are noe papists in this parish.
8 Dissenters There are noe dissenters.
9 Gentry &c. There are noe noblemen, gentlemen or persons of note.
10 Schools We have noe endowed schoole.
11 Charities We have no charities given to the parish, nor any hospitals.
12 Post-towns The next post-town is Andover.

83 Fareham 21M65/B4/1/2 fo.43
Daniel Wavell, vicar 1721/2–1738 30 August 1725
1 Area The compass of the parish is supposed to be about 9 miles.
2 Population The number of souls are computed at 1,300.
3 Marriages &c. The marriages (*communibus annis*) are 8; births 35; burials 28.
4 Patron The patron of the living is the Lord Bishop of Winchester.
5 Chapels There is no chapell in the parish.
6 Lecturer The cure is served, at present, by William Du-Gard AM.
7 Papists The number of Papists is 4; all women and of no consequence.
8 Dissenters The meetings of protestant dissenters consist of about 100. Some few are Anabaptists.
9 Gentry &c. Persons of distinction are Sir Brocas Gardiner Bt., and Richard Chaundiler Esq.
10 Schools Mr Price of this parish, lately deceased, is said to have bequeathed by will, an estate of about £100 p.a. for founding a free-school, for teaching children to read English only, and for other charitable uses; but his will being not yet proved, and the whole not settled, I cannot be particular.
11 Charities Sir John Clobery deceased hath left a charity of £40, the interest whereof is appointed, yearly, to be distributed amongst such poor people as do not receive collection from the parish.
12 Post-town Fareham is a post-town.

An extract of the last will and testament of William Price of Fareham, lately deceased, so far as it relateth to a charity-school to be erected and maintained in the town of Fareham aforesaid.

The said William Price oblidgeth John Price, his heir at law, to acknowledge his said will by a writing under his hand and seal, to be duly executed within 3 months after his decease, and giveth by his said will severall parcells of land to the value of about £100 p.a. to the minister and churchwardens of Fareham and their successors for ever, who are to apply the clear rents and proffits of the said lands to the maintenance of a charity-school which is to be for 30 boys and girls to be chosen out of the poor of the parrish of Fareham aforesaid, by the minister and churchwardens for the time being, to be taught to read in the English Bible, and to be instructed in the doctrine and principles of the Church of England.

The schoolmaster is to be chosen by the minister and churchwardens for the time being or the major part of them, and to have a sallary of £35 yearly. The children are to be cloathed yearly with an upper garment of blue cloth of such goodness as the estate (all other expenses defrayed) will purchase. 40*s*. yearly are allowed for buying books for the said children, and the same for sea-coal for the use of the school.

The summe of £6 is to be paid yearly to the minister and churchwardens for the time being for their trouble and pains in inspecting the said school.

The said testator hath likewise given a dwelling-house garden and severall household goods for the use of the schoolmaster and an house for the school, both which the said schoolmaster is to keep in good repair.

4 trustees are appointed for fitting up the dwelling-house and school-house who are to receive out of the growing proffits of the estate the summe of 8 guineas in equall proportions for their trouble.

In case any overplus of rents shall remain, it shall be distributed by the minister and churchwardens among the poor widows belonging to Fareham and to no other use or purpose whatsoever.

And in default of performance of these his directions according to the true meaning of his said will, the said testator Price giveth and bequeatheth the said estate to Christ Church Hospitall for ever.

84 Farley Chamberlayne 21M65/B4/1/2 fo.335

John Pretty, rector of 'Farley St John' 1709–29

1 Area The parish of Farley is in length about 2 miles, in breadth 1.

2 Population The number of souls [is] near 4 score.

3 Marriages &c. The marriages, not so much as 1 every year. The births and burialls may amount to one each, though I have known 4 years together in which not one has dyed in the parish.

4 Patron The patron of the living [is] Ellis St John Esq.

5 Chapels, 6 Lecturer No chapel, curate or lecturer in the parish.

7 Papists No Papist.

8 Dissenters No meeting of dissenters.

9 Gentry &c. No nobleman or person of quality. Ellis St John hath a house in it, but at present dwells elsewhere.

10 Schools A small school where a woman teaches to read.
11 Charities No hospitall or settled charity.
12 Post-town Winchester [is] the nearest post-town.

85 Farlington 21M65/B4/1/2 fo.48
Edmund Cornewall, rector 1689–1726
William Lamerton, curate
1 Area Glebe 2 acres; parish contains 1,100 [including] a great extent of forest.
2 Population Number of souls, 180.
3 Marriages &c. Marriages 1, births 3, burialls 3.
4 Patron Thomas Dacre Esq. Thomas Smith Esq. [added in another hand].
5 Chapels Chapell, none.
6 Lecturer None.
7 Papists 2 but of noe account.
8 Dissenters Meeting of protestant dissenters, none.
9 Gentry &c. None.
10 School None.
11 Charities None.
12 Post-town To William Lamerton, curate of Farlington, near Havant, Hampshire, per Midhurst bagg.
[This reply is headed 'Under the visitation of the Archdeacon of Hampshire'.]

86 Farnborough 21M65/B4/1/1 fo.238
William Halstead, rector 1724–1725/6 15 August 1725
1 Area The parish of Farnbro is 3 miles in length, in some places 1½ miles broad, and in others not so much. Most of the parish is heath.
2 Population The number of souls, according to the best computation I can get, is 257.
3 Marriages &c. At a medium, one year with another, the marriages are 3 or 4, births 8, burials 6.
4 Patron The Right Hon. Arthur Earle of Anglesey.
5 Chapels None.
6 Lecturer No.
7 Papists No Papists live in the parish.
8 Dissenters There are no meetings of protestant dissenters. The dissenters of all denominations from the Church are about 17.
9 Gentry &c. The Right Hon. the Lady Elizabeth Gayer, Robert Gayer Esq., and their 2 daughters, viz. Miss Ann and Miss Mary.
10 Schools There are no schools endowed in the parish.
11 Charities No charities have been given, nor are there any hospitals in the parish.
12 Post-town Bagshot bag is the next post-town.

Farnbro, 1724 Marriages

William Burt of Cove in the parish of Yately and Jane Brown of Frimley were married by virtue of a license April the 23d.

William Cobbat of Stoke in the county of Surrey and Joan Linton of Farnbro were married after due publication of the bans in both parish churches April the 28th.
James Gosden of Windlesham in the county of Surrey and Elizabeth Legg of the same parish were married by virtue of a licence January 31st.

Births

Thomas of Thomas and Elizabeth Hunt April the 20th.
John of Thomas and Joan Luvin July the 1st.
George of George and Elizabeth Gosden July 28th.
Ann of John and Ann Harrison October the 30th.

Burials

Thomas Hunt an infant was buried April 13th, affidavit made the same day.[12]
James Cobbat an infant was buried May 17th, affidavit made the same day.
Ann Harrison an infant was buried January the 13th and affidavit made the 14th.

87 Farringdon 21M65/B4/1/1 fo.69

Stephen Hales STB, rector 1722–61
1 Area The shortest diameter of this parish from north to south, viz. from Chawton to Newton, is about 1 mile; the longest diameter from east to west, viz. from Hartley to Rapley [Ropley], is about 2½ miles. Hence the compass of the parish may be computed, at 3 mean diameters, to be 5¼ miles.
2 Population The number of souls here is 273. The number of families, 64.
3 Marriages &c. The number of marriages at a medium for these last 20 years is 1 p.a.; of births 7¼ p.a.; of burials 4½ p.a.
4 Patron William Gage Esq., of Milgate near Maidstone in Kent, is the patron of this living.
5 Chapels Here is no chapel in this parish.
6 Lecturer Here is no lecturer. The Revd Mr Benjamin Blisset is curate here.
7 Papists Here are no Papists.
8 Dissenters Here are no protestant dissenters nor Quakers.
9 Gentry &c. Here are no noblemen, gentlemen, or persons of note.
10 Schools Here are no endowed schools, but only little dames' schools where all the children are taught to read, being furnished with all books needfull for that purpose by the rector, for their greater encouragement.
11 Charities Here have been three several small charities, given to this parish, viz. one of 16*s*. p.a., another of 20*s*. p.a., for the payment of both which land is tyed. And £25 in money, the interest of which, with the 16*s*. and 20*s*., are annually distributed among the poor by their overseers.
12 Post-town Alton is the next post-town.

88 Fawley 21M65/B4/1/2 fo.280

William Bradshaw, Bishop of Bristol 1724–32, rector 1722–32
Joseph Ward, curate 23 August 1725
1 Area According to the best information I can gett it is computed at 7 miles long and 3 over.

2 Population According to the strictest examination and inquiry I could make, it consists of men, women and children, 692.

3 Marriages &c. The proportion is as follows from 1714 to 1724.

	Marriages	Births	Burials
1714	4	45	22
1715	10	34	39
1716	2	34	18
1717	3	26	16
1718	9	37	26
1719	2	39	34
1720	12	26	27
1721	7	41	30
1722	9	38	31
1723	8	41	52
1724	1	32	33
Tottal	67	389	370

4 Patron The Bishop of Winchester.

5 Chapels We have here one chapel called by the name of Exbury, served by Mr James Price for £30 p.a. The nomination is by the Bishop of Bristol, the present rector.

6 Lecturer The curate of the parish is Joseph Ward MA and his curacy [is] worth £40 p.a.

7 Papists There are noe Papists or any popishly affected in the parish.

8 Dissenters There is a dissenting meeting of Anabaptists, but of small note; the families [being] but 5 in the parish, and the number not exceeding 15.

9 Gentry &c. There are neither noblemen, gentlemen or any above the degree of yeomen of either sex.

10 Schools As to the number of schools, they are 5; yet none of any certain foundation, or certain number of scholars. The chiefe is that of Fawley, which was promoted by the Bishop of Bristol, the present rector of Fawley, at the desire of the parishioners; to which his honour contributes £6 p.a. for the education of poor children. It is taught by Mr Price, curate of Exbury. As for the rest they are taught by women in there several tythings for the conveniency of those places, to read, knit and sow. The names of the said mistresses are Mrs Scullard of Heith; Mrs King at Harley; Mrs Phillips at Fawley and Mrs Broaded at Ower.

11 Charities As to the charities given to the parish, they are, first a certain house consisting of 4 apartments, commonly called Church House, joyning to the churchyard; these are disposed of when a vacancy falls by a vestry of the parish. But who was the donor, I can by noe means inform myself, nor is there the least information of its founder, by any of our parish books.

A 2nd is a legacy given by Mr James Osee of one mark p.a., 1686, to be paid out of certain lands laying at Butts Ash, to be given to poor widows at the feast of Easter.

A 3rd charity is about an acre of land in the hands of Henry Etheridge senior, laying near Ashlet, rented at 6*s*. p.a. The giver of it is unknown, but the money is distributed among the poor at Easter.

A 4th charity is a parcel of lands given immemorially to the parish, now in the occupation of Jacob Langer, laying in Ashlet; it is rented at £1 8*s*. p.a. and this also is distributed among the poor at Easter by the collectors for the poor.
The 5th and last legacy was given by one John Pinhorn AD 1667, a codicil of whose will as it was taken out of the Archdeacon's register, is as follows. 'I give to the poor of the parish of Fawley 10s. p.a. for ever to be payd out of my lands at Rimehall, on the feast of the Annunciation of our blessed Lady St Mary; and to be given and distributed by the minister of the parish and the collectors for the poor, to such as they shall find most need'. This was subscribed *vera copia*, Charles Truffles.
From this will I must inform Your Lordship and desire your advice and assistance in it. Be it known then that the legacy has not been paid for some years last past. The reason is that the lands of the said John Pinhorn being divided between two, Francis Gill and Edward Brixey, coheirs. The said Edward Brixey having one part is ready to pay his share. But the said Francis Gill, selling his right in 2 parcels, one to Henry Etheridge, son, who covenanted and agreed with the said Francis Gill to be exempted from paying any part of the said legacy and gave £5 for his exemption. Besides the said purchase of Henry Etheridge lays not in Rimehall as the said will specifies, tho a part of Pinhorn's land. Now the last purchace was made by John Light without any such covenant of exemption.
Query then whether or not it is incumbent upon the said John Light to pay the other moyety.
Your Lordship's decision in this case will be a great obligation to the parish in general, the poor in particular, and will prevent a chargeable suit of law. Therefore we humbly beseech your honour to be assistant to us in so good and charitable a work.
12 Post-town The next post-town to Fawley is Southampton.
My Lord, I must not in gratitude omitt to return you hearty thanks for the great honour you have done to your clergy in permitting them to address themselves to your honour upon all occasions which is an indulgence never granted by your predecessors; but were always obliged to apply only to there officials to the great damage of our affairs, the expence of our fortunes and the discredit of our order. Therefore with all duty I must acknowledge my obligations for so great favour.

89 Fordingbridge 21M65/B4/1/2 fo.125

Gregory Doughty, vicar 1724–42
1 Area About 10 miles.
2 Population About 1,700.
3 Marriages &c. Marriages about 8, births 40, burials 34.
4 Patron Provost and scholars of King's College, Cambridge.
5 Chapels Ibsley: in compass about 4½ miles; about 220 souls; marriages 2, births 6, burials 7. Served by vicar or curate of Fordingbridge. No Papists, 2 protestant dissenters. Gentlemen or persons of note, Edward Lisle Esq. and Jeremiah Cray. No publick school. Charity, 6s. to be distributed yearly on New Year's Day at the discretion of parish wardens and minister.

6 Lecturer The Revd Mr John Berjew, curate.
7 Papists 3 of no consequence or estate.
8 Dissenters 2 meetings. Dissenters [are] in number about 377.
9 Gentry &c. Sir Dewey Bulkeley Kt.
10 Schools No school endowed.
11 Charities Lands given to the parish, about £5 p.a. and £5 every third year to bind a poor child apprentice.
12 Post-town Fordingbridge [is] a post-town.

90 Freshwater [IoW] 21M65/B4/1/2 fo.173
Edmund Brome BD, rector 1723–45 4 March 1724/5
1 Area The compass of ground in the parish is supposed, in the whole, to contain about 18 or 20 miles.
2 Population The number of souls herein, according to the best informacion that I can reasonably get, are computed to be between 4 and 500.
3 Marriages &c. The marriages, births and burials in this parish, taking one year with another, I find to be about 30.
4 Patron This living is in the patronage of St John's College in Cambridge.
5 Chapels Here are no chapels in, or belonging to, this parish.
6 Lecturer Here is no lecturer or curate at present.
7 Papists There are no Papists in this parish that I know, or have ever heard of.
8 Dissenters Nor any one meeting of protestant dissenters.
9 Gentry &c. There are no persons of quality in this parish; and the chief gentlemen are Arthur Morgan Esq. (the present deputy-governor) and David Urrey Esq.
10 Schools We have 1 free school in this parish, endowed with a yearly salary of £10 p.a., and a convenient dwelling house and garden. The number of scholars required to be instructed therein are 16 poor children of the said parish. The persons appointed by will to nominate the master are Colonel Holmes of Yarmouth, Mr Urrey of Afton in this parish, and Mr Edward Hayles of Newport, gent.
11 Charities We have 1 charitable legacy belonging to the parish, the gift of Edward Adkins (late of Freshwater, deceased), viz. £50 in money to be put to interest upon good security for the raising a stock of money towards the apprenticing of the children of such parents as dwell in the aforesaid parish, and do not receive alms of the same, and yet are not able to place out their children themselves: and 'tis further provided by this will, that after the death of the executors, the said sum of £50 be put into the hands of the rector, churchwardens and overseers for the poor of the said parish of Freshwater for the time being to dispose of the said interest to the end and uses aforesaid. Provided still that the said £50 be reserved and remain whole and entire to be improved for the said end and use. This will bears date, December 28, AD1691.
12 Post-town The nearest and most ready post-towns for conveying letters to Freshwater are Lemington or Newport.

91 Froyle 21M65/B4/1/1 fo.71
John Greenway, vicar 1719–34
1 Area Our parish is supposed to be 9 miles in compass.

2 Population 400 souls or thereabouts.
3 Marriages &c. 4 marriages, 5 births and 3 buryalls.
4 Patron William Draper of Froyle Esq.
5 Chapels Not any.
6 Lecturer Not any.
7 Papists Not any.
8 Dissenters Not any meetings in our parish, we have 15 familys of Quakers.
9 Gentry &c. Not any noblemen. Hewer Edgly Hewer Esq., Mrs Hewer, William Draper Esq., Mrs Draper.
10 Schools Not any schools.
11 Charities Not any charitys have been given, not any hospitall.
12 Post-town Alton.

92 Fyfield 21M65/B4/1/1 fo.139
Samuel Torrent, rector 1684–1733 20 August 1725
1 Area I suppose the compass of our parish is 9 miles.
2 Population I suppose the number of souls therein are 60.
3 Marriages &c. The number of marriages, births and burials, *communibus annis*, I take to be 6.
4 Patron The Lord Keeper is my patron.
5 Chapels There is no chapel in this parish.
6 Lecturer No lecturer nor curate.
7 Papists No Papist.
8 Dissenters No meeting of protestant dissenters.
9 Gentry &c. No nobleman. Gentlemen, Mr Hugh Winckworth, Mr Joseph Winckworth, Mr John Hayward Winckworth, his lady and grandmother Mrs Winckworth, and mother Mrs Woodrofe and Mrs Ann Hayward. And Mrs Aubery.
10 Schools No school.
11 Charities Here is a charity given by one Mr Rogers to this parish and Thruxton jointly distributed by Trustees.
12 Post-town Andover is the next post-town to this parish.

93 Gatcombe [IoW] 21M65/B4/1/2 fo.177
John Worsley, rector 1708–64
1 Area As to the compass of ground in the parish, 'tis supposed to be about 6 miles in circumference.
2 Population There are about 120 souls in it.
3 Marriages &c. There is near 1 marriage, and 2 or 3 births and burials at a medium, one year with another.
4 Patron The patron of the living is John Worsley Esq.
5 Chapels There is a little chapel called St Radegunde, under the same roof with the chapel of Whitwell, one family belongs to it, and the new vicar of Godshil is allowed 4 nobles[13] a year for their hearing him.
6 Lecturer No lecturer, nor curate.

7 Papists No Papists.
8 Dissenters Nor any meeting of protestant dissenters.
9 Gentry &c. No noblemen, but 2 gentlemen's families.
10 Schools There is an English school endowed with £8 p.a. and about 20 little children go to it. The mistress is nominated by the minister of the parish: her name is Elizabeth Godden.
11 Charities There are no charities, nor hospitals.
12 Post-town The post-town is Newport.

94 Godshill [IoW] 21M65/B4/1/2 fo.179
Barnabas Simson, vicar 1700–34 23 August 1725
1 Area Upon the best estimat[e that] can possibly be made, the parish of Godshill (lying very crooked, and intermixed with other parishes, as Arreton and Gatcomb) is in circuit 30 miles and upwards.
2 Population The said parish contains inhabitants to the number of 1,800 or 2,000, if all sexes and conditions be to be taken into the account.
3 Marriages &c. Our register runs for births and buryals generally at 15 or 20, plus [or] minus, yearly, and our marriages at 5 or 6; some years we have none.
4 Patron The said parish of Godshill is under the patronage of Queen's College, Oxford. [The] value, *communibus annis*, £50.
5 Chapels There is a chapel within this parish, in the quarter of Whitwell, standing upon ground belonging to the rector of Gatcomb, which was, I conceive, originally served by the said rector. It was very small at first, but was, as I have been informed, enlarged by the inhabitants of the quarter of Whitwell, or by some others, for their use and convenience; this quarter of the parish of Godshill lying somewhat remote from the parish church. The rector of Gatcomb pays to the vicar of Godshill *£1 6s. 8d. p.a., which is all the consideration the vicar has for the service of the whole year.* In the college presentation to Godshill, Whitwell is allso mentioned. But this I receive for no other reason than that the tithes of that quarter may not by neglect or disuse be allienated from the parish; because Queen's College, I presume, can have no other right to the chapel; it standing on ground, as observed before, belonging to the rectory of Gatcomb, under a different patron. Besides to the clearing of this matter, I must observe that this quarter of Witwell, by *agreement* with the quarter of Godshill, maintain their own poor distinctly, but contribute nothing to those of Godshill, nor to the repair of the church; and yet retain a right of burying in the churchyard. Lastly all bills, bonds &c. to or from any person in this quarter, run allways to or from such or such a person of the quarter of Whitwell in the parish of Godshill, and all the [small] tithes belonging to or being in the parish of Godshill, are payd to the vicar, notwithstanding that the land from which they are payd be situated in the quarter of Whitwell. For the more clear understanding of what goes before, I desire it may be observed that the parish of Godshill is divided into 2 quarters. The first takes its denomination from the chief part of it, and is therefor called the quarter of Godshill, which again is subdivided into 4 more quarters, viz. Stenbury, Sandford,

Rookly and Rood; the other general quarter into which Godshill is divided is that of Whitwell, which quarter is again divided into 3, the first is Whitwell, the second is Witcomb, and the third Netlecomb.

6 Lecturer Here are no lecturers nor curats. We have 12*s*. given by one Gibbert for a sermon on the resurrection on Ash Wednesday.

7 Papists No Papists.

8 Dissenters One meeting of dissenters; the teacher Brown, a quondam taylor, as I am informed, but of what sect, or denomination I know not, nor can I be informed.

9 Gentry &c. We have no noblemen in this parish. One baronet and his family, viz. Sir Robert Worsley; Edward Worsley Esq. and his family, a branch of the same family.

10 Schools We have 1 free school, endowed with salarys for a master to teach grammar, and an usher to teach English and arithmetick. The salary of the first is £20 p.a.; who hath no scholars; this post was endowed by the Lady Anne Worsley. The usher's salary is £10 p.a., the one moiety given by one Gard, and the other by the parish of Godshill. The usher has a good number of children under his care, which I could wish were *greater*. The master is the Revd Mr James Nutting, rector of St Laurence; the usher, Thomas Farthing, of whom I can say nothing but that he is licenced.

11 Charities We have had more charitys, I am informed, than are now to be found; but what they were I can get no information. We have yet one remaining of £1 10*s*. p.a., to be distributed to poor labourers, not yet become chargeable to the parish. It is paid from an estate called Blackpan. We had 20*s*. more very lately, I mean in the memory of some yet living in the parish; but the foundation having bin thrown away by or upon a law suit, I mean the £20 being by the then churchwardens spent in law, their successors now, *especially the churchwardens of the last year*, are so charitable, as absolutely to refuse the payment of the interest according to the intent of Mr Legg the donor. After I had obtained a transcript of the will, which I have still by me, I perswaded the parish officers to continue the payment of it, I think, for about 10 years, and was never refused till by, as I sayd before, by the last year's churchwardens; this charity was allso designed for the same kind of poor laborers as the former. We have one alms-house founded by the ancestors of Sir Robert Worsley, and is still maintained by him. It is for 6 [originally 8] poor people, such as are past labor, of either sex. They have each a chamber, a garden, and £9 in money yearly divided among them.

12 Post-town Newport is the nearest post-town to us.

Right Revd Father in God,

These are the most distinct answers I can at present frame to Your Lordship's queries. Should the least scruple arise from the obscurity or ambiguous sense of any of them, or not full satisfaction be given, Your Lordship's commands to explain any particular or to fulfill the defects when made known shall no sooner be layd than readily, punctually and with all due respect observed by ... your lordship's most dutyfull and obedient son and most humble servant.

95 Goodworth Clatford 21M65/B4/1/1 fo.141
Thomas Hardy, vicar 1709–37
1 Area The compass of ground in the parish is about 11 miles.
2 Population There are about 200 souls in the parish.
3 Marriages &c. There are about 2 marriages, 6 births and 6 burials yearly.
4 Patron Sir John Fryer Bt. of Wherwell is patron of the living.
5 Chapels There is no chapel in the parish.
6 Lecturer There is no lecturer or curate in the parish.
7 Papists There is not one Papist in the parish.
8 Dissenters There is no meeting of protestant dissenters in the parish. There are about 3 or 4 families of Presbyterians who go to the meeting at Andover.
9 Gentry &c. There are no noblemen, gentlemen or persons of note living in the parish.
10 Schools There is no endowed school in the parish.
11 Charities There have been no charitys given to the parish.
12 Post-town The nearest post-town is Andover.

96 Grateley 21M65/B4/1/1 fo.143
Richard Jenks, rector 1699–1731 20 August 1725
1 Area There are about 1,200 acres of ground within the said parish, the which [is] about 9 miles in compass.
2 Population About 83.
3 Marriages &c. Very seldom any marriage, and about 1 or 2 births and burialls in a year.
4 Patron Mr Souch is supposed to be patron.
5 Chapels There is noe chapel in the said parish.
6 Lecturer I have no lecturer, but the Revd Mr Richard Tyrell is my curate of the said parish.
7 Papists There is no Papist in the said parish.
8 Dissenters There are noe meetings of such persons in the parish and but 2 protestant dissenters, under the denomination of Presbyterians.
9 Gentry &c. There are none.
10 Schools There is no school.
11 Charities Noe charity has been given, neither is there any hospital.
12 Post-town Andover is the next post-town.

97 Greatham 21M65/B4/1/1 fo.75
Edmund Yalden AM, rector 1717–46 16 August 1725
1 Area The compass of ground in the parish of Greatham is about 7 miles.
2 Population The number of souls in the parish is about 130.
3 Marriages &c. One year with another there is about 1 or 2 marriages, 3 or 4 births, and 2 or 3 burials.
4 Patron Richard Love of Basing in the parish of Froxfield and country of Southampton Esq. is patron of the living.
5 Chapels There is no chapel in the parish.

6 Lecturer There is no lecturer or curate in the parish.
7 Papists There are no Papists in the parish.
8 Dissenters There is no meeting of protestant dissenters, or protestant dissenters of any kind in the parish.
9 Gentry &c. There is no nobleman, gentleman or person of note in the parish.
10 Schools There is no school in the parish endowed or maintained by collection.
11 Charities There has been no charity given to the parish, and there is no hospital in the parish.
12 Post-town Petersfield is the next post-town.

98 Hambledon 21M65/B4/1/2 fo.50
John Sutton, vicar 1719–65
1 Area The parish is generally computed to be 5½ mile[s] long, and 2 broad.
2 Population According to the best information they are supposed to be 700 and upwards.
3 Marriages &c. The burials, *communibus annis*, are about 20, the births nigh the same, and marriages 6.
4 Patron The Lord Bishop of Winton.
5 Chapels No.
6 Lecturer No.
7 Papists There are 19 who openly profess themselves such, but of little consequence as to their estates.
8 Dissenters There are about 14 Anabaptists who assemble once a fortnight in a house in the frontier of the parish, which is rented for that purpose.
9 Gentry &c. There are 3 gentlemen who at present reside in the parish viz. Counsellor Garway, Captain Alkins and John Conduit Esq., all 3 in [the] commission of the Peace.
10 Schools There are no schools that are endowed.
11 Charities There was formerly land worth £10 p.a. left for the relief of poor widows, but this is now much reduced and in the hands of trustees, who of late have not accounted for it. There are also 2 little meadows given towards the repair of the church, which is duly paid every year into the hands of the churchwardens. There are no hospitals.
12 Post-town Fareham.

99 Hannington 21M65/B4/1/1 fo.241
John Nicoll MA, rector 1721–28 16 August 1725
A peculiar of the Lord Bishop of Winchester.
1 Area About 1,000 or 1,200 acres of land.
2 Population About 120.
3 Marriages &c. By the register there appear to be in 8 years, marriages 7, births 32, and burials 21.

4 Patron The Right Revd Father in God the Lord Bishop of Winchester.
5 Chapels None.
6 Lecturer Lecturer none, curate John Pierce.
7 Papists One, a woman of no consequence or estate.
8 Dissenters None.
9 Gentry &c. None.
10 Schools None.
11 Charities None.
12 Post-town The next post-town to Hannington is Basingstoke.
The present rector lives in the Little Cloysters in Westminster Abby.

100 Harbridge 21M65/B4/1/2 fo.135
George Harris, vicar of Ringwood 1723–46
Thomas Price, curate
A chappel of ease to Ringwood.
1 Area Compass of ground, 2 miles long, 1 broad, 6 in circumference.
2 Population I find the number to be, according to the best information I can get, about 250.
3 Marriages &c. I suppose we may have in all about 12 marriages, births and burials.
4 Patron The parish of Harbridge is annexed to Ringwood, and the right of patronage is in King's College, Cambridge.
5 Chapels Our said parish of Harbridge has but one place more immediately set apart for divine service which is called the chappel of Harbridge, and which is annexed to Ringwood as above mentioned; this place is served alternately by the vicar of Ringwood and a curate who has an yearly salary allowed him by the said vicar.
6 Lecturer In this place there is no lecturer, but a curate, as already intimated.
7 Papists There is not one Papist here that I know of.
8 Dissenters We have not any meetings, and but one protestant dissenter.
9 Gentry &c. We have but one person of note in our parish, who is the Hon. Sir Thomas Hoby Bt.
10 Schools We have no schools in this place.
11 Charities We know not of any charities that have been given to the parish, and have no hospitals therein.
12 Post-town The next post-town to this place is Ringwood.

101 Hartley Mauditt 21M65/B4/1/1 fo.77
William Avery, rector 1713/4–1736
1 Area Compass of ground about 2 miles in length, and 1 miles in breadth, a great part of which is wood ground, and covered with tall trees.
2 Population Number of souls about 60. Men and their wives, 16. Widowers and widows, 3. Young people, grown up and servants, 27. Children, 14.
3 Marriages &c. Number of marriages and burials, about 1 of each; and births about 2, one year with another.

4 Patron Patron of the living is Sir Simeon Steward Bt.
5 Chapels No chapel or chapels in the parish.
6 Lecturer No lecturer. The curate Charles Long, ordained priest and licenced by Your Lordship.
7 Papists No Papist in this parish.
8 Dissenters No meeting of protestant dissenters nor yet one dissenter in this parish.
9 Gentry &c. Persons of note &c. Sir Simeon Steward and his lady. 2 daughters now at home, women grown. One other daughter and 3 sons; all young.
10 Schools Not any school in this parish.
11 Charities Every Michaelmas Day 20s. are paid to the minister for preaching a sermon on death, resurection or jud[g]ment. And 30s. given to such poor people who hear the said sermon. Hospitals none.
12 Post-town The next post-town to Hartly is Alton, being about 2 miles distant.

102 Hartley Wespall 21M65/B4/1/1 fo.245
Miles Stanton, rector 1720/1–1753
1 Area The compass of ground about 1,000 acres.
2 Population The number of souls about 170.
3 Marriages &c. Burials, one year with another, 3; marriages 1; births 5.
4 Patron Patrons of the church [are] the Revd Dean and Canons of Windsor.
5 Chapels, 7 Papists, 8 Dissenters, 9 Gentry &c., 10 Schools [No reply.]
6 Lecturer The present curate [is] Mr Pyrke.
11 Charities Charities to the church and poor £10 5*s*. p.a. Another charity given for the use of the poor in money £10.
12 Post-town Your Lordship may be pleased to direct for me at Eton near Windsor.

103 Hartley Wintney 21M65/B4/1/1 fo.248
Charles White, vicar 1718–26
[Parish] so-called from a monastery formerly in it, named Wintney monastery, suppressed by Harry the eighth among the rest of the lesser monasteries.
1 Area, 2 Population The said parish is in circumference by computation about 11 miles, and contains in it between 400 and 500 souls.
3 Marriages &c. It apears by the parish register for 7 years last past, one year with another, that there has been yearly 2 marriages, 7 burials and 11 births.
4 Patron The presentation to the vicarage is in the right of Mr James Field of Odiham, attorney-at-law; some time since in the gift of James Zouch Esq. of the same place.
5 Chapels There is no chapel of any kind within the said parish.
6 Lecturer No lecturer or curate.

7 Papists Neither is there any papist of any degree.
8 Dissenters As to dissenters, we have but a small number, viz. one family of Presbyterians and 2 or 3 of Quakers, and but one of Anabaptists, and all these persons of no consequence.
9 Gentry &c. There is no nobleman, gentleman or person of any considerable note of either sex, except Colonel Henry Harvey, now in His Majesty's service, lately settled amongst us.
10 Schools Here is no publick school endowed, and but one otherwise, which is only to teach children to write and read.
11 Charities The chief benefaction in this parish has been lately settled upon the vicarage by the Governours of the Bounty of her late Majesty Queen Anne, in conjunction with Frederick Tylney Esq., Edward Colstone Esq., the present vicar and some others.[14] There is likewise a small charity given for ever by Mr Robert Ray of 60 ells[15] of canvas, another of a sack of wheat or 20s. payable at Christmas out of Wallers Farm, now the estate of Frederick Tylney Esq., and one more small one of 6*s* 8*d* payable from a house called Black house; all well payed.
12 Post-town There is a post-house in the said parish, and when occasion requires I shall not fail to trouble Your Lordship with a line, whom God long preserve with your fatherly care over this diocese. So prayeth Your Lordship's most obedient and dutifull son and servant.

104 Havant 21M65/B4/1/2 fo.52
Ralph Baddely AM, rector 1723–7
Havant is a peculiar in the deanery of Droxford.
1 Area About 10 miles in compass.
2 Population About 780.
3 Marriages &c. 3 marriages, 22 births, and 30 burials.
4 Patron The Lord Bishop of Winton.
5 Chapels No chapel or chapels.
6 Lecturer Mr Howel is curate.
7 Papists 50 reputed Papists, of no great consequence, said to meet frequently at Middle Ligh in the parish of Havant with divers others.
8 Dissenters One meeting-house belonging to Prisbyterian dissenters, consisting of about 120 persons that live in the parish. Anabaptists 20, but no meeting-house.
9 Gentry &c. None at all.
10 Schools None at all.
11 Charities One hospital disposed of by the churchwardens.
12 Post-town Havant is a post-town.

105 Hayling 21M65/B4/1/2 fo.54
Alexander Smith, vicar 1721–31 30 August 1725
1 Area This parish is an island, and is, taking straight direct courses, computed to be much about 12 miles in compass.
2 Population The number of souls in this parish, according to my best information, is 363.

3 Marriages &c. The number of births in this parish, one year with another, I judge about 12; burials 11, and marriages 2.
4 Patron The patron of this living is John Anstis Esq., Garter.
5 Chapels There is in this parish, besides the parish church, a chappel or church called Northwood. It is served once a day either morning or evening, by the vicar. [It] has neither any separate maintenance nor right of nomination. [It] is supported and kept in repair by the northern, as the parish church is by the southern, division of the parish.
6 Lecturer We have no other lecturer nor curate.
7 Papists There are none in this parish that are Papists, or reputed to be such.
8 Dissenters There is not in this parish, any meeting of protestant dissenters of any kind, and but 4 persons only, professed dissenters.
9 Gentry &c. We have none, neither noblemen, gentlemen nor persons of note of either sex, in this parish.
10 Schools We have no school, nor endowment for any in this parish.
11 Charities Last year a charity of £5 was left by Anne Moulas widow, deceased, and distributed to the poor of this parish by John Moulas, her executor, and this year a charity of £10 by John Moulas, deceased, and distributed to the poor of the parish by his widow and executrix.
12 Post-town The next post-town is Havant in Hampshire. Letters come there from London by the Midhurst bagg.

106 Headbourne Worthy 21M65/B4/1/2 fo.337
Samuel Lindsey, rector 1724-38
Called also Worthy Mortimer
1 Area My parish is about 10 miles in compass.
2 Population According to the best information I can get, there are about 115 souls in the parish.
3 Marriages &c. There is about 1 marriage and 4 births and burials, at a medium, one year with another.
4 Patron The Vice-Chancellor of Oxford, the 2 divinity professors, the Rector of Lincoln College, and the Master of University College, to which it is a benefaction of Dr Ratcliff's.
5 Chapels There is no chapel in the parish.
6 Lecturer There is no lecturer. My curate is Thomas Hodgson MA of Queen's College in Oxford.
7 Papists There are no Papists in the parish.
8 Dissenters There are no meetings of protestant dissenters in the parish.
9 Gentry &c. There are no noblemen, gentlemen or persons of note in the parish.
10 Schools There is no school in the parish.
11 Charities There is a charity of £4 p.a. given to be distributed amongst the poor of the parish by the churchwardens and overseers of the poor. There is no hospital in the parish.
12 Post-town Winchester is the next post-town to Headborn Worthy.

107 Headley 21M65/B4/1/1 fo.81

George Holme DD, rector 1718–65

1 Area About 10 miles, being near 4 miles long and 3 broad, but consisting of much heath and forest land.

2 Population About 450.

3 Marriages &c. 3 marriages, 12 births and 9 burials.

4 Patron The Provost and Fellows of Queen's College in Oxford.

5 Chapels None.

6 Lecturer None.

7 Papists None.

8 Dissenters There are no meetings and only 5 Quakers.

9 Gentry &c. None.

10 Schools None.

11 Charities Only £10 given by one Varndel time out of mind, the interest whereof is distributed amongst the poor house-keepers.

12 Post-town Letters are directed for this place near Farnham in Surry.

108 Heckfield 21M65/B4/1/1 fo.252

Augustine Goodwin, vicar 1724–27

1 Area I suppose my parish to be 20 miles in compass.

2 Population I do suppose them, upon my best information, to be about 700.

3 Marriages &c. Our marriages, att a moderate computation, may be reckoned one year with another, 4, our births 16, burials 20.

4 Patron New College in Oxford.

5 Chapels I have one chapel in my parish, called Mattingley Chapel, served by Mr [Stephen] Wheatland, maintained by the income of the small tythes of the said hamlet, and nominated to by New College in Oxford.

6 Lecturer Lecturer I have none. I have a curate whose name is Mr [Stephen] Wheatland.

7 Papists I have no Papist in my parish, n<or> estate held by a papist.

8 Dissenters I have no meeting-house in my parish. I have 7 protestant dissenters, commonly called Presbyterians.

9 Gentry &c. I have no nobleman; gentlemen, I have Sir Anthony Sturt Kt., and Bryan Richards Esq.

10 Schools I have one school, endowed with £12 p.a., the master's name is John Burgess, the number of scholars is 20, 10 boys and as many girls. The nomination to it i<s> in the vicar, the churchwardens and the tenant <of> the great tythes.

11 Charities Here is £8 p.a. left by Mistress Howell, 40*s*. by Mr Woodcock p.a., and 2 small yearly sums, the one 6*s*. 8*d*., the other 5*s*., but the names of the persons who bestowed these benefactions are not remembered. These charities are distributed once a year by the minister, churchwardens and others who attend the vestry.

12 Post-town The nearest post-town to Heckfeild is Hartford Bridge.

109 Herriard 21M65/B4/1/1 fo.256

Richard White, vicar 1683–1736

1 Area The parish is about 10 miles in ... circumference.

2 Population The number of souls therein is about 250.
3 Marriages &c. There have been in the parish for some years past (*communibus annis*) 1 marriage, 5 births and 3 burialls.
4 Patron The vicaridg is in the gift of [the] Duke of Bolton.
5 Chapels There is no chapell in my parish.
6 Lecturer There is no lecturer nor curat in my parish.
7 Papists There are no Papists in my parish.
8 Dissenters There is no meeting of protestant dissenters in my parish.
9 Gentry &c. Thomas Grevile Esq., a Justice of the Peace, lives in my parish.
10 Schools There is no school in my parish.
11 Charities There are no charities given to my parish nor any hospitall.
12 Post-town The next post-town to Herriard is Basingstoke.

110 Highclere 21M65/B4/1/1 fo.145
Hastings Lloyd, rector 1723–57
A peculiar.
1 Area According to the best computation we can make, it is about 9 miles in compass.
2 Population About 300.
3 Marriages &c. 1 or 2 marriages; 6 or 7 births; and 5 or 6 burials.
4 Patron The Hon. Robert Herbert, second son of the Earl of Pembroke.
5 Chapels There is no chapel in the parish.
6 Lecturer I have neither lecturer nor curate.
7 Papists I cant find upon the strictest enquiry I can make that there is one Papist in the parish.
8 Dissenters There is neither a meeting-house nor dissenter, as I can find, in the parish.
9 Gentry &c. The Hon. Mr and Mrs Herbert.
10 Schools There is never a school endowed in the parish.
11 Charities There have no charities been given, neither are there any hospitals.
12 Post-town [Address to] R[ector of] Highclear, near Newbury, Berks.

111 Hinton Ampner 21M65/B4/1/1 fo.34
William Browne, rector 1717–58
1 Area The parish is about 6 miles in compass.
2 Population It contains about 200 souls.
3 Marriages &c. One year with another, there are about 6 births, 4 burials and 1 marriage.
4 Patron The Bishop of Winchester is patron of the living.
5 Chapels There is no chapel.
6 Lecturer No lecturer or curate.
7 Papists There are 4 Papists, very poor.
8 Dissenters No protestant dissenters.
9 Gentry &c. The Hon. Edward Stowell Esq. His wife and her sister are the only persons of note in the parish.

10 Schools There is no school.
11 Charities Lady Stewkeley, lately deceased, left to the minister of the parish for the time being, the yearly interest of £100, to be laid out in teaching poor children of the parish to read; but the charity is not to take place whilst her niece, Mrs Bayley, is living.
12 Post-town The nearest post-town is Alresford.

112 Holdenhurst 21M65/B4/1/2 fo.119
Gabriel Ayscough, curate
1 Area The circumference of the parish of Holdenhurst is about 8 miles.
2 Population [The] number of inhabitants therein about 400.
3 Marriages &c. The number of marriages in the year 1724, 5; of births 9; of burials 10.
4 Patron Dean and Chapter of Winchester are patrons.
5 Chapels Holdenhurst is the chappel of ease to Christchurch, maintained by the church of Winchester.
6 Lecturer No lecturer or curate but myself.
7 Papists There is but one Popish family in the parish of little estates and as little consequence.
8 Dissenters There are 3 families of protestant dissenters in the parish.
9 Gentry &c. No noblemen, no gentlemen, nor persons of note in the parish.
10 Schools There is no school that is endowed in the parish.
11 Charities No charitys have been given to the parish, neither are there any hospitals.
12 Post-town The next post-town is Christchurch.

113 Houghton 21M65/B4/1/2 fo.226
Dr Charles Woodroffe, rector 1720–26
A peculiar
1 Area There are between 15 or 1600 acres in the said parish.
2 Population There are about 2 or 300 souls in the said parish.
3 Marriages &c. There are about 2 or 3 marriages, 5 or 6 births, 4 or 5 burials.
4 Patron The Lord Bishop of Winton is patron of the said rectory.
5 Chapels There is no chapel in the said parish.
6 Lecturer Mr Gilbert Bull is curate of the said parish.
7 Papists There are no Papists in the said parish.
8 Dissenters There are no meetings of protestant dissenters, only 2 Anabaptist inhabitants.
9 Gentry &c. There are no noblemen, gentlemen or persons of either sex living in the said parish.
10 Schools There is no endowed school in the said parish.
11 Charities There are no hospitals or other charities given to the said parish.
12 Post-town Rumsey is the nearest post-town to the said parish, but Winchester [is] the most convenient, whenever your lordship is pleased to honour me with a letter.

114 Hound, Bursledon and Hamble 21M65/B4/1/2 fo.286

Dummer Andrews, vicar 1720–61, 'and also minister of the contiguous parishes of Bursledon and Hamble, under the peculiar visitation of the rector of Bishop's Waltham.' 23 August 1725

1 Area The compass of ground in the parish of Hound is supposed to be about 6 or 7 miles; Bursledon about 1½ miles; Hamble about 2 miles.

2 Population		
	In the parish of Hound	205 souls
	In Bursledon	213
	In Hamble	258
	In all	676

3 Marriages &c. In Hound, one year with another, marriages 6; births 10; burials 10. In Bursledon marriages 4; births 8; burials 6. In Hamble marriages 1; births 9; burials 7.

4 Patron The college of Winchester is patron.

5 Chapels In the parish of Hound antiently there were 2 chappels, only some small ruines now remaining of either of them; one of them called Netley chappel still pays an annual procuration[16] to the Archdeacon of Winchester.

6 Lecturer No lecturer or assistant in any of the parishes. Hound supplyed with prayers and sermon every Sunday morning; Bursledon and Hamble with the same alternately every Sunday in the afternoon, except in the depth of winter, and then every Sunday morning all three are supplyed by turns.

7 Papists In the parish of Hound there is only 1 Papist, a poor widow woman; in Bursledon and Hamble none.

8 Dissenters There is no meeting of dissenters of any kind in any of the 3 parishes.

9 Gentry &c. There is no person of note or distinction in any of the parishes.

10 Schools No endowed school or any of note in the parishes.

11 Charities No charities of any kind belong to any of the parishes.

12 Post-town The nearest post-town is Southampton.

115 Hursley and Otterbourne 21M65/B4/1/2 fo.339

Edward Griffith, vicar 1719–27 3 September 1725

Hursley

1 Area The parish of Hursley is generally computed to be 28 miles or 30 in circumference.

2 Population The number of souls, according to the best information I can get, is about 750.

3 Marriages &c. As for marriages, *communibus annis*, there may be about 4, births 14, burials 11.

4 Patron William Heathcote Esq. is patron of the living of Hursley *cum cappella annexa de* Otterbourne. Though 2 distinct parishes they are allways joyned in one presentation and goe allways together, and are esteemed but one living.

5 Chapels I have no other chappel belonging to the parish of Hursley except Otterbourn.

6 Lecturer I usually supply both myself, as my predecessors did. But at present there is a curate whose name is Pierce.
7 Papists There is about 3 or 4 Papists in the parish of Hursley, in mean circumstances.
8 Dissenters There are no meetings of any kind in my parish nor above 3 or 4 protestant dissenters.
9 Gentry &c. William Dawsonne Esq. lives constantly in my parish, as [also] William Heathcote Esq. and Lady Betty when in the country. And John Cundright Esq. and lady.
10 Schools No endowed schools in the parish of Hursley.
11 Charities Lady Wyndham gave £20 lately to purchase land. The annual rent is for the use of the poor, the executrix Mrs Elizabeth White, eldest daughter of the aforesaid Lady Wyndham has lately paid that sum to Richard Fielder, a farmer, in the parish of Hursley, and then one of the churchwardens which said sum of £20 lyes now in Feilder's hands, and he pays interest for it, and it is annually distributed amongst the poor at the discretion of the church officers.
12 Post-town Winchester is the next post-town to Hursley.

Otterbourne
1 Area The parish of Otterbourn is about 3 miles in circumference.
2 Population The number of souls [is] about 194.
3 Marriages &c. Marriages 1; births 6; burials 5.
4 Patron, *5 Chapels*, *6 Lecturer* [No reply; but see under Hursley.]
7 Papists Papists about 50 in 12 families, all mean and inconsiderable.
8 Dissenters No meetings.
9 Gentry &c. One Mr Down the only gentleman in the parish.
10 Schools No schools endowed.
11 Charities No charities.

116 Hurstbourne Priors and St Mary Bourne 21M65/B4/1/1 fo.147
Charles Warner, vicar 1724–45
A peculiar.
1 Area The parish in circumference measures 30 miles and is divided into 9 tythings.[17]
2 Population I do suppose according to the best account I could get that there are about 800 souls in the parish.
3 Marriages &c. There are about 12 marriages, 26 births, 22 burials, one year with another.
4 Patron The Lord Bishop of Winchester.
5 Chapels One chapel [is] called St Mary Bourne and is annext to the mother church at Husbourn Priors and served by the vicar of that church. No fixt salary.
6 Lecturer There is no lecturer or curate in the parish.
7 Papists Not one Papist in the parish.
8 Dissenters There is no meeting of any kind in the parish, but about 36 dissenters.
9 Gentry &c. The Right Hon. the Lord Viscount Lymington. No other of any estate or rank.

10 Schools There is one school at Husbourn Priors free for the boys of that parish, endowed with £20 p.a. by the Hon. Sir Berkley Lucy Bt., who has the nomination of a master, who at present is William Munday. There is another at St Mary Bourne free for 20 poor boys, endowed with £10 10s. p.a. by the Right Hon. the Lord Viscount Lymington, who nominates the master and the boys. The present master's name is Alexander Neave under whose care is 40 boys.
11 Charities Sir Robert Oxenbridge gave £25 to the parish of Husbourn Priors, and £75 to the parish of St Mary Bourne; and the Lady Dorothy Wallop, widdow, gave £25 to the parish of Husbourn Priors; the interest of all which is distributed annually among the poor of both parishes. There is no hospital.
12 Post-town The next market-town is Andover.

117 Hurstbourne Tarrant and Vernham Dean 21M65/B4/1/1 fo.151
Samuel Heskins, vicar 1686–1732/3
1 Area The whole compass of the parrish including Fernhams Dean is supposed to be about 17 miles.
2 Population The number of souls according to the best information [is] above 1,200.
3 Marriages &c. The numbers of marriages uncertaine; but at a medium in both parishes, one year with another about 8 or 10. The number of christenings, one year with another about 26, and soe likewise of burials.
4 Patron The patron of the liveing is a prebend of the church of Sarum, who at present is Mr Benjamin D'Aranda.
5 Chapels No chappel in the parrish but that of Fernhams Dean aforementioned, which is served every Sunday by the vicar of Husburn.
6 Lecturer No lecturer or curate in the parrish.
7 Papists No Papist but one family lately come into the parrish, of not great consequence or estate.
8 Dissenters No meeting of protestant dissenters nor protestant dissenter in the whole parrish.
9 Gentry &c. No nobleman. One gentleman, Mr Giles Lifford, one gentlewoman, Mrs Elizabeth Powlett.
10 Schools, 11 Charities No endowed schools, no charity, no hospital.
12 Post-town The next post-town is Andover.
[The above responses are renumbered to match the order of the queries.]

118 Itchen Abbas 21M65/B4/1/1 fo.36
John Newey, rector 1714–35 3 September 1725
1 Area The said parish is about 3 miles in length and 2 in breadth.
2 Population The number of souls in it are about 117, 92 men and women, and the rest children.
3 Marriages &c. The number of marriages at a medium, one year with another, not above 1, of births and burials about 3; of the former, rather more.

4 Patron My Lord Duke of Bolton is patron.
5 Chapels No chapel.
6 Lecturer No lecturer or curate.
7 Papists 2 families of Papists of no consequence, 9 in number, 5 of them children.
8 Dissenters No meetings of any sort.
9 Gentry &c. No nobleman or person of note of either sex.
10 Schools No school endowed.
11 Charities No charities, except 10*s*. which is out upon bond and the interest given to the poor.
12 Post-town Alresford is the next post-town, from whence I shall be glad at any time to receive Your Lordship's commands.

119 Kimpton 21M65/B4/1/1 fo.153
George Greenway, rector 1719–40 20 August 1725
1 Area The parish is supposed to contain about 8 miles in compass.
2 Population The number of souls in the parish is 196.
3 Marriages &c. By a medium of 7 years, marriages 1 a year, births 5, burials 3.
4 Patron The patroness of the living is Mrs Anne Foyle, relict of Robert Foyle Esq.
5 Chapels There is no chapel in this parish.
6 Lecturer There is no lecturer or curate.
7 Papists There is no Papist in the parish.
8 Dissenters There are no dissenters.
9 Gentry &c. The are no noblemen or persons of note.
10 Schools There is no school endowed.
11 Charities There are no settled charitys.
12 Post-town The nearest post-town is Andover.

120 Kingsclere 21M65/B4/1/1 fo.258
Ambrose Webbe AM, vicar 1682–1732
1 Area Upon the best computation that can be made of the parish of Kingsclere, inclusive of Echenswell and Sidmonton, it is 5 miles in length and 5 miles in breadth.
2 Population In the parish of Kingsclere and the 2 chappelries of Echenswell and Sidmonton there are 2000 souls.
3 Marriages &c. About 10 marriages, 40 births and 40 burials.
4 Patron The Duke of Bolton.
5 Chapels There are 2 chappels, called by the name of Echenswell and Sidmonton chappels, both served by the vicar of Kingsclere or his curate, and maintained by the respective parishes.
6 Lecturer There is no lecturer, but a curate whose name is Thomas Ball.
7 Papists There is but one woman of no consequence or estate.
8 Dissenters There is only 1 meeting of protestant dissenters, called Presbyterians, but at present in a very declining way. Their number may be about 3 score.

9 Gentry &c. There is but 1 gentleman liveth in the parish, William Kingsmill Esq.
10 Schools There is only one grammer free-school, of £20 p.a., founded by Sir James Lancaster Kt. The present master's name is Thomas Ball, who is also curate. The number of boys seldom exceeds 20. There have been great strife about the right of nomination, the vicar claiming a right to himself, and the churchwardens and chief of the parish a right to themselves. My predecessor was curate to the vicar, as well as master of the free school, into whose place I succeeded without any dispute. There are 2 or 3 English schools besides in the town for reading and writing.
11 Charities There have been several charities given to the parish. The chief are these following. 10 acres of field land given to the repairs of the church. Mr Thomas Smith in the 17th year of Henry VIIIth gave a piece of ground called Crooked Mead to the repair of the church. Mr Andrew Chamberlaine gave £1 to the church, and £3 to the poor p.a. Sir James Lancaster Kt., about the year 1618, gave £20 p.a. to the school master and £10 p.a. to the poor. John Fauconer Esq. gave to be laid out in communion plate £30. Item he gave £12 p.a. to 12 poor housekeepers. Item he gave £3 p.a. towards the repairs of the church. Robert Higham, deceased 1724, left by will in lands to the value of £40 or £50 p.a. for clothing poor people, schooling and maintaining 4 poor children and putting them out apprentises to some honest trades. There are a few other small charities kept in a table (with the above-mentioned) set up in the church for that purpose.
12 Post-town The next post-town to Kingsclere, is Newbury, Berks.

121 Kings Somborne 21M65/B4/1/2 fo.254
Peter Needham, vicar 1690–1733
1 Area I suppose it to be at least 16 miles round this parish, it being about 5 miles in length and about 3 miles athwart, one place with another.
2 Population The number of souls I suppose to be at least 1,000.
3 Marriages &c. The births and burials here, *communibus annis*, maybe 40 each, marriages 4.
4 Patron Sir Richard Mill Bt. is the patron of this living.
5 Chapels There are 2 chapels, one at Stockbridge and the other at Little Somborn, which have no other names that I know but what they take from the places in which they stand. These chapels are served by me, that at Stockbridge every Sunday in the afternoon, that at Little Somborn, the first Sunday in every month (except the months of December and January).
6 Lecturer I have no lecturer or curate.
7 Papists There are about 11 Papists, numbering men, women and children, who have no considerable estate among them.
8 Dissenters I know not of any person in the parish who is a protestant dissenter.
9 Gentry &c. There is no noblemen or person of quality of either sex, in this parish.
10 Schools There is no endowed school in this parish.
11 Charities There is no hospital or estate given in or to this parish for charitable uses.

12 Post-town The next post-town is Winchester.

122 Kingston [IoW] 21M65/B4/1/2 fo.183
John Godsall, rector 1684–1752 25 August 1725
1 Area The compass of ground in this parish is about 5 miles.
2 Population There are 26 inhabitants.
3 Marriages &c. None have been baptized or marryed for 7 years past, and only 1 buried.
4 Patron Lady Meux is the patrones[s].
5 Chapels There is noe chapel.
6 Lecturer There is noe lecturer nor curate.
7 Papists There is noe Papist.
8 Dissenters There is noe dissenter, nor are there any meetings of protestant dissenters.
9 Gentry &c. There is noe person of quality or of note.
10 Schools There is noe school endowed.
11 Charities There is noe hospital nor publick charity.
12 Post-town The next post-town is Newport.

123 Kings Worthy 21M65/B4/1/1 fo.49
Henry Tittle, rector 1721–35
1 Area The parish is supposed to contain 2,500 acres of land.
2 Population 162 souls are in the parish.
3 Marriages One year with another are 3 marriages, 3 births and 3 burials.
4 Patron The Duke of Bedford is patron of the living.
5 Chapels No chapel in the parish.
6 Lecturer No lecturer or curate in the parish.
7 Papists There are 6 Papists but of no consequence or estate.
8 Dissenters No meeting of protestant dissenters, nor one such dissenter in the parish.
9 Gentry &c. No noblemen, gentlemen or persons of note of either sex live in the parish.
10 Schools There is no school endowed.
11 Charities No charities have been left to the parish.
12 Post-town Winchester is the next post-town.

124 Knights Enham 21M65/B4/1/1 fo.131
Samuel Read, rector of 'Enham' 1716–41 2 August 1725
1 Area According to the best information, the compass is about 6 miles.
2 Population About 62.
3 Marriages &c. Of marriages and burials, not one yearly. Of births about 1.
4 Patron The Provost and Fellows of Queen's College, Oxford.
5 Chapels None.
6 Lecturer None.

7 Papists None.
8 Dissenters None.
9 Gentry &c. One gentleman.
10 Schools We have only a woman, who, in her own private house, teaches young children to read.
11 Charities None.
12 Post-town Andover.

125 Lainston 21M65/B4/1/2 fo.346
Walter Garrett, rector 1707–37
[*Reply given in letter form*]
I believe the parish is about 2 miles in compass. There is in it but one house and one family, Mr Merrill's, a Member of Parliament, who may reside here about 4 months in the year. There has bin but 1 christening, but 3 marriages and no burial, for these 18 years last past. The next post-town is Winchester, within 2½ miles or thereabouts.

126 Lasham 21M65/B4/1/1 fo.83
Thomas Hinton, rector 1713–30
1 Area Our parish may be about 2 measured miles in length, and something more than 1 measured mile over.
2 Population I believe there may be near 120 souls in the parish.
3 Marriages &c. We have about 3 births, 2 burialls, and some times never a marriage in 3 or 4 years.
4 Patron The patrone of the living is William Guidott Esq. of Lincoln's Inn.
5 Chapels We have no chappell in the parish.
6 Lecturer We have no lecturer nor curate.
7 Papists We have never a Papist in the parish.
8 Dissenters We have no meeting of protestant dissenters, nor no sort of protestant dissenter.
9 Gentry &c. We have no nobleman, gentleman, or person of note, of either sex, living in our parish.
10 Schools We have no endowed school in the parish.
11 Charities We have no hospitall, nor settled charity.
12 Post-town The next post-towne is Alton.

127 Laverstoke 21M65/B4/1/1 fo.262
Samuel Baker, rector 1715–30 16 August 1725
1 Area The parish of Laverstoke is about 5 or 6 miles in length, and may contain as I suppose about 1,200 or 1,400 acres of land.
2 Population The number of souls in my parish is about 60.
3 Marriages &c. I seldom have more than 1 marriage in 2 or 3 years, or more than 1 birth or buriall in one year.
4 Patron The Lady Shuckburgh of Shuckburgh in Warwickshire is patron of the living.

5 Chapels I have only one church in my parish.
6 Lecturer I have no lecturer nor curate in my parish.
7 Papists I have no Papists in my parish.
8 Dissenters Neither is there any meeting of protestant dissenters of any denomination in my parish.
9 Gentry &c. The only persons of distinction in my parish, are William Guidott Esq., and Jane his wife.
10 Schools I have no school in my parish.
11 Charities In 1693 died the Lady Trott of this parish who left a legacy of £100 to the poor. The interest thereof to be distributed amongst them every year at Christmas; which interest has been distributed accordingly by myself and the churchwardens for the time being.
12 Post-town The next post-town to me is Basingstoke.

128 Leckford 21M65/B4/1/2 fo.229
George Hayward, vicar 1708–59
1 Area 6 miles.
2 Population 120.
3 Marriages &c. *Communibus annis*, marriages 1, births 3, burials 2.
4 Patron Patron of the prebend[18] St John's College, Oxford; patron of the vicarage, the prebendary in being.
[No reply to remaining questions, except]
12 Post-town Andover.

129 Linkenholt 21M65/B4/1/1 fo.155
Robert Worgan, rector 1709–27 19 August 1725
1 Area I suppose it to be between 6 and 7 miles in compass.
2 Population Betweext 60 and 70 souls.
3 Marriages &c. I have been rector of this place 16 years and never married more than 8 couples, baptized 25 souls, buried 22 persons in the whole time.
4 Patron Mr Worgan.
5 Chapels We have none.
6 Lecturer We have none.
7 Papists I know of none.
8 Dissenters I know of none.
9 Gentry &c. Not one.
10 Schools We have none.
11 Charities I know of none.
12 Post-town The next post-town to me is Andover.

130 Liss 21M65/B4/1/1 fo.85
William Jackson, curate after 1719–1727
1 Area The parish is about 6 miles in compass.
2 Population The number of souls [is] about 270.

3 Marriages &c. There are very few marriages. Births and burials are at a medium, one year with another, 12.
4 Patron It is an appropriation[19] belonging to the Chancellor of Salisbury which Esquire Tilney holds by purchase.
5 Chapels None.
6 Lecturer None.
7 Papists None.
8 Dissenters No meetings of protestant dissenters, only 2 families of Quakers in the parish.
9 Gentry &c. Charles Cole Esq.
10 Schools None endowed.
11 Charities No charities nor hospitals.
12 Post-town The next post-town is Petersfield.

131 Litchfield 12M65/B4/1/1 fo.159
Hugh Wallington, rector 'of Ludshelf alias Litchfield' 1718/9–1727
1 Area The extent of the parish of Ludshelf from east to west is about 3 miles, and from north to south about 2½ miles.
2 Population The number of souls therein is about 64.
3 Marriages &c. Births (one year with another) may be 4, and marriages and burials, of each may be 1.
4 Patron William Kingsmill Esq. (a lunatick) is the patron of the living, but by reason of his lunacy the right of presentation thereunto is at this time vested in the Lord High Chancellor of Great Britain.
5 Chapels There is no chappel in the parish.
6 Lecturer There is no lecturer or curate in the parish.
7 Papists There is no Papist in the parish.
8 Dissenters There is no meeting of any kind of protestant dissenters in the parish.
9 Gentry &c. There is no nobleman, gentleman nor any person of note in the parish.
10 Schools There is no free school nor charity school of any kind in the parish.
11 Charities There have been no charities given to the parish nor is there any hospital in it.
12 Post-town The nearest post-town is Whitechurch.

132 Littleton 21M65/B4/1/2 fo.348
Thomas Brereton, curate 1719–26
A peculiar exempt from archidiaconal jurisdiction.
1 Area The compass of ground in this parish is about 4 computed miles.
2 Population The number of souls here is about 70.
3 Marriages &c. There is no marriage and not more than 1 birth or burial here in a year's time.
4 Patron My living is called an impropriate rectory in the gift of the Dean and Chapter of Winchester.

5 Chapels There is no chappel in my parish.
6 Lecturer There is no lecturer nor curate but myself.
7 Papists There is no Papist in my parish.
8 Dissenters There is no meeting-house nor protestant dissenter of any kind in this parish.
9 Gentry &c. There is no nobleman, gentleman nor persons of note, but 4 substantial farmers living in my parish.
10 Schools There is no school in this parish.
11 Charities There is no charity given to this parish, nor hospital.
12 Post-town The Post Office in the city of Winchester.

133 Longparish 21M65/B4/1/1 fo.161
Corbett Shelbery, vicar 1722–34 20 August 1725
1 Area My parish is 27 miles in compass; [it] contains about 4,740 acres.
2 Population There are about 500 souls in my parish.
3 Marriages &c. There are in my parish, *communibus annis*, of marriages about 3, of births about 13, of burials about 13.
4 Patron The Duke of Bolton presents the prebendary, and the prebendary presents the vicar of my parish. [MS marginal note adds: 'Prebendary of Middleton [John Pretty, 1724–9] presents to the vicarage of Middleton *alias* Longparish.']
5 Chapels No chappel is in my parish, but a parish church onely.
6 Lecturer There is no lecturer or curate in my parish.
7 Papists There are no Papists in my parish.
8 Dissenters There are no meetings of protestant dissenters in my parish. There are 2 licensed houses, but no congregations have lately assembled in them.
9 Gentry &c. There are no gentlemen of quality or distinction in my parish.
10 Schools There are no publick schools in my parish. There are 3 women, who, in a private capacity, teach children to read.
11 Charities There appear to have been no charities given to my parish, neither are there any hospitals erected.
12 Post-town Andover is the next post-town to my parish.
My Lord,

I have answered the 1st, 2d and 3d queries to the best light I can gather, and all the rest to a punctual exactness. I wish Your Lordship's predecessors had been animated with a desire equal to their power of enquiry into the affairs of this diocese. I speak this the more feelingly because I share in the highest degree the fate of poor vicars, whose endowments are cast away by neglect or design, whose small dues, buryed in oblivion are wrongfully detained, and those wrongs made lawfull by custome. The expensive suit I now maintain against a powerful adversary (Sir John Fryer) and the difficulty I labour under through want of my endowment, as it makes me to lament the remissness of former ages so it imprints a deeper sense of Your Lordship's care ... Corbett Shelbery.

134 Longstock 21M65/B4/1/2 fo.232

John Burbank, vicar 1695–1733

This paper humbly representeth that John Burbank MA is the present vicar of Longstock alias Longstock Priors. To which vicarage he the said John Burbank was instituted and inducted in the year of our Lord 1695. And that he hath duly resided ever since on the said vicarage, which is under the Archdeaconry of Winchester, and Deanery of Kingsomborn.

1 Area That as to the compass of ground supposed to be within the limits of the said parish, it may contain in circuit between 6 and 7 miles. Being bounded on the east by the parishes of Leckford and Stockbridge, on the south by the parish of Houghton, on the west by the parishes [of] Broughton and Lower Wallop, on the north by the parishes of Lower Cladford and Whorwell.

2 Population As for the number of souls within the said parish, reckoning 50 families to be there constantly resident, and supposing 5 persons to be in each family, taken one with another, there must be the number of 250.

3 Marriages &c. As for the number of marriages, births and burials, there may at a medium, one year with another be reckoned 2 marriages, 6 births, and as many burials.

4 Patron That the patron of this living is the Hon. Sir Richard Mill Bt., of Woollbedding in the county of Sussex.

5 Chapels That there is no chappel belonging to the said parish.

6 Lecturer That there is no lecturer or curate in the said parish, but it is constantly supplyd by myself.

7 Papists That there is no Papist or reputed Papist residing in the said parish.

8 Dissenters That there is no meeting of protestant dissenters within the said parish, nor do any of the parishioners (so far as I know) resort to any such meeting without the said parish.

9 Gentry &c. That there is no nobleman, gentleman or person of note of either sex living in the said parish.

10 Schools That there is no endowed school within the said parish.

11 Charities That the summ of £5 p.a. is given for ever out of the manner of Longstock Harrington for the better support of the honest poor of the said parish, who maintain themselves and familes without receiving collection from the overseer of the parish. Which charity money was given for the aforesaid use by Henry Smith Esq. in 24 Charles I, AD1648. And the said money is annually distributed at the discretion of the churchwardens, overseers and chief inhabitants of the said parish. And the yearly receipts of the said charity money are duly made and registered by the minister of the said parish.

12 Post-town That the next post-town to the parish of Longstock is Andover.

135 Long Sutton 21M65/B4/1/1 fo.270

Temple Rose, curate 1696–before 1736 16 August 1725

1 Area The parish of Long Sutton is in compass 6 miles.

2 Population The number of souls, according to the best information is about 150.
3 Marriages &c. At a medium, one year with another, the marriages may be 2, births 2, burials 2.
4 Patron The patrons are at present in number 5, vid. [sic] Mr Samuel Blundell, rector of Codford near Salisbury; Mr Isaac Knight, an attourney in London, Mr Thomson att Petersfield, Thomas Eeds in Long Sutton, Mrs Blundell vid. in London. Sutton is an impropriation held by virtue of 3 lives from the Master of St Cross Hospital near Winchester.
5 Chapels None.
6 Lecturer No.
7 Papists None.
8 Dissenters None.
9 Gentry &c. None.
10 Schools There are no endowed schools in the parish.
11 Charities No charities have been given to the parish, nor are there any hospitals in the parish.
12 Post-town Odyham is the next post-town.

136 Lymington 21M65/B4/1/2 fo.109
Thomas Jenner, rector of Boldre 1724–30
Francklyn Powell, curate
1 Area The parish of Lymington is in circumference about 4 miles.
2 Population Number of souls therein about 1,500.
3 Marriages &c. Number of marriages, at a medium, one year with another, about 15; births 47; burials 26.
4 Patron Lymington is a chappel to Boldre of which Mr John Howel is patron.
5 Chapels, 6 Lecturer [No reply.]
7 Papists Number of Papists 10. No estates.
8 Dissenters Meetings of protestant dissenters 2, the one Presbyterian, the other Anabaptist. Number of such dissenters about 200.
9 Gentry &c. The Hon. the Lord William Powlet, Sir Robert Smyth Bt., William Tulse Esq., Thomas Bower Esq., Charles Bulkley Esq., John Burrard Esq., Mrs Sarah Jefferies, Robert Knaplan, Odber Knaplan gent., Captain Patrick Heren, Mr Roger Beor, Mr Henry Hackman, Mr John Northover, Mr William Vessey, Mr John How, Mr Phineas Wright, Mr Benjamin Bevis, Mr William Cole.
10 Schools 6, 1 of them a free school, endowed with lands in Dorsetshire of the value of £10 p.a. by Mr Fulford deceased. Master Mr John Rigg. Trustees remaining Sir Robert Smyth and William Tulse Esq. The other 5 private schools are kept by Mr Samuel Belbin, an Anabaptist preacher, Mrs Coleman, Mrs Mussen, Mrs Cook, Mrs Brent.
11 Charities [No reply.]
12 Post-town Lymington is a market- and post-town.

137 Martyr Worthy 21M65/B4/1/1 fo.47
William Moss, rector 1722–48 3 September 1725
1 Area My parish is about 2 miles in length, and 1½ miles in breadth.

2 Population The number of souls in my parish is about 4 score and fiveteen.
3 Marriages &c. The number of marriages in my parish is about 1 in 2 years, of births 2 in a year, and of burials 1 in a year.
4 Patron The patron of my living is the Bishop of Winchester.
5 Chapels I have no chapel in my parish.
6 Lecturer I have no lecturer or curate in my parish.
7 Papists There is one poor woman, a papist in my parish.
8 Dissenters There are no protestant dissenters of any denomination in my parish.
9 Gentry &c. There are no noblemen or gentlemen that live in my parish.
10 Schools There is a free school in my parish given for the benefit of 10 boys of the parish. It is endowed with the yearly salary of £6 13*s*. 4*d*. belonging to it. The present schoolmaster's name is Thomas Baker. The number of scholars belonging to the school in the whole is about 20. The nomination of the master is in the minister and churchwarden.
11 Charities There is but [a] pound given to the minister which is put out to use; and the interest of it yearly added to the church rate.
12 Post-town My nearest post-town is Winchester from whence I should be glad to receive Your Lordship's commands.

138 Meonstoke 21M65/B4/1/2 fo.58
Abraham Markland DD, rector 1684–1728
1 Area The parish of Meonstoke is about 8 miles in compass.
2 Population According to the best information, there are in the parish 225 souls.
3 Marriages &c. There are, one year with another, about 2 marriages, 5 births and 4 burials.
4 Patron The Bishop of Winchester is the patron of the living.
5 Chapels There is no chapel, for Soberton is a distinct parish and the living consolidated. The present curate of Soberton is Mr Michael Ainsworth.
6 Lecturer There is no lecturer, but a curate whose name is Edward Bodington.
7 Papists There are no Papists in this parish.
8 Dissenters There are no meetings, nor protestant dissenters of any kind.
9 Gentry &c. There are no gentlemen nor persons of note of either sex living in the parish.
10 Schools There is no settled school, but Dr Markland the present rector pays for the schooling of 12 children of the parish who are taught to read.
11 Charities I know of no charities given to the parish, nor is there any hospital therein.
12 Post-town The next post-town is Bishop's Waltham, but letters are directed by Fareham bagg.

139 Micheldever 21M65/B4/1/2 fo.238
John Imber, vicar 1721–1735/6
1 Area The parish of Micheldever is computed to be more than 30 miles in compass.

2 Population The vicarage of Micheldever consists of 7 tythings, viz. Micheldever alias Southbrook, Northbrook, Weston, West Stratton, East Stratton, Popham, and Northington. The inhabitants of the first 4 tythings do resort to the church of Micheldever. The inhabitants of:

Micheldever, males	70 years old and upwards	13
	from 14 years old to 70	174
	under the age of 14	73
		260
Micheldever, females	70 years old and upwards	17
	from 14 years old to 70	127
	under the age of 14 years	84
		228
East Stratton, males	70 years old and upwards	5
	from 14 years old to 70	66
	under the age of 14	36
		107
East Stratton, females	70 years old and upwards	4
	from 14 years old to 70	66
	under the age of 14	32
		102
Popham, males	70 years old and upwards	2
	from 14 years old to 70	19
	under the age of 14	6
		27
Popham, females	70 years old and upwards	1
	from 14 years old to 70	15
	under the age of 14	4
		20
Northington, males	70 years old and upwards	4
	from 14 years old to 70	55
	under the age of 14	29
		88
Northington, females	70 years old and upwards	4
	from 14 years old to 70	45
	under the age of 14	29
		78

In the whole parish of Micheldever:

Males	70 years old and upwards	24	Females	70 years old and upwards	25
	from 14 years to 70	314		from 14 years to 70	253
	under the age of 14	144		under the age of 14	149
		482			428

In all 910.

3 Marriages &c. Micheldever	1721	Marriages 1	Births 12	Burials 1
	1722	2	14	5
	1723	7	13	11
	1724	2	14	7

	Stratton	8	21	13
Since July 1721	Popham	1	4	3
	Northington	3	25	15

NB Thos[e] who die within the chapelries of Stratton and Popham are buried at Micheldever; the register of thos[e] burials is kept in each chapel. The dead at Northington are buried there.

4 Patron The most noble Wriothesly, Duke of Bedford is patron.

5 Chapels In this parish are now standing 3 chapels, viz. East Stratton, Popham and Northington. There was formerly a chapel at West Stratton. Besides thes[e] in a large tract of land called Norrington (about 4 miles in length in the tything of Northington, though separated from Northington by the lands of another parish) heretofore stood a chapel. The spot of ground whereon it stood, with some adjacent parts is known by the name of Stanchester, now ploughed by husbandmen, as far as the foundations will permit.

Two of the chapels now standing are served by a curate, the other I serve myself. My predecessor caused this too to be served by a curate for that his income would allow it, he having likewise another living which at his death was separate from this. The case was thus. The late Revd Mr Swaine was possessed of 2 livings, viz. the rectory of Kings Worthy and the vicarage of Micheldever, both in the presentation of the Right Hon. Lady Russel, since deceased. In the year 1716 I was nominated by Lady Russel to be curate of Stratton and Popham, chapels belonging to the vicarage of Micheldever. After I had been curate some time, my Lady Russel was pleased to give her promise, that in case I should be then living at Stratton and she did survive Mr Swayne, I should certainly succeed to him as rector of Kings Worthy and vicar of Micheldever. Upon my Lady Russel's repeated assurances of my succeeding to the 2 livings I tarried at Stratton til[l] the death of Mr Swayne, 13 July 1721, when I waited on her ladiship (then at Stratton) at which time she did again assure me I should have the livings, adding withal 'no other person can have any claim or pretensions to ask them'. Notwithstanding this, before I could procure proper stamps (there being none in the country) my Lady Russel was prevailed upon by servants to give the rectory of Kings Worthy to an utter stranger to her family to hold it till the next spring when Mr Swayne's son would be of age to enter into holy orders. Mr Tittle, the person whom lady Russel presented, was asked to give bond of resignation, which he refused, but engaged himself solemnly by promissory words to resign it in a year's time, or whenever after it should be required, either by Lady Russel, or in case of her death, by her heirs. This was particularly put to him on my account it being still my Lady's purpose that in case Mr Swayne did not enter into holy orders, that Mr Tittle should resign the rectory for me. Mr Swayne is not in holy orders. Lady Russel died in September 1723, Mr Tittle not being called upon to resign. Since her decease I have applied myself to His Grace the duke of Bedford, who is now heir to Lady Russel. He was pleased to tell me, it was his desire I should have the living, and bad[e] me to acquaint Mr Tittle therewith. This I have done. Mr Tittle deteins the living—*justi judicant.*[20]

Return now to answer the remaining part of the 5th querie. Whatever curate or curates serve at either of the chapels they are maintained and supported at the charge of the vicar, who has the right of nomination; though if the patron would desire to nominate a curate to either chapel (in case he kept any at call) I suppose the vicar would scarce refuse to accept him with license of his diocesan. This was the case when I was appointed curate.

6 Lecturer The Revd Mr Luke Imber is curate of Stratton and Popham.

7 Papists 1 woman the wife of a labouring man in the tithing of Northington is the only Papist in this parish.

8 Dissenters There is no meeting of protestant dissenters in this parish. The miller's wife at Weston is a Quaker, she [is] the only protestant dissenter.

9 Gentry &c. His Grace the Duke of Bedford hath a mansion house at Stratton; Robert Bristow Esq. at Micheldever; James Hunt Esq. at Popham; Anthony Henly Esq. at the Grange in the tything of Northington.

10 Schools In this parish is no school endowed.

11 Charities — Pink gave £50 to be placed out in some safe hands, and the interest thereof to be distributed yearly unto and among the poor of Micheldever; meaning the 4 first tythings above-mentioned. — Cordery gave £10 to be placed out and the interest thereof to be distributed yearly. — Dudeny left to poor 5*s*. p.a. — Cooper left 15*s*. p.a. John Harding by his last will 'gave to the poor of the 4 tythings which are relieved by the overseers of the poor of Micheldever 20*s*. a year to be paid yearly by his executrix thereinafter named, her executors, administrators or assigns at the feast of the nativity of our Lord God commonly called Christmas. And the said yearly payment is to continue during the natural lives of Rebecca Harding, daughter of William Harding of Sutton Scotney in this county, taylor, and Mary Harding, daughter of Thomas Harding of Easton in the said county, yeoman, and for and during the life of the longest liver of them. By whose lives his leasehold by indenture dated the 9th day of August 1653 granted to him by Thomas Earle of Southampton after his decease will be holden for the residue of of 4 score and 19 years thereby granted if they or either of them shall so long live.

NB the above-mentioned Rebecca Harding is now [27 August 1725] living, being about 85 years of age. The legacy hath not been paid for about 20 years past. Thomas Perry of this parish, yeoman, is the assignee.

The Right Hon. Rachel Lady Russel, dying 29 September 1723, by her last will gave to the poor of the parish of Micheldever the sum of £50 which said sum of £50 was afterwards, to wit, on the 2 and 20th day of April 1725 paid into the hands of the vicar, churchwardens and overseers of the poor of the said parish, and was by them distributed unto and amongst the said poor on the 17th day of July following. — Pink gave a sum of money to be placed out and the interest of it to be distributed yearly among the poor of East Stratton. How much the sum first given was I cannot be informed. Part thereof is lost. The sum remaining is £17. John Winkworth gave the sum of £5 to be placed out and the interest thereof to be distributed among the poor of East Stratton. The Right Hon. Henry Earle of Galway who died in September 1720, by his last will gave the sum of £10 to the poor of East Stratton. This legacy is not yet paid. The Right Hon. Rachel, Lady Russel,

by her last will gave £50 to the poor of the tything of East Stratton, which sum of £50 was paid into the hands of the vicar, churchwardens, and overseers of the poor of the said tything, and by them distributed among the said poor.
12 Post-town Micheldever near Winchester.

The extended income of the vicarage of Micheldever June 1722.

Northington let for	£20	10*s.*	0*d.*
Norrington	1	5*s.*	0*d.*
Popham	10	0*s.*	0*d.*
Lady Russel's garden tyths	2	0*s.*	*d.*
Her ladiship's addition	20	0*s.*	0*d.*
Wool	32	10*s.*	0*d.*
Hop-ground	1	0*s.*	0*d.*
Tyth of calves, pigs &c.	10	17*s.*	6½*d.*
Hay	6	0*s.*	0*d.*
Corn, the last year, 1721	25	0*s.*	0*d.*
	129	2*s.*	6½*d*
Certain charge	74	0*s.*	1*d.*
Remain to the vicar	55	2*s.*	5½*d.*

Certain yearly charge on the vicar

Curate of Stratton and Popham	£40	0*s.*	0*d.*
Curate of Northington	16	0*s.*	0*d.*
Tenths	2	13*s.*	4*d.*
Recei[p]t			6*d.*
Land Tax	4	10*s.*	9*d.*
Window Tax		6*s.*	0*d.*
Poor Rates		17*s.*	6*d.*
Charges in gathering the tyths	9	12*s.*	0*d.*
	74	0*s.*	1*d.*

Corn in the year	1722	£13	1*s.*	0½*d.*
	1723	17	15*s.*	6*d.*
	1724	21	4*s.*	1*d.*

140 Michelmersh 21M65/B4/1/2 fo.236
Charles Cranley AM, rector 1712–38
1 Area We compute the extent of the parish to be about 6 miles, the breadth about 3.
2 Population There are in the said parish, consisting of 3 hamlets, viz. Abridge, Brashfield and Michelmersh, about 110 families, containing upon the best information I can gett, about 550 souls.
3 Marriages &c. Births and burials there are at a medium, one year with another, about 12 of each, and 3 or 4 marriages.
4 Patron The patron of the said rectory is the Lord Bishop of Winchester.

5 Chapels There is no chappell in the said parish.
6 Lecturer There is no lecturer or curate.
7 Papists There are no Papists in the said parish.
8 Dissenters There is 1 small family of protestant dissenters, but no meeting-house.
9 Gentry &c. There is but one gentleman of note inhabiting in the said parish, viz. Joseph Moyle Esq., clerk of the signet to His Majesty.
10 Schools There are in the said parish of Michelmersh 2 small schools for teaching poor children to read, but no school endowed.
11 Charities The summe of £120 has been left at several times by will of severall parishioners to the said parish which money is laid out upon a mortgage in the said parish and the interest is annually distributed and paid by the minister and churchwardens for poor children's schooling and to buy them books, or in bread according to the directions of the donors. There is not any hospital in the said parish.
12 Post-town The said parish of Michelmersh is distant from Rumsey, a post-towne, about 3 miles.

141 Milford 21M65/B4/1/2 fo.127
Leonard Milbourne AM, vicar 1723–46
1 Area Compass of ground: 3 miles in length, 2½ broad.
2 Population Number of souls therein, 507.
3 Marriages &c. Number of marriages 10; number of births 15; number of burials 10.
4 Patron Patronage therof in Queen's College, Oxford.
5 Chapels Chapels thereto belonging, Herdwel and Milton; Herdwel 2 miles in length and 3 in breadth, number of souls therin 157; number of marriages 3; number of births 5; number of burials 5. Served by the vicar of Milford. Milton chapel served by Mr Smith; both in the nomination of the vicar of Milford.
7 Papists Number of Papists in Milford and Herdwel 23; Richard White and John Lacy worth £4,000.
8 Dissenters Meetings of protestant dissenters 2. Anabaptists in number 79, edified by Simon the thatcher and John the cooper.
9 Gentry &c. Persons of note: the Revd Mr Atkinson, a Franciscan, confined in Hurst Castle for life, AD 1700, for acting as a Romish priest.
10 Schools [No reply.]
11 Charities Charities given to Milford. To the poor thereof, indiscriminately, £23 p.a., whereby the parish rates are rather lessened, than the poor relieved. To be distributed by the hands of the vicar £1 5*s*. p.a.
12 Post-town Post-town next to Milford, Lymington.

142 Millbrook 21M65/B4/1/2 fo.291
Bernard Brougham, rector 1721–50
1 Area The said parish is about 7 miles in compass.
2 Population There are about 480 souls in it.

3 Marriages &c. About 5 marriages, 14 births, and 12 burials, one year with another.
4 Patron The Bishop of Winton is patron.
5 Chapels There is no chapel in it.
6 Lecturer There is no lecturer. Mr William Wheeler is curate.
7 Papists There are no Papists.
8 Dissenters There are no meetings of dissenters, but [there are] 20 Quakers and 17 Presbiterians.
9 Gentry &c. There are no noblemen, gentlemen or persons of note in it.
10 Schools There is no endowed school, only a private one kept by a mistress, whom the present rector pays for teaching 8 poor children of the parish.
11 Charities No charities have been given to the parish, nor is there any hospital in it.
12 Post-town Southampton is the next post-town.

143 Milton 21M65/B4/1/2 fo.129
Leonard Milbourne, vicar of Milford 1723–46
William Smith AB, curate
1 Area Compass of ground, 17½ miles.
2 Population Number of souls, 400.
3 Marriages &c. Number of marriages 4; number of births 12; number of burials 12.
4 Patron, 5 Chapels [No reply.]
6 Lecturer The grand tythes and small [tithes are] impropriated. [There is] allowed to the officiating curate from the impropriators £4 3*s.* 0*d.* p.a. The rest paid by contributions. The church yard and vicarage plot [are] in possession of the impropriators of the small tythes.
7 Papists, 8 Dissenters, 9 Gentry &c., 10 Schools, 11 Charities [No reply.]
12 Post-town Post-town next to Milton, Christchurch.

144 Minstead 21M65/B4/1/2 fo.294
Edward Midleton, rector 1714–33
1 Area The circumference of the parish of Minsteed is thought to be about 5 miles; of Lyndhurst where the chappel of ease is, to be about 4 miles.
2 Population The number of inhabitants in both parishes is computed to be about 500.
3 Marriages &c. The number of marraiges, births and burials to be about 60, *communibus annis.*
4 Patron Mr Compton is the patron of the living.
5 Chapels [No reply, but see no. 1.]
6 Lecturer No lecturer or curate.
7 Papists No Papists in either parish.
8 Dissenters 1 Anabaptist meeting in the parish of Lyndhurst, the number supposed to be 30, most of them upon certificate.

9 Gentry &c. Lord Forrester has a seat in the parish of Lyndhurst.
10 Schools 2 mothar schools in each parish. 24 girls are kept at school and cloathed yearly by Her Grace the duchess dowager of Bolton.
11 Charities The interest of £20 p.a. given by Mrs Bennet to the parish of Lyndhurst to be distributed amongst the poor widows at Easter. The interest of £50 p.a. given by Mr Brown to be distributed among the poor of Minstead at Christmas. No hospital in either parish.
12 Post-town The next post-town to the parish of Minstead is Southampton.

145 Monk Sherborne 21M65/B4/1/1 fo.299
Laurence Farington, vicar 1722–50
William Deane, curate
1 Area What compass of ground is in the parish is a question difficult to be nicely answered, by reason there are several parcels of distant lands interspersed among the lands of other parishes; one great parcel of which is a farm called Chinham near Basingstoke. The main body of the parish is thought to extend itself above 1½ miles from north to south, and more than 1 mile from east to west.
2 Population It is thought that the number of souls may be upwards of 200.
3 Marriages &c. It appears by the register book that for these 10 years last past, one with another there have been 1 or 2 marriages, 6 or 7 christenings, 3 or 4 burials.
4 Patron The living is in the patronage of Queen's College in Oxford.
5 Chapels There is an old chapel at Chinham aforesaid, but disused and desecrated, the family resorting to the neighbouring church of Basingstoke.
6 Lecturer No lecturer or curate, save only at present to supply the vicar's absence whilst gone into the north.
7 Papists 1 woman, a reputed Papist, having an estate in a neighbouring parish of £40 p.a.
8 Dissenters No meeting-house, and only 1 protestant dissenter.
9 Gentry &c. No nobleman or gentleman; farmers only and servants and labourers.
10 Schools One school for 24 children to be taught; supported by yearly charitable contributions; the master, Richard Coperthwait, chosen by the subscribers.
11 Charities One charity of 50s. p.a. issuing out of lands left by Thomas Simson, to be distributed to the poor by the minister and churchwardens at two half-yearly payments; which is done accordingly.
12 Post-town The nearest post-town, Basingstoke.
Given in by William Deane, supplying at present the absence of the vicar.

146 Monxton 21M65/B4/1/1 fo.165
Dr Thomas Rothwell, rector 1723/4–1749 20 August 1725
1 Area Our parish is computed to be 9 miles in circumference.

2 Population The number of souls in our parish is 161.
3 Marriages &c. There are about 2 marriages, 6 births, and 3 burials at a medium.
4 Patron Our living is in the gift of King's College in Cambridge.
5 Chapels, 6 Lecturer We have no chapel nor lecturer; the curate is Henry O'Neale.
7 Papists We have not one Papist in the parish.
8 Dissenters We have 2 families of protestant dissenters, but no meeting-house.
9 Gentry &c, There is no nobleman, gentleman, nor person of note in the parish.
10 Schools, 11 Charities We have no school, no hospital, nor charities given to the parish.
12 Post-town Our next post-town is Andover.
[Signed by] Henry O'Neale.

147 Morestead 21M65/B4/1/2 fo.350
Charles Braxtone, rector 1722–32
1 Area About 1,200 acres.
2 Population 52.
3 Marriages &c. 5 marriages in 11 years; 2 births yearly, and 6 burials in 10 years.
4 Patron The Right Revd Father in God the Bishop of Winchester.
5 Chapels None.
6 Lecturer None.
7 Papists 1, the wife of a labouring man.
8 Dissenters None.
9 Gentry &c. None.
10 Schools None.
11 Charities None.
12 Post-town Winchester.

148 Mottisfont 21M65/B4/1/2 fo.244
Edward Jones, rector 1722–73
1 Area The parish is about 4 miles in length and 2½ over.
2 Population There are in it between 5 and 600 souls.
3 Marriages &c. There are about 20 births, 15 burials, and 4 or 5 marriages, one year with another.
4 Patron The advowson having belonged to one of the late South Sea directors, is now vested in that company, but must be sold.
5 Chapels There are 2 chapels of ease, Lockerly and East Dean, which are supplied by a resident curate, at present Mr William Barlow.
6 Lecturer There is no lecturer in it.
7 Papists There is but one family of Roman Catholics, who are renters.
8 Dissenters There is no meeting of protestant dissenters, nor are there any of them in it.

9 Gentry &c. There is in it only one gentleman's seat (formerly a priory of Augustine monks) which belongs to Sir Richard Mill Bt., who very seldom resides at it.
10 Schools There are no schools in it except some private ones for teaching children to read.
11 Charities There are no charities given to, nor is there any hospital in, it.
12 Post-town The nearest post-town is Rumsey.

149 Mottistone [IoW] 21M65/B4/1/2 fo.185
Harry Constantine, rector 1699–1744 25 August 1725
1 Area The compass of the ground in my parish is about 1½ miles in length and 1 mile in breadth.
2 Population The number of souls inhabiting therein is about 60 or 70.
3 Marriages &c. The number of marriages at a medium, one year with another, [is] 1, births 2, and burials 2.
4 Patron The patron of the rectory is John Leigh Esq.
5 Chapels There is no chapel therein.
6 Lecturer My curate is the Revd Mr John Woodford.
7 Papists There is no Papist therein.
8 Dissenters No protestant-dissenting meetings, or dissenter of any kind.
9 Gentry &c. There is no person of any note therein.
10 Schools There is no schole therein.
11 Charities No charity nor hospital.
12 Post-town The next post-town is Newport.

150 Nately Scures 21M65/B4/1/1 fo.272
Thomas Fenton, rector 1719–43 16 August 1725
1 Area The circumference of the parish is about 11 miles.
2 Population The number of souls therein is about 120.
3 Marriages &c. There have been in the parish, *communibus annis*, for the last 10 years, 1 marriage, 3 births, and 2 burials.
4 Patron The patron of the living is Anthony Henley Esq.
5 Chapels There is no chapel in my parish.
6 Lecturer There is no lecturer in my parish. Mr William Sealy, curate of Rotherwick, and domestic chaplain to Frederick Tylney Esq., at Tylney Hall, about a mile distant from my parish church, supplies the cure of my parish for the greatest part of the year.
7 Papists There are no Papists in my parish.
8 Dissenters Nor protestant dissenters of any kind.
9 Gentry &c. Nor any persons of note.
10 Schools Nor any schools.
11 Charities Nor any charitable benefactions, nor hospitals.
12 Post-town The next post-town to Nately-Scures is Basingstoke in Hampshire.

151 Nether Wallop 21M65/B4/1/1 fo.181
Francis Barry, vicar 1722–9 20 August 1725
1 Area About 5,500 acres.

2 Population About 500.
3 Marriages &c. Of marriages 4, of births 22, of burials 14.
4 Patron Vicars Choral of the cathedral of York.
5 Chapels None.
6 Lecturer None.
7 Papists 1, a labourer of no consequence.
8 Dissenters No meeting, but there are 6 families of Anabaptists.
9 Gentry &c. The Lady Sudbury.
10 Schools We have no school endowed.
11 Charities £20 have been given to the parish by Mr Smith, £20 by Mr Complin, £10 by Mr Pile, £5 by Mr Faithfull, the interest of which sums is duly paid to the poor widows, and those of the parish who have more children born in wedlock than they can maintain by their honest labour. We have likewise 40s. p.a. paid to the parish by the parishioners of Tangly. The gift of Sir William Read. We have no hospital.
12 Post-town Andover is the next post-town.

152 Newchurch [IoW] 21M65/B4/1/2 fo.187
William Kelway, vicar 1695–1732 25 August 1725
1 Area The compass of the ground around the parish is by estimation about 26 miles.
2 Population We have of people in the parish, men, women and children, about 800 or 900.
3 Marriages &c. We have, one year with another, about 8 or 9 marriages; births about 16 or 18; burials about 10 or 12.
4 Patron The patron of this living is the Bishop of Bristol.
5 Chapels We have a chapel at Ride in this parish built by Mr Player and the people of that place, which was consecrated by your predecessor, Bishop Trelawney, the 27th day of June 1719. The said Mr Player, who then lived in that place but since deceased, endowed it with £10 p.a. which his estate at Ride by the instrument given His Lordship is bound to pay.
6 Lecturer No lecturer or curate.
7 Papists No Papist.
8 Dissenter No dissenting meeting-house, nor but 1 dissenter, who is a Presbyterian.
9 Gentry &c. In this parish is the seat of the Dillingtons, Knighton by name. Sir Tristram Dillington, the last male of that family died about 3 or 4 years ago. His mother and 2 sisters are now living in the parish. Mrs Player, the widow of Mr Player above-named, lives at Ride aforementioned.
10 Schools No endowed school.
11 Charities No hospital. There was given (but not now in the memory of man) by one Mr Guard 20*s*. p.a. to the poor of this parish not receiving alms, which an estate near this place called Black-pan is bound for the payment of. The minister and churchwardens as by virtue of the will have the giving of it to the poor. Besides we have an acre of land belonging to the poor of 10*s*. p.a. at Princelet in this parish.
12 Post-town Newport in this island is our next post-town.

If I am not so full in my reply to the enquiries as Your Lordship may expect, I shall be ready submissively to give answer what I can to any enquiry which your lordship at any time hereafter may think fit to order me to give a reply to.

153 Newnham 21M65/B4/1/1 fo.276
Michael Hutchinson DD, rector 1718/9–1740 16 August 1725
1 Area The rectory of Newnham, consists of 1,730 acres by a measurement I was at the charge of making.
2 Population It consists of about 70 families, which may contain above 200 souls.
3 Marriages &c. We have not above 5 or 6 marriages in a year; and about 10 or 12 births, and as many burials.
4 Patron The patronage is in Queen's College, Oxford.
5 Chapels There is a chapel belonging to my rectory called Maple Dorwell at which I or my curate read prayers and preach every afternoon on Sundays.
6 Lecturer I have a curate who resides constantly in the parsonage whose name is Thomas Skelton.
7 Papists I have no Papists in my parish.
8 Dissenters I have no meetings in the parish, and but one family of protestant dissenters.
9 Gentry &c. I neither have any noblemen or gentlemen in my parish.
10 Schools There is no endowed school in the parish.
11 Charities We have a small charity of £4 p.a. given by the Duke of Bolton's family and distributed annually to 3 poor families, not receiving parish alms.
12 Post-town Address to Rector of Newnham near Basingstoke.

154 Newton Valence 21M65/B4/1/1 fo.89
Edmund Yalden AM, vicar 1718–46 16 August 1725
1 Area The compass of ground in the parish of Newton Valence, alias Hawkley, is about 13 miles.
2 Population The number of souls is about 2 hundred and 4 score.
3 Marriages &c. There is, one year with another, about 2 or 3 marriages, 7 or 8 births, and 5 or 6 burials.
4 Patron The Revd Mr Edmund Yalden, the incumbent, is patron of the living.
5 Chapels There is one chapel in the parish called Hawkley, served by the vicar of Newton-Valence alias Hawkley, maintained by the vicarage tythes of the place, and annext to the vicarage of Newton-Valence alias Hawkley.
6 Lecturer There is no lecturer, [but] there is one curate the Revd Mr Richard Lissett AM.
7 Papists There are no Papists in the parish.
8 Dissenters There is no meeting of protestant dissenters, or protestant dissenters of any kind in the parish.

9 Gentry &c. There is no nobleman, gentleman or person of distinction in the parish.
10 Schools There is no school in the parish endowed or maintained by collection.
11 Charities A charity of £30 was given to the parish about a hundred years since, which has been lost for many years by being put out upon bad security, and that there is is no hospital in the parish.
12 Post-town That Alton is the next post-town.

155 Niton [IoW] 21M65/B4/1/2 fo.189
John Thomson, rector 1716–35
1 Area About 6 miles.
2 Population 214.
3 Marriages &c. 1 marriage, 5 births, 4 burials.
4 Patron Queen's College in Oxford.
5 Chapels, 6 Lecturer, 7 Papists, 8 Dissenters, 9 Gentry &c., 10 Schools [All] none.
11 Charities Only £5 p.a. distributed by the rector and churchwardens among the poor of the parish about Christmas. No hospitals.
12 Post-town Newport.[21]

156 North Stoneham 21M65/B4/1/2 fo.302
Timothy Owen, rector 1723–49
1 Area The parish is about 15 miles in circumference or something more.
2 Population Between 3 and 400 souls in it.
3 Marriages &c. At a medium, one year with another, I suppose there may be 2 marriages, 11 births, and 7 burials.
4 Patron Richard Fleming Esq. is the patron.
5 Chapels There is no chapel.
6 Lecturer No lecturer or curate.
7 Papists Only 2 Papists; one receives alms, the other a servant.
8 Dissenters No meetings or dissenters of any kind.
9 Gentry &c. No noblemen and only 2 gentlemen.
10 Schools No schools endowed, nor any other but such as teach young children to read.
11 Charities I find that in 1687 there was at interest £73 belonging to the poor; but by whom given, or whether by an particular appointment, neither appears by our parish books, nor can I learn by any informacion. Since which time there has been given by several persons, the sum of £95, £50 of which is directed to be disposed of to those who are *frequenters of the church and constant communicants*. The interest of all which money has been distributed, as I am informed, to the poor of the parish, in general, according to their various wants and necessities, by the minister, churchwardens and overseers, part upon St Thomas Day, the other upon Good Friday. No hospital.
12 Post-town The next post-town is Southampton.

157 North Waltham 21M65/B4/1/1 fo.278
Richard Walton, rector 1682–1730 30 July 1725
A peculiar in the Archdeaconry of Winchester.
1 Area This parish of North Waltham is solely in Your Lordship's tenure as Lord Bishop of Winchester. It is near 1 mile in length and half a mile in breadth, containing therein 57 yardland, or 1,710 acres.
2 Population Upon the strictest calculation at present [it] hath in it 180 soules.
3 Marriages &c. At a medium here, births are yearly 6, burialls 2, and marriages 2.
4 Patron The Lord Bishop of Winchester is patron of this living.
5 Chapels No chappell in this parish.
6 Lecturer No lecturer nor curate in this parish.
7 Papists No Papist here.
8 Dissenters No dissenters, nor meeting of any such here.
9 Gentry &c. No noblemen here. Gentlemen there are 2 (who cohabit together), viz. Mr George Yate and Mr Cary Hunt; one gentlewoman, Mrs Mary Pinck, widow.
10 Schools No school endowed here.
11 Charities In the yeare 1636 there was a charity of £50 given to this parish, by one Mr Walter Pinck, the interest whereof by his will appropriated to prenticing out of poor children of this parish, to which use it has been applied ever since.
12 Post-town I shall be glad to receive and obey Your Lordship's commands at any time, but if by letter I presume to aquaint your lordship that all my letters are directed for me at North Waltham, to be left at Deangate near Basingstoke, which is the next post-town to me.

158 Nursling 21M65/B4/1/2 fo.298
Henry Lambe, rector 1715–1727/8
1 Area About 5 miles [in compass] as near as I can guess.
2 Population 200 souls.
3 Marriages &c. 2 or 3 marriages, 4 or 5 births, 2 buryals.
4 Patron The Lord Bishop of Winchester.
5 Chapels No chapel.
6 Lecturer No lecturer. Mr Newcome is curate.
7 Papists No Papists.
8 Dissenters No meetings. One family of Presbyterians; 2 small familys of Quakers.
9 Gentry &c. No noblemen, but 1 gentleman, Henry Knollys Esq.
10 Schools No school.
11 Charities No hospital. I have not heard of any charities given to the parish.
12 Post-town Rumsy is the next post-town.

159 Nutley 21M65/B4/1/1 fo.42
John Waterman, perpetual curate 1671–1726
1 Area We have about 1000 acres of land in o[u]r parish.

2 Population We have about 50 souls in our parish.
3 Marriages &c. We have not above 1 marriages, births nor burials, one year with another.
4 Patron The Dean and Chapter of Winchester is the patron of my curasee.
5 Chapels Our chapel is called as before writen Nutley chapel and served by Mr Thomas Ealls and repaired by the parish.
6 Lecturer I have no lecturer. Mr Thomas Ealls is my curatt.
7 Papists We have no Papists in our parish.
8 Dissenters We have no protestant dissenters in our parish.
9 Gentry &c. We have no gentlemen nor persons of note in our parish.
10 Schools We have no schools in our parish.
11 Charities Norten Pollett Esq. gives 40*s*. p.a. to the poor of the parish.
12 Post-town Al[re]sford is the niest post-town to me.

160 Odiham and Greywell 21M65/B4/1/1 fo.282
James Finmore, vicar 1708–30
Odiham
1 Area Compass of ground in the said parish, at a moderate computation, is *about* 12 miles, at least.
2 Population Number of souls *about* 1,230.
3 Marriages &c. At a medium, 5 marriages in a year (besides many out of the parish by licences), 40 births, 24 burials.
4 Patron Patron and rector, the Chancellour of the church of Sarum.
5 Chapels No chapel (certainly known to be such). However, there is a way in Northwarnborow-tything called Chapel-Way, and a little house called Chapel-House and a piece of building at the parsonage (now made use of to dry cloaths, and lay wood in) which looks at first sight, to all strangers, like a chapel, and is often called so (I am told) by some in the house.[22]
6 Lecturer No lecturer nor curate.
7 Papists No Papist.
8 Dissenters 1 meeting *now* of Presbyterians and Independents (if they were ever really divided on that account)[23] very lately united. Number of persons about *180*. 1 meeting of Anabaptists, number of persons *7*. 4 Quakers, no meeting *now*.
9 Gentry &c. The most noted persons [are] Mr James Feild, attourney, senior, Mr Thomas Rawlinson, tenant of the great tithes (for 3 lives).[24]
10 Schools One school endowed for writing, reading and casting accompt (as is generally understood). Schoolmaster, the Revd Mr William Allen, curate of Dogmersfeild; *particulars* of the *endowment* in Mr May's and Mr Zouch's charity, mentioned in the fourth sheet.
11 Charities 1608 Mistress Francis Clark, widow, (late wife of Mr Roger Clark, citizen and Alderman of London) by a deed dated 13th February 1608, gave to the poor of Odiham (the place where she was born) £10 p.a. for ever.
1623 Sir Edward Moor Kt., by his last will, dated 24th August 1623, gave the almshouses and gardens thereunto belonging to 8 poor aged people,

widowers or widows; and to each of them 1*s*. 6*d*. a week for ever, payable out of the lands and housing belonging to the said almshouses, lying in the town and parish of Odiham, now lett at £32 p.a. The poor of the almeshouses are to be ordered according to the orders of Emmanuel Hospital in Westminster. Query, how those orders run. (Maidens, I suppose, excluded, and dissenters; though both have been putt in by the town churchwarden.) The rents I now hear are sunk a little.

1626 Henry Smith Esq. in 1626, 2 Car. I, by his last will gave to this town (out of the manner farm and rectory of Longney in Gloucestershire) £10 p.a. for ever to several pious and charitable uses therein mentioned, and under the particular restriction and limitation of a bond to be given by the churchwardens of every year to the parson or vicar, and a certificate of such bond to be made by the parson or vicar to the governours of Christ's Hospital, London, before the rents are to be received. Every churchwarden also to keep a stock in hand, wherewith to set to work such as are able. Several other things to be done upon pain of forfeiting one year's rent to the poor of Christ's Hospital aforesaid.

1630 John Vaus gent., by his last will in 1630, gave £20 p.a. for ever for several pious uses, but chiefly to place poor children to service payable out of the houses and land belonging thereunto within the said parish of Odiham. In the hands of certain trustees in the town, of whom there should be 12. There are now 5 only surviving. Mr James Feild snr, Mr Thomas Rawlinson, John Harding, Mr Richard Hooker, Mr William Wakeford snr (the 2 last [being] dissenters).

1638 Richard Gurney Esqr (afterwards Sir Richard Gurney Kt. and bart, alderman of London, at the instance of his lady Elizabeth Gurney who was born in this town) by a deed bearing date February 18th, 1638, in 14 Car. I, gave to this town and parish 8½ acres of land lying in the parish of Fulham near Hammersmith in Middlesex for ever (valued then at £10 p.a.) which land was lett in the year 1699 for 60 years then to come at £13 p.a. (excepting all the trees and timber growing thereon) to be layd out in manner following, viz. £3 in bread, and meat to be given to the poor on Good Friday; £10 in cloth, for cloathing 6 poor men, and 6 poor women who have lived in the town or parish of Odiham 12 years; to be given every year at the feast of All Saints, the overplus (if any) to go to such as have the cloaths.

1674 Robert Ray of Hartley Wintney gent., by a deed dated March 24th, 1674, gave an annuity of £3 p.a. forever, to buy canvas, to be given every Good Friday to such poor people of Odiham as do not receive collection. Payable out of the brick-kiln and the land thereunto belonging, belonging to Odiham.

1694 Robert May gent., born in this town, deceased February 5th 1694, gave by his last will and testament £600 for ever, for the maintenance of a free school in this town, for the educating of 20 boys (I suppose to read, write and cast accompt). And he gave £200 for ever, the interest whereof is to put forth to trades such children as shall be educated in the said free school. The present trustees are John Limbrey Esq., Benjamin Rudyeard Esq., Mr James Feild senior, attourney, Mr Thomas Rawlinson, Mr Richard

Hooker, Mr William Wakeford (the 2 last dissenters). How many more there ought to be I cannot tell. Many of them are dead since I came to this place.
1702 James Zouch Esq., lord of the mannor of Odiham, deceased November 1708, by a deed bearing date May 6th, 1702, (which deed was confirmed by a decree in Chancery on March 4th, 10 Anne) gave to the master of the free school of Odiham, for 500 years, £10 p.a.; to 4 schoolboys (added to the 20 on Mr May's foundation) £20 p.a. for binding out 2 of the 4 every year apprentices; to every trustee for the same term of 500 years, £20 p.a.; of which trustees he appointed 3, Thomas Jervoise Esq., Benjamin Rudyeard Esq., Mr James Feild, attourney; and the remainder of his estate after his debts were payd, to the poor of Odiham, to be disposed of, I think, in such manner, for their use, as his trustees shall think fit.
1703 Frederique Tylney Esqr (who is reported to have an estate in this parish worth about £1000 p.a.) begun to give on the last Sunday in March 1723, and has to this time continued to give, on the last Sunday in every moneth since, 60 3d.-loaves (made and baked at his own house, that they might not be lessened by the charge of baking), ordering them to be given by the minister, church-wardens and overseers to the poorest persons in the parish, who are honest and keep [to?] their church. And we hope he will make it perpetual.
12 Post-town We have a post-bag at Odiham every Sunday, Wednesday and Friday.

Greywell (Grewell)
1 Area Compass of ground about 4½ miles.
2 Population Number of souls, about 246.
3 Marriages &c. Marriages 1 (besides such as are married out of the parish by licence); births about 7; burials about 5.
4 Patron Included, though not mentioned by the patron, in the presentation to Odiham.
5 Chapels Wherefore I take it for a chapel of ease to Odiham; the great tithes payd to the same tenant of the chancellor of Sarum as those of Odiham, and the small [tithes] to the vicar of Odiham. Their being served with prayers and sermon once every Sunday depends upon a subscription they have made to my predecessor and me.
6 Lecturer At present one assists me there, because I would have double service at Odiham, and particularly keep up catechizing, in a church belonging to a market-town, and to take away all pretence from my people for going to any separate meeting in the town, though I lose above £10 a year by so doing.
7 Papists No Papist.
8 Dissenters No meeting of dissenters. The number of those called Presbyterians, not 20. No Independent, no Anabaptist, no Quaker.
9 Gentry &c. Ashburnham Toll Esq., who has a small mannor there; the great mannour belongs to Anthony Henley Esq., who dos not inhabit there.
10 Schools No school endowed.

11 Charities No charities.
12 Post-town By Odiham bag.
PS I think I have reason to be confirmed in my opinion that Grewell is only a chapel of ease to Odiham, because the churchwardens of Grewell do, in the name of the parish, or tithing of Grewell, maintain four score feet of rails about the churchyard of Odiham. And in virtue of that payment [they] have a right of burying in the said churchyard. Which they do accordingly, without paying any fee to the vicar, as foreigners use to do.

All foreigners paying 6*s*. 8*d*. as a double fee for burying there. Tho' I know not how it come to pass that no single fee has been payd by the people of Grewell or by any of the undoubted parishioners of Odiham, for performing the office of burial there.

161 Old Alresford, New Alresford and Medstead 21M65/B4/1/1 fo.5
William Needham BD, rector of 'Old Alresford with the chappelries of New Alresford and Meidstead annexed' 1691–1727
Alresford is a peculiar[25] and deanery.
1 Area The whole parish including the 2 chappelries, and an hamlet of 7 houses called Harmsworth, is near 6 miles in length, and 2 in breadth, though in some places 'tis not so broad.
2 Population There are in Old Alresford, as well as I can reckon, about 40 familys, Harmsworth included, which at 4 to a family makes the number of souls 160.
3 Marriages &c. 3 marriages, 5 births and 4 burials.
4 Patron The Lord Bishop of Winton.
5 Chapels 2 as above. New Alresford [is] supported well by the inhabitants, but the chancel [is maintained] by the rector. Served by Mr Ralph Baddely MA of Oriel College, Oxford. Pensioned and nominated by the rector. Meidstead also maintained by the inhabitants, but the chancel by the rector. Served by Mr Stephen Stephens MA of Christ Church, Oxford. Pensioned and nominated by the rector. Both curates are resident upon their respective cures.
6 Lecturer No lecturer. Curates as before.
7 Papists Only one poor family in the hamlet called Harmsworth.
8 Dissenters None at all.
9 Gentry &c. None.
10 Schools Noe school at all.
11 Charities I think £15 in money. The principal is placed out at interest amongst the parishioners, and the interest, at every 2 years' end, is divided amongst poor families for buying them shoes. There is no hospital.
12 Post-town New Alresford is a post-town.

New Alresford 21/M65/B4/1/1 fo.9
William Needham, rector of Old Alresford
Ralph Baddely AM, curate
Alresford is a deanery and peculiar.
1 Area About 4 miles in compass, being included in the rectory of Old Alresford.

2 Population About 800 souls.
3 Marriages &c. Marriages 1, births 22, burials 18.
4 Patron New Alresford is a chapel belonging to Old Alresford.
5 Chapels New Alresford is anext to Old Alresford.
6 Lecturer Ralph Baddely is curate, pentioned and nominated by the rector of Old Alresford.
7 Papists No intire families, but 4 reputed Papists of no great consideration.
8 Dissenters One meeting house built for the use of the Quakers, but they being but a few, not above 3 families, and they of small consideration, rarely hold any meetings. There are no other profest dissenters.
9 Gentry &c. None at all.
10 Schools One grammer school lately founded by Dr Perin, and endowed with lands to the value of £27 p.a., besides the school-house settled upon trustees (gentlemen in the country) who have the nomination of the master, who is at present Mr John Church AM, Fellow of Pembroke College in Oxford. The school is in good order.
11 Charities £3 p.a. given by one Mr Todd to thee poor of New Alresford to be distributed on Good Friday by the churchwardens and overseers, £1 p.a. given by one Mr Widders to poor widoers and widows to be distributed by the baliff of New Alresford. £1 p.a. to be payd out of the common [sic] of New Alresford, and to [be] distributed to the poor on St. Thomas, his day, by the churchwardens and overseers.
12 Post-town New Alresford is a post-town.

Medstead 21M65/B4/1/1 fo.11

William Needham, rector of Old Alresford
Stephen Stephens AM, curate
Meidstead [is] a peculiar in the deanery of Alresford.
1 Area Meidstead is about 2½ miles long, 1½ broad.
2 Population The number of souls is about 200.
3 Marriages &c. Marriages 2; births 11; burials 2, at a medium, one year with another.
4 Patron Meidstead is a chapel of ease to Old Alresford [i.e. the patron is the rector of Old Alresford].
5 Chapels None.
6 Lecturer No lecturer.
7 Papists No Papist.
8 Dissenters No meeting, and but 2 dissenters, 1 Quaker and 1 Presbyterian.
9 Gentry &c. No nobleman, gentleman, nor person of note.
10 Schools No school endowed.
11 Charities No charities given to the parish. No hospital.
12 Post-town Alton is the next post-town.

162 Overton and Tadley 21M65/B4/1/1 fo.289

Dr Nicholas Clagget, rector of 'Overton with the chappel of Tadley' 1721-46

Richard Russell, vicar 1719–71

1 Area This parish is about 12 miles in compass.

2 Population It contains about 730 souls.

3 Marriages &c. There are about 3 marriages, 21 christenings, and 15 burials.

4 Patron The Bishop of Winton is patron of the rectory; the rector of the vicaridge.

5 Chapels A chappel in a tything called Quidhampton, unserved and unmaintained.

6 Lecturer No lecturer or curate in the parish.

7 Papists No Papists.

8 Dissenters No dissenters.

9 Gentry &c. No persons of note.

10 Schools A private school kept by John Lake, a weaver, where children are taught to read and write.

11 Charities Charities to the church, as follow, viz. the interest of £17; the interest of £5 left by Ann Worsum; 10*s*. p.a. charged on houses left by Mr Dowse; and 5*s*. p.a. charged on houses left by Mr Denbigh; 7 acres of land let for £1 3*s*. p.a.; an house let for £1 6*s*. p.a.; all which summs are laid out yearly on the repair of the church. Charities to the poor, as follow, viz. the interest of £40 left by Mrs Ann Holdripp to buy 6 coats, 3 for widowers and 3 for widows; the interest of £10 left by Mr Henry Hasker and the interest of £50, which are given to the poor yearly at Xmas.

12 Post-town Basingstoke is the next post-town.

Tadley

1 Area, 2 Population This parish is about 6 miles in compass, and contains about 400 souls.

3 Marriages &c. Marriages 3, christenings 8 and burials 8 in a year.

4 Patron, 5 Chapels [No reply.]

6 Lecturer Mr George Gibson, curate.

7 Papists One poor woman a Papist.

8 Dissenters About 3 Quakers, and a meeting of protestant dissenters consisting of about 50.

9 Gentry &c. No persons of note.

10 Schools No school.

11 Charities No hospital. £2 10*s*. p.a. charged on lands left by one Simpson, and yearly given to the poor at Xmas.

12 Post-town [No reply.]

163 Over Wallop 21M65/B4/1/1 fo.185

Richard Burd DD, rector 1701–1729/30

1 Area 12 miles containing about 3,000 acres of arable land and 3,000 acres of down, pasture for sheep.

2 Population 300.
3 Marriages &c. Marriages 2, births 8, burials 6.
4 Patron The Right Hon. the Lord Viscount Lymington.
5 Chapels None.
6 Lecturer None.
7 Papists None.
8 Dissenters One meeting of the denomination of Annabaptis and about 10 in number.
9 Gentry &c. 1 gentlewoman, Elizabeth Swanton, widow.
10 Schools 1 school-mistress that teaches to read English. About 20 scholars, children. Some paid for by their parents and other poor children by myself.
11 Charities £100 given by — Pyle gent. The interest to be paid yearly to the poor, and 50*s*. p.a. being a quite rent given by Sir Richard Read to the poor. Hospitals none.
12 Post-town Andover.

164 Ovington 21M65/B4/1/1 fo.38
John Barrett MA, rector 1697–1744
[Ovington is] a peculiar.
1 Area The parish of Ovington is supposed to be 9 miles in compass.
2 Population There are in the parish aforesaid about 136 souls.
3 Marriages &c. The number of marriages, births and burials may be att a medium, one year with another, of each sort about 2.
4 Patron The Bishop of Winchester is patron of the living.
5 Chapels There is no chapel in the parish.
6 Lecturer No lecturer or curate.
7 Papists There are 2 familys of Papists in the parish, 7 persons in number, 3 in the one and 4 in the other, one a maltster and the other a labourer.
8 Dissenters No protestant dissenters of any kind.
9 Gentry &c. No nobleman, gentleman or person of note of either sex.
10 Schools No school.
11 Charities There are 3½ acres of ground belonging to the parish, the rent of which has time out of mind been used in the repairs of the church, but no other charitie belonging to the parish.
12 Post-town The next post-town is Alresford.

165 Owslebury 21M65/B4/1/2 fo.343
Walter Mildmay, vicar of Twyford and Owslebury 1700–44
1 Area [It is] supposed to be about 20 miles round.
2 Population About 80 families, consisting of about 300 souls.
3 Marriages &c. Marriages about 2; births 15; burials 3.
4 Patron Emmanuel Colledge in Cambridge.
5 Chapels Owslibury chappel, served by Walter Mildmay, maintained and supported by small tythes and offerings. Emmanuel Colledge in Cambridge has the right of nomination to it.

6 Lecturer None.
7 Papists Not any Papists.
8 Dissenters There is no meeting, but about 5 persons that call themselves Presbiterians.
9 Gentry &c. Thomas Davies Esq. and George Carpenter Esq.
10 Schools There is no school.
11 Charities None.
12 Post-town Winchester.

166 Pamber 21M65/B4/1/1 fo.291
Laurence Farington, vicar 1722–50 16 August 1725
George Gibson, curate
1 Area The parish is supposed to consist of about 1,000 acres of land, exclusive of the forrest and common.
2 Population The number of souls are something upwards of 150.
3 Marriages &c. There have been but 17 marriages for the last 20 years. We have about 2 christenings in a year, and as many burials.
4 Patron Queen's College in Oxford.
5 Chapels No chapel.
6 Lecturer No lecturer or curate besides the above named.
7 Papists We have no Papists in the parish.
8 Dissenters No meeting of protestant dissenters, but a small number of such supposed to be Presbyterians.
9 Gentry &c. We have no persons of distinction in the parish except Mrs Wither, whose house stands part in the parish of Tadley and part of it in this.
10 Schools We have no endowed school.
11 Charities We have no charities belonging to the parish, except £1 3*s*. 4*d*. paid by Queen's College in Oxford, and £2 10*s*. at 2 several payments left to the poor by one Thomas Smith. Both these sums are regularly paid and distributed.
12 Post-town Basingstoke is the next post-town.

167 Penton Mewsey 21M65/B4/1/1 fo.167
John Border, rector 1706–1731/2
1 Area The compass of ground in this parish is supposed to be about 6½ miles.
2 Population The number of souls in this parish is computed at 140.
3 Marriages &c. The marriages are about 1 a year. Births about 5, and burials about 4 or 5.
4 Patron The patron of this living is Sir Philip Medows.
5 Chapels We have no chapel in this parish.
6 Lecturer We have no lecturer or curate in this parish.
7 Papists We have no Papist in this parish.
8 Dissenters Here is no meeting of protestant dissenters in this parish. We have but one dissenter in it, who is an Independent.
9 Gentry &c. Here are no noblemen, gentlemen or persons of note of either sex in this parish.

10 Schools We have a little school, endowed by one John Read, a citizen and carpenter of London. He left by will £6 p.a. for the teaching of the poor children of this parish, and of the parish of Weyhill. We are to be paid by the master, wardens and assistants of the Carpenters' Company in London, but they have kept back half the money every year for above 16 years last past, without giving us a satisfactory reason for so doing. The number of scholars are about 14 or 16. The schoolmaster's name is John Cradock. The schoolmaster is to be chosen by the ministers, churchwardens and overseers of both parishes.
11 Charities The same John Read did likewise give 40*s*. p.a., 20 to the poor of this parish, and 20 to the poor of the parish of Weyhill,to be paid by the same persons; but have kept back half of this too, for the same reason as they do the other, and for as long a time. What money we do receive is distributed to the poorest sort of people in each parish. We have no hospital in this parish.
12 Post-town The next post-town to this parish is Andover.

168 Petersfield 21M65/B4/1/2 fo.19

George Aylmer, curate
1 Area The compass or circuit of ground belonging to the parish of Petersfield, is generally computed to be about 5 miles more or less.
2 Population The number of souls supposed to be within the said parish are reckoned to be between 8 or 900, there being more than 200 families.
3 Marriages &c. The marriages both by lycenses and bannes one year with another, upon careful examination of the register, are found to be not more than 8, the births somewhat under 40, the burials somewhat exceeded by the christ[e]nings.
4 Patron, 5 Chapels, 6 Lecturer The church is a chapel belonging to the parish of Buriton, and has a curate ma[i]ntained and supported by the rector of Buriton who has the right of nominating him, and his name is above-written.
7 Papists The number of Papists is inconsiderable, there being not above 2 or 3 families, one whereof is a gentleman whose name is Mr Henry Mathews of about 4 or 500£ p.a. estate. The other[s] are poor people.
8 Dissenters There is a meeting of protestant dissenters of the Presbyterian persuasion, very lately erected, consisting of about 7 or 8 families, and have their preacher living in the parish whose name is Mr William Henry, an Irishman, as he saith himself.
9 Gentry &c. As to gentlemen and persons of note living in the said parish, there are Edmund Miller serjeant-at-law and Member of Parliament for the town of Petersfield, Robert Michel Esq., and William Graham Esq. and others I know not.
10 Schools There are 2 schools, the master of one of which teaches Latin, writing and arithmetique, the other writing and arithmetique only. The name of the former is Mr John Finden. The other is Mr Richard Colebrook. There is no endowment.
11 Charities There is lately given by the will of Mr Richard Churcher of the parish of Petersfield aforesaid, a benefaction of £3000 for building and

founding a mathematical school to consist of 1 master and 10 or 12 scholars to be instructed in navigation, under the instruction of neighbouring gentlemen who are appointed trustees for that purpose.
12 Post-town [No reply.]

169 Portchester 21M65/B4/1/2 fo.62
Thomas Carew, vicar 1693–1745/6 10 August 1725
1 Area As to the compas of ground in Porchester, I suppose [it] to be about 1500 acres.
2 Population As to the number of souls, about 300.
3 Marriages &c. About 2 marriages, 4 births and 3 burials, at a medium one year with another.
4 Patron The presentation belongs to the Crown.
5 Chapels We have no chappell, only the parish church.
6 Lecturer We have no lecturer or curate.
7 Papists We have no Papists.
8 Dissenters We have one Quakers' meeting-house, only 3 women in the parrish of that perswasion.
9 Gentry &c. We have no noblemen or persons of note of either sex.
10 Schools We have no school.
11 Charities There is 5*s*. p.a. given to the poor of this parrish by Richard Norton Esq. which is distributed as the minister and churchwardens think convenient. Here is no hospitall.
12 Post-town The next post-town is Fareham.

170 Portsea 21M65/B4/1/2 fo.64
Evan Jones, vicar 1716/7–1738
1 Area The compass of ground in the said parish of Portsea is computed to be between 4 and 500 acres.
2 Population The number of souls according to the best information is about 1,500.
3 Marriages &c. The number of marriages since the peace and the great discharges at the Dock are about 50 p.a., and about 140 children baptized yearly, and about 100 buried.
4 Patron This vicaridge is in the gift of the college of Winchester.
5 Chapels There is one chapel in His Majesties Dockyard within this parish, called St Ann's, built in the year 1704 for the use of the officers and artificers belonging to the said Dock, as also for the officers and men belonging to the ordinary of the navy in this harbour. The present chaplain is Mr John Fetherston and warranted by the Lords of the Admiralty.
6 Lecturer I have one curate, viz. Mr William Scott.
7 Papists Here is no Papist of any consequence, and I believe not above 2 or 3 labouring persons that are such.
8 Dissenters There is one meeting-house of the Anabaptist persuasion within this parish, and, I do believe, the number of protestant dissenters here may be near 200.

9 Gentry &c. There are no noblemen, gentlemen or persons of distinction of either sex in this parish, except Sir Isaac Townsend, one of the Commissioners of the Navy who presides in the dockyard, and is Commander-in-Chief of all the men-of-war in this harbour.
10 Schools There are no endowed schools in this parish.
11 Charities Nor are there any charities or hospitalls.
12 Post-town The next post-town is Portsmouth, which is about a mile distant.

171 Portsmouth 21M65/B4/1/2 fo.68
Anthony Bliss, vicar 1724–38
1 Area This parish contains but about 5 acres of ground, beside what the town stands upon.
2 Population We are computed to have about 8,000 souls in this parish.
3 Marriages &c. The christ[e]nings, marriages and burialls are much less numerous at present than they were in the time of warr; the following table will give the best account of this matter:

Year	Christnings	Marriages	Burialls
1707	239	114	212
1708	227	112	271
1709	202	74	231
1710	227	64	235
1711	217	80	269
1712	187	90	180
1713	202	72	126
1714	177	54	186
1715	185	40	109
1716	172	48	162
1717	160	45	122
1718	181	46	129
1719	143	45	268*
1720	132	79	254
1721	137	67	258
1722	146	44	235
1723	152	47	260
1724	145	48	182

*NB This year the soldiers began to be buried in St Mary's or Colewort Garden where formerly there was a chappell.
4 Patron The colledge of Winchester is the patron of this living.
5 Chapels We have one chappel in the parish called the Garrison Chappel or God's House. Mr Cooper is the chaplain, Mr Nathaniel Jones serves it as his curate. The sallary is 6*s*. 8*d*. *per diem*, paid by his Majesty, who is the patron.
6 Lecturer At present here is no curate or lecturer.
7 Papists We have but 2 familys of proffessed Papists and those mean and obscure.

8 Dissenters We have one meeting of Presbyterian dissenters, consisting of about 700 persons, about 500 of which belong to this parish. The rest come from adjacent parishes, but mostly from the place called the Common in the parish of Portsea. We have also a meeting of Arminian Baptists, consisting of about 150 persons, but not more than 100 of them belong to this place; and a third [meeting] of Quakers not exceeding 20 persons. Beside these wee have about 20 families of Calvinistical Baptists, which belong to a meeting held in the aforesaid place called the Common.
9 Gentry &c. The persons of cheife note in the parish are Colonel Hawker, our Lieutenant Governor, John White Esq., the present mayor, Sir John Suffield Kt., Thomas Ridge, Thomas Missing, Henry Stannyford, John Vining Esqs., William Smith and Samuel Brady MD.
10 Schools We have no endowed school either for boyes or girls. We have 1 Latin school which the vicar nominates to, who generally nominates his curate.
11 Charities Thomas Winter Esqr gave £200; Mr Thomas Mills gave £100; which sums are in the hands of the corporation who annually pay the interest. Mr John Mounsher gave £100; Mr John Timbrell gave £50; the executors of the respective testators pay the interest of these sums. Mr William Branden gave £200. NB The interest of this last £200 was paid for some time by the executors, but has been discontinued ever since the year 1709 on account of demand from the government upon the testator, who was agent victualler of this place which there are not assets to discharge.
12 Post-town [No reply.]

172 Preston Candover 21M65/B4/1/1 fo.43
John Waterman, vicar 1671–1726
1 Area We have about 3,000 acres of ground in our parish.
2 Population We have about 240 souls in our parish.
3 Marriages &c. We have about 2 marriages and 2 births and 2 burials, one year with another, in our parish.
4 Patron The Dean and Chapter of Winchester is the patron of my vicarage.
5 Chapels We have no chapel in our parish.
6 Lecturer Lecturer I have none. Mr Thomas Ealls is my curate.
7 Papists We have no Papists in our parish,
8 Dissenters We have no protestant dessenters in our parrish.
9 Gentry &c. We have gentelmen in our parish 2, Mr John Cooper and Mr Thomas Oades.
10 Schools We have no schools in our parish.
11 Charities We had forme[r]ly given to our church t[w]eenty sheep, but lost for many years. We had given more to our church t[w]eenty acres of ground, but sold since by the churchwardens for 3 lives. We had given by one Mr Joyner, formerly minister of this parish, the use of £5 to be given to a widdow and widower of this parish once a year, which mon[e]y Mr Thomas Oades of Mounsmor have and gives itt constantly every year. There is likewise given to the poor of this parish fower pound a year and

teen shillens for ever. Robbard Lickscom decesed of this parish gave itt and tied sertan land for the payment of it, this money is payd every year att 2 equael porshons unto Mr Thomas Oades of Mounsmor and he has the giving and ordering of itt to the poor peopple. Likewise we had now lately given unto the poor of this parish teen pounds by Mr Jams Oades of London, lately deceased, which mon[e]y is given to the poor by Mr Thomas Oades of Mounsmor, brother to the aforesaid Jams Oades.
12 Post-town Al[re]sford is the niess post-towen to me.
This was writen by me John Powell by the orders of the Revd John Waterman, viccar of Presen Candover, [who] have aproufed of all herein writen.

173 Quarley 21M65/B4/1/1 fo.171
George Lewis, rector 1719–34
1 Area We have about 1,000 acres in our parish.
2 Population There are about the number of 100 souls in our parish.
3 Marriages &c. We have about 6 or 7 births and burialls in our parish, *communibus annis*. [No mention of marriages.]
4 Patron The Hospitall of St Catherin near the Tower in London have the patronadge of the living and presented me to it. The valew of the rectory is about £106 p.a.
5 Chapels We have no chappell in our parish.
6 Lecturer We have no lecturer, but I have a curate, one Mr Robert Atkinson, lately [1724] licensed and approved by Your Lordship.
7 Papists We have no Papist in our parish.
8 Dissenters We have no meeting and not one dissenter. My Lord, I have 2 more parishes in Wiltshire, one as bigg again as Quarly, and the other 5 or 6 times as bigg, and but 1 dissenter in 'em both.
9 Gentry &c. We have no nobleman or gentlemen that dwells now in our parish. We have one Mr Hoare, son of the late Henry Hoare Esq., the famous banker. That gentleman comes now and then, and stays a little while with us in the hunting seasons. He has an estate in our parish about £200 p.a., and is lord of the mannor under the Hospitall of St Catherins.
10 Schools We have no schoolmaster or mistress at present that I know of.
11 Charities We have no charities nor hospitalls. We want a charity-school and a benefaction for that purpose which might be of great use to the poor. The late Mr Hoare and Squire Benson were considerable benefactors to me and to the parish in building the east end of the chancell and putting in a north Venetian window. The late Mr Hoare and myself contributed to the seating the chancell.
12 Post-town Andover is the nearest market- and post-town to our parish, And if Your Lordship shall please at any time to honor me with a letter, I will give proper orders and direcions to my curate to take care that it may safely come to my hands. My Lord these are the best answers that I am capable to give to your lordship's queries.

174 Ringwood 21M65/B4/1/2 fo.131

George Harris DD, vicar 1723–46

1 Area The length of the parish is 8 miles, the breadth from 2 to 5 miles, by which I take the compass of the parish of Ringwood to be more than 25 miles.

2 Population The number of souls may be reasonably inferred to be 2,000, there being 540 families.

3 Marriages &c. The births at a moderate computation are 88; burials 64; marriages 12.

4 Patron The patron is the Provost and Scholars of King's College in Cambridge.

5 Chapels There is a chaple at Harbridge consolidated to the vicarige of Ringwood, served by myself and curate. (The particulars of Harbridge [are] under that name.)

6 Lecturer There is a curate, the Revd Mr Price.

7 Papists The number of Papists may be 10, and of little or no consequence.

8 Dissenters There are several meetings of protestant dissenters, viz. Presbyterians, Anabaptists and Quakers, in number according to a moderate computation 800, of which the Presbyterians are more than 600.

9 Gentry &c. Bistern House belonging to the relict of Henry Compton Esq., is the only gentleman's house in the parish; now uninhabited.

10 Schools One small school, the endowment £14 p.a. Mr Rice [is] the schoolmaster, number of schollars 20. The nomination to it [is] in Mr James Willys of Ringwood.

11 Charities A few small charities have been given, not amounting to £8 p.a. (the school excepted).

12 Post-town Ringwood is a post-town.

175 Rockbourne 21M65/B4/1/2 fo.139

Thomas Durnford AM, perpetual curate 1714–46 23 August 1725

1 Area I suppose there may be contained in the compass of the parish about 3,670 acres.

2 Population The number of souls therein are about 300.

3 Marriages &c. We have at a medium yearly about 1 marriage, 8 births, 8 burials.

4 Patron The Duke of Manchester nominates the curate.

5 Chapels There is no chapel in the parish.

6 Lecturer There is no lecturer or other curate in the parish.

7 Papists There is no Papist living in it.

8 Dissenters There are no meetings of protestant dissenters. There are in the parish 18 such dissenters, viz. 2 Quakers, 16 Presbyterians.

9 Gentry &c. There is no person of note living in the parish.

10 Schools There is no school that hath any endowment.

11 Charities No charities have been given to the parish.

12 Post-town Fordingbridge is the next post-town to Rockborn.

176 Romsey 21M65/B4/1/2 fo.246

William Mayo, vicar 1689/90–1727

1 Area The compass of ground in the parish of Rumsey is supposed to be near 20 miles.

2 Population The number of souls is supposed to be 5,000.

3 Marriages &c. The number of births, take one year with another is between 50 and 60; the number of burials between 40 and 50; the number of marriages between 20 and 30.

4 Patron The Dean and Chapter of Winchester.

5 Chapels Only one great church, no chapel. The vicarage worth but £50 p.a. An augmentation of 20 marks[26] p.a. from the church of Winchester.

6 Lecturer No lecturer; one curate, Mr Miller.

7 Papists No Papists in the parish.

8 Dissenters 1 Presbyterian and 1 Anabaptist meeting. The number of these dissenters is supposed to be 400.

9 Gentry &c. Not one nobleman nor lady of quality and but few gentlemen of note.

10 Schools 2 schools—a free school endowed with 20 marks[26] p.a., and a charity school with £25 p.a. besides a few subscriptions. 12 scholars in the free school, and 20 in the charity. The trustees nominate the masters.

11 Charities No hospital in the parish.

12 Post-town Rumsey is a post-town in Hampshire.

[Letter enclosed with return]

John King to the Bishop of Winchester, Rumsey, November 14, 1741

(21M65/B4/1/2 fo.247)

In answer to Your lordship's commands which I was favoured with the 9th of this month, I humbly acquaint you, that we have in Rumsey a free school, but the terms of its erection I cannot inform you. It was endowed above a hundred years ago by one Mr Robert Brackley, a gentleman of this parish, with the sum of £6 6*s*. 8*d*. which money is paid yearly by the mayor of this corporation to the master of the free school. Mr Robert Brackley, as appears by his monument in the church, died August 14, 1628. This free school had another endowment made to it by Sir William Petty, born in Rumsey, of £7 p.a., payable out of the rents of his lands and houses in this parish. The time when this benefaction was made, or the conditions, if any, required by the donor I cant find out. But this sum is paid by order of Sir William's only surviving son, the Lord Shelburne, to the schoolmaster, by the mayor and vicar, who sign a certificate of the payment made to him, and also the distribution of some charities given to poor widows and housekeepers of the town, which certificates are sent to Lord Shelburne. The present schoolmaster's name is Mr Job Beardsley, clerk. There is no person in the parish who teaches the learned languages but he.

But there are other schoolmasters in the town who teach children to read, write and cast accounts, the chief of which is the master of our charity school. This school for the educating and cloathing poor boys was first set up on the free contributions and voluntary subscription of several gentlemen in the neighbourhood and others of the town and parish. The late Sir John St Barbe was a great encourager of this goodwork, and at his death, by will, setled a legacy of £25 p.a., in the manner following, taken from his will.

'Item, I give and bequeath unto the treasurer and governours of the charity school of Rumsey, and their successours forever, the sum of £25 p.a., to be paid out of the rents and profits of my farm of Broadlands, and applied and disposed of in the following manner, viz. the sum of £10 p.a., part thereof to the use of the schoolmaster of the said school and his successours for the time being, so long as he or they, shall continue to teach and instruct the full and compleat number of 10 poor boys, equally to be chosen out of the said farm of Broadlands and the mayor and minister of Rumsey for the time being, and other £10 p.a., other part thereof, towards cloathing them in blue cloaths, as others now belonging to the said school are now cloathed, and £5 p.a., the remaining part of the aforesaid £25 p.a. towards cloathing such poor boys so chosen and instructed as aforesaid when they shall at any time, with the consent of the said owner of Broadlands, mayor and minister of Rumsey, be placed out to trade or service.'
Sir John St Barbe died September 7, 1723. The present owner of Broadlands is the Hon. Lord Viscount Palmerston, a nobleman most exemplary in piety and liberality. He most punctually with his own hand pais this legacy.

Though I had made a larger trespass on Your Lordship's time I wish I could have given you the particulars of the benefactions made to the free school, as clearly and particularly, as that setled by Sir John St Barbe on the charity school.

With all duty and submission, I subscribe myself your lordship's most obedient and humble servant.

177 Rotherwick 21M65/B4/1/1 fo.293

William Sealy AM, perpetual curate 1723–27 14 August 1725

1 Area The parish of Rotherwick is in compass about 7 miles.

2 Population The number of souls in it is about 250.

3 Marriages &c. At a medium one year with another, there is 1 marriage, 8 births and 6 burials.

4 Patron The tithes of the said parish both small and great were appropriated, in the reign of King John, to the chancellor of the church of Sarum. From him Frederick Tylney Esq. holds them by lease of three lives, and by the said lease is obliged to allow a small yearly stipend for the supply of the church.

5 Chapels There is no chappell in the parish.

6 Lecturer There is no lecturer. William Sealy is the present curate, and supplys the church by appointment of Frederick Tylney Esq.

7 Papists There is no Papist in the parish.

8 Dissenters There is no protestant dissenter of any kind.

9 Gentry &c. The only gentlemen of note, is Frederick Tylney.

10 Schools The said Frederick Tylney Esq. has lately erected and endowed a charity school for instructing 10 boys and 10 girls in reading, writing and accounts. He has given £10 p.a. for ever, for a maintenance to the schoolmaster, issuing out of a certain farm and lands called Joyce, lying

in Rotherwick, and also a very good school-house, an orchard and one piece of land worth together about £5 p.a. more. The present master is Mr Richard Waller, who has in his schools generally about 30 scholars besides the charity children. The nomination of the master is in Mr Tylney during his life; after his decease in such person as shall be in possession of the said lands called Joyce.
11 Charities There have been 3 several charities left to the said parish. A mark yearly for ever towards repairing the church, which the churchwardens constantly receive and account for. 72 ells of linnen cloth, to be distributed by the churchwardens on every Good Friday for ever to such poor people as receive no collection money; and 5*s*. at the same time to 5 poor women. The books and parchments that might have enabled me to give a better account of these charitys, are at present in the custody of William Milton and Richard Freemantell both of the said parish; the latter of whom, *Freemantell*, could not be prevailed upon to attend at any seasonable time for examining the said writings, and, when summoned by the churchwardens (the proper officers to assist the minister in all enquirys of this nature) to give them his key, for the purpose mentioned in the querys, refused to deliver it.
12 Post-town The next post-town is Hartford-bridge.

178 Rowner 21M65/B4/1/2 fo.72
John Burbydge, rector 1692–1728
1 Area It contains, as appears by a survey lately taken, 1,200 acres, and is in breadth from east to west 7 furlongs, and in length from north to south 20 furlongs.
2 Population 90 or a hundred at most.
3 Marriages &c. Marriages 5 or 6; 2 or 3 born, and the same number buryed, though some years less.
4 Patron Charles Brune Esq. of Plumbar neare Blandford in the county of Dorset.
5 Chapels We have none.
6 Lecturer We have none.
7 Papists Not one.
8 Dissenters No meetings of dissenters, but we have 3 in the parish that frequent their assemblies.
9 Gentry &c. There are none.
10 Schools We have no schools.
11 Charities None.
12 Post-town Fareham or Gosport are equally distant from us, and a letter sent either way will not miscarry.

179 St Laurence [IoW] 21M65/B4/1/2 fo.197
James Nutkins, rector 1709–34 25 August 1725
1 Area The parish of St Laurence is about 1 mile in length and three quarters of a mile in breadth.

2 Population The number of souls in this parish is 39.
3 Marriages &c. We have had for the space of 10 years past in the whole 4 marriages, 9 births, and 2 burials.
4 Patron The patron of the living is Sir Robert Worsley Bt.
5 Chapels There is no chapel in this parish.
6 Lecturer There is no lecturer or curate.
7 Papists There are no Papists in this parish.
8 Dissenters There is no protestant dissenter in this parish.
9 Gentry &c. There is no nobleman, gentleman, or person of note living in this parish.
10 Schools There is no school here.
11 Charities No charities have been given to the parish.
12 Post-town The next post-town is Newport.

180 Selborne 21M65/B4/1/2 fo.91
Gilbert White, vicar 1681–1728
1 Area 'Tis judged to be about 5 miles long, and in the widest place about 3 miles broad, but a great part is heathy, waste and uninhabited, called Wulmer Forrest.
2 Population About 500.
3 Marriages &c. About 3 marriages, 14 births, and 10 burials.
4 Patron The President and Scholars of St Mary Magdalen College in Oxford.
5 Chapels We have none.
6 Lecturer We have none.
7 Papists We have none.
8 Dissenters We have none of any kind.
9 Gentry &c. None.
10 Schools We have no endowed school.
11 Charities Hospitals we have none, but we have 3 charities. The 1st is 10 bushels of wheat given every St Thomas's day out of East Worl[d]ham parsonage by Magdalen College aforesaid; the 2nd, £4 p.a. paid out of Bin's parsonage (a portion of impropriate tithes in the parish belonging to Magdalen College) to put out poor children apprentices and servants with, by the nomination of the vicar, and the owners or tenants of 5 farms here, viz. Grange, Priory, Upper Temple, Blackmoor, and Oakhanger House; and the 3d is the interest of an £100, £80 of which was given by Mr Richard Byfield, late vicar here, and £20 by one Henry Holloway, and both to the same uses as the former, and to be distributed by the same persons.
12 Post-town The next post-town to our parish is Alton.

181 Shalden 21M65/B4/1/1 fo.95
Anthony Lynch, rector 1704–25
1 Area I do suppose there are 1200 acres of ground in the parish.
2 Population There are about 120 souls.
3 Marriages &c. At a medium, one year with another, there are about 3 births, 2 marriages, and 2 burials.

4 Patron My Lord Chancellor [is] the patron.
5 Chapels No chappel.
6 Lecturer No lecturer; John Siddon, curate.
7 Papists No Papists.
8 Dissenters No meeting of protestant dissenters of any kind. Only 1 dissenter.
9 Gentry &c. No noblemen, gentlemen or persons of note of either sex.
10 Schools No school.
11 Charities No charity nor hospital.
12 Post-town Alton [is] the next post-town.

182 Sherborne St John 21M65/B4/1/1 fo.297
Ezekiel Lion, vicar 1699–1732
1 Area I suppose that the compass of ground in the parish of Sherbourn St Johns is about 9 miles.
2 Population The number of souls in the said parish I suppose to be about 350.
3 Marriages &c. The number of marriages is very uncertain. In some years there is none. In other years there may be 3 or 2 or but 1. The number of births and burials may be about 9 at a medium, one year with another.
4 Patron Anthony Chute Esq., is the patron of the vicarage and of the rectory also.
5 Chapels There is a chapel of ease in the patron's house, formerly a chantry. But there is no allowance made to any clergyman to serve there.
6 Lecturer There is no lecturer or curate in the said parish.
7 Papists I know no popish family in the said parish.
8 Dissenters There are no meetings of any protestant dissenters, in the parish of Sherbourn St Johns.
9 Gentry &c. Anthony Chute Esq. lives in the said parish at his seat called The Vine. There is another gentleman's seat called Beaurepaire, belonging to Thomas Brocas Esq. who seldom lives there.
10 Schools There are no schools in the said parish.
11 Charities I dont know of any charities given to the parish, but that of one Simson who gave 50*s*. p.a. to our parish about 50 years ago for ever, to be distributed to the poor on 2 distinct days, viz. the feast of St Thomas the Apostle, 25*s*., and the rest on Thomas Becket day.
12 Post-town The next post-town to the parish of Sherbourn St Johns is Basingstoke.

183 Sherfield English 21M65/B4/1/2 fo.248
William Kingsman AM, rector 1707–37
1 Area About 3½ miles round.
2 Population Number of souls 150.
3 Marriages &c. Marriages 2 or 3; births 5; burials 3 or 4.
4 Patron Mr Henry Eyre of Weddington near Devises, Wilts.
5 Chapels No chappel.

6 Lecturer A curate, Mr Richard Head.
7 Papists 2 small familys Papists, poor people.
8 Dissenters No meeting. One family of Presbyterians.
9 Gentry &c. No person of note.
10 Schools No school.
11 Charities No charitys nor hospital.
12 Post-town Romsey [is the] nearest market- and post-town.

184 Sherfield on Loddon 21M65/B4/1/1 fo.301
Charles Sutton, rector 1708–30 16 August 1725
1 Area, 2 Population Sherfield Lodon or Lodden as 'tis generally called by the inhabitants from the river Lodon or Lodden which runs by it, is 4 miles NNE from Basingstoke which is the nearest post-town, and is supposed to contain about 7 square miles, and has in it 382 souls or thereabouts.
3 Marriages &c. The marriages, one year with another, usually amount to 2, the births to 10, and the burials to 6.
4 Patron The Duke of Bolton is the patron of it.
5 Chapels, 6 Lecturer It has no chapel or lecturer, and it is at present served by the rector.
7 Papists There is 1 Papist in it, who is wife to a farmer, who rents about £30 p.a., and has no children, nor is likely to have any.
8 Dissenters It has no protestant dissenter, but there are 6 Quakers, 1 of which is a man of a weak understanding, and but one degree above an idiot. 2 of the other 5 are an old day-labourer and his wife, and the remaining 3 are a thatcher and his wife, and son.
9 Gentry &c., 10 Schools There is no person of note of either sex living in the parish, neither are there any schools, but 2 or 3 private ones for the teaching children to read.
11 Charities There is no hospital, but this parish has a share in a charity left by the late Duke of Bolton, grandfather to the present [duke], amounting to £15 one year and £12 another, to be distributed to some poor £6, and to others £3 at the discretion of the minister who is a trustee for the whole charity left to this and 5 other neighbouring parishes amounting in the whole to £102 p.a., deducting taxes.

185 Shorwell [IoW] 21M65/B4/1/2 fo.191
John Godsall, vicar 1680–1733 25 August 1725
1 Area The compass of ground in the parish is about 10 miles.
2 Population There are about 310 inhabitants.
3 Marriages &c. There have been, one year with another for several years past, about 6 or 7 births and burials and 2 marriages.
4 Patron John Leigh Esq. is patron of the vicaridge.
5 Chapel There is noe chapel.
6 Lecturer There is noe lecturer nor curate.
7 Papists There is noe Papist.
8 Dissenters There is noe meeting of protestant dissenters, only 1 man and his wife who are Presbiterians.

9 Gentry &c. There are noe gentlemen, but John Leigh Esq. and Maurice Morgan Esq.
10 Schools There is noe school endowed.
11 Charities There is noe hospital, nor publick charitys.
12 Post-town The next post-town is Newport.

186 Silchester 21M65/B4/1/1 fo.303
Richard Taylor, rector 1719–26
1 Area There are about 1900 acres of land in the parish, including the commons, the wastes and coppices, which are about 400 acres.
2 Population There are about 216 souls in the parish.
3 Marriages &c. There are about 5 births, 4 burials, and 2 marriages, annually, one year with another.
4 Patron The Right Hon. William, Lord Viscount Mountjoy, of the kingdom of Ireland, is patron of the living.
5 Chapels There is not any chapel in the parish.
6 Lecturer There is not any curate or lecturer in the parish.
7 Papists There is not any Papist in the parish.
8 Dissenters There is not any meeting-house, and but 1 dissenting family of the Presbyterian sect in the parish.
9 Gentry &c. There is not any nobleman or gentleman in the parish.
10 Schools There is not any publick school in the parish.
11 Charities There are about £4 p.a. distributed to the poor, of which legacy some of the parishioners are the trustees.
12 Post-town Reading is the post-town, and letters are directed to be left at the turnpike in that town.

187 Soberton 21M65/B4/1/2 fo.60
Abraham Markland, rector 1684–1728
Michael Ainsworth, curate
1 Area The parish of Soberton is about 10 miles in compass.
2 Population In this parish according to the best information I can get, are 460 souls.
3 Marriages &c. There are in this parish at a medium, one year with another, 3 marriages, 17 births, and 7 burials.
4 Patron The parish is part of the rectory of Meonstoke in the gift of the Bishop of Winchester.
5 Chapels The church is a chapel of ease to that of Meonstoke, and there is no other chapel in the parish.
6 Lecturer There is no lecturer. There is a curate whose name is Michael Ainsworth.
7 Papists There are 3 families of Papists in this parish, who are all farmers.
8 Dissenters There are no meetings of protestant dissenters of any kind in this parish.
9 Gentry &c. There is no nobleman in this parish. Thomas Lewis Esq., Member of Parliament for Southampton, is the only gentleman or person of note in this parish.

10 Schools There is no settled school in this parish, but Dr Markland, the present rector, pays for the schooling of 12 poor children, who are taught to read.
11 Charities There is a charity of £12 p.a. given to the parish by the Lady Laurence which is distributed quarterly by the churchwardens and overseers of the poor. There is no hospital in this parish.
12 Post-town The next post-town is Bishop's Waltham, but letters are generally directed by Fareham-bag.

188 Sopley 21M65/B4/1/2 fo.141
Thomas Stephens, vicar 1690/91–1728
1 Area The circumference of the parish of Sopley [is] about 8 miles.
2 Population The number of inhabitants therein [is] about 400.
3 Marriages &c. The number of marriages in the year 1724, 5; of burials 11, baptismes 15, and in preceding years much the same.
4 Patron Mr James Willis now patron.
5 Chapels But 1 parish church.
6 Lecturer Nil.
7 Papists There are 4 popish familys, but of small estates.
8 Dissenters Nil.
9 Gentry &c. About 10 farmers, but of no great estates.
10 Schools Nil.
11 Charities Nil.
12 Post-town Christchurch [is] our next market-town.

189 Southampton, All Saints 21M65/B4/1/2 fo.304
William Purbeck, rector 1716–1739/40
1 Area The parish is near 2 miles long, the fields and common adjacent to the town included. The inhabited part of the parish is about ¼ mile square, and consists chiefly of part of 2 streets which meet in a right angle. Upon which stands the church.
2 Population There are much about 700 souls in the parish.
3 Marriages &c. There are at a medium 6 or 7 marriages in a year, 26 births, and about 20 burials.
4 Patron The rectory is in the gift of the Crown.
5 Chapels No chapel.
6 Lecturer No lecturer nor curate.
7 Papists One family only of Papists, the master of it a poor gardiner.
8 Dissenters There is one meeting-house of Presbyterians or Independents, and another for Quakers, to which they resort from all parts of the town. Of each in the parish, the Presbyterians are about 4 score and 10, the Quakers are only 2 familys.
9 Gentry &c. No persons of note in the parish.
10 Schools No schools endowed in the parish.
11 Charities Alexander Ross, formerly master to the grammar school, left 40*s*. to the poor, and 6*s*. to the minister of All Saints parish, to be given them

yearly upon Xmas Eve. Mr Mylles left 20*s*. the first of May and 20*s*. the first of November yearly to the poor. Mr Seal the elder left 50*s*. p.a. to put out a poor boy of the parish an apprentice. Mr Stepto gave £3 to the poor of the parish and 40*s*. to the minister, to be given them yearly on May 3d. Mrs Palmer gave £5 p.a. to the poor. These charitys are in trust with the corporation. Besides which particular gifts, there are some general legacys to the poor of the town, of which the poor of this parish have a share. There is likewise an almshouse, but not endowed, for 6 poor people.
12 Post-town Southampton in which is situated the parish of All Saints is a post-town, where I shall always think myself honoured with Your Lordship's commands.

190 Southampton, Holy Rood 21M65/B4/1/2 fo.307
Bernard Brougham, vicar 1702–50
1 Area The parish contains about half the High Street in Southampton.
2 Population There are about 750 souls in it.
3 Marriages &c. About 8 marriages; 27 births and 23 burials.
4 Patron The Provost and Fellows of Queen's College, Oxford, patrons.
5 Chapels St Julian's, commonly called God's House chapel, belonging to an hospital of that name. The vicar of Holy Rhood serves it with morning prayer, Wednesdays and Fridays by appointment of Queen's College above-mentioned, which likewise supports and maintains the said chapel and grants the use of it on Sundays during pleasure, to the conforming part of the French.[27]
6 Lecturer There is no lecturer or curate.
7 Papists 2 Papists.
8 Dissenters No meeting but one of French refugees. 35 Presbyterians and 3 Anabaptists.
9 Gentry &c. Persons of any distinction are Maurice Buckland Esq., Charles Tyrrel Esq., Colonel Bellor and Major Speed.
10 Schools There is no endowed school, but one maintained by a subscription of £40 p.a. to a master for teaching 50 poor boys, 40 whereof are cloathed.
11 Charities There is a charity of £20, the interest whereof is distributed to the poor by the minister and churchwardens, the gift of the late Archbishop Lamplugh. The hospital of God's House, wherein are 4 brothers and 4 sisters nominated by the Provost of Queen's College, Oxford, and have each 2*s*. per week allowed them by the College, besides some other advantages.
12 Post-town It is in Southampton, a post-and market-town.

191 Southampton, St Laurence and St John 21M65/B4/1/2 fo.311
Bernard Brougham, sequestrator[28] 1702–50
1 Area These 2 united parishes[29] are but of small extent in the town of Southampton.
2 Population There are about 520 souls in them.

3 Marriages &c. About 4 marriages; 10 births and 13 burials.
4 Patron The Crown is patron, but both [parishes] being of small value, they have been held by sequestration from the bishop's court time out of mind by the vicar of Holy Rhood in the same town.
5 Chapels There is no chapel in them.
6 Lecturer No lecturer or curate.
7 Papists No Papists.
8 Dissenters No meetings of dissenters, but 5 Anabaptists and 80 Presbiterians.
9 Gentry &c. Persons of any distinction are Dr Speed, a physician, and the widow of John Eyre Esq.
10 Schools In the parish of St John there is a free school endowed with £15 p.a. and a good house. The Revd William Kingsman is master; the number of scholars between 50 and 60. The corporation of Southampton elect the master.
11 Charities There is £1 13*s*. 4*d*. distributed quarterly in St Laurence church by the mayor to the poor of the whole town, and 5*s*. to the minister of the parish for a sermon; the gift of Mr Sendy. In the parish of St John there is a workhouse, endowed with £40 p.a. for a master to maintain and instruct 6 poor boys in the clothing trade: it is under the care and direction of the Corporation of Southampton, the benefaction of Mr Major. There is likewise in the parish of St Lawrence a gift of £100 towards the apprenticeing of 2 children a year with the interest thereof.
12 Post-town The two parishes are in Southampton, a post- and market-town.

192 Southampton, St Mary 21M65/B4/1/2 fo.314
Ralph Brideoake, rector 1702–1742/3
1 Area The parish of St Mary's is divided by the River Itchin, that comes from Winchester, into two parts. That part of the parish that lyes on the east side of the river consists of these severall hamlets, viz. Weston, Itchin Ridgway and part of Bittern. The extent of all which from north to south in its longest line (the common excluded) is about 1½ miles in length, and about 1 mile in bredth. And the whole number of acres, arable and pasture, may be computed at about 700. The common ground on that side of the river is about 2 miles square. That part of the parish which lyes on the west side of the river is about a mile in length in its longest line (the common excluded) and ½ a mile in bredth and the whole number of acres, arable and pasture, may be computed at about 500.The common ground belonging to the parish on the west side of the river, jointly with the other parishes of the town of Southampton, is about 1 mile square.
2 Population The number of houses in the east side of the parish is nearly the same with that on the west, viz. about 45 each, in the whole 90, which containing about 5 each, one with another, may have in all 450 persons.
3 Marriages &c. The number of births, one year with another, may be about 10, of marriages 5, and of burials 7.
4 Patron The Lord Bishop of Winchester is the patron of St Mary's. All the tiths and lands belonging to the rectory of St Mary's (which has the

rectory of South Stoneham united to it, and has the tiths of all the lands that lye without the walls of the town of Southampton) were in danger of being alienated from the church by a lease of 100 years that was granted of the said tiths and lands in the latter end of Edward VI by Poinet,[30] then Bishop of Winchester, and the rector of St Mary's at that time; upon which lease £18 p.a. were reserved for the service of the church of St Mary's. For the person possessed of this lease did by another grant made of the same tiths and lands from the Crown (under pretence that they belonged to a chantry that was dissolved) endeavour to carry away the title of them from the church of St Mary's. But Dr Clutterbuck being collated by Bishop Morley to the rectory of St Mary's soon afer the Restoration, did eject the person that claimed under the grant from the Crown and quietly enjoyed all the tiths and lands belonging to the said rectory to his death, and so they have been enjoyed since his time.

5 Chapels The ground upon which the town of Southampton within the walls is situate did formerly belong to the parish of St Mary's, so that all the churches in Southampton (though they are now made parochiall, and have instituted ministers) were no other originally than chappells of ease to the church of St Mary's; and in token of that dependance which they had formerly upon St Mary's as the mother church, all the parishes of the town of Southampton bury their dead in the churchyard of St Mary's, there being no churchyard belonging to those churches. These churches therefore in Southampton do not as I conceive fall under this quere, but are referred to their particular ministers, who will (no doubt) give an account of them. But there is a chappell of ease situate on the east side of the river, called Jesus chapple, erected by one Captain Smith about 2 years since for the convenience of those that live on that side; who by particular provision in the deed of consecration are to maintain a minister at their own cost. The nomination to the curacy of the said chappell is now in Francis Mylles Esq. who lives near it. Mr Andrews, lecturer of Hexham in Northumberland, and living there, has the right to the curacy; but it is served at present by Mr John Mylles, brother to Mr Francis Mylles, who reads prayers and preaches there once in a fortnight.

There is a house let at 40*s*. yearly which was built for the curate, and belongs to him, and there is the interest of £100, formerly given to the chappell and a pension of 40*s*. yearly paid him for serving it.

6 Lecturer The rector of St Mary's has no curate, but does the duty of his cure himself.

7 Papists There are 2 families of Papists in St Mary's parish. The mistress of one of them is widdow of Brigadier Boles, and the master of the other is a taylor by trade, and unmarried. The number of persons in both families may be 10.

8 Dissenters There is no meeting-house for dissenters in the parish. There is one woman, the widow of an Anabaptist teacher, who is also an Anabaptist that lives in a poor cottage, and is supposed to be very poor, and she has one person with her in her house.

9 Gentry &c. The persons of distinction on the east side of the river are Evans, Lord Carbery of the kingdom of Ireland, Francis Mylles Esq., and 2

families whose names are St Barbe. On the west side are Mrs Boles before mentioned, and Mr Winter, a shipbuilder.
10 Schools There is no grammar school in the parish but only schools where children are taught to read and write. There is one school of this sort on the east side of the water, where William Blunford teaches, and another on the west side where William Earl teaches. The children are taught for 2*d.* per week, and the children of such parents as are in mean condition are usually paid for by the rector, if they will be taught.
11 Charities There are no hospitals within the parish, but there are 2 almshouses repaired by the corporation of Southampton which are filled with poor who have no other allowance than what the parish thinks fit to make them. Then there are some small charities bestowed at Xmas upon the poor of this and of the other side of the water, of which the corporation of Southampton have the trust. But the whole of them does not amount to £5.
12 Post-town St Mary's (where old Southampton formerly stood) is nigh unto the present town of Southampton, and the direction to the rector of St Mary's near Southampton will bring such commands as your Lordship is pleased to honour him with.

193 Southampton, St Michael 21M65/B4/1/2 fo.318
William Kingsman AM, curate
A very small vicarage held by sequestration.
1 Area It stands compact in the west side of the town consisting chiefly of 3 streets containing 132 houses.
2 Population Number of souls 517.
3 Marriages &c. Marriages 6; births 18; burials 16.
4 Patron In the gift of the Crown.
5 Chapels No chappel.
6 Lecturer No lecturer &c.
7 Papists One family of Papists, Mr Tichborn, about £200 p.a.
8 Dissenters A meeting-house lately built for Anabaptists, though not above 3 or 4 of that sect live in the parish, poor people. No Quakers, about 40 Presbyterians.
9 Gentry &c. No nobleman, gentleman or person of note.
10 Schools No school &c.
11 Charities No charitys nor hospital.
12 Post-town In a post-town.

194 South Stoneham 21M65/B4/1/2 fo.320
George Prince, vicar 1714–43 23 August 1725
Richard Scott, curate
1 Area According to the best account I can gett, the parish must be near 30 miles in circumference.
2 Population About 697.
3 Marriages &c. Marriages 7; births 20; burials 19.

4 Patron The rector of Saint Maries for the time being.
5 Chapels None.
6 Lecturer Richard Scott, curate.
7 Papists 2, both old women.
8 Dissenters No meetings, but 4 dissenters, viz. 2 Quakers and 2 Presbyterians; so happy are we that notwithstanding our parish is so very populous, we have no more than these 2 Roman Catholicks, 2 Presbyterians and 2 Quakers that dissent from the church of England, and no more of our people that are in the least inclined either to Popery or schism.
9 Gentry &c. We have but one gentleman's seat in the parish, belonging to William Nicholas Esq., a minor.
10 Schools None endowed, but 4 others, one a writing school taught by — Cob. In the other 3, children are only taught to read English, and they have for their mistresses Goodwife Sharp senior, Goodwife Sharp junior, Goodwife White.
11 Charities The interest of £50 for ever to as many poor widows as are in the parish, to be disposed of by the minister and churchwardens. The principal [was] lodged by the benefactor in the hands of the churchwardens. And the interest of £40 more for ever, given by an ancestor of Thomas Dummer Esq. of North Stoneham, to be distributed to such poor housekeepers of South Stoneham as are not relieved by the parish, and paid out of an estate of Mr Dummer's called Barns Land in the parish of South Stoneham.
12 Post-town [No reply.]

195 South Tidworth 21M65/B4/1/1 fo.173
Samuel Heskins, rector 1703–1732/3
1 Area The whole compass of the parish is supposed to be about 10 miles.
2 Population The number of souls [is] about 60.
3 Marriages &c. The number of marriages, births and burials uncertain; sometimes 1 or 2 in a year, sometimes none in 3 or 4 years.
4 Patron The patron of the living is Thomas Smith Esq., son and heir of the Right Hon. John Smith, deceased.
5 Chapels No chappell in the parrish.
6 Lecturer No lecturer; the curate at present is Mr Daniel Stockwell.
7 Papists No Papist but one, a gardner of no great consequence.
8 Dissenters No meeting of protestant dissenters, no protestant dissenters in the parish.
9 Gentry &c. No person of note but Mrs Ann Smith, widdow of the Right Hon. John Smith.
10 Schools, 11 Charities No schools, charities or hospitals.
12 Post-town The next post-town is Andover.

196 South Warnborough 21M65/B4/1/1 fo.305
Lawrence Smith, rector 1694–1727 16 August 1725
1 Area My parish is I suppose in length on all sides about 4 miles. Some few of the parishioners dwell a mile from the church, which is in good

repair, both church and chancel, and in comely ornament suitable to the place of divine worship. But the much greater number of parishioners live within ¼ mile of the church.
2 Population I suppose the number to be 150.
3 Marriages &c. In the year 1724 were 3 persons buried, 8 baptized, not one married. In the present year 1725 were 4 baptized, not one married or buried hitherto.
4 Patron The President and 10 Senior Fellows of St John Baptist's College in Oxford, are the patrons who presented me to my living.
5 Chapels I have none.
6 Lecturer I have neither of them [lecturer or curate], am constantly resident, make no change with others in my course of officiating, keep no curate, though of considerable advance in years, and have been 30 years incumbent on my living.
7 Papists None.
8 Dissenters But 5 in the whole.
9 Gentry &c. None but Robert Graham Esq., lord of the mannor of Southwarmborough; a person well affected to His Majesty King George, and to our most happy constitution in church and state.
10 Schools We have 2 schoolmistresses, teachers of the young children, who are all of them under the age of 14 years, well instructed in the church catechism, but unqualified for confirmation according to Your Lordship's order and direction, they being under-aged. Those above 14 years of age going out of the parish into service. The grown persons of greater age who know the nature and great consequence of the solemn vo<ws> and engagements made in their name at their baptism, and which they are to renew and take upon themselves at confirmation, have been, the greatest part of them, already confirmed, and I have earnestly exhorted any who have not been confirmed to receive confirmation from Your Lordship, shewing them the great spiritual benefit thereof, in two sermons.
11 Charities We have but one charity of an £100, the principal of which is lodged in the lord of the mannor's hands, and the interest thereof by him and the trustees distributed to the poor of the parish every year at Christmas.
12 Post-town That Your Lordship may be able to write to me, as occasion shall require, to next post-town to me, is Odiham in Hampshire; within 2 miles of Southwarmborough.

197 Sparsholt 21M65/B4/1/2 fo.355
William Baker, vicar 1685–1731 3 September 1725
1 Area The compass of ground I suppose may be 8 miles.
2 Population The number of souls according to the best information I cann gett are 220.
3 Marriages &c. Att a medium one year with another, [the] number of marriages 2, births 7, burials 4.
4 Patron Patron is the king.
5 Chapels I have not any chappell.

6 Lecturer I have not any lecturer or curat.
7 Papists There is not any Papist an inhabitant in my parish.
8 Dissenters There are not any meetings or protestant dissenters in my parish.
9 Gentry &c. There is not any nobleman, gentleman or person of note of either sex in my parish.
10 Schools There is not any school endowed in my parish.
11 Charities £5 given by Richard and Robert Sims for the use of the church. £5 given by the same persons for the use of the poor. £5 given by the family of the Wades for the use of the poor. £5 given by Richard Bricknell for the use of the poor. £5 given by Mary Sims, widdow, for the use of the poor, all to be putt out att interest by the vicar and churchwardens.
12 Post-town The next post-town is Winchester.

198 Steventon 21M65/B4/1/1 fo.309
Richard Wright, rector 1720–27 16 August 1725
1 Area The parish of Stevington, according to the best information I can have, is about 3 miles in length, and three quarters of a mile in breadth.
2 Population We have in our parish about 80 souls.
3 Marriages &c. We have, one year with another, marriages about 1 or 2, births about 3 or 4, burials 1 or 2.
4 Patron Madam Knight of Chawton, my patronesse.
5 Chapels No chapel.
6 Lecturer No lecturer or curate.
7 Papists No Papist.
8 Dissenters No meeting of any sort.
9 Gentry &c. No nobleman, gentleman or person of note.
10 Schools No school.
11 Charities No charity or hospital.
12 Post-town Basingstoke is the next post-town.

199 Stoke Charity 21M65/B4/1/2 fo.250
Joshua Reynolds, rector 1716–35
Alias Old Stoke, which also is the only name it goes by in all the maps of Hampshire, *alias* Old-Stoke-Charity
1 Area The parish itself is an exact paralellogram, almost as regular as could be drawn by a line. It is about 2¼ miles in length, and 1 mile (or very little more) in breadth.
2 Population All the houses and cottages (including the parsonage house) are 16. The number of souls, men, women, and children, servants as well as housekeepers (not reckoning my own family, nor that of Sir Peter Mew, who is only here sometimes occasionally) are at this time (viz. August 12, 1725) 68.
3 Marriages &c. During the time that I have been rector, which is above 9 years, there have been marriages 6; births 14; burials 11.
4 Patron The patronage belongs to Corpus Christi College in Oxford.

5 Chapels No chapel.
6 Lecturer No lecturer nor curate.
7 Papists No Papists in the parish.
8 Dissenters No protestant dissenters.
9 Gentry &c. Sir Peter Mew, Chancellor of the diocese of Winchester, comes hither only (as was said before) sometimes occasionally, having but an old decayed mansion house to receive him.
10 Schools No schools.
11 Charities No charities.
12 Post-town Letters are always directed to me at Stoke Charity, near Winchester.

200 Stratfield Saye 21M65/B4/1/1 fo.311
Walter Chapman, rector of 'Stratfield Sea' 1705–51 16 August 1725
1 Area The parish of Stratfield contains in compass of ground about 10 miles.
2 Population The number of souls therein are computed to be about 300.
3 Marriages &c. One year with another, the marriages (by me celebrated) are not above 2, our births are reckoned at 10, our burials at 6.
4 Patron The patron of the living is George Pitt Esq.
5 Chapels In our said parish there is no chapel.
6 Lecturer Nor any lecturer or curate.
7 Papists Nor any Papist.
8 Dissenters In a remote tything of the parish is held an Independent meeting of protestant dissenters, containing of the parishioners about 20.
9 Gentry &c. In the said parish lives no nobleman, but the gentlemen or persons of note are George Pitt Esq., Francis Baber Esq., George Clark Esq. The 2 latter only tenants upon lease.
10 Schools We have no endowed or settled charity school, but a few poor children taught by private contribution.
11 Charities We have no considerable charities given or belonging to the parish, but by placing out the summs given upon small legacys, we are endeavouring by degrees to raise a parish-stock for the better maintenance of the poor.
12 Post-town The post office nearest to this parish is att Hartford Bridge.

201 Stratfield Turgis 21M65/B4/1/1 fo.313
John James, rector 1717–1732/3
1 Area The parish of Stratfield Turges is computed to be about 10 miles in compass, more or less.
2 Population The parish consists of about 22 families of all sorts, in which there may be about 110 souls, masters, mistresses, children and servants.
3 Marriages &c. Marryed of the parishioners since 1717, the time that I have been incumbent, but 2 couple. Baptized in that time 27, males and females together. Buryed 6.
4 Patron George Pitt Esq. of Stratfieldsea.

5 Chapels Chappels, none.
6 Lecturer Lecturer or curate, none.
7 Papists None.
8 Dissenters None.
9 Gentry &c. Noblemen or gentlemen, none.
10 Schools None.
11 Charities There has been given in money by severall persons for the use of the poor £20 at [different] times*, the interest whereof is paid to them yearly at Christmas. Hospitalls none.
12 Post-town The nearest posthouse to this parish is Hartfordbridge.
*There has been given in money by George Pitt Esq. £10; by John Nevil £2; by Abraham Wheeler £2; by John Chase junior £2; by Mr Stephens £2; by John Chase senior £4; the money in the hands of Robert Coats, yeoman, the interest paid yearly as above.

202 Swarraton 21M65/B4/1/1 fo.51
William Box, rector 1719–33
1 Area 700 acres.
2 Population 60.
3 Marriages &c. Of each kind [i.e. marriages, births, burials] 1.
4 Patron Anthony Henly Esq.
5 Chapels One, by the name of Godsfield, not served or endowed, adjoining to a farm of the same name, and (as pretended) tithe-free, the estate of Sir Berkly Lucy.
6 Lecturer None.
7 Papists None.
8 Dissenters None.
9 Gentry &c. None.
10 Schools None.
11 Charities None.
12 Post-town Alresford.

203 Tangley 21M65/B4/1/1 fo.137
Francis Eyre, rector of Faccombe 1706–38
S. White, curate
1 Area Compass of ground, about 4 miles.
2 Population Number of souls, according to the best information, 130.
3 Marriages &c. Marriages, births and burials, at a medium, one year with another, 3.
4 Patron Sir Bar[kly] Lucy.
5 Chapels None.
6 Lecturer Lecturer, none; curate as above said.
7 Papists None.
8 Dissenters None.
9 Gentry &c. None.
10 Schools None.

11 Charities None.
12 Post-town Andover.

204 Thruxton 21M65/B4/1/1 fo.175
William Pretty, rector 1720–1747/8 20 August 1725
1 Area The parish is in length about 3 miles, in breadth about half a mile.
2 Population There is in it about 152 souls, including men, women and children.
3 Marriages &c. The number of births about 3; of burials 2, one year with another; marriages seldome any.
4 Patron The patronesses of the living are 3 sisters and executrixes of the late Secretary Crags deceased,[31] viz. the widow Newsome, the widow Elliott, and the now lady of Sir John Hynde Cotton.
5 Chapels There is no chapel in the parish.
6 Lecturer Nor any lecturer or curate.
7 Papists There is but 1 Papist in the parish, and she a poor woman, without any family.
8 Dissenters There is no meeting, nor but 2 protestant dissenters in the parish.
9 Gentry &c. There is no person of note of either sex residing in the parish.
10 Schools There is no endowed school in the parish, nor any but a private one; where children are taught to spell and read.
11 Charities There has been a charity given to the parish by Henry Rogers Esq. deceased, sometime lord of this mannor, viz. he gave to the parishes of Thruxton and Fifield the sum of £300 to raise a stock and working-house for the maintainance of such poor in the 2 several parishes as have been long inhabiting there, and have not been new incomers, or intruders. Which sum being too inconsiderable for so great a design, the trustees obtained a decree in Chancery whereby they were impowered to lay out the aforesaid money on land, which they have since done, purchased with it an estate of £13 p.a. know[n] by the name and title of Mankhorn estate. The rent of which is annually divided between such poor people as do not receive collection of the two parishes aforesaid. The charity is vested in the hands of 9 or more trustees, which shall be substantial freeholders, leaseholders or copyholders inhabiting in or near the 2 parishes. And are to be chosen by the lords of the mannors of Thruxton and Fifield, and by the minister, churchwardens and overseers of the 2 several parishes. Of which 9 or more trustees, there are but 3 now living, but we hope to come to an election of others, the ensuing winter.
12, Post-town The nearest post-town is Andover.

205 Titchfield 21M65/B4/1/2 fo.76
Vicarage vacant and sequestrated.
William Hailes, curate
1 Area The parish of Tichfield is supposed to extend itself about 30 miles in compass.

2 Population According to the best information that can reasonably be got, the number of souls are reckoned to be at least 1,500.
3 Marriages &c. At a moderate computation, by looking back in the register-book, there are, one year with another, about 6 or 8 weddings, between 40 and 50 christenings, and the number of burials seldom exceed 30.
4 Patron The Dukes of Portland and Beaufort present alternately to the living.
5 Chapels There is a chapel in the parish called Crofton chapel, which is served by the minister of Tichfield, and seems to have no separate maintenance, or distinct nomination from the parish church.
6 Lecturer The curate is Mr William Hailes, who was appointed by the late Bishop of Winchester in November 1721, and now supplies the cure during the sequestration of the living, which at present is void by the death of Mr Alexander Bruce, the late incumbent.
7 Papists There are said to be 2 women in the parish that are Papists; they are of no estate or consequence.
8 Dissenters We have no meeting-house in the parish; but of Presbyterians, and Anabaptists, commonly so-called, there are about 30 in number.
9 Gentry &c. The Dukes of Beaufort and Portland have a seat here called Tichfield House.
10 Schools There are 2 schools. In one the present schoolmaster, Clement Walcott, has £10 p.a. to teach 12 boys to read write and cast account. The other has a schoolmistress, one Dame Adams, who is allowed £4 p.a. to teach the same number of children the English tongue. The minister with the trustees nominate the master; the present mistress was appointed by will.
11 Charities There are 4 several charitys that have been given to the parish, one of £20, another that has been improved to £10, another of £4, and the last £6 10*s*. p.a. The first and second are appropriated to the use of the schoolmaster, and cloathing, and, as occasion offers, apprenticing out the boys; the third the mistress has for teaching the children to read; and the fourth is distributed to poor widows every year, who have no maintenance from the parish.
12 Post-town [Address to] The minister of Tichfield, near Fareham.

206 Tunworth 21M65/B4/1/1 fo.315
John Graile, rector 1713/14–1728
1 Area I suppose the parish to be about 4 mile in compass.
2 Population The number of souls are about 70.
3 Marriages &c. The number of marriages, births and burials is, at a medium, one year with another, 6.
4 Patron Mr Thomas Hall, a minor, is patron of the living.
5 Chapels We have no chapel.
6 Lecturer No lecturer or curate.
7 Papists No Papist.

8 Dissenters No meeting. One dissenter, a Presbyterian.
9 Gentry &c. No person of note.
10 Schools No school.
11 Charities No charities given to the parish.
12 Post-town The next post-town is Basingstoke.

207 Twyford 21M65/B4/1/2 fo.361

Walter Mildmay, vicar 1700–44
1 Area [Twyford is] supposed to be about 20 miles round.
2 Population About 80 families, consisting of about 300 souls.
3 Marriages &c. Marriages about 2; births 15; burials 3.
4 Patron Emmanuel College in Cambridge.
5 Chapels Owslebury chappel, served by Walter Mildmay, supported and maintained by small tythes and offerings and the right of nomination to it is Emmanuel Colledge in Cambridge.
6 Lecturer None.
7 Papists 10 families consisting of about 90 souls. The only landed man amongst them is Henry Wills Esq., who is supposed to have in several counties about £1000 p.a.
8 Dissenters There are no meetings, but about 3 persons that call themselves Presbiterians.
9 Gentry &c. James, Duke of Montross [Montrose], and Henry Wills Esqr.
10 Schools There is no free school in the parish, but a writing school consisting of about 20 scholars, John Waller, master. And likewise a supposed Papist school, consisting of about 20 boarders, John Manly, supposed master, and Mr Corbat supposed usher.
11 Charities £18 p.a. for the use of the poor of the parish in the hands of Humphrey Mildmay Esq.
12 Post-town Winchester.

208 Upham and Durley 21M65/B4/1/2 fo.80

John White, rector after 1719–1746
1 Area The parish of Upham is towards 3 miles in length and ½ mile in breadth.
2 Population There are about 200 souls in Upham.
3 Marriages &c. Births and burials about 2 in a year; marriages scarce one.
4 Patron The Right Revd the Lord Bishop of Winchester is patron.
5 Chapels The chappellry of Durly is parochial, supplied by a resident licenced curate. The present [curate] is the Revd Mr John Rogers. He is nominated and maintained by the rector; his salary is £30 p.a. besides surplice fees and Easter offerings.
6 Lecturer The rector resides constantly at Upham and does the duty there.
7 Papists There is no Papist of any consequence in Upham, only 1 poor man and 3 women besides a few children.

8 Dissenters Not one protestant dissenter of any kind in Upham.
9 Gentry &c. No person of note in Upham.
10 Schools No endowed school in Upham.
11 Charities No charity or hospital in Upham.
12 Post-town When Your Lordship shall please to favour me with your pleasures, the direction is to Mr White at Upham near Bishop's Waltham by Waltham bag.

209 Upper Clatford 21M65/B4/1/1 fo.179

Peter Terry, rector of 'Upclatford' 1709–27
1 Area The compass of ground in the parish is about 8 miles.
2 Population There are about 200 souls in the parish.
3 Marriages &c. There are about 6 births, 6 burials and 1 marriage yearly.
4 Patron Thomas Jervoise Esq. of Herriot is patron of the living.
5 Chapels There is no chapel in the parish.
6 Lecturer There is no lecturer or setled curate in the parish.
7 Papists There is not one Papist in the parish.
8 Dissenters There is no meeting of protestant dissenters of any kind in the parish. There are about 3 or 4 families of Presbyterians or Independents who go to the meeting at Andover.
9 Gentry &c. There are no noblemen, gentlemen or persons of note, of either sex living in the parish.
10 Schools There is no endowed school in the parish.
11 Charities There have been no charities given to the parish.
12 Post-town The nearest post-town is Andover.

210 Upton Grey 21M65/B4/1/1 fo.317

Lancelot Jackson, perpetual curate 1722–30
1 Area The parish is about 7 miles in compass.
2 Population The number of souls [is] about 160.
3 Marriages &c. There are very few marriages. Births and burials are at a medium 8 one year with another.
4 Patron Queen's College in Oxford.
5 Chapels None.
6 Lecturer None.
7 Papists None.
8 Dissenters No meetings; one family of Presbyterians.
9 Gentry &c. John Limbrey Esq.
10 Schools None endowed.
11 Charities No hospitals. There are £30 given for the use of the poor, which is distributed by John Limbrey Esq. and George Knight, gent.
12 Post-town The next post-town is Odiham.

211 Warblington 21M65/B4/1/2 fo.90

Vincent Bradston, rector 1720–40
1 Area The compass of ground in my parish is supposed to be about 6 miles.

2 Population The number of souls in my parish according to the best information I can get, is about 500.
3 Marriages &c. I have, one year with another, 4 marriages, 16 births and 10 burials.
4 Patron The present patron of my living is William Cotton Esq.
5 Chapels I have no chapel in my parish.
6 Lecturer I have neither lecturer nor curate.
7 Papists There are 20 Papists in my parish, persons of no estates or consequence.
8 Dissenters There are no meetings in my parish of any kind, but there are 4 persons that frequent the Presbyterian assemblies in other places.
9 Gentry &c. There do[e]s not live in my parish any nobleman, gentleman or person of note of either sex.
10 Schools There is no school in my parish.
11 Charities There have been no charities given to the parish, neither are there any hospitals.
12 Post-town The next post-town to me is Havant.

212 Warnford 21M65/B4/1/2 fo.94
James Baddely, rector 1704–31
1 Area The parish of Warnford is about 5 miles in compass, being about 1½ miles long and 1 mile broad.
2 Population In this parish, according to the best information I can get, are about 160 souls.
3 Marriages &c. There are in this parish at a medium, one year with another, not above 2 marriages, 6 births, and 6 burials.
4 Patron The legal patronage at present is in John Harvey Esq. and Mr Richard Searl in trust for the Lady Desbouverie, wife of Sir Christopher Desbouverie.
5 Chapels There is no chapel in this parish.
6 Lecturer There is no lecturer or curate in this parish.
7 Papists There is no Papist in this parish.
8 Dissenters There is no meeting of protestant dissenters of any kind in this parish.
9 Gentry &c. There is no nobleman, gentleman or person of note.
10 Schools There is no school in this parish.
11 Charities There is a charity of 40*s*. p.a. to be distributed by the rector and churchwardens among such poor as receive no collection. There is no hospital.
12 Post-town The next post-town is Bishop's Waltham, but letters come by Westmeon bag.

213 Weeke 21M65/B4/1/2 fo.390
George Fern, rector of 'Wyke alias Weeke' 1719–34
1 Area The compass of ground in the parish according to the nearest computation is 507 acres.

2 Population The number of souls doth not exceed 60.
3 Marriages &c. Marriages, births and burials, about 2 of each in a year.
4 Patron The Bishop of Winchester is patron.
5 Chapels There is no chapel in the parish.
6 Lecturer No lecturer or curate.
7 Papists No Papists.
8 Dissenters No meeting of protestant dissenters.
9 Gentry &c. No noblemen or gentlemen.
10 Schools No school endowed.
11 Charities £40 have been given in charities to the parish by several persons, which are annually distributed to the poor.
12 Post-town The next post-town is Winchester.

214 Wellow 21M65/B4/1/2 fo.260
Peter Newcome MA, vicar 1715–44
1 Area The ground of the parish is supposed to be in compass 3 miles long, and about 2 miles in breadth, the major part consisting of woods and heath-commons.
2 Population The number of souls reasonably computed to be therein is about 400.
3 Marriages &c. One year with another, the number of marriages [is] 3, of births 9, and of burials 8.
4 Patron The patron is His Grace James Duke of Chandos.
5 Chapels No chapel in the parish.
6 Lecturer No lecturer nor curate in the parish.
7 Papists 1 family of Papists, of no consequence or estate.
8 Dissenters No meetings of protestant dissenters, but the number of such dissenters in the parish are about 5 or 6.
9 Gentry &c. No persons of note live in the parish.
10 Schools No schools &c.
11 Charities The charities given to the parish have been:
1. viz. 5 small tracts of land, the whole not above 1½ acres, the rent applyed towards the repairs of the church, time immemorial.
2. viz. £10 given by the Duke of Chandos AD1718 towards the ceiling and adorning of the church, a guinea towards the same by William Stanley Esq. of Paultons, a guinea given by the Revd Mr Newcome, vicar, and £3 by the widow of the late vicar, the Revd Mr Tim Goodacre, which sums of money were applyed to the purposes aforesaid. Also a silver paten given by Mr Goodacre's widow.
3. viz. £147 given by His Grace the Duke of Chandos AD1720 for the buying of a house and land, the quantity of 5 acres, called Sankys, adjoining to the glebe, and supposed to have belonged formerly thereunto, now in possession by me, and by His Grace settled upon the vicar of the church for ever. No hospitals in the parish.
12 Post-town The next post-town is Rumsey.

215 West Cowes [IoW] 21M65/B4/1/2 fo.171
John King, lecturer of West Cowes chapel
1 Area West Cowes chappel in the archdeaconry of Winton was built AD1657. The said chappel stands about 5 miles distant from the parish

church of Carisbrooke. Mr Richard Stephens, the principal and chief benefactor towards it gave 1 acre of ground to sett the said chappel on, and to be a yard or litten[32] to it, and also endowed it with, and setled upon it £5 p.a., payable out of his estate lying in West Cowes. This chappel built by the inhabitants, at their request, was consecrated by the Right Revd Father in God George Morley, late Lord Bishop of Winchester in his primary visitation AD1662. Being then so slenderly endowed, and having no other setled incomb to support and maintain a minister to officiate in it, the said Right Revd Father, out of concern for and tender care of them, charitably proposed to settle £20 p.a. for ever towards the maintenance of a lecturer of and in the said chappel, if the inhabitants of West Cowes would by contribution or any other way raise, allow and pay unto the said lecturer for the time being the full sum of £40 p.a. Which proposal of the said Revd Father the said inhabitants accepting of and consenting to, he thereupon setled the said £20 p.a. upon such lecturer. And the said inhabitants did by a contract and agreement made between diverse of them and the said Lord Bishop oblige themselves to raise and pay to the said lecturer the full sum of £40 p.a. The above-mentioned exhibition of £20 p.a. setled on the lecturer is charged on and to be paid out of a fee-farm rent[33] of £51 p.a. issuing out of the late Priory of the Holy Trinity of Mottesfont in the county of Southampton, purchased by the said George, late Lord Bishop of Winton of his late Majesty, King Charles II his trustees for the sale of fee-farm rents. The said exhibition is to be paid half-yearly viz. at Our Lady and Michaelmas to the lecturer of West Cowes by the housekeeper of Woolsey House in Winchester. The original deed both of the purchase and settlement of the said exhibition are deposited in the chapter house adjoining to the cathedral church of the Holy Trinity in Winchester and are also enrolled in His Majesty's high court of Chancery.
2 Population [The] number of souls in the town of West Cowes, according to the best information, [is] about 1,300.
3 Marriages &c. Number of marriages about 10; of births between 20 and 30; of burials about 18, one year with another.
4 Patron The patron of this chappel is the Lord Bishop of Winchester. NB The inhabitants name the person, to be approved and licenced by the bishop.
5 Chapels, *6 Lecturer* [No reply, but see answer no. 1.]
7 Papists No Papists in the town.
8 Dissenters 10 dissenters, viz. 7 Presbyterians, 2 Sabbatarians, one Quaker.
9 Gentry &c. 3 gentlemen's families in the town.
10 Schools 2 schools for the instruction of children in reading writeing and accounts. The masters' names, Oliver Gibbs, Edward Kervell.
11 Charities No publick charities given or hospitals built.
12 Post-town A deputy post-office [is] in the town, the principal at Newport, 4 miles distant from West Cowes.
[These responses are renumbered and rearranged in the order of the bishop's questionnaire.]

216 West Meon 21M65/B4/1/2 fo.96

Stephen Unwin MA, rector 1720–72

A peculiar in the deanery of Drockinsford.

1 Area The parish of Westmean consists of 2 distinct tythings called Westmean, Woodland and Privett. Westmean and Woodland 2 miles long, 1 ½ miles broad. Privett is 1½ miles long and a ½ mile broad. I take the division of Woodland with Westmean, by reason that, in the assessments to church, poor and king's tax, they are rated together; but for the repairs of Redbridge and other county taxes it is rated with Privett.

2 Population Westmean and Woodland contain 403 souls; Privett 132.

3 Marriages &c. There has been, one year with another, for 7 years past, in Westmean and Woodland 4 marriages, 12 christenings, 10 burials; in Privett, 1 marriage, 4 christenings and one burial.

4 Patron The patron of the living is my Lord Bishop of Winchester.

5 Chapels There is onely 1 chapel and that in the tything of Privett, served by the rector or his curate. It is at this time served by the Revd Mr John Heighes, to whom I allow for maintenance and support thirto £5 p.a., E[a]ster offerings, a convenient dwelling-house adjoining to the church-yard and surplice fees.

6 Lecturer The present curate of Westmean is the Revd Mr Lubbridge Woods, to whom I allow £40 p.a., E[a]ster offerings and surplice fees.

7 Papists I have not one Papist in my parish of Westmean, tything of Woodland or chapelry of Privett.

8 Dissenters We have no meeting of protestant dissenters, and no more than 2 dissenters who are Anabaptists.

9 Gentry &c. There is neither nobleman, gentleman or person of note of either sex in my chapelry or parish, the parishioners, being, all of them, rack-renters under Mr Foxcroft, who lives at Yately in the county of Southampton, or coppy-holders under him. Punsholt Farm must here be excepted, which is a distinct mannor of itself, and is reported to have been a religious house; but is now the property of — Bulbeck, a farmer of Warnford.

10 Schools I have no endowed school in my parish, but William Chase, clerk of Westmean, instructs the children (few in number) to read, write and cast accompts.

11 Charities I have no hospital in my parish, nor any charitable donation whatever.

12 Post-town Westmean about 4 years ago was appointed, and at present continues a post-town.

217 Weston Patrick 21M65/B4/1/1 fo.321

Temple Rose, perpetual curate 16 August 1725

1 Area The parish of Weston Patrick is in compass 5 miles.

2 Population The number of souls, according to the best information, is about 3 score and 10.

3 Marriages &c. 1 marriage, 1 birth, 1 burial.

4 Patron Frederick Tylney Esq. The tithes both great and small, were appropriated in the time of King John to the Chancellor of the church of Sarum. Mr Tylney holds them from him by a lease of 3 lives.

5 Chapels None.
6 Lecturer No.
7 Papists None.
8 Dissenters None.
9 Gentry &c. None.
10 Schools There are no endowed schools in the parish.
11 Charities There are no hospitals in the parish, and but 1 charitie of £3 p.a. given by His late Grace the Duke of Bolton to the poor of Weston Patrick for ever.
12 Post-town Odyham is the next post-town.

218 West Tisted 21M65/B4/1/1 fo.103
George Knibb BD and fellow of Magdalen College, Oxford, perpetual curate 1729–31
1 Area About 5 miles [in compass].
2 Population About 100 souls.
3 Marriages &c. Marriages 1, births 3, burials 1.
4 Patron The president and fellows of Magdalen College nominate the curate.
5 Chapels, 6 Lecturer None, the church of West Tysted is served by George Knibb, curate.
7 Papists None.
8 Dissenters None.
9 Gentry &c. None.
10 Schools None.
11 Charities None.
12 Post-town New Alresford is a post-town.

219 West Tytherley 21M65/B4/1/2 fo.258
William Kingsman AM, rector 1708/9–1737
1 Area About 4 miles in compass.
2 Population Number of souls, 214.
3 Marriages &c. Births 5, burials 4 or 5, marriages 2.
4 Patron Richard Whithead Esq., living in the parish.
5 Chapels No chappel.
6 Lecturer A curate Mr Thomas Mundy.
7 Papists No Papist.
8 Dissenters No meeting nor dissenter of any sort.
9 Gentry &c. No nobleman nor any person of note but the patron.
10 Schools No school.
11 Charities No charitys nor hospital.
12 Post-town Romsey [is the] nighest post-town.

220 West Worldham 21M65/B4/1/1 fo.78
William Avery, curate 12 August 1725
1 Area Compass of ground—about 2 miles in length and a mile in breadth.

2 Population Number of souls, about 35 men, and their wives 14. 1 widow. Young people grown up and servants 13. Children 7.
3 Marriages &c. Number of marriages &c, seldom above 1 of each in a year.
4 Patron This is a lease from the college of Winchester to John Fisher of Bristol, gent. I preach here myself every first Sunday in the month, Mr Long reads prayers every other Sunday at two in the afternoon. The sacrament is administered thrice in the year. It is very near Hartley church and for serving here Mr Fisher pays me £10 p.a.
5 Chapels No chapel or chapels in this parish.
6 Lecturer No lecturer; Charles Long, curate.
7 Papists No Papist in this parish.
8 Dissenters No meeting of protestant dissenters, nor one dissenter in this parish.
9 Gentry &c. No noblemen, gentlemen or persons of note of either sex in this parish.
10 Schools No school in this parish.
11 Charities No charity has been given to, nor is any hospital in, this parish.
12 Post-town The next post-town is Alton, but 1 miles distant.

221 Weyhill 21M65/B4/1/1 fo.189
Joseph Todhunter, rector 1722–1731/2 20 August 1725
1 Area The parish is generally supposed to be about 7 miles in compass.
2 Population The number of souls herein is about 240.
3 Marriages &c. It appears from the register that at a medium, one year with another, the number of marriages is 3; of births is 5; and of burials 4.
4 Patron The right of patronage is in Queen's College, Oxford.
5 Chapels We have no chapel in this parish.
6 Lecturer There is no lecturer or curate.
7 Papists There is no professed Papist, nor
8 Dissenters Any meeting of protestant dissenters.
9 Gentry &c. There are only 2 gentlemen and their families living in this parish, viz. Thomas Drake and Robert Pyke Esqs.
10 Schools There is no school endowed.
11 Charities There is a charity given to this parish for the support of a schoolmaster which equally concerns the next [parish,] viz. Penton where the school is kept, and was given by Mr John Read, citizen and carpenter of London, who by his will made AD1651 left £6 p.a. to be paid for the encouragement of a master to teach the poor children of both, and 20*s*. p.a. to the poor of both parishes, and 10*s*. p.a. to the minister and clark of Penton. But the company have for several years last past kept back half of the money they are obliged to pay. Several representations and applications have been made to them, but without success. A member of the company was here at Michaelmas and came with directions to inquire about this affair. We gave him (what he then seemed to own) full satisfaction as to the justice of our demands, which he promised to acquaint the company with,

and to send us their answer immediately. But we never heard from him or anyone else since as to the subject of our complaint. Our worthy diocesan's advice or interposition on this occasion, if thought proper, is most humbly requested, and will be most thankfully acknowledged.
12 Post-town Andover is the next post-town.

222 Wherwell 21M65/B4/1/1 fo.191
Samuel Ogden, vicar 1698–1719
William Dowse, curate
1 Area The compass of ground in the parish of Wherwell is supposed to be between 5 or 6 miles.
2 Population The number of souls according to the best information I can get, are supposed to be herein about 390.
3 Marriages &c. We have herein about 5 or 6 marriages, 7 or 8 births, and 10 or 11 burials, at a medium one year with another.
4 Patron Sir John Fryer Bt. has the disposal of the prebend and the prebendary [John Jackson] prefers the vicar.
5 Chapels There are 2 chapels annexed to the parish of Wherwell, Bullington and Tufton. The number of souls in each are about 100. They are served by the vicar of Wherwell, and maintained by the tyth[e]s that grow in each chapelry.
6 Lecturer The above-named Mr Samuel Ogden hath been under a state of lunacy some years, and the vicarage under sequestration, so that the mother church and 2 chapels are served by a curate, who is the Revd Mr William Dowse [licensed 1719].
7 Papists We have no Papists in the parish.
8 Dissenters There are no meetings of protestant dissenters in our parish of any kind; and the number of such dissenters are few.
9 Gentry &c. Sir John Fryer Bt. is the only person of note in this parish.
10 Schools We have no schools that are endowed in our parish.
11 Charities I find a stone fixed to the east end of the church with this inscription, given by Philadelphia Whitehead, 12*s*. to be paid to 6 poor men and 6 poor women at Christmas for ever. Edmund Bolter Esq. left 20*s*. for the ringing of a bell at 8 of the clock in the evening and five in the morning between the feasts of St Michael the Archangel and the Annunciation of the Blessed Virgin.
12 Post-town The next post-town to Wherwell is Andover.
[Signed by William Dowse, curate.]

223 Whippingham [IoW] 21M65/B4/1/2 fo.199
John Gilbert, rector 1717–62
1 Area I suppose the parish of Whippingham to be about 6 miles long and 2 miles broad, comparing one part with the other.
2 Population According to the best information I can get, I suppose there may be near 500 souls in it.
3 Marriages &c. At a medium, one year with another, we have about 4 marriages, 7 or 8 births, and 6 burialls.

4 Patron The Lord Chancellor is the patron of my living.
5 Chapels No chappel.
6 Lecturer No lecturer or curate.
7 Papists No Papist.
8 Dissenter No licensed meeting-house that I know of. There is sometimes an assembly of people called Quakers at the house of one Daniel Hollis, a farmer. There are 2 familys Quakers and 2 familys Presbyterians.
9 Gentry &c. William Stephens Esq., MP for Newton, his lady and family. Robert Blachford Esq, Mr Benedict Ball, Mr Thomas Cole and his grandaughter Mrs Elizabeth Rook, Mr Isaac Newland, merchant, and his lady, Mrs Chapman, Mr Newland Reynolds, collector of His Majesty's customs, his wife and son.
10 Schools No endowed school.
11 Charities John Mann Esq. gave by his last will and testament to the parish of Whippingham,the summ of £23 p.a. towards the maintenance and setting up of poor orphan children and for want of such to poor lame and impotent people within the said parish, to be distributed by the minister, churchwardens and major part of the inhabitants.
12 Post-town Newport [is] the next post-town.

224 Whitchurch 21M65/B4/1/1 fo.195

Joseph Wood, vicar before 1691–1732
1 Area As to the compass or extent of the parish of Whitchurch, 'tis computed about 4½ miles from north to south, and near 3 from east to west.
2 Population This parish may contain in it in all i.e. men, women and children, near 1,500 souls.
3 Marriages &c. The number of marriages, births and burials may be about 50, one year with another.
4 Patron The patron of the vicarage of Whitchurch is the Right Revd Father in God the Lord Bishop of Winchester.
5 Chapels The[re] is a chapel about 1½ miles from Whitchurch called Freefolk Chapel which has always been served by the vicar of Whitchurch. NB This chapel is in the gift of the Master of St Cross [Hospital] and since [has been] given to the chaplain of St Cross. *Service* only *once a month.*
6 Lecturer There is no lecturer or curate belonging to the vicarage of Whitchurch.
7 Papists There is but one Papist in the whole parish who is a barber-surgeon.
8 Dissenters There are 3 meetings of dissenters in this parish, of Anabaptists, Independents, and Quakers, who altogether may make up near 400.
9 Gentry &c. The 2 chief gentlemen who have inhabitations in this parish are Thomas Vernon Esq., Member of Parliament for this burrough, and William Petre Esq.
10 Schools There is no school endowed in this parish of Whitchurch.
11 Charities There is no hospital in the parish of Whitchurch, but there is a charity of £30 p.a., settled by a decree of [the] high court of Chancery, to buy cloathing for the poor of the parish for ever.

12 Post-town There is a by-bagg allowed from the General Post- Office to this town. So that a letter directed to any person in Whitchurch in Hampshire cannot easily miscarry.

225 Whitsbury 21M65/B4/1/2 fo.143
Thomas Durnford AM, vicar 1714–46 23 August 1725
1 Area I suppose there may be contained in the compass of the parish about 1,800 acres.
2 Population The number of souls therein are about 100.
3 Marriages &c. We have at a medium yearly between 1 and 2 marriages, between 1 and 2 births, 1 burial.
4 Patron The Duke of Manchester is the patron of the vicaridge.
5 Chapels There is no chapel in the parish.
6 Lecturer There is no lecturer or curate.
7 Papists There is no Papist living in the parish.
8 Dissenters There are no meetings of protestant dissenters; there are only 3 such dissenters in the parish (Presbyterians).
9 Gentry &c. There is no person of note living in the parish.
10 Schools There is no school that hath any endowment.
11 Charities No charities have been given to the parish.
12 Post-town Fordingbridge is the next post-town to Whitsbury.

226 Wickham 21M65/B4/1/2 fo.100
Samuel Palmer, rector 1705–30 30 August 1725
1 Area The parish of Wickham is supposed to be 2 miles long from east to west, and 2 miles from north to south.
2 Population According to the best computation I can make, the number of souls therein may amount to about 550.
3 Marriages &c. At a medium for the last 7 years, the births have been about 17, the burials 14, the marriages 3 p.a.
4 Patron William Nicholas of South Stoneham Esq., a minor, is the patron of Wickham.
5 Chapels There is no chapel in the parish of Wickham.
6 Lecturer There is noe lecturer nor currat.
7 Papists There is 1 Papist, who rents about £6 p.a., and he has a wife and 3 small children.
8 Dissenters There is 1 protestant dissenter, a shop keeper who has a wife and 3 small children.
9 Gentry &c. The gentlemen are Mr William Russell, Mr Samuel Powel and Mr Paul Garnier, and the gentlewomen Mrs Beverley, Mrs Wynn and Mrs Lock.
10 Schools There is a school not endowed, the master of which is Charles Ford who teaches to read, write and cast accounts, and he has about 20 scholars.
11 Charities The Right Hon. Charles, Earl of Carlisle, has given £100 by way of charity, the interest of which according to His Lordship's appointment is yearly distributed by the rector and churchwardens to such poor

householders and inhabitants of the parish as have no alms from it. There is another charity of 20*s*. p.a. given by John Pearson, yeoman, and distributed. And a third charity of 20*s*. p.a. called Rushmore which is appropriated to poor widdows, among whom the churchwardens divide the money. There is no hospital in the parish.
12 Post-town <The nearest post-town to Wickham> is Fare<ham.>

227 Widley and Wymering 21M65/B4/1/2 fo.102
23 September 1725

William Chichely, 'rector of Widley and vicar of Wimering, united, held by one presentation', 1716–37
[A disorderly response, presented as follows:]
Widley From Sheepwash to Ports Bridge in length 3 miles, in breadth 1.
Papists none; dissenters none.
Christened in the year 1724, 4.
Married none. Patrons, Mr Norton's heirs who are obliged by an antient agreement with the college of Winchester confirmed in the Exchequer in James I's time to present one out of four which the college name to them, they renewing their lease under the college always at a fine certain.
Schools, midwives, surgeons, none.
Next post-town, Portsmouth.
Wimering From the Guildables to Sheep Wash in length 4 miles. From Pauls Grove to Drayton Gate in breadth 3 miles.
Papist familys 2. John Blonden and his wife and 3 children. George Knight his wife and 1 child. The Hon. Mr Dormer, Papist, his estate about £20 p.a., but not resident. The tenant protestant.
Schools, midwives, surgeons none.
One Almshouse given by Honor Wait in the year 1600 for 4 poor widows. The trustees Richard Norton Esq. and the vicar of Wimering for the time being.
Next post-town, Portsmouth.
Married in the year 1724, 10.
Buried 8.

228 Wield 21M65/B4/1/1 fo.12

Stephen Stephens AM, curate
Weild [is] a peculiar in the deanery of Alresford.
1 Area Weild is 2 miles long, 1½ broad.
2 Population The number of souls is about 150.
3 Marriages &c. Births 2, burials 1 at a medium, and but 6 marriages in 24 years.
4 Patron Weild is a lay impropriation in the possession of the Lord Limington.
5 Chapels None.
6 Lecturer No lecturer.
7 Papists No Papist.

8 Dissenters No meeting nor protestant dissenter.
9 Gentry &c. No nobleman, gentleman, nor person of note.
10 Schools No school endowed.
11 Charities No charities given. No hospital.
12 Post-town Alresford is the next post-town.

229 Winchester, St Bartholomew Hyde 21M65/B4/1/2 fo.326
Walter Garrett, minister of 'St Bartholomew in Sokam commonly called Hyde Street near the Citty of Winchester', 1718–37
1 Area The parish is between 5 and 6 miles in compass.
2 Population It contains about 350 souls.
3 Marriages &c. There are yearly at a medium about 8 christenings, about 8 burials, about 3 marriages.
4 Patron The king (as I am informed) is the patron.
5 Chapels There are no chappels &c.
6 Lecturer There is no curate or lecturer.
7 Papists There are 5 families Papists; I believe of no consequence.
8 Dissenters There is no meeting of any kind and but 2 families of dissenters.
9 Gentry &c. There is no nobleman or gentleman of note.
10 Schools There is no endowed school in the parish.
11 Charities There are no public charities.
12 Post-town The next post-town is Winchester.

230 Winchester, St Faith 21M65/B4/1/2 fo.364
Abraham Markland DD, Master of St Cross, rector 1694–1728
1 Area It is supposed that the parish may be 7 miles in compass.
2 Population The number of souls is about 140.
3 Marriages &c. There may be at a medium, one year with another 2 marriages, 3 births, 4 or 5 burials.
4 Patron The Lord Bishop of Winchester is patron of the living as annexed to the Hospital of St Cross.
5 Chapels There is onely a chapel called the chapel of the Hospital of St Cross, served by a chaplain, maintained supported and nominated by the Master of the Hospital of St Cross.
6 Lecturer No lecturer or curate.
7 Papists There are 6 Papists in the parish of no consequence or estates.
8 Dissenters No protestant dissenters.
9 Gentry &c. There are no noblemen, gentlemen or persons of note of either sex in the parish.
10 Schools No school.
11 Charities No charities given to the parish. One hospital of St Cross for maintaining 13 men called brethren; the government of the hospital belongs to the Master.
12 Post-town Next post-town Winchester.

231 Winchester, St John 21M65/B4/1/2 fo.366

Thomas Brereton, 'minister of St John's parish in the Soak' near Winchester, 1719–52[?]

1 Area The compass of ground in this parish is about 2 computed miles.

2 Population The number of souls here is 436.

3 Marriages &c. The number of marriages is about 4, births 16, and burials 12, *communibus annis*.

4 Patron The patron of my living is the Lord Keeper, but though it be in the gift of the Crown, yet it is always holden under Your Lordship's sequestration.

5 Chapels There is no chappel in my parish.

6 Lecturer No person officiates in my parish but myself.

7 Papists There are 3 distinct large families who are profest Papists of no considerable note nor substance, and some more poor people who have been seduced by the rich Roman Catholicks in the city and, maintained by their allowances, embrace their commmunion and go to their mass, as I am informed.

8 Dissenters There is no meeting-house in the parish. The number of protestant dissenters is about 32, viz. of the Presbyterian sect.

9 Gentry &c. There is no nobleman nor gentleman living in my parish; the only chief persons are 10 substantial traders, the rest very poor and needy.

10 Schools There are 2 schools in which young children are taught by mistresses to read.

11 Charities The charities given to the poor inhabitants are: 1. Mr Smith's benefaction of £20 p.a. divided between both the parishes of St John's and St Peter's; being the interest of an estate he left at Shaldron in this county of Southampton, to be paid yearly.

2. Mr Johnson's benefaction, viz. the interest of £20 he left. Besides considerable sums arising from quit-rents[34]&c. I am credibly informed that the right of disposing these charities is left to the minister and church-wardens, but they will never admitt me to see how they distribute them. I have often desired a schedule of the papers reposited in the parish chest, and though Mr Archdeacon has interposed his authority to oblige them to a compliance, yet they disobey his order, and abuse me for enquiring after it. There is no hospital nor almshouse.

12 Post-town The Post Office is in the city of Winchester. I live in the suburbs near it.

232 Winchester, St Lawrence 21M65/B4/1/2 fo.378

John Price, rector 1703–33 3 September 1725

1 Area The compass of ground in the parish, I suppose to be half a mile.

2 Population The number of souls I suppose to be about 160.

3 Marriages &c. 3 marriages; 4 births; and 2 burials.

4 Patron The Lord High Chancellor is patron.

5 Chapels There is no chapel.

6 Lecturer There is no lecturer or curate. I serve the cure myself.

7 Papists There are 2 Papists, George Wright, alehouse-keeper, and his wife.

8 Dissenters There are no meetings of protestant dissenters; 21 persons that are called Presbyterians (including children) dissent from the church.
9 Gentry &c. John Ecton Esq., George Fern clerk, Richard Serle, Guilbert Wavell, Arthur Good and John Blake gentlemen, live in the parish.
10 Schools There is a school founded by William Over MD deceased, in the year 1702, endowed with £21 p.a., a rent-charge upon the estate of Sir John St Barb deceased, of Broadlands in the parish of Rumsey, Hants, for the teaching of 24 poor boys of the city and suburbs of Winton, in the grounds of the latin, grammar, writing and arithmetick, the children to be put in by the mayor and aldermen of Winton. The present master is Ambrose Holloway. The nomination of the master is in the mayor and aldermen of Winchester for the time being.
11 Charities The church was augmented in the year 1720 with £200, the bounty of Queen Anne[35] in conjunction with a £100, the benefaction of Edward Colston Esq., late of Mortlake, deceased, and £100 the benefaction of John Price, clerk, the present incumbent. The interest of Mr Colston's money has not been paid [to] the minister for 4 years last past; nor the interest of Queen Anne's Bounty of £100 upon pretence that Mr Colston's is not paid; so that the incumbent has but £8 p.a. out of £16 due. Mr Colston's executors pretend there must be lands bought before they can pay their £100 to the governours of the Bounty, which will never be done upon the foot the governours require, and as the value of land is in this country, we can expect to bye free land for no less than 25 years' purchase. This is humbly offered to your lordship's consideration.
There is given by the will of Edward Grace of this city, draper, deceased in the year 1713, £5 4*s*. payable quarterly out of his farm in the parish of Martyr's Worthy, Hants; to the churchwardens of this parish to be distributed by 2 shillings' worth of bread to the poor every Sunday in the said church after morning prayers are ended, for ever, which is never done. The mayor of Winton inspects this charity.
There is given to the poor of Winton by the will of Mrs Neale of Winton, deceased 40*s*. payable by a rent-charge for ever from a farm in Kent. This charity is under the administration of the churchwardens of this parish, and is duely executed.
In the year 1651 Mr Nathaniel Mills of Southton by his will gave 20*s*. payable by a rent-charge yearly for ever from his mannor of Woolstone to the poor. This charity is under the administration of the churchwardens of this parish, and duely executed.
In the year 1620, George Pemberton, gentleman, of Winton, gave out of his estate in Houghton, in this county, 20*s*. for a sermon to be preached upon St George's Day in this church; and £3 at the same time to be distributed to the poor for ever. This charity is under the direction of the mayor and aldermen of this city, and is duely executed.
In the year 1586, Peter Symonds of London, mercer, gave 6*s*. 8*d*. to be paid for a sermon at this church upon Good Fryday for ever, payable by the Company of Mercers in London; and at the same time 6*s*. 8*d*. to be given to the poor. This charity is under the direction of the mayor and aldermen of this city. No hospitals.

12 Post-town The parish is in Winchester, a post-town.

233 Winchester, St Maurice (with St Mary Kalendar, and St Peter Colebrook) 21M65/B4/1/2 fo.381

Daniel Wavell, 'rector of St Maurice and St Mary Calender, and sequestrator of St Peter's Colebrook' 1721–38 3 September 1725

[The parishes of] St Maurice and St Mary Calender [were] united by Bishop Morley by virtue of an Act of Parliament. All 3 parishes [lie] contiguous.

1 Area The compass of the parishes is about 1 mile.

2 Population The number of souls in St Maurice is 680; in St Mary Calender is 398; in St Peter's Colebrook 115.

3 Marriages &c. Marriages yearly are 5; births 38; burials 45.

4 Patron The patron is the Lord Bishop of the diocese.

5 Chapels There is one church only for the 3 parishes.

6 Lecturer There is no curate or lecturer.

7 Papists There are 9 Papists, reputed, in St Maurice. In St Peter's Colebrook 1, of no consequence.

8 Dissenters There is a meeting of protestant dissenters in the parish of St Mary Calendar; about 12 families of whom dwell in the 3 parishes. 1 family is Anabaptistic, another Quaker.

9 Gentry &c. Persons of note are Henry Penton Esq., Thomas Coward Esq., recorder of Winchester, and Edward Hooker Esq.

10 Schools We have 1 charity school (for reading and writing) maintained by subscription. Mr Duel teacheth it.

11 Charities Charities are a pension of £25 p.a. to the rector and £6 2*s*. p.a. from the Crown; 20*s*. to him yearly for preaching a sermon before the mayor and aldermen on All Saints Day, left by — Budd Esq., who hath bequeathed other charities in common to this city. Hospitals are, St John's for 6 sisters, appointed by the mayor and aldermen, founded by Sir John Lamb. Pension 2*s*. 6*d*. per week each. They have some other small allowances for firing &c. St Mary Magdalene hospital, for 4 brothers and 4 sisters at 14*d*. per week pension. They have, over and above, 10 groats[36] every quarter; and somewhat at Xmas, which amounts, in the whole, to £4 p.a. each. They are appointed by the master of the hospital, who is collated by the Bishop of Winchester.

12 Post-town There is a post-house in this city.

234 Winchester, St Michael 21M65/B4/1/2 fo.370

John Broadway, rector of 'St Michaels in the Soke near the City of Winchester' 1723–26 3 September 1725

1 Area 'Tis supposed there are 160 acres of ground in my parish.

2 Population There are 409 souls in my parish.

3 Marriages &c. I have 6 marriages, 8 births, and 11 burials, one year with another, in my parish.

4 Patron The Right Revd the Lord Bishop of Winton is the patron of my living.

5 Chapels There is no chapel in my parish.
6 Lecturer No lecturer or curate.
7 Papists There are 21 Papists in my parish, but of no consequence or estate which I know of.
8 Dissenters There are no meetings of protestant dissenters in my parish, nor any such dissenter living in it.
9 Gentry &c. There is no nobleman in my parish. There are 14 houses wherein are families of distinction.
10 Schools There are 3 schools in my parish. The mistress of one is Mrs Keel, who has about 20 scholars. The mistress of another [is] Mrs Lewis who has about 10 scholars. The mistress of the third [is] Mrs Westcomb who has about 20 scholars. But neither of the schools is endowed.
11 Charities There have been no charities given to my parish, neither is there any hospital in it.
12 Post-town [No reply.]

235 Winchester, St Peter Chesil 21M65/B4/1/2 fo.374

Thomas Brereton, 'minister of St Peter's Cheeshill in the Soak near Winton' 1717–28
1 Area The compass of ground in this parish is equal to the adjoining parish of St John's, about 2 computed miles.
2 Population The number of souls here is 408.
3 Marriages &c. The number of marriages is about 2, births 16, and burials 12, *communibus annis*.
4 Patron The right of nomination is vested in the power of the Right Revd the Lord Bishop of Winchester by sequestration.
5 Chapels There is no chappel nor place of publick worship but the parish church.
6 Lecturer No person performs any parochial duty here but myself.
7 Papists There are about 8 profest Papists of no considerable note nor substance who go to gentlemen's houses in town where mass is said; and some others who do not openly own the irreligion receive weekly or monthly contributions from them. I find a predominant spirit of Popery among many of my parishioners which urges me the more strenuously to confute their errours in almost all discourses. But though I preach with as discreet zeal and moderation as I can, yet I am abused, insulted and persecuted by the prevailing party of rich Papists and their correspondents who instigate the common people to revile me in the street.
8 Dissenters There is no meeting-house of protestant dissenters, but there about 30 Presbyterians and 5 Quakers who are the most substantial tradesmen in this parish.
9 Gentry &c. There is no nobleman. The only persons of note living in my parish are 2 gentlemen and 1 gentlewoman, who enjoy estates. The most part of the inhabitants are very poor.
10 Schools There are 2 schools in which poor young children are taught by mistresses to read.
11 Charities The chief benefaction given to this parish is that equal dividend of rents (viz. £10 p.a.) paid yearly out of an estate Mr Smith left at

Shaldron, which I believe is distributed rightly and duly to the uses and purposes designed by him as putting children prentices to some good trades or relieving poor housekeepers. There are other small gifts disposed of in bread and meat according to the will of the benefactors which I have seen at certain times appointed. There is no hospital nor almshouse.
12 Post-town The Post Office is in the city of Winchester, I live in the suburbs near it.

236 Winchester, St Swithin 21M65/B4/1/2 fo.372
John Broadway, minister 1723–26 3 September 1725
1 Area Tis supposed there are 30 acres of ground in my parish.
2 Population There a[re] 147 souls in my parish.
3 Marriages &c. I have 1 marriage, 4 births and 2 burials, one year with another, in my parish.
4 Patron The archdeacon of Surry is the patron of my living.
5 Chapels There is no chapel in my parish.
6 Lecturer No lecturer or curate.
7 Papists There is no Papist in my parish.
8 Dissenters There is no meeting of protestant dissenters, nor any such dissenters living in my parish.
9 Gentry &c. Wolvesey House, the palace of the Lord Bishop of Winchester is in my parish, and there are 4 other houses wherein are families of some distinction.
10 Schools There are 2 schools in my parish. The Revd Mr Tittle, the master of one, who has about 40 scholars; and Mrs Whitehead the mistress of the other who has about 20 scholars. But neither of those schools are endowed.
11 Charities There have been no charities given to my parish, neither is there any hospital in it.
12 Post-town [No reply.]

237 Winchester, St Thomas 21M65/B4/1/2 fo.385
William Jefferies, rector 1718–35 2 September 1725
1 Area The parish is about 2 miles in circumference.
2 Population The number of souls therein is between 8 and 900.
3 Marriages &c. Marriages about 16; births about 20; burials 15, one year with another.
4 Patron The Lord Bishop of Winchester [is] patron.
5 Chapels No chapel.
6 Lecturer No lecturer or curate.
7 Papists Papists or reputed Papists, about 40 or 50, the chief of whom are William Sheldon Esq., George Bolney Esq., Rowland Bellasis Esq., Mrs Smith. These have considerable estates, but not in this parish. The houses Mr Bolney and Mrs Smith inhabit are their own.
8 Dissenters No meeting. Presbiterians between 20 and 30.
9 Gentry &c. No nobleman living in the parish, but there is a royal palace of His Majesties unfinished. Gentlemen, James Cross Esq., Richard Warr Esq., John Foyle Esq.

10 Schools No endowed school.
11 Charities Thomas Brooker gave £40 p.a. for ever to the poor to be distributed in bread. One hospital called Christ's Hospital, founded by Peter Symonds, citizen and mercer of London in the year 1586 for 6 poor men, 4 boys, 1 woman of the city of Winchester. The conservator or governour, the Warden of the College for the time being, and 6 citizens of the city of Winchester. The present [governours] are Mr Thomas Godwin, Mr Thomas Fussel, Mr John Tarrant, Mr John Purdue, Mr William Spearing and Mr Francis Smith.
12 Post-town The Post Office is in the parish.

238 Winchfield 21M65/B4/1/1 fo.323
Thomas Pretty, rector 1684–1725
1 Area About 5 miles circumference.
2 Population About 150.
3 Marriages &c. Very few marriages; births and burials not exceeding 4, one year with another.
4 Patron Benjamin Rudyard Esq. lord of the manour of the said parish.
5 Chapels None.
6 Lecturer Noe lecturer; but Mr White vicar of Hartley Row supplyes as churate.
7 Papists None.
8 Dissenters Noe meeting nor any dissenter that is a housekeeper in this parish.
9 Gentry &c. Only Mr Rudyerd's family aforesaid, and a few substantial farmers.
10 Schools None.
11 Charities None.
12 Post-town Hartford-Bridge.

239 Winnall 21M65/B4/1/2 fo.389
Luke Imber, rector 1722–53 3 September 1725
1 Area The compass of ground is about 3 miles, 1 mile in length and half a mile over.
2 Population The number of souls are generally between 40 and 50.
3 Marriages &c. Strangers are often privately married at the church, 5 or 6 in the year. Births in the year 2; burials in the year 2.
4 Patron My Lord Bishop of Winchester is patron.
5 Chapels There is no chapell belonging to it.
6 Lecturer There is no lecturer, but at present the church is served by Mr Broadway as curate.
7 Papists, 8 Dissenters, 9 Gentry &c. No Papists nor dissenters of any kind, nor gentlemen of distinction live in the parish.
10 School There is no school.
11 Charities There are no charities setled, or any hospitall.
12 Post-town [No reply.]

240 Winslade 21M65/B4/1/1 fo.325
John Pepper, rector 1717–47 16 August 1725
1 Area 10 miles in circumference.
2 Population About 3 score.
3 Marriages &c. Few marriages; births and burials 2 or 3 in a year.
4 Patron Charles, Duke of Bolton.
5 Chapels None.
6 Lecturer None.
7 Papists None.
8 Dissenters None.
9 Gentry &c. None.
10 Schools There is a charity school maintained by Her Grace Anne, Dutchess of Bolton, consisting of 10 girls, who are cloathed annually by Her Grace, and are taught to read and to work all manner of plainwork. The salary is £6 p.a.; the present mistresse [is] Mrs Aimy Hockley.
11 Charities There is a charity of £6 p.a. payable out of the personal estate of His Grace, Charles, Duke of Bolton, which is regularly payed and is disposed off according to the tenor of the will in that behalf made to 2 families who do not receive collection. The trustees are the mayor of Basingstoke for the time being, the rector of Winslade for the time being, the steward of Basing for the time being.
12 Post-town Basingstoke is the only post-town which is convenient and brings letters safe, Winslade being only 2 miles from it.

241 Wolverton 21M65/B4/1/1 fo.329
William Robbins MA, rector 1719–59 Chelsea, 4 March 1724/5
1 Area Wolverton parish contains about 1,300 acres.
2 Population In which are now living, servants included, 126 souls.
3 Marriages &c. And it appears that there have been 2 burials, between 2 and 3 marriages, and between 3 and 4 baptized at a medium p.a.
4 Patron Jemmett Raymond Esq. is the patron.
5 Chapels There is no chapel in the parish.
6 Lecturer Nor lecturer nor curate.
7 Papists Nor any Papist.
8 Dissenters Nor dissenter of any kind.
9 Gentry &c. Nor any person of note.
10 Schools Nor any school. But
11 Charities Sir George Brown Kt. bequeathed by his last will and testament an estate called Bewshons in the said parish, value £6 10*s*. p.a. to Sir Adam Brown, Sir William Meux and to Sir James Worsely and their heires in trust to the only use of the poor of the said parish. And the minister, churchwardens and overseers of the poor of the said parish for the time being are empowered by the said will to receive and distribute the profitts, which hath been hitherto regularly observed.
12 Post-town Newbury is the next post-town.

242 Wonston 21M65/B4/1/2 fo.264
John Sturges, rector 1723–40
1 Area The extent of the parish is generally computed to be from north to south about 5 miles, and from east to west about 3.

2 Population According to the best information I can get, we are supposed to have about 350 souls.
3 Marriages &c. For the 7 years last past, one with another, there have been about 3 marriages, 10 births and 12 burials.
4 Patron The Lord Bishop of Winchester is patron.
5 Chapels No chapel or chapels.
6 Lecturer No lecturer or curate at present.
7 Papists No Papists.
8 Dissenters No meeting of protestant disenters; there are 3 or 4 persons who go sometimes to the meeting and sometimes go to church.
9 Gentry &c. No nobleman, gentleman or person of note.
10 Schools No school endowed. I give (as my predecessor did) £5 p.a. to a woman for teaching the children of the parish.
11 Charities No charity that I can learn given to the parish, excepting £20 by the late Dr Newey and £20 by 2 other hands, the interest of which sums is annually distributed among the poor.
12 Post-town Winchester is the next post-town if Your Lordship should have occasion to write.

243 Woodcott 21M65/B4/1/1 fo.160
Hugh Wallington, perpetual curate 1718–27
1 Area The extent of the parish of Woodcot from east to west is about 2½ miles, and from north to south is about one mile.
2 Population There are about 40 souls in this parish.
3 Marriages &c. There may be 1 birth, one year with another, and a wedding and burial once in 2 or 3 years.
4 Patron This is now no presentative living, but the committee of the estate of William Kingsmill Esq. (the lunatick) in whose hands (as impropriator) are the tiths of the parish pays me a yearly stipend for performing once in a fortnight (as has been usual) divine service there.
5 Chapels There is no chappel in the parish.
6 Lecturer There is no lecturer, but I officiate as curate there.
7 Papists There is no Papist in the parish.
8 Dissenters There is no meeting of any kind of protestant dissenters in the parish.
9 Gentry &c. There is no nobleman or gentleman nor any person of note in the parish.
10 Schools There is no free school nor charity school of any kind in the parish.
11 Charities There have been no charities given to the parish nor is there any hospital in it.
12 Post-town The next post-town is Whitchurch.

244 Wootton, St Helens and Binstead [IoW] 21M65/B4/1/2 fo.193
Francis Deacon, 'rector of Wootton, curate of the donative of St Helens, and sequestrator of Binsted', 1718/19–1734 25 August 1725
Wootton
1 Area The compass of ground belonging to the parish of Wootton is

about 2 miles, consisting only of 2 farms which are at 7 miles distance. The tenant of the farm contiguous to the church conforms to the Church of England as by law established, the other is an Independent.
2 Population The number of souls is 12.
3 Marriages &c. Of marriages, births and burials perhaps 1 of each in 7 years.
4 Patron The patron of the living is Edward Lisle Esq.
5 Chapels No chapel.
6 Lecturer The curate is Mr Thomas Dickonson.
7 Papists No Papist.
8 Dissenters No protestant dissenter but as above-sayd.
9 Gentry &c. No person of note.
10 Schools No school.
11 Charities No charity given to the parish.
12 Post-town The next post-town is Newport.
Binstead, which is contiguous to Wootton
1 Area The parish of Binsted is about 2 miles in compass.
2 Population Number of souls 60.
3 Marriages &c. Marriages 1; births 3; burials 2.
4 Patron The patron of the living is the Lord Bishop of Winchester.
5 Chapels No chapel.
6 Lecturer The curate is Mr Thomas Dickonson.
7 Papists No Papist.
8 Dissenters No protestant dissenters.
9 Gentry &c. No person of note.
10 Schools No school.
11 Charities No charity given to this parish.
12 Post-town The next post-town is Newport.
St Helens
1. Area The parish is about 3 miles in compass.
2 Population The number of souls is 80.
3 Marriages &c. Marriages 2; births 5; burials 6.
4 Patron The patron of the living is Eaton College.
5 Chapels No chapel.
6 Lecturer No lecturer nor curate.
7 Papists No Papist.
8 Dissenters No protestant dissenter.
9 Gentry &c. 1 gentleman, viz. Mr William Stygant.
10 Schools No school.
11 Charities No charity but 10*s*. p.a. which was given by one Mr Richard Gard to the poor labourers of the parish.
12 Post-town The next post-town is Newport.

245 Wootton St Lawrence 21M65/B4/1/1 fo.266
Thomas Fenton, vicar 1723–43 16 August 1725
1 Area The parish is about 16 miles in circumference.

2 Population The number of souls therein is about 290.
3 Marriages &c. There have been in the parish, *communibus annis*, for the last 10 years, 2 marriages, 6 births, and 4 burials.
4 Patron The vicarage is in the gift of the Dean and Chapter of Winchester.
5 Chapels There is no chapel in my parish.
6 Lecturer There is no lecturer nor curate in my parish.
7 Papists There are no Papists in my parish.
8 Dissenters There is no meeting of protestant dissenters in my parish; but there is 1 family of dissenters of the Presbyterian persuasion.
9 Gentry &c. 2 of His Majesty's Justices of the Peace live in my parish, viz. William Wither Esq. and John Limbry Esq.
10 Schools There are no schools in my parish.
11 Charities There are 50*s*. p.a. left to the poor of this parish for ever, by Mr Thomas Sympson of Sherburne St John's, deceased, payable out of his lands at Monk Sherburne, to be distributed half-yearly by the minister and churchwardens; and the yearly interest of £50 for ever, left to this parish by Mr Walter Pincke of Kempshot in the parish of Winslade, deceased, to be disposed of by the churchwardens and overseers of this parish, for binding poor children to apprenticeships. There are no hospitals in this parish.
12 Post-town The next post-town to St Laurence Wootton is Basingstoke in Hampshire.

246 Worting 21M65/B4/1/1 fo.331
Henry Bigg, rector 1724–31 16 August 1725
1 Area The said parish of Worting is supposed to contain between 1,000 and 1,100 acres in its whole extent.
2 Population The number of souls therein may be reasonably computed at about 50 or 60.
3 Marriages &c. Marriages and burials are hardly found to exceed 1, nor births 2, at a medium of one year with another.
4 Patron The patron of this living is William Wither Esq. of Manydown in the parish of Wotton adjoyning.
5 Chapels There is no chappell in this parish.
6 Lecturer In my absence the cure is supplyed by the Revd Mr Thomas Fenton, vicar of St Laurence Wotton, who lives near, within half a mile's distance of any house in my parish.
7 Papists There is no Papist in this parish.
8 Dissenters Nor any protestant dissenter, of any denomination whatsoever.
9 Gentry &c. Thomas Hodges Esq., having lately purchased an estate herein, resides some part of the year.
10 Schools There is no endowed school in the parish.
11 Charities It does not appear that any charitys have been given to this parish.
12 Post-town The next post-town to it is Basingstoke.

247 Yarmouth with Shalfleet and Thorley [IoW] 21M65/B4/1/2 fo.204
Robert Harvey, 'minister of the borough of Yarmouth, vicar of Shalfleet and Thorley', 1698–1730
1 Area Yarmouth [is] in circumference about half a mile; Shalfleet about 14 [miles]; Thorley about 4.
2 Population In Yarmouth about 300; in Thorley about 75; in Shalfleet about 320.
3 Marriages &c. In Yarmouth about 25; in Shalfleet about 30; in Thorley about 9.
4 Patron Yarmouth and Shalfleet [in] the gift of the Crown. Patron of Thorley is Thomas Goter, gent.
5 Chapels None.
6 Lecturer None.
7 Papists Not one.
8 Dissenters No meetings. In Yarmouth no dissenters, in Thorley none, in Shalfleet about 5.
9 Gentry &c. In Yarmouth Henry Holmes Esq., and David Urry, gent. Shalfleet none. Thorley, Benjamin Leigh, gent.
10 Schools [A] poor widow teaching to read in the parish of Shalfleet; Yarmouth one woman; Thorley none.
11 Charities None.
12 Post-town Newport, Isle of Wight.

248 Yateley 21M65/B4/1/1 fo.333
John Thomas, curate 1707–30
1 Area About 16 miles in circumference.
2 Population About 800.
3 Marriages &c. 3 or 4 marriages; 16 or 17 births; about 13 or 14 burials.
4 Patron The M[aste]r of St Cross [Hospital] has let by lease to John Limbrey Esq. the rectory and the nomination of the curate.
5 Chapels, 6 Lecturer No chappell, no lecturer, no curate but myself.
7 Papists Not one.
8 Dissenters No meeting of protestant dissenters. About 22 dissenters, of which 1 is a Quaker, the rest Presbiterians, Independants and Anabaptists.
9 Gentry &c. Thomas Windham, Henry Foxcroft Esqs.
10 Schools A third part of an estate at Sunninghill, Berkshire, which is let for £10 10*s*. p.a. was left for ever to the parish by Mrs Barker of Egham to pay for the teaching of 6 boys to read English, and 6 girls to read knit and doe plain-work. The nomination of a master or mistress is invested in her trustees and at present 2 poor women teach them.
11 Charities 1 meadow in Finchamstead, Berkshire, of £9 p.a. left to the parish for ever by Mr Peter South which is let, the rents received and disposed of to the poor at the discretion of the trustees who are 5 or 6 substantial inhabitants in the parish. Halfe an estate at Sandhurst, Berkshire, let for £6 15*s*. p.a. left to the parish for ever by [donor's name wanting] to be disposed of annually by the same trustees. Some lands in Yately let for £3 p.a. left by the Lady Rieves and is disposed by the

overseers of the poor of the parish. 10*s*. p.a. payable from an house, and is disposed of to the poor by the possessor of the house.
12 Post-town Hartforde Bridge.

249 Yaverland [IoW] 21M65/B4/1/2 fo.201
William Griffin, vicar of Arreton 9 May 1726
I, William Griffin, vicar of Arreton, understanding that Your Lordship requires a speedy answer from the minister of Yaverland to your several queries, have thought it my duty to make to your lordship the following representation.
1 Area The compass of Yaverland is adjudged to be 7 English miles.
2 Population The number of souls in Yaverland are about 60.
3 Marriages &c. That not meeting with any register book in the parish, I cannot *exactly* tell the number of marriages, births and burials, one year with another. But that within the last twelve moneth there have been in the parish church of Yaverland, 1 marriage, 2 christenings and no more that I know of.
4 Patron The patron of the living is Edward Richards Esq., whose residence is at Compton in Berkshire.
5 Chapels There is no chapel in the parish unless the parish church may be called a chapel, since they bury their dead at Brading, and pay (to my best remembrance) 10*s*. p.a. to the impropriator thereof on the account. I may add that there have been 2 persons belonging to Yaverland and buried at Brading within this twelve moneth.
6 Lecturer There is no lecturer or curate in the parish, but in the absence of the minister the church hath been supplied of late alternately by the vicars of Arreton and Newchurch at the request of the inhabitants.
7 Papists There are no Papists.
8 Dissenters No meetings of protestant dissenters.
9 Gentry &c. No noblemen, gentlemen or persons of note of either sex.
10 Schools No schools that are endowed. But I believe there may be some children taught to read English.
11 Charities There are no charities or hospital.
12 Post-town The nearest post-town is Nuport.
If there hath been any omission of what I ought to have made Your Lordship acquainted with, it is not wilful, and I hope Your Lordship will believe that it will be a pleasure to me to approve myself, if I can. Humbly craving your blessing.

The Visitation of 1765
Hampshire

John Thomas (1696–1781), Bishop of Winchester 1761–1781. Engraving by Richard Houston from a painting by B. Wilson, published 1771. (Hampshire Record Office, Winchester City Archives, W/K2/4/29)

Episcopal Visitation, 1765

Printed Articles of Inquiry

Articles of Inquiry, which the clergy of the diocese of Winchester are desired to answer, and deliver to the Register at the Visitation.

1 Is your church or chapel, with its chancel, in good and sufficient repair: and are all things necessary provided for the celebration of divine service, and the administration of the holy sacrament?

2 Is divine service performed in your church twice on every Sunday? And if not, declare the reason of such omission.

3 Is the sacrament administered so often in each year, that every parishioner may receive the communion at least three times?

4 Have you a register book for christenings and burials: and also a register-book for marriages pursuant to the directions contained in the Act of Parliament, *for the better preventing of clandestine marriages?*

5 Have you a true and perfect terrier of all the glebe-lands, gardens, orchards, &c., and a note in writing of all the pensions and other dues, belonging to your parsonage or vicarage? And, if you have, hath an authentick copy of such terrier and note been delivered into the registry for safe custody?

6 Is your church-yard sufficiently fenced and decently kept? and hath any person incroached upon it?

7 Hath the fabrick of the church been altered in any respect? and have any pews been erected, galleries built, vaults dug, or dead bodies removed without a licence or faculty from your ordinary for so doing?

8 If you are possessed of a curacy, what is the stipend allowed by the impropriator, and what is the computed yearly value of the impropriation? Is the stipend the same which hath usually been allowed, and is it adequate to the duty to be performed?

9 Is your parsonage or vicarage house, with the barns, out-houses, and other buildings thereunto belonging in proper repair?

10 Do you reside upon your parsonage or vicarage? and if not, what is the cause of your non-residence? And have you a constant resident curate, who hath been licenced to act as such within your parish?

11 Are there any dissenters in your parish of any denomination? and, if there are, have they any meeting-house or place for divine worship?

12 Do you know of any benefaction which hath been witheld from those for whom it was designed? Or of the abuse of any charity, which regards either the church or the poor?

13 Have any of the ecclesiastical officers misbehaved themselves by taking undue fees, or in any other manner: and do the church-wardens, clerk, sexton, and the other officers of your church perform their respective duties?

John [Thomas] Winchester, 1765

250 Abbotts Ann 21M65/B4/2/31
John Burrough, rector 1730–74 3 September 1765
1 Repair of church In very good repair, and everything necessary is provided for the purposes mentioned.
2 Services It is always performed twice, except in case of illness, or if called upon to assist a neighbour very short or upon any extraordinary occasion.
3 Sacrament It is administered 5 times every year.
4 Register We have every book necessary for the purposes mentioned.
5 Terrier There are no pensions or dues but those arising from the great and small tithes of the parish, a terrier of which was given in, when Mr Archdeacon Lowth visited parochially.
6 Churchyard It is decently kept and fenced sufficiently, nor hath there been any encroachments upon it.
7 Alterations There has been no alteration in any respect in the church, either as to the fabrick, vaults, galleries or bodies removed.
8 Impropriation I serve no other church, but that of my own parish.
9 Repair of parsonage They are all in good repair.
10 Residence I constantly reside in my parish.
11 Dissenters There is not more than one, a Presbyterian. No meeting-house in the parish.
12 Loss of benefactions I know of none. There is a legacy of £3 p.a. left some time since by one Mr Thomas Crisswick and payable out of his freehold estate at Little Anne which is constantly paid, and applied to the instruction of poor children in reading and needlework.
13 Misbehaviour I dont know that any ecclesiastical officer has in any respect misbehaved. And the churchwardens and clerk do their respective duties.

251 Amport 21M65/B4/2/32
Thomas Ball, Dean of Chichester, vicar 1754–70
Thomas Sheppard, curate
1 Repair of church The church is in good repair and everything necessary is provided for the celebration of divine service and the administration of the sacrament.
2 Services Yes.
3 Sacrament Yes.
4 Registers Yes; yes.
5 Terrier A terrier of the house and glebe-lands was some time ago required to be given to the registry of the Archdeacon by Dr Lowth, and, I believe, it may be presumed was delivered agreeable to that injunction.

6 Churchyard It is well fenced and no incroachment hath been made.
7 Alterations No.
8 Impropriation Amport is a vicaridge endowed with the great tithes.
9 Repair of parsonage Yes.
10 Residence The Dean of Chichester is the vicar. But there is a resident curate at Amport.
11 Dissenters No.
12 Loss of benefactions No.
13 Misbehaviour No; yes.

252 Andover 21M65/B4/2/33
Rice Price LLB, vicar 1761–5
[Unsigned.]
1 Repair of church Yes.
2 Services Yes.
3 Sacrament Yes.
4 Registers Yes.
5 Terrier I do not know.
6 Churchyard It is.
7 Alterations No.
8 Impropriation [No reply; not applicable.]
9 Repair of parsonage I do not know.
10 Residence I have a resident curate.
11 Dissenters There are dissenters and they have a meeting-house.
12 Loss of benefactions No.
13 Misbehaviour Not that I know of.

253 Appleshaw 21M65/B4/2/34
Thomas Ball, vicar of Amport 1754–70
Thomas Sheppard, curate
1 Repair of church The chapel is in good repair and everything necessary is provided for the celebration of divine service and the administration of the sacrament.
2 Services Yes.
3 Sacrament Yes.
4 Registers Yes; yes.
5 Terrier There is no glebe-land belonging to the chapelry of Appleshaw.
6 Churchyard It is in good repair and no incroachment has been made.
7 Alterations No.
8 Impropriation [No reply; not applicable.]
9 Repair of parsonage Yes.
10 Residence There is a constant curate for Appleshaw who resides at Amport of which Appleshaw is only a hamlett.
11 Dissenters No.
12 Loss of benefactions There was a benefaction of £50 left by Mrs Frances Offley about two years since, for teaching poor children to read, which has not yet taken place but will do, I presume, in some time.

13 Misbehaviour No; yes.

254 Ashley 21M65/B4/2/174

John Butler LLB, rector 1749/50–1777
[Unsigned.]
1 Repair of church Church etc. in good repair.
2 Services Service duly performed.
3 Sacrament Sacrament administered 3 times a year.
4 Registers We have 2 register books.
5 Terrier I know nothing of a terrier of lands. I am curate.
6 Churchyard The churchyard is in decent order.
7 Alterations The fabrick of the church hath not been altered.
8 Impropriation I serve the curacy of Ashley at the yearly stipend of £30.
9 Repair of parsonage The parsonage-house etc. in good repair.
10 Residence This must be answered by the rector.
11 Dissenters There is no dissenter.
12 Loss of benefactions I know of none.
13 Misbehaviour I have no complaint under this article.

255 Avington 21M65/B4/2/1

George Fern MA, rector 1743–69
J. Dennis, curate
1 Repair of church The church is not in good repair. As for the other articles, all is well.
2 Services Yes, except every fifth Sunday on which I am to preach at the Cathedral in the afternoon.
3 Sacrament Yes.
4 Registers Yes.
5 Terrier I know not.
6 Churchyard It is sufficiently fenced and I know of no incroachments.
7 Alterations I know not.
8 Impropriaton I receive £30 p.a. for serving the cure of Avington.
9 Repair of parsonage I believe so, as they have very lately been repaird.
10 Residence I cannot reside being obliged to attend at the Cathedral.
11 Dissenters I know of none.
12 Loss of benefactions The benefactions I think are prudently dispensed.
13 Misbehaviour As far as I know they are not chargeable with any misconduct in any respect.

256 Barton Stacey 21M65/B4/2/120

William Jourd, vicar 1738–77
1 Repair of church Yes.
2 Service Divine service is usually performed twice on every Sunday.
3 Sacrament Yes.
4 Registers Yes.

5 Terrier There is a perfect terrier of the glebe. 52 acres. This terrier has formerly been delivered to the Archdeacon.
6 Churchyard The churchyard is properly fenced.
7 Alterations A vault has lately been dug under a pew in the south [a]isle, belonging to the lord of the manour.
8 Impropriation A stipend is paid to my curate, the same as always hath been allowed.
9 Repair of parsonage The vicarage house and barn are lately rebuilt; the house not quite fitted up on the inside.
10 Residence I have a constant resident curate.
11 Dissenters There is no family of dissenters in my parish.
12 Loss of benefactions Nothing of this kind has come to my knowledge.
13 Misbehaviour The churchwardens and officers of the church perform their duties.

257 Basingstoke 21M65/B4/2/60
William Henchman BD, vicar 1745/6–1768
[Unsigned. No replies.]

258 Bedhampton 21M65/B4/2/86
Thomas Dyer MA, rector 1736–80
Isaac Hodgson, curate
1 Repair of church Yes.
2 Services Once only according to custom.
3 Sacrament Yes.
4 Registers Yes.
5 Terrier I know not.
6 Churchyard Yes without incroachment.
7 Alterations 2 pews have been erected for private families at their own expence, without any inconvenience to the parishioners.
8 Impropriation Curacy £25 p.a. What the impropriation is, or what was usually allowed, I know not.
9 Repair of parsonage Yes.
10 Residence No; I know not; no, he resides at Havant at a mile distance.
11 Dissenters No dissenters' [meeting-]house in the parish.
12 Loss of benefactions I know of no such thing.
13 Misbehaviour The officers have behaved very well.

259 Bentley 21M65/B4/2/175
Richard Cheese, curate 1760–71
1 Repair of church The great rains and violent winds which we had last year have made some repairs necessary, which the churchwardens and parishioners have promised shall be done this summer.
2 Services Twice every Sunday.
3 Sacrament Yes.

4 Registers Yes.
5 Terrier As to this inquiry I am totally ignorant.
6 Churchyard The fences of the churchyard have time immmemorial been maintained not by a parish rate, but by the several lands and farms within the parish. Hence it frequently happens that some part or other wants repairing which is the case at present. But I have received assurances from the parties concerned that the repairs shall be done as soon as possible. I have heard of no incroachments.
7 Alterations Not that I know of.
8 Impropriation £28 p.a. It has been augmented with £400. The tyths are held by lease under the Archdeacon of Surrey, the yearly value of which I never heard. The stipend I presume is the same as has been usually allowed, whether adequate or not, I am an improper judge.
9 Repair of parsonage I never heard of any building belonging to the parsonage but a barn, which, being constantly used, is I imagine in tenantable repair.
10 Residence I reside in the parish.
11 Dissenters None.
12 Loss of benefactions No.
13 Misbehaviour I know of no offence that has been committed against this article of inquiry.

260 Bighton 21M65/B4/2/2
William Sealey, rector 1732/3–1767
1 Repair of church Yes.
2 Services Yes.
3 Sacrament Yes.
4 Registers Yes.
5 Terrier [No reply].
6 Churchyard It is well fenced and there hath been no incroachment.
7 Alterations Not that I know of.
8 Impropriation Bighton is a rectory.
9 Repair of parsonage Yes.
10 Residence The incumbent resides, but as he is infirm the duty is performed by a curate.
11 Dissenters No.
12 Loss of benefactions No.
13 Misbehaviour As to the first part of the quaere, not that I know of; as to the second, they have all I believe performed their respective duties.
[Signed] W. Sealy junior, for my father.

261 Binsted 21M65/B4/2/16
Grimshaw Smith, vicar 1740–66
[Unsigned.]
1 Repair of church Yes.
2 Services According to the usual custom both here and at Kingsley.

3 Sacrament Yes.
4 Registers Yes.
5 Terrier None ever came into my hands.
6 Churchyard Yes.
7 Alterations No.
8 Impropriation Yes, with a stipend of £30 a year for this and Kingsley.
9 Repair of parsonage [It] is to be repaired.
10 Residence Yes.
11 Dissenters No.
12 Loss of benefactions No.
13 Misbehaviour No.

262 Bishops Sutton and Ropley 21M65/B4/2/3
William Howley, vicar 1757–96
[This return is unsigned and contains no replies to any of the questions.]

263 Bishopstoke 21M65/B4/2/143
Thomas Yale Caverley, rector 1746–70
1 Repair of church Yes.
2 Services Yes.
3 Sacrament Yes.
4 Registers Yes.
5 Terrier No terrier that I ever heard of.
6 Churchyard No.
7 Alterations No.
8 Impropriation [No reply.]
9 Repair of parsonage Yes.
10 Residence The rector resides.
11 Dissenters Many Papists, but no meeting house in my parish.
12 Loss of benefactions I do not.
13 Misbehaviour Not as I know of.

264 Bishops Waltham 21M65/B4/2/87
James Cutler, rector 1753–82
Joseph Challoner Bale, curate
1 Repair of church Yes.
2 Services It is performed twice.
3 Sacrament Yes.
4 Registers We have each according to the several Acts of Parliament thereto relating.
5 Terrier [No reply.]
6 Churchyard All therein well.
7 Alterations No.
8 Impropriation [No reply.]
9 Repair of parsonage Yes.

10 Residence The curate is constantly resident.
11 Dissenters One family of dissenters, but no meeting-house.
12 Loss of benefactions No.
13 Misbehaviour No; yes.

265 Blendworth 21M65/B4/2/176
John Aiskew, rector 1741–89 7 September 1765
1 Repair of church Yes.
2 Services No. I suppose owing to the smallness of the living.
3 Sacrament Yes.
4 Registers Yes.
5 Terrier No.
6 Churchyard Yes; no incroachment that I know of.
7 Alterations The church has been entirely rebuilt within about 7 years.
8 Impropriation I am curate to the Revd Mr Harris at Widley and the Revd Mr Powell at Porchester; the impropriation of the latter is in lay hands, and the stipend at present allowed is £21. It has been more, is not adequate to the duty performed; but the vicarage is very small, and its <as> much, I think as Mr Powell can well afford.
9 Repair of parsonage They are.
10 Residence I do not, for at present I cannot afford it; the living is small; it is served by the Revd Mr Williams, the vicar of Catherington to which it was joined many years before I had it. In respect to my answer to this article, I cannot in this public manner be very particular. If His Lordship requires it, I shall be ready to lay it before himself, whenever he pleases to command it.
11 Dissenters No dissenters; there may be a Roman Catholic, but of no consequence; no place of worship but the established church.
12 Loss of benefactions There is a charity. I know of no abuse as I am not concerned in it; but to prevent any misapplication of it, or its being lost, I some years ago laid the whole circumstances of it before the Revd Dr Eden, who thought proper to take no further notice.
13 Misbehaviour Not as I know of; as to the officers of my particular church, I believe they do.

266 Boldre 21M65/B4/2/107
William Hawkins, vicar 1751–77
1 Repair of church Yes.
2 Services Once every Sunday at Boldre, the mother church, and once in the chapple of Brockenhurst.
3 Sacrament Yes.
4 Registers Yes.
5 Terrier An authentic copy of a terrier has been delivered into the Registry and I have one in my custody.
6 Churchyard The fence of the churchyard is now sufficiently repairing.
7 Alterations The fabric of the church has not been altered nor any part belonging to it.

8 Impropriation [No reply; not applicable.]
9 Repair of parsonage Yes.
10 Residence Yes.
11 Dissenters There are dissenters in the parish, but there is no meeting-house.
12 Loss of benefactions No.
13 Misbehaviour No.

267 Botley 21M65/B4/2/132
Thomas Kingsman, rector 1748–80
1 Repair of church Yes.
2 Services Yes.
3 Sacrament Yes.
4 Registers Yes.
5 Terrier Yes.
6 Churchyard It is; no.
7 Alterations No. The gallery has been enlarged.
8 Impropriation I am not.
9 Repair of parsonage In very good repair.
10 Residence I do reside.
11 Dissenters Not one of any denomination.
12 Loss of benefactions I do not.
13 Misbehaviour No; they do.

268 Bradley 21M65/B4/2/4
Joseph Hoole BD, rector 1763–83
1 Repair of church Both in good repair, and there are all things necessary provided for, etc.
2 Services Divine service is performed twice every Sunday.
3 Sacrament Yes.
4 Registers We have.
5 Terrier We have a perfect terrier of the glebe-lands &c.
6 Churchyard The church yard is in good repair, and nobody hath incroached upon it.
7 Alterations There hath been no alteration in the fabric of the church.
8 Impropriation The duty is performed by the rector.
9 Repair of parsonage All in excellent repair.
10 Residence I reside constantly.
11 Dissenters There is not one dissenter.
12 Loss of benefactions [No reply.]
13 Misbehaviour The parish officers do their duty.

269 Bramdean 21M65/B4/2/5
Thomas Durnford MA, rector 1741–92
1 Repair of church Our church and chancel are in exceeding good repair, and all things necessary are provided for the celebration of divine service, and administration of the Holy Sacrament.

2 Services Divine service is performed in our church twice every Sunday.
3 Sacrament The sacrament is administered three times every year.
4 Registers We have a register-book for christenings, burials and marriages.
5 Terrier I have no true terrier of the glebe-lands &c.
6 Churchyard The churchyard is not sufficiently fenced nor decently kept. The persons to whom the fence belongs promise to repair it speedily.
7 Alterations The fabric of the church has not been altered lately, nor have any pews been erected, gallaries built, vaults dug, or dead bodies removed.
8 Impropriation [No reply; not applicable.]
9 Repair of parsonage The parsonage house with barns, outhouses and other buildings are in uncommon good repair, very large sums of money having been laid out upon them.
10 Residence I reside upon my parsonage at Bramdean about 9 months in the year. When I am absent I have a constant resident curate. The remainder of the year I reside upon my other parsonage.
11 Dissenters There are 3 Roman Catholicks in my parish; they have no place for divine worship that I know of. There are no other dissenters of any denomination.
12 Loss of benefactions I know of no abuse of any charity in the parish.
13 Misbehaviour I know of no misbehaviour of any ecclesiastical officer. The churchwarden and clerk perform their respective duties.

270 Brockenhurst 21M65/B4/2/108
William Hawkins, vicar of Boldre 1751–77
1 Repair of church Yes.
2 Services Once every Sunday at the mother church, Boldre, and once every Sunday in the chapple of Brockenhurst.
3 Sacrament Yes.
4 Registers Yes.
5 Terrier An authentic copy of a terrier has been delivered into the Registry and I have one in my custody.
6 Churchyard The churchyard is sufficiently fenced and no one has encroached.
7 Alterations The church has not been altered in any respect, but a new tower or spire was built thereon by a faculty from the late bishop.
8 Impropriation [No reply.]
9 Repair of parsonage Yes.
10 Residence Yes, I reside upon the vicarage.
11 Dissenters There are dissenters in the parish but no meeting-house.
12 Loss of benefactions No.
13 Misbehaviour No.

271 Broughton 21M65/B4/2/178
Robert Thistlethwayte, rector 1744/5–1767
[Little remains of this return.]
2 Services Service is performed twice on every Sunday, and also two sermons are preached in the church of Broughton every Sunday.

3 Sacrament The sacrament is administered often enough for every parishioner to receive the same 3 times at least in each year.
4 Registers There is a register book for christenings and burials, and a new register book for marriages etc.
7 Alterations The p<ews have not> been altered as appears, n<either> have there been any other <alter>ations.
8 Impropriation I have not a curacy.
9 Repair of parsonage The parsonage-house, barns etc., are in good repair.
12 Loss of benefactions < ... > pose< ... sc>hool in the parish foun<ded by ... > Dowse Esq. about <...>years ago, the indowment of which is very considerable, supposed to be near £40 p.a. The management of which has fallen into the hands of certain persons called trustees, and they are suspected greatly to have misapplied this charity, at least as long as I have been concerned in the parish. The schoolmaster's place is now vacant, and its reported they are now filling it up with a person by no means qualified for that office.
13 Misbehaviour I have no complaint against the ecclesiastical officers; the churchwardens, clerk, sexton do their duty.

272 Bullington 21M65/B4/2/179
Richard Ring, 'vicar of Wherwell' 1763–91, 'and curate of Bullington and Tufton annexed'
1 Repair of church Yes.
2 Services Once a fortnight only, it being a chapel belonging to the mother church of Wherwell.
3 Sacrament Yes.
4 Registers Yes.
5 Terrier A terrier of the vicarage was delivered in about 7 years ago.
6 Churchyard Well fenced and no encroachment. Since my signing this, part of the fence has been broken down, which, if not mended, the churchwardens will take notice of.
7 Alterations No.
8 Impropriation The curate hath the small tythes, but the value of the impropriation I do not yet know.
9 Repair of parsonage No house nor barn etc.
10 Residence I reside at Wherwell in the vicarage-house.
11 Dissenters No.
12 Loss of benefactions No.
13 Misbehaviour I know no officer who has taken undue fees nor anyone who has neglected his duty.

273 Burghclere 21M65/B4/2/177
Thomas Lisle DD, rector 1737–67 31 August 176<5>
John Davies, curate
[This return has suffered extensive damage.]

1 Repair of church The church and chancel are <in> good repair and everything contained in the question properly pr<ovided>.
2 Services Divine service is co<nstantly per>formed in my chur<ch> morning and eve<ning>.
3 Sacrament It is admini<stered ... times> in each year.
4 Registers We have <all these> books here.
5 Terrier There are no pensions or other extraordinary dues belonging to my parsonage. I have a terrier of the glebe-lands etc. but whether the Registry has any <su>ch or no I am ignorant.
6 Churchyard The churchyard is well fenced, and decently kept, and I know of no encroachments on it.
7 Alterations The <fabric of> the church <has> received no <alterations;> the pews are very near <as I> found them; there are no <galleries built; no d>ead bodies have been re<moved nor> vault dug, to which I know no farther.
8 Impropriation <The stipen>d allowed the <curate is entirel>y adequate to the <duty perform>ed and is the same his <predecessor ha>d. As the computed yearly value of the impropriation must vary <with the> harvest, it is difficult to fix or ascertain it. John Davies, curate.
9 Repair of parsonage <In corre>ct repair.
10 Residence I reside upon my parsonage a great part of the year, and throughout the whole have a constant resident curate.
11 Dissenters There are a few Presbyter<ian> dissenters in our parish who have no meet<ing->house or place for divine worship therein; however they resort to the town of Newbury in Berkshire, where there is a meeting-house for that purpose.
12 Loss of benefactions I know of none such. John Davies, curate.
13 Misbehaviour <I kno>w not <hat the ecclesiasti>cal officers have anyw<ay misbe>haved themselves, or that the parish officers have neg<lected their> duties.

274 Buriton 21M65/B4/2/88
Philip Barton BD, rector 1751–96
Jonathan Rashleigh, curate
1 Repair of church The church and chancel are in good repair, and all things necessary are provided for the service and the sacraments.
2 Services Divine service is performed twice on every Sunday.
3 Sacrament The sacrament is administered 5 times in each year.
4 Registers We have a register of baptisms and burials, and a distinct register of marriages.
5 Terrier There is no antient terrier to be found in the registry or elsewhere. If I live, I hope to provide a new terrier to be made out, properly attested, and delivered into the registry.
6 Churchyard Our churchyard is well fenced and kept. There is no incroachment upon it.
7 Alterations Our church was entirely new pewed and a gallery built 30 years ago. The north side of it was handsomely rebuilt last summer. The

form and property of some of the pews were altered by a faculty from Bishop Hoadly. There are 2 burying vaults in the church of antient date, both, I believe, dug by permission of the ordinary.
8 Impropriation [No reply; not applicable.]
9 Repair of parsonage The parsonage-house and outhouses are in decent and good repair.
10 Residence I reside on my parsonage the greater part of the year. My duty, as residentiary at Exeter, obliges me to be absent at least 3 months. I have at present a resident curate, Mr Jonathan Rashleigh, Fellow of All Souls College. He hath no licence.
11 Dissenters No dissenters of any sort.
12 Loss of benefactions I know of none.
13 Misbehaviour I know of no complaint on these heads.

275 Bursledon (Brissleden Chapelry) 21M65/B4/2/133
[Unsigned.]
[No replies.]

276 Catherington 21M65/B4/2/89
John Williams, vicar 1740–78
1 Repair of church The chancel which belongs to Mr John Brett, a minor, is greatly out of repair. We have everything else that is necessary in good order.
2 Services The vicarage of Catherington is not £50 p.a., and I serve a curacy in the neighbourhood; so that we have service but once every Sunday. The parishioners had service but once on every Sunday in my predecessor's time.
3 Sacrament The sacrament is administered 4 times a year.
4 Registers Yes.
5 Terrier No. All the land belonging to this church is only a garden and a little court.
6 Churchyard It is tolerably well fenced, and not encroached upon.
7 Alterations There has been no alteration since I was instituted into the living.
8 Impropriation I have all the small tithes. The impropriation is about £250 p.a., as I have been told.
9 Repair of parsonage Yes, I have laid out £150 upon them.
10 Residence I am now, and have been always, resident upon my vicarage, but never kept a curate.
11 Dissenters There is no meeting-house in this parish, and not above 2 dissenters.
12 Loss of benefactions There is no benefaction belonging to this church, but there is a charity school managed by a trustee.
13 Misbehaviour I know of no misbehaviour in any of them.

277 Chalton 21M65/B4/2/90
William Denison BD, rector 1756–86
Richard Keats, curate
1 Repair of church [No reply.]

2 Services Once only according to custom.
3 Sacrament It is administered 5 times every year.
4 Registers Yes.
[Questions 5–13, no reply.]

278 Chawton 21M65/B4/2/17
John Hinton BA, rector 1744–1802
1 Repair of church Yea.
2 Services Service is performed twice every Sunday.
3 Sacrament Yea.
4 Registers Yea.
5 Terrier <I h>ave a true <terrier of> all <the> glebe <l>ands, and <a co>py <th>ereof has been delivered into <th>e registry.
6 Churchyard The churchyard is sufficiently fenced; and noone hath incroached upon it.
7 Alterations The fabric of the church hath not been altered, nor anything done that required a faculty.
8 Impropriation I have no curacy.
9 Repair of parsonage The parsonage house and other buildings are in proper repair.
10 Residence I r<eside i>n my parson<age>.
11 Dissenters There is no dissenter in my parish.
12 Loss of benefactions I know of no benefaction that hath been withheld, nor of the abuse of any charity with regard to the church or poor.
13 Misbehaviour [No reply.]

279 Cheriton 21M65/B4/2/6
Robert Ashe, rector 1753–
[Unsigned.]
1 Repair of church Yes.
2 Services Yes.
3 Sacrament Yes.
4 Registers Yes.
5 Terrier There is a terrier, but I dont find that there is any copy of it in the Registry. I will take care to send one.
6 Churchyard Yes; no.
7 Alterations In the year 1744 this church was burnt and rebuilt much after the same manner as before; and, as I am informed, everything was done agreeably to order.
8 Impropriation This does not concern me.
9 Repair of parsonage Yes.
10 Residence I reside during summer, for 7 months. In the winter I reside upon my prebend. There is a curate constantly resident, but not licenced.
11 Dissenters There are no dissenters; but there are a few Roman Catholic families, the principal of which is Sir Henry Tichborne's.
12 Loss of benefactions I know of none.

13 Misbehaviour No; yes.

280 Chilbolton 21M65/B4/2/121

Jonathan Shipley DD, rector 1760–69[?]
John Osborne, curate

1 Repair of church Yes.
2 Services Yes, morning and afternoon.
3 Sacrament Yes, 4 times in the year, viz. at the 3 grand festivals, and about Michaelmas.
4 Registers Yes.
5 Terrier The glebe is but small, but I think no terrier has been taken according to the canon.
6 Churchyard Yes and no incroachment.
7 Alterations No.
8 Impropriation [This is] a rectory with a resident curate upon it.
9 Repair of parsonage Yes.
10 Residence A resident curate upon it, who has resided upon it almost 40 years, viz. from Michaelmas 1725 to this time.
11 Dissenters None.
12 Loss of benefactions Dr Layfield's benefaction is now determined in Chancery and the parish likely to receive the same very soon for the benefit of the poor. The principal money being about £208 and interest to receive for the time past amounting to £57. 4*s*. 4*d*. And for the future from the South Sea annuities an interest of £6. 5*s*. p.a.
13 Misbehaviour I know of no complaints that can be made of this kind.
Signed by the resident curate in the absence of the rector.

281 Chilcomb 21M65/B4/2/144

Richard Wavell, rector 1750/51–1779

1 Repair of church My church with its chancel is in good repair; and all things necessary for the celebration of divine service etc. are provided.
2 Services Divine service is performed in my church but once on every Sunday. It has not usually, as I am informed, been performed oftener by my predecessors.
3 Sacrament The sacrament is administered so often in each year, that every parishioner may receive the communion 3 times.
4 Registers I have a register book for christenings and burials; and also a register book for marriages etc.
5 Terrier I have no terrier.
6 Churchyard My churchyard is sufficiently fenced and decently kept; neither hath any person incroached upon it.
7 Alterations, 8 Impropriation [No replies.]
9 Repair of parsonage My parsonage-house and barn are in good repair.
10 Residence I do not reside, having the care of St Maurice P[arish] etc. in Winchester. I have a curate who lives in Winchester, to the suburbs of which city the parish of Chilcomb is adjoining.

11 Dissenters I do not know of any dissenters in my parish.
12 Loss of benefactions I do not.
13 Misbehaviour I know of no reason to complain of any person mentioned in this article.

282 Church Oakley 21M65/B4/2/61
[No replies. Subscribed:] I am only curate of Church Oakley.

283 Clanfield 21M65/B4/2/91
William Denison BD, rector 1755–86
Richard Keats, curate
1 Repair of church [No reply.]
2 Services Divine service is performed twice every Sunday.
3 Sacrament The sacrament is administered 4 times every year.
4 Registers Yes.
[Questions 5–13, no reply.]

284 Colemore 21M65/B4/2/18
Thomas Harrison, rector 1758–67
1 Repair of church The church is in a ruinous condition.
2 Services Divine service is performed alternately, morning and evening with Prior's Dean, a chapelry annexed, once a day according to custom time immemorial.
3 Sacrament Yes.
4 Registers Yes.
5 Terrier Yes.
6 Churchyard It is [fenced], and no incroachments have been made.
7 Alterations No.
8 Impropriation I have no curacy.
9 Repair of parsonage Yes.
10 Residence Yes.
11 Dissenters No.
12 Loss of benefactions No.
13 Misbehaviour Not that I know of. Every officer, I believe, performs his respective duty, unless the churchwardens in neglecting to present the church.

285 Combe 21M65/B4/2/35
Thomas Hill, vicar 1754–72
1 Repair of church The church with its chancel is in sufficient repair and all things provided for divine service and administration of the sacrament.
2 Services Divine service performed once every Sunday. It has been usual, the vicarage being small, to serve another church.
3 Sacrament The sacrament is administered 3 times a year.

4 Registers There are registers for christenings and burials and another for marriages according to a late Act of Parliament to prevent clandestine marriages etc.
5 Terrier No glebe-lands, no terrier.
6 Churchyard The churchyard is sufficiently fenced, and no incroachments made.
7 Alterations There has been no alterations in the fabric of the church, pews erected etc.
8 Impropriation Hold no curacy in this diocese from any impropriation.
9 Repair of parsonage The vicarage-house and outhouses in proper repair.
10 Residence Always reside.
11 Dissenters No dissenter of any denomination.
12 Loss of benefactions There are no benefactions or charities belonging to the poor.
13 Misbehaviour I know of no misbehaviour of any ecclesiastical officers, and the churchwardens etc. perform their respective duties.

286 Compton 21M65/B4/2/145
Robert Shipman, rector 1765–75
1 Repair of church In good repair. Divine service and the holy sacrament duly provided for.
2 Services Twice constantly.
3 Sacrament It is.
4 Registers We have.
5 Terrier No glebe etc. belonging to this rectory.
6 Churchyard Decently fenced and kept, and no encroachments.
7 Alterations No alterations of this sort have taken place.
8 Impropriation [No reply; not applicable.]
9 Repair of parsonage Repairs of the whole nearly compleated.
10 Residence The rector performs all his duty himself constantly.
11 Dissenters None of any sort.
12 Loss of benefactions Benefactions and charities annually and faithfully disposed of by the rector and churchwarden.
13 Misbehaviour No misbehaviour of the ecclesiastical or the church officers that I know of.

287 Corhampton 21M65/B4/2/180
John Upton, 'curate and schoolmaster, licenced by the late bishop'
1 Repair of church Church in good repair and things necessary for the sacrament provided.
2 Services Only once a fortnight during the summer season, the endowment being very small.
3 Sacrament Once a year only.
4 Registers Register books provided and duly kept.
5 Terrier No glebe belonging to the minister. No tythes or salary from the parish.

6 Churchyard Lately repaired, and no incroachments.
7 Alterations No alterations except necessary repairs.
8 Impropriation The tythes belong to the impropriator about £50 p.a.; reputed glebe of greater value. The endowment only £40, settled upon estates at several miles distance from Corhampton, partly for the church, and partly for taking care of a free school.
9 Repair of parsonage [No reply.]
10 Residence The minister resides in a free-school house, near the church.
11 Dissenters No dissenters in the parish.
12 Loss of benefactions Nothing to be compained of.
13 Misbehaviour Nothing to be complained of.

288 Crawley and Hunton 21M65/B4/2/146
Henry Taylor, rector 1755–85
1 Repair of church They are.
2 Services It is.
3 Sacrament It is.
4 Registers I have.
5 Terrier No.
6 Churchyard It is and hath no encroachment.
7 Alterations No.
8 Impropriation [No reply; not applicable.]
9 Repair of parsonage The house is in good repair. The barn and some other buildings are burnt down.
10 Residence I do reside.
11 Dissenters Not as I know.
12 Loss of benefactions I do not.
13 Misbehaviour Not as I know; I believe they do.

289 Crofton 21M65/B4/2/92
Gilbert Jackson BD, vicar of Titchfield 1734–79
1 Repair of church The chapel is in sufficient repair, and all things necessary for the celebrating of divine service are duly provided.
2 Services Divine service is performed in the chapel once every Sunday.
3 Sacrament It is.
4 Registers There are no weddings or burials at Crofton, and the christenings are registered in the parish register of Titchfield.
5 Terrier There are no lands that I know of belonging to this chapel.
6 Churchyard The churchyard is sufficently fenced, nor do I know of any incroachments.
7 Alterations No.
8 Impropriation I take it the church of Winchester are obliged to find a curate at Crofton and the vicar of Titchfield has always been paid for serving it, by the person who has from that church the lease of the great tithes.
9 Repair of parsonage There is no house belonging to that chapel.

10 Residence [No reply; answer implied in reply to no. 9.]
11 Dissenters [No reply.]
12 Loss of benefactions No.
13 Misbehaviour All do their duty.

290 Crondall 21M65/B4/2/62
John Bourne, vicar 1750–76
John Jones, curate
1 Repair of church All is well in this respect.
2 Services It is.
3 Sacrament It is.
4 Registers We have both.
5 Terrier There is no terrier.
6 Churchyard All is well in this respect.
7 Alterations The fabric of the church has not been altered, nor have any material alterations been made.
8 Impropriation [No reply; not applicable.]
9 Repair of parsonage It is.
10 Residence There is a constant resident curate, but not licenced.
11 Dissenters There is a Quakers' meeting-house.
12 Loss of benefactions We know of none.
13 Misbehaviour All is well in this respect.

291 Crux Easton 21M65/B4/2/36
John Burton, rector 1751–77
1 Repair of church Yes.
2 Services Yes.
3 Sacrament Yes.
4 Registers Yes.
5 Terrier There is no terrier.
6 Churchyard As usual, the greater part of the fence being only a dead hedge.
7 Alterations No.
8 Impropriation This question relates not to a rectory.
9 Repair of parsonage The house lately built, all the outhouses in good repair.
10 Residence Attendance at Winchester prevents the residence of the rector. There is a constant curate resident very near the parish, which contains but 8 houses.
11 Dissenters No dissenters or meeting-house.
12 Loss of benefactions None is known.
13 Misbehaviour No misbehaviour in the officers. The churchwarden and clerk doe their duty.

292 Deane 21M65/B4/2/63
William Hillman MA, rector 1757–73
1 Repair of church Yes.

2 Services Yes.
3 Sacrament Yes.
4 Registers There is a register for christenings and burials, but none for marriages.
5 Terrier No.
6 Churchyard No.
7 Alterations No.
8 Impropriation [No reply.] Query. If the stipend be the same as hath been usually paid and not adequate to the duty performed, where is the curate to apply for an increase [?]
9 Repair of parsonage Yes.
10 Residence Yes.
11 Dissenters There are no professed dissenters.
12 Loss of benefactions No.
13 Misbehaviour [No reply.]

293 Dibden 21M65/B4/2/134
Thomas Burman, rector 1758–84
1 Repair of church In good repair.
2 Services Twice every Sunday.
3 Sacrament 4 times every year.
4 Registers Registers of both kinds regularly kept.
5 Terrier An old terrier, but not exact, a new house having been built, but a new terrier presented.
6 Churchyard Some of the railing not good, but directed to be repaired.
7 Alterations No alteration.
8 Impropriation No curacy.
9 Repair of parsonage All in good repair.
10 Residence I do reside.
11 Dissenters None that I know of.
12 Loss of benefactions There is no benefaction that I have heard of.
13 Misbehaviour I have no concern with any ecclesiastical officers, and the churchwardens and other officers respectively perform their duty.

294 Dummer 21M65/B4/2/64
Thomas Stockwell, rector 1742–81
1 Repair of church They are in sufficient repair and everything provided etc.
2 Services It is.
3 Sacrament It is.
4 Registers I have.
5 Terrier A terrier of glebe-lands etc. is kept in the Registry, but as alterations has been made in the glebe-lands, another will shortly be made out and delivered.
6 Churchyard It is.
7 Alterations No.

8 Impropriation I serve the church myself.
9 Repair of parsonage They are.
10 Residence I reside myself.
11 Dissenters There are no dissenters.
12 Loss of benefactions I know not of any.
13 Misbehaviour I know not of any. Churchwardens etc. perform their respective duties.

295 East Dean 21M65/B4/2/122
Edward Jones, rector before 1734–1775
John Evans, curate
1 Repair of church Yes, the chapel has lately been put into very good repair.
2 Services Once a day only, [it] being a chapel annexed to Mottisfont.
3 Sacrament Yes.
4 Registers Yes.
5 Terrier I dont know.
6 Churchyard Yes; no.
7 Alterations No.
8 Impropriation The stipend paid me for the Sunday duty of the chapel, £30 p.a.
9 Repair of parsonage Yes.
10 Residence A school obliges me to reside at Romsey. Another gentleman takes care of Mottisfont, at present the rector.
11 Dissenters No.
12 Loss of benefactions No.
13 Misbehaviour No; yes.

296 East Meon (with chapels) 21M65/B4/2/93
Andrew Lewis Boisdaune, vicar 1763–88
1 Repair of church Yes.
2 Services Yes.
3 Sacrament The sacrament is administered 5 times every year.
4 Registers Yes.
5 Terrier [No reply.]
6 Churchyard The churchyard is well fenced, and there have been no incroachments.
7 Alterations All is well.
8 Impropriation [No reply; not applicable.]
9 Repair of parsonage Yes.
10 Residence I am doing duty at Haslar Hospital on His Majesty's service, and have a resident curate at my vicarage at £40 p.a.
11 Dissenters There is no meeting-house or place of worship for dissenters; and there are very few, if any, in the parish.
12 Loss of benefactions I know of no such thing.
13 Misbehaviour I know of no misbehavior of the ecclesiastical officers; and the officers of my church faithfully perform their respective duties.

297 Easton 21M65/B4/2/7

Charles Monckton, rector 1731–76
1 Repair of church Yes.
2 Services Yes.
3 Sacrament Yes.
4 Registers Yes.
5 Terrier Yes; I will enquire.
6 Churchyard Yes.
7 Alterations No.
8 Impropriation I reside in person upon a rectory.
9 Repair of parsonage Yes.
10 Residence Yes.
11 Dissenters William Mount Esq., lord of the mannor.
12 Loss of benefactions No.
13 Misbehaviour No.

298 East Tisted 21M65/B4/2/19

Thomas Brickenden, rector 1760–67
1 Repair of church Yes.
2 Services It is.
3 Sacrament It is.
4 Registers Yes.
5 Terrier [No reply.]
6 Churchyard The churchyard is sufficiently fenced and decently kept.
7 Alterations No.
8 Impropriation I am not possessed of a curacy.
9 Repair of parsonage Yes.
10 Residence I reside upon my parso<nage>.
11 Dissenters No dissenters in the parish.
12 Loss of benefactions No.
13 Misbehaviour No ecclesiastical officer has misbehaved. The churchwardens and other officers perform their duties.

299 East Woodhay (and Ashmansworth chapel) 21M65/B4/2/37

Henry Stephens, rector 1756–72
1 Repair of church The pews of the church are out of repair, as is the tower. The parishioners have agreed to repair the last.
2 Services Divine service is regularly performed twice a day.
3 Sacrament The sacrament is administered 4 times in each year.
4 Registers There is a proper register book etc.
5 Terrier I am informed a terrier <h>as formerly been delivered in.
6 Churchyard The churchyard is sufficiently fenced, and there have been no incroachments upon it.
7 Alterations No.
8 Impropriation [No reply; not applicable.]
9 Repair of parsonage All in repair.

10 Residence I reside upon my parsonage.
11 Dissenters No dissenters in the parish.
12 Loss of benefaction No benefaction witheld.
13 Misbehaviour [No reply.]

300 East Worldham 21M65/B4/2/20
Richard Jackson DD, vicar 1742/3–1779
[Unsigned.]
1 Repair of church Yes.
2 Services According to the usual custom.
3 Sacrament Yes.
4 Registers Yes.
5 Terrier None ever came into my hands.
6 Churchyard Yes.
7 Alterations No.
8 Impropriation Yes, with a stipend of £24 p.a.
9 Repair of parsonage Yes.
10 Residence No, but constantly attend.
11 Dissenters No.
12 Loss of benefactions No.
13 Misbehaviour No.

301 Ecchinswell 21M65/B4/2/65
Erlysman Peachy MA, vicar 1752–69
[Unsigned.]
1 Repair of church In sufficient repair.
2 Services Every other Sunday, being annexed to Kingsclere.
3 Sacrament As often as is customary.
4 Registers Yea.
5 Terrier No lands belong to the chapel.
6 Churchyard Sufficiently fenced.
7 Alterations No.
8 Impropriation It is annexed to Kingsclere.
9 Repair of parsonage In good repair.
10 Residence [No reply; answer implied in replies to questions 2 and 8.]
11 Dissenters None.
12 Loss of benefactions No.
13 Misbehaviour In no fault.

302 Eling (and Ower chapel) 21M65/B4/2/135
Samuel Speed, vicar 1757–75
[Unsigned.]
1 Repair of church All in good repair.
2 Services Divine service is performed twice every Sunday.
3 Sacrament The sacrament is administered 5 times in the year.

4 Registers Register books are provided.
5 Terrier No perfect terrier ever came to my sight, but I shall endeavour to procure one as soon as possible.
6 Churchyard The churchyard is sufficiently fenced and decently kept.
7 Alterations No alteration in the fabrick etc. of the church, but repaired as often as occasion.
8 Impropriation Not possessed of a curacy.
9 Repair of parsonage The parsonage-house is in very good repair.
10 Residence I do not reside in the vicarage, having licence from the bishop to reside upon another parsonage. And keep a curate not licenced.
11 Dissenters 2 or 3 families of dissenters.
12 Loss of benefactions I do not know of any abuse of charity.
13 Misbehaviour I have had no concern with any ecclesiastical officers. The churchwardens and other parish officers perform their respective duties.

303 Ellisfield 21M65/B4/2/66
Edward Peck, rector 1734–76
1 Repair of church Yes.
2 Services Performed twice on every Sunday, except in case of illness, or to assist a neighbour.
3 Sacrament At least three times in a year administered.
4 Registers We have both.
5 Terrier I have a copy of a terrier taken out of the office a few years ago.
6 Churchyard The churchyard is sufficiently fenced and decently kept, and no encroachment made.
7 Alterations No.
8 Impropriation [No reply; not applicable.]
9 Repair of parsonage Yes.
10 Residence I reside upon my parsonage constantly.
11 Dissenters No dissenters.
12 Loss of benefactions No abuse in this article.
13 Misbehaviour I have no complaint to make on this article.

304 Empshott 21M65/B4/2/21
Richard Newlin, vicar 1728/9–1772
1 Repair of church It is, and all things necessary are provided for the celebration of divine service, and the administration of the holy sacrament.
2 Services Divine service is performed in this church but once on every Sunday, morning and evening alternately; never known to be twice on a Sunday. The revenue of the vicarage being but £30 p.a.. The parish is very small and the houses are so situated, that there is scarce any one much more than a mile distant from some other church where there is divine service on the other part of the day.
3 Sacrament It is.
4 Registers I have the several register books required; and also one for banns and marriages according to the late Act.

5 Terrier <Th>ere is but little more than three <acr>es of glebe land, besides the garden <and o>rchard, belonging to this vicarage.
6 Churchyard It is.
7 Alterations No.
8 Impropriation I am possessed of the curacy of Liss, and apprehend that the stipend allowed by the impropriator is but £20, though the computed yearly value of the impropriation is above £150. I served the cure some years for that stipend, but since the Right Hon. Earl of Tilney have been in possession of the tithes, I have been paid £24 p.a., and of late have been allowed £30 (the parish being extensive and populous), though my Lord accounts what he gives above £20 as his own free gift.
9 Repair of parsonage The vicarage house (there being no other building belonging thereunto) is in proper repair.
10 Residence I do not reside upon the vicarag<e>, having leave from Your Lords<hip> to reside in the parsonage hou<se> of Greatham, and to serve that cure, which is situate between Empshott and L<iss> about a mile distant from each of those churches, which I regularly supp<ly>. The vicarage house of Empshott is a mean cottage, and never known to be inhabited by <the> vicar, it being lett for 30*s*. a year to a family kept by the parish.
11 Dissenters There are none.
12 Loss of benefactions I know of none.
13 Misbehaviour No; the officers of the church perform their respective duties.

305 Eversley 21M65/B4/2/67
Richard Cope BA, rector 1745/6–
[Unsigned.]
1 Repair of church Yes.
2 Services Yes.
3 Sacrament Yes.
4 Registers Yes.
5 Terrier [No reply.]
6 Churchyard Yes. No incroachment.
7 Alterations No.
8 Impropriation [No reply; not applicable.]
9 Repair of parsonage Yes.
10 Residence Yes.
11 Dissenters No.
12 Loss of benefactions No.
13 Misbehaviour [No reply.]

306 Ewhurst 21M65/B4/2/68
Thomas Obourn, rector 1762–99
[Unsigned.]
1 Repair of church In sufficient repair.

2 Services As often as is customary.
3 Sacrament As often as is customary.
4 Registers There is a register book.
5 Terrier No lands belong to the rector.
6 Churchyard Sufficiently fenced.
7 Alterations No.
8 Impropriation It is a rectory.
9 Repair of parsonage No house.
10 Residence [No reply; answer implied in return to no.9.]
11 Dissenters None.
12 Loss of benefactions No.
13 Misbehaviour In no fault.

307 Fareham 21M65/B4/2/94
Thomas A. Woolls, vicar 1739–89
1 Repair of church My church with its chancel is in good repair — and all things necessary are provided for the celebration of divine service, etc.
2 Services Divine service is performed in my church twice every Sunday.
3 Sacrament I administer the sacrament every month.
4 Registers There is a register-book for christenings and burials, and also a register book for marriages etc.
5 Terrier I have no terrier.
6 Churchyard My churchyard is sufficiently fenced and decently kept; and I know not of any incroachments.
7 Alterations [No reply.]
8 Impropriation [No reply; not applicable.]
9 Repair of parsonage My vicarage-house has been entirely rebuilt, at my own expense.
10 Residence I do reside etc.
11 Dissenters There *are* dissenters in my parish.
12 Loss of benefactions I do not know of any benefaction which hath been witheld from those for whom it was designed; nor of the abuse of any charity.
13 Misbehaviour The ecclesiastical officers have not misbehaved themselves by taking undue fees etc. The churchwardens, clerk, sexton, and other officers perform their respective duties.

308 Farley Chamberlayne 21M65/B4/2/147
John St John, rector 1765–86
[Unsigned.]
1 Repair of church Yes.
2 Services Yes.
3 Sacrament Yes.
4 Registers Yes.
5 Terrier No.
6 Churchyard No.

7 Alterations, 8 Impropriation [No replies.]
9 Repair of parsonage No.
10 Residence Yes.
11 Dissenters None.
12 Loss of benefactions No.
13 Misbehaviour [No reply.]

309 Farlington 21M65/B4/2/181
Peter Evans, rector 1737–81 6 September 1765
1 Repair of church Our church and chancel are in good repair. And so are all things necessary for divine service, and both the sacraments.
2 Services I do myself perform divine service in the church twice every Sunday; and once on every holiday throughout the year.
3 Sacrament I baptize every child that is brought to the church to be baptized, and do administer the Lord's Supper 4 times in the year.
4 Registers We have a paper register book for christenings and burials, and have also a printed and ruled register book for marriages pursuant to the said Act of Parliament.
5 Terrier We have a terrier of all the glebe-lands, <bu>t no pensions or any other dues that the law gives us any right to, belonging to this parsonage. I delivered a copy of the terrier signed by myself and the churchwardens to Mr Archdeacon Eden at his parochial visitation on the 9th of May 1745.
6 Churchyard Our churchyard is well fenced, and free from any incroachments.
7 Alterations Our church hath been no otherwise altered than from a ruinous condition to a good and decent repair.
8 Impropriation I am rector of this parish and have the tythes great and smal[l] for my stipend.
9 Repair of parsonage My parsonage-house and outhouses are all in very good repair, for I built them all new since I had the rectory in the year 1737 at about £1,000 expence.
10 Residence I do reside upon my parsonage, and have been resident upon it ever since the house was finished and fit to dwell in, which was in the year 1740.
11 Dissenters We have no professed dissenters, and consequently no meeting-house in the parish; and yet alas we have more absentees from the church than I could wish.
12 Loss of benefactions I find a memorandum in an old parish book April 23, 1711, that £20 were given by one Mr Winter, the interest whereof to be distributed to such poor widows of Farlington as had no relief from the parish. And in another book I find that at a vestry held in the year <...> it was agreed by the parishioners that they would divide the principal money among themselves, and sink it into their own pockets, which I believe was done, for I could get no further account of it. I shewed these memoranda to Mr Archdeacon Eden at his parochial visitation, who deemed the money irrecoverably lost.
13 Misbehaviour We have had no litigation to try the moderation of the officers of the ecclesiastical court since I have been in this parish, 28 years.

Our clerk does his duty very well; we have no sexton; and our church-wardens from time to time would do their duty full as well as they do, if they were not sworn to it.

310 Farringdon 21M65/B4/2/22

William Roman, rector 1761–82

[Unsigned.]

1 Repair of church In decent repair.

2 Services Yes.

3 Sacrament The sacrament is administered 4 times.

4 Registers There are proper registers.

5 Terrier [No reply.]

6 Churchyard The fences are decently kept up.

7 Alterations The fabric has not been altered, or galleries built; one pew erected.

8 Impropriation Faringdon parsonage is not an impropriation.

9 Repair of parsonage Repairing for some years past.

10 Residence The rector resides at his other parsonage of Clatford. The curate at Selborne, the next parish to Faringdon.

11 Dissenters None.

12 Loss of benefactions I know of none.

13 Misbehaviour None that I know of. The churchwardens etc. have not behaved amiss.

311 Fordingbridge 21M65/B4/2/109

William Barford DD, vicar 1762–73

1 Repair of church Yes.

2 Services Divine service is performed in the church twice every Sunday.

3 Sacrament The sacrament is administered at the 3 great festivals, and on the Sunday after Michaelmas each year.

4 Registers Yes.

5 Terrier No terrier having been delivered to the present incumbent, he is now preparing one. No pensions are due to the vicarige.

6 Churchyard Yes.

7 Alterations No.

8 Impropriation It is an appropriated vicarige, augmented with a portion of the great tythes.

9 Repair of parsonage Left in bad repair to the present incumbent; but the repairs almost finished.

10 Residence The incumbent resides at present only 4 months in the year; His Lordship having been pleased to give him leave to be absent on account of an office he holds in the University of Cambridge. He has 2 constantly resident curates.

11 Dissenters The most numerous class of dissenters is that of the Presbyterians. Besides them are many Independents, and a few Anabaptists. They all assemble at the same place for divine worship. There are 5 families of Quakers.

12 Loss of benefactions No.
13 Misbehaviour No ecclesiastical officers have behaved amiss. The churchwardens, clerk, etc. discharge their duties properly.

312 Froyle 21M65/B4/2/23
Thomas Loggin, vicar 1734–72
1 Repair of church Yea.
2 Services Yea.
3 Sacrament Yea.
4 Registers Yea.
5 Terrier Orchard and garden only.
6 Churchyard The churchyard is fenced and I know of no incroachment.
7 Alterations The fabrick of the church has not been altered, nor anything done requiring a faculty.
8 Impropriation I am possessed of no curacy.
9 Repair of parsonage Vicarage house etc. in proper repair.
10 Residence Reside.
11 Dissenters Quakers, and no meeting-house.
12 Loss of benefactions I know not of any benefaction withheld, or of the abuse of any charity regarding either the church or poor.
13 Misbehaviour [No reply.]

313 Fyfield 21M65/B4/2/38
Henry White MA, rector 1762–88
[Unsigned.]
1 Repair of church All in good repair.
2 Services Every other Sunday.
3 Sacrament Yes.
4 Registers Yes.
5 Terrier None to be found.
6 Churchyard Yes.
7 Alterations No.
8 Impropriation [No reply; not applicable.]
9 Repair of parsonage Repairing.
10 Residence Yes.
11 Dissenters None.
12 Loss of benefactions No.
13 Misbehaviour All well.

314 Goodworth Clatford 21M65/B4/2/39
George Snell, vicar 1749–82
1 Repair of church In good repair; all provided.
2 Services Twice every Sunday.
3 Sacrament It is.
4 Registers We have both.

5 Terrier Truly made and delivered.
6 Churchyard Decently fenced and kept without incroachment.
7 Alterations Not in my time.
8 Impropriation [No reply; not applicable.]
9 Repair of parsonage In proper repair.
10 Residence I do reside.
11 Dissenters One only.
12 Loss of benefaction [I know] of none.
13 Misbehaviour Not that I know; perform well.

315 Greatham 21M65/B4/2/24
Richard Yalden, rector 1754–85
1 Repair of church It is.
2 Services It is.
3 Sacrament It is.
4 Registers We have.
5 Terrier I have.
6 Churchyard It is.
7 Alterations No.
8 Impropriation The rectory £95. The curacy £40 p.a.
9 Repair of parsonage They are.
10 Residence A resident curate.
11 Dissenters No.
12 Loss of benefactions No.
13 Misbehaviour Not that I know of.

316 Harbridge 21M65/B4/2/110
John Maule MA, vicar of Ringwood 1750–78
[Unsigned.]
1 Repair of church They are and all things necessary for those purposes are provided.
2 Services It is performed twice, except in the months November, December, and January, when it has been customary to have service only in the morning.
3 Sacrament It is administered 4 times in the year.
4 Registers Books necesssary for the said purposes are provided.
5 Terrier Upon enquiry, no terrier to be found in the bishop's office. The composition for the vicarage of Ringwood at large in Ecton.[37]
6 Churchyard All is well.
7 Alterations No alteration. None.
8 Impropriation [No reply; not applicable.]
9 Repair of parsonage They are.
10 Residence The vicar of Ringwood is resident.
11 Dissenters None.
12 Loss of benefaction None.
13 Misbehaviour [No reply.]

317 Hartley Mauditt 21M65/B4/2/25

Richard Willis, rector 1714–83
[Unsigned.]
1 Repair of church Church etc. under repair by the patron. All things necessary are provided in a sumptuous manner.
2 Services Performed twice.
3 Sacrament It is.
4 Registers We have.
5 Terrier An exchange of glebe has been made, much to the advantage of the incumbent.
6 Churchyard Now under repair by the patron.
7 Alterations Nothing hath been altered.
8 Impropriation I am possessed of the curacy of West Wordelham, for which I receive the old stipend £10 p.a. Duty once a Sunday; prayers, a sermon once a month — apprehend the impropriation might afford a larger stipend.
9 Repair of parsonage Lately new built by the patron.
10 Residence I serve the church myself.
11 Dissenters No dissenters.
12 Loss of benefactions I know of none.
13 Misbehaviour None have misbehaved to my knowledge. Churchwardens etc. do their respective duties.

318 Hartley Wespall 21M65/B4/2/69

Roger Huggett, rector 1762–69
1 Repair of church It is in very good repair; and all things are necessary [sic] for celebration of the divine services.
2 Services It is performed twice every Sunday; except in cases of sickness etc.
3 Sacrament It is.
4 Registers There are register books proper for the several occasions of marriages, christenings and burials.
5 Terrier I find no terrier of the glebe etc., nor any note of pensions; nor can I learn that any copies of such were ever delivered into the Registry.
6 Churchyard It is; nor hath any person to my knowledge at any time incroached upon it.
7 Alterations It hath not been altered, nor pews erected, nor vaults dug, nor dead bodies removed, since my incumbency.
8 Impropriation I am possessed of no curacy.
9 Repair of parsonage The parsonage-house, with the barns and all other the buildings, are in very proper repair.
10 Residence I do; except when I attend on duty in the King's Free Chapel within the castle of Windsor: at which time I either supply my church from thence, or get it regularly supplied by some neighbouring clergyman.
11 Dissenters There are neither dissenters, nor conventicle of any denomination within the parish.
12 Loss of benefactions I know of no abuse of any charitable benefactions to this parish.

13 Misbehaviour I am emboldened by the question being thus put to answer, that upon an inquiry of your clergy, Your Lordship may fully know whether, or how far, the ecclesiastical office<rs> may have herein misbehaved themselves, either by demanding as a fee what may not be in the table of fees injoyned by the canons; or demanding more than the said canons have ordered to be paid for such fees as are by them regularly established.

319 Havant 21M65/B4/2/95
Richard Bingham, rector 1727–65
Isaac Hodgson, curate
1 Repair of church Yes.
2 Services Yes.
3 Sacrament Yes.
4 Registers Yes.
5 Terrier I know not.
6 Churchyard The yard is well fenced; Thomas Pollington has made a road into a celler through part of it.
7 Alterations Not since I had the care of the church.
8 Impropriation I am possessed of the cure of Havant with a stipend of £50 p.a. The value of the impropriation is upwards of £200 p.a.
9 Repair of parsonage Yes.
10 Residence The rector does not reside, nor has the curate taken a licence for Havant, but will if required.
11 Dissenters Too many! There is a dissenting meeting-house as well as a mass-house.
12 Loss of benefactions I know of no such thing.
13 Misbehaviour Very well.

320 Hawkley 21M65/B4/2/26
Richard Yalden, curate 1761–85
1 Repair of church It is.
2 Services Once [a Sunday], being a chappel.
3 Sacrament It is.
4 Registers I have.
5 Terrier I have.
6 Churchyard It is.
7 Alterations No.
8 Impropriation Impropriation £100; curacy £30.
9 Repair of parsonage They are.
10 Residence I do.
11 Dissenters No.
12 Loss of benefactions No.
13 Misbehaviour None that I know of.

321 Hayling South and Hayling North
Isaac Skelton, vicar 1745–73 21M65/B4/2/96
1 Repair of church In decent repair. They are.

2 Services There are a church and [a] chapel in Hayling, and divine service is commonly performed twice every Sunday; at one in the forenoon, and the other in the afternoon, alternately.
3 Sacrament It is.
4 Registers We have.
5 Terrier There are in Hayling-South about 40 acres of glebe-land; but there is no terrier that I know of.
6 Churchyard Sufficiently fenced; but Thomas Rogers of Hayling-North made his fence last year about 12 inches further into the chapel-yard than it was before; and cut down a tree that was in the ditch of the chapel yard.
7 Alterations I think not.
8 Impropriation I am not possessed of a curacy.
9 Repair of parsonage In proper repair.
10 Residence I officiate in my parish, but reside, at present, at Havant on account of my health.
11 Dissenters There is one Roman Catholic family in Hayling; but there is no meeting-house there.
12 Loss of benefactions I do not know of any.
13 Misbehaviour I believe not.

322 Headbourne Worthy 21M65/B4/2/148
Thomas Nelson MA, rector 1758–71
[Signed] John Lucas, 'officiating minister for Mr Kerby'
1 Repair of church Yes.
2 Services Yes.
3 Sacrament Yes.
4 Registers Yes.
5 Terrier [No reply.]
6 Churchyard The churchyard [is] in good order and no one hath incroached upon it.
7 Alterations No.
8 Impropriation The stipend is £35 p.a., the same as has usually been allowed.
9 Repair of parsonage Yes.
10 Residence Yes.
11 Dissenters No.
12 Loss of benefactions No.
13 Misbehaviour No.

323 Heckfield 21M65/B4/2/70
John Goodwin LLB, vicar 1763–67
[Unsigned.]
1 Repair of church Yes.
2 Services Yes.
3 Sacrament Yes.
4 Registers Yes.

5 Terrier There is no terrier.
6 Churchyard Yes.
7 Alterations No.
8 Impropriation No stipend allowed by the impropriator.
9 Repair of parsonage Repaired by the present vicar.
10 Residence The vicar resides.
11 Dissenters No.
12 Loss of benefaction No.
13 Misbehaviour No.

324 Highclere 21M65/B4/2/40
Richard Davies, rector 1757–97
1 Repair of church The church and chancel are in sufficient repair, and all things necessary for the celebration of divine service and administration of the holy sacrament provided.
2 Services Divine service is performed in Highclere church twice every Sunday.
3 Sacrament The sacrament is administered so often in each year, that every parishioner may receive it more than three times.
4 Registers We have a register book for christenings and burials; and also Fox's New Register Book for marriages.
5 Terrier I have no terrier of the glebe-lands etc.
6 Churchyard The churchyard is properly fenced and kept without any encroachments.
7 Alterations No.
8 Impropriation I have no curacy.
9 Repair of parsonage The parsonage house etc. are in proper repair.
10 Residence I reside on my parsonage and keep no curate.
11 Dissenters I know of no dissenters in the parish; and am sure there is no meeting-house.
12 Loss of benefactions I know of no benefaction at all, nor of the abuse of any charity.
13 Misbehaviour I neither know nor have heard of any misbehavior in any of the ecclesiastical officers, and I have nothing to lay to the charge of the officers of my parish.

325 Hinton Ampner 21M65/B4/2/182
Thomas Wingfield DD, rector 1758–73
1 Repair of church They all are, and supplied with all things necessary.
2 Services It is.
3 Sacrament It is.
4 Registers I have both, but wish the late act was repealed, because I think it is attended with very bad consequences, having not had any one marriage for more than seven years, the time that I have been rector of this church.
5 Terrier I have, and likewise have secured a plan of the glebe-lands to be drawn which I intend to leave for the benefit of my successors.

6 Churchyard It is, nor hath any encroachment been made upon it.
7 Alterations There hath been a large vault dug in the chancel under the communion table by Lady Howell for the burial of the late Mr Legge, for which I received no composition, I desire this may be received and entered as a *caveat* in the court against any faculty or licence for the same being granted to the said Lady Howell till I have certified the court of my being satisfied for the same.
8 Impropriation [No reply; not applicable.]
9 Repair of parsonage My house with all things belonging to it is in very good and excellent repair, [I] having expended a great sum thereon since my being possessed thereof.
10 Residence I do not constantly reside on account of my health, labouring under a very grievous paralytic disorder, for which I am advised by the physician to be in London all the winter, for the sake of warmth, being not able to endure the cold here in the country in the winter season. And in my absence, as well as when I am personally resident at my parsonage-house (for as yet I am incapable of doing much duty, saving that now and then, occasionally, I read prayers) the Revd Mr Durnford, rector of Bramdean, who is my very near neighbour, does all the duty of my parish (it being the custom to begin service at his church much later than it is at mine, by which he is enabled to serve <my church> and for which I allow him a sufficient stipend; and finding myself growing much better I desire by continuing the same regimen I have hitherto observed, in time to gain a perfect cur<e>.
11 Dissenters There are no dissenters of any denomination in my parish, nor is there any meeting-house.
12 Loss of benefactions I do not; but all that I do know of are distributed regularly, according to the will of the benefactors.
13 Misbehaviour I have no complaint on this head.

326 Hordle 21M65/B4/2/111

Bolton Simpson DD, vicar 'of Milford and Hordle' 1759–86
1 Repair of church Yes.
2 Services Divine service is performed at Hordle only in the afternoon and at Milford in the morning.
3 Sacrament Yes.
4 Registers Yes.
5 Terrier I have no glebe-lands etc. at Hordle. It is only a chapel.
6 Churchyard No incroachments on the churchyard. Well fenced.
7 Alterations No.
8 Impropriation I have no curacy.
9 Repair of parsonage No house at Hordle. I reside at Milford.
10 Residence I reside upon my vicarage at Milford.
11 Dissenters A very few dissenters. They have no meeting-house and frequently attend the chapel.
12 Loss of benefactions I know of no benefaction which hath been withheld or abused.
13 Misbehaviour I dont know that any ecclesiastical officers have misbehaved themselves, and the parish officers, I believe, have done their respective duties.

327 Houghton 21M65/B4/2/123

R. Hinckesman, rector

1 Repair of church Our church and chancel are in very good repair. And everything is regularly provided for the celebration of divine service, and the administration of the holy sacrament.

2 Services Divine service is performed twice on every Sunday in our church.

3 Sacrament The sacrament is administered 4 times in every year.

4 Registers We have a register book for christenings and burials, and also a register book for banns and marriages, pursua<nt> to the directions of the Act of Parliament.

5 Terrier I have a copy of the terrier of the glebe-lands etc., which I took out of the <R>egister's office.

6 Churchyard Our churchyard is sufficiently fenced, decently kept, and not incroached upon.

7 Alterations The fabrick of our church and chancel have not been at all altered, but have been lately very handsomely repaired and beautified.

8 Impropriation The rector of Houghton is possessed of all great and small tythes.

9 Repair of parsonage My parsonage house, barns, out-houses and other buildings thereunto belonging are in proper repair.

10 Residence I am constantly resident on my parsonage when my ill-health will permit me. When I am absent, Mr Powell, my next neighbour at Broughton, supplys my church twice on every Sunday.

11 Dissenters We have no dissenters of any denomination in our parish.

12 Loss of benefactions We have a yearly benefaction of £2. 6*s*. 8*d*. left to the poor of our parish, which is regularly disposed of by myself and the parish officers. We have likewise an acre of meadow ground belonging to the poor, lying in a meadow called Oakley Meadow; the rent of which is yearly disposed of as above among the poor.

13 Misbehaviour I dont hear of any complaints against the ecclesiastical officers. And our own parish officers perform their respective duties in a proper manner.

328 Hound 21M65/B4/2/136

James Scott, vicar 1761–1811

[Unsigned.]

[No replies.]

329 Hursley and Otterbourne 21M65/B45/2/149

William White MA, vicar 1747–80

1 Repair of church The churches and chancels both at Hursley and Otterbourn are in good repair; and nothing is wanting for the celebration of divine service or the administration of the sacrament.

2 Services There are two churches belonging to the same living, in each of which divine service is performed once every Sunday.

3 Sacrament The sacrament is administered in each church 4 times in every year.
4 Registers There is a register book in each parish for christenings and burials, and another for marriages.
5 Terrier There is no terrier of the glebe-lands, nor note in writing of the pensions and dues belonging to the vicarage. If it be necessary I will procure them.
6 Churchyard The churchyards both at Hursley and Otterbourn are sufficiently fenced.
7 Alterations Nothing of this sort has been done without a faculty.
8 Impropriation I have no curacy.
9 Repair of parsonage I apprehend the vicarage-house with the out-buildings are in proper repair.
10 Residence I reside upon my vicarage.
11 Dissenters There are no dissenters in either of <my paris>hes.
12 Loss of benefactions I know of no s<uc>h be<ne>faction, or of abuse of any charity.
13 Misbehaviour I know of no cause of complaint in either of these respects.

330 Hurstbourne Priors 21M65/B4/2/41
John Blair, vicar 1745/6–1783
[Unsigned.]
1 Repair of church In pretty good repair.
2 Services The stated service is only once a Sunday. The income is very small.
3 Sacrament It is.
4 Registers Yes.
5 Terrier There is no terrier.
6 Churchyard It is.
7 Alterations No.
8 Impropriation It is a vicarage.
9 Repair of parsonage There is no house.
10 Residence Mr Blair serves the church from Whitchurch.
11 Dissenters There are no dissenters in the parish.
12 Loss of benefactions No.
13 Misbehaviour I believe not. The parish officers perform their duties.

331 Ibsley 21M65/B4/2/112
William Barford, rector 1762–73
1 Repair of church Yes.
2 Services Yes.
3 Sacrament The sacrament is administered on the three chief festivals and at Michaelmas.
4 Registers Yes.
5 Terrier There is no glebe-land; a cottage only with a small garden. There are no pensions belonging to the parsonage.

6 Churchyard Yes.
7 Alterations No.
8 Impropriation Ibsley is joined with Fordingbridge in one presentation, and has all the tythes.
9 Repair of parsonage The parsonage, which is a small cottage, with the outhouses, is in a sufficient state of repair.
10 Residence The residence of the minister and his curate is at Fordingbridge. The present incumbent is there 4 months in the year.
11 Dissenters No dissenters in the parish.
12 Loss of benefactions No.
13 Misbehaviour The parish officers perform their respective duties properly.

332 Idsworth 21M65/B4/2/97
Richard Keats, curate
1 Repair of church [No reply.]
2 Services It is performed once only, according to custom.
3 Sacrament It is administered 4 times every year.
4 Registers Yes.
[Questions 5–13 no reply.]

333 Itchen Abbas 21M65/B4/2/8
John Burton DD, rector 1735–74
[Unsigned.]
1 Repair of church Yes.
2 Services Yes.
3 Sacrament Yes.
4 Registers Yes.
5 Terrier No terrier.
6 Churchyard Yes.
7 Alterations No.
8 Impropriation [No reply; not applicable.]
9 Repair of parsonage Yes.
10 Residence The rector resides. His attendance at Winchester being necessary, he has a resident [curate].
11 Dissenters No dissenters.
12 Loss of benefactions No.
13 Misbehaviour None have misbehaved.

334 Itchen Stoke 21M65/B4/2/9
John Burroughs, rector 1730–74
Ellis Jones, curate
[Unsigned.]
1 Repair of church The church of Itchenstoke is in good repair, but the chancel far otherwise; and has been presented at several visitations.

2 Services Yes.
3 Sacrament Yes.
4 Registers Yes.
5 Terrier A terrier of the glebe is delivered to the Register.
6 Churchyard Yes; no.
7 Alterations No.
8 Impropriation No curacy.
9 Repair of parsonage Yes.
10 Residence The Revd Mr Ellis Jones is constant resident curate.
11 Dissenters None.
12 Loss of benefactions None.
13 Misbehaviour Yes.

335 Kimpton 21M65/B4/2/42
Edward Foyle, rector 1750–84
1 Repair of church Yes.
2 Services Yes.
3 Sacrament Yes.
4 Registers Yes.
5 Terrier I have a terrier of the glebe belonging to my parsonage.
6 Churchyard The churchyard is well fenced, and no incroachments have been made upon it.
7 Alterations The fabric of the church not altered in any respect, except the windows, which are some of them enlarged to give better light.
8 Impropriation Mine is a rectory.
9 Repair of parsonage Yes.
10 Residence I reside at present at Salisbury and have a constant resident curate at Kimpton.
11 Dissenters I have no dissenters in my parish.
12 Loss of benefactions I do not.
13 Misbehaviour The ecclesiastical officers have not misbehaved that I know of, and the parish officers, I believe, do their duty.

336 Kingsclere 21M65/B4/2/183
[Unsigned.]
1 Repair of church In good repair.
2 Services Yea.
3 Sacrament Yea.
4 Registers Yea.
5 Terrier No glebe-lands besides a small meadow adjoining to the vicarage-house.
6 Churchyard Sufficiently fenced.
7 Alterations No.
8 Impropriations It is a vicarage, endowed.
9 Repair of parsonage The vicarage-house is in sufficient repair, and the dove house also, the only building belonging to it.

10 Residence The vicar res[i]des upon his rectory of Faccomb and has a resident curate at Kingsclere.
11 Dissenters No.
12 Loss of benefactions No.
13 Misbehaviour In no fault.

337 Kings Somborne 21M65/B4/2/124
Sir Charles Mill, vicar 1747–93
[Unsigned.]
[No replies.]

338 Kings Worthy 21M65/B4/2/184
John Imber LLB, rector 1735/6–1768
1 Repair of church King's Worthy church, with its chancel, is in good repair; and all things necessary are provided for the celebration of divine service and the administration of the holy sacraments.
2 Services Divine service is performed in the church of King's Worthy twice every Sunday ordinarily.
3 Sacrament The sacrament of the Lord's Supper is administered at least 3 times in the year, and every parishioner is exhorted to communicate.
4 Registers Here is a register book for christenings and burials; and also a register book for marriages pursuant to the directions conteined in the famous Act of Parliament *for the better preventing of clandestine marriages*.
5 Terrier A terrier of all the glebe-lands etc. is delivered to the Register.
6 Churchyard The churchyard is sufficiently fenced and no incroachment on it that we know of.
7 Alterations The fabric of the church hath not been altered in any respect, save the addition of a cieling to the body of the church at my own expense about 28 years ago; and a gallery built by subscription 24 or 25 years ago.
8 Impropriation No curacy.
9 Repair of parsonage The parsonage-house, with the barns, stable, etc., is in proper repair.
10 Residence I have resided on the parsonage of King's Worthy ever since January 1735/6, except when at my vicarage of Itchenstoke.
11 Dissenters No dissenters in the parish, but one, a Papist, Widow Gaiger.
12 Loss of benefactions None.
13 Misbehaviour [No reply to first question;] yes.

339 Knights Enham (Enham) 21M65/B4/2/43
William Haygarth MA, rector 1747/8–1782
[Unsigned.]
Answers to questions 1–4 'yes'; to questions 5–12, 'all right'.

340 Leckford 21M65/B4/2/125
Nehemiah Ring, vicar 1760–66
William Lynch, curate
1 Repair of church The church etc. are in good repair.

2 Services Divine service never was performed but once on a Sunday at Leckford.
3 Sacrament Yes.
4 Registers Yes; yes.
5 Terrier The terrier is in the hands of the prebend and St John's College, Oxford.[38]
6 Churchyard Yes, and no encroachment made upon it.
7 Alterations No.
8 Impropriation [No reply.]
9 Repair of parsonage The parsonage-house etc., repaired this summer. The vicarage-house lately rebuilt.
10 Residence The curate lives very nigh, but not in the parish.
11 Dissenters No.
12 Loss of benefactions No.
13 Misbehaviour No.

341 Liss 21M65/B4/2/27
[Signed] Richard Newlin, curate
1 Repair of church It is, and all things very decent for their proper services.
2 Services Divine service but once on every Sunday. On my first admission to this curacy, I offered to apply to the impropriator for an augmentation of the stipend for the performance of divine service twice on every Sunday; and was then told by the chief of the parish that they were satisfied with the usual service, and desired no alteration. The service is on the morning and evening alternately.
3 Sacrament It is.
4 Registers Yes.
5 Terrier [No reply.]
6 Churchyard It is; no.
7 Alterations No.
8. Impropriation I apprehend that this stipend allowed by the impropriator for serving this cure is but £20 p.a.; that the yearly value of this impropriation is above £150. I served it for some years for that stipend, but since the Right Hon. Earl of Tilney have been in possession of the tithes, I have been paid £24; and of late have been allowed £30 p.a. (the parish being extensive and populous) though my lord accounts what he gives above £20 as his own free gift [cf. above, *sub* Empshott no. 304].
9 Repair of parsonage There is no parsonage-house. The barn and other buildings are in proper repair.
10 Residence I do not reside on this curacy, there being no house belonging to the minister; but live in the parsonage in Greatham, the parish between Liss and Empshot [Cf. above, *sub* Greatham no. 315].
11 Dissenters There is one family Roman Catholic, and one of the people called Quakers, but no meeting-house.
12 Loss of benefactions I know of none.
13 Misbehaviour Each church officer regularly performs his respective duty.

342 Litchfield 21M65/B4/2/44

Edmund Elyott, rector of 'Ludshelfe alias Litchfield' 1757–81

1 Repair of church Yes.

2 Services Service has always been performed at Woodcotts every other Sunday in the afternoon, and on those Sundays there has never been afternoon service at Litchfield, the congregations being made up in a great part of the same people.

3 Sacrament Yes.

4 Registers Yes.

5 Terrier Yes.

6 Churchyard Churchyard fenced but at present a little out of repair, which may be easily mended by a few rails which is all that is wanting.

7 Alterations No.

8 Impropriation [No reply; not applicable.]

9 Repair of parsonage Yes.

10 Residence I reside at Whitchurch, 2 miles from Litchfield, and serve it myself, the parsonage-house being but a cottage.

11 Dissenters None.

12 Loss of benefactions No.

13 Misbehaviour No misbehaviour. Officers do their duty.

343 Littleton 21M65/B4/2/150

Thomas Rees, curate –1769

1 Repair of church Yes.

2 Services Once only by custom.

3 Sacrament Yes.

4 Registers Yes.

5 Terrier There is no glebe that I know of.

6 Churchyard It is and there is no incroachment.

7 Alterations Not to my knowledge.

8 Impropriation The stipend is £20 p.a.

9 Repair of parsonage The house is, so far as I know, in good repair.

10 Residence I reside in Winchester on account of attending the duty of the cathedral.

11 Dissenters There are no dissenters of any denomination.

12 Loss of benefactions I know of none.

13 Misbehaviour I know of no misbehaviour nor have I cause of complaint against any ecclesiastical officer.

344 Lockerley 21M65/B4/2/126

Edward Jones, rector before 1734–1775

John Evans, curate

1 Repair of church Yes.

2 Services Once only, [it] being a chapel annexed to Mottisfont.

3 Sacrament Yes.

4 Registers Both.

5 Terrier I dont know.
6 Churchyard Yes.
7 Alterations No.
8 Impropriation I serve the c[h]apel on Sunday, the gentleman generally resident at Mottisfont does the weekly duty.
9 Repair of parsonage Yes.
10 Residence A school obliges me to reside at Romsey.
11 Dissenters Some few Anabaptists who have built a room to assemble in.
12 Loss of benefactions No.
13 Misbehaviour No; yes.

345 Longparish 21M65/B4/2/45
Henry Binfield MA, vicar 1762–5
George Ryves Hawker, curate
[Replies given to only the following questions]
5 Terrier There is no terrier.
8 Impropriation Stipend for the curacy is £35 p.a. Value of the living small and uncertain.
11 Dissenters There is a licenced meeting-house for the Anabaptists.

346 Lymington 21M65/B4/2/113
William Hawkins, vicar of Boldre 1751–77
Thomas Winbolt, curate
1 Repair of church All in good and sufficient repair; and everything necessary for both purposes.
2 Services Twice on every Sunday.
3 Sacrament The first Sunday of every month, besides festivals.
4 Registers We have both.
5 Terrier A curacy.
6 Churchyard Sufficiently fenced and decently kept, without incroachment.
7 Alterations Enlarged about 10 years since by virtue of a faculty. A few graves in the churchyard of a larger kind than usual, but cannot with propriety be called vaults.
8 Impropriation A curacy maintained principally by the voluntary contribution of the inhabitants.
9 Repair of parsonage No house etc.
10 Residence A resident curate, but not licenced.
11 Dissenters An abundance of Presbyterians and Anabaptists, who have their respective meeting-houses.
12 Loss of benefactions None.
13 Misbehaviour Entirely to satisfaction.

347 Lyndhurst 21M65/B4/2/114
James Willis LLB, rector 1759–70
Colston Carr, curate
1 Repair of church Yes.

2 Services Service is performed alternately with Minsteed.
3 Sacrament Yes.
4 Registers Yes.
5 Terrier [No reply.]
6 Churchyard The churchyard is properly fenced and kept, and no one has incroached on it.
7 Alterations No.
8 Impropriation [No reply.]
9 Repair of parsonage No parsonage house.
10 Residence [No reply. Answer implied in 9.]
11 Dissenters There are several Anabaptists who have a meeting-house.
12 Loss of benefactions I know of none.
13 Misbehaviour All right.

348 Mapledurwell 21M65/B4/2/71
Joseph Richmond DD, rector 1762–1816
[Unsigned.]
1 Repair of church Yes.
2 Services Divine service is performed in the morning at Newnham, and in the evening at Mapledurwell according to custom.
3 Sacrament Yes.
4 Registers Yes.
5 Terrier No.
6 Churchyard Yes; no incroachments upon it.
7 Alterations No.
8 Impropriation I am not possessed of a curacy.
9 Repair of parsonage Yes.
10 Residence I reside upon the parsonage at Newnham.
11 Dissenters No.
12 Loss of benefactions No.
13 Misbehaviour No; yes.

349 Martyr Worthy 21M65/B4/2/10
Samuel Speed MA, rector 1748–75
[Unsigned.]
1 Repair of church All is well.
2 Services It is performed twice.
3 Sacrament It is.
4 Registers Yes.
5 Terrier A terrier was some few years ago delivered into the Registry Office of the Archdeacon.
6 Churchyard It is well fenced and not incroached on.
7 Alterations No alteration for some years past.
8 Impropriation I am not [possessed of a curacy].
9 Repair of parsonage In good repair.
10 Residence I do reside.

11 Dissenters There are none.
12 Loss of benefactions I know of none.
13 Misbehaviour I have had no concern with the ecclesiastical officers. The parish officers do their duty well.

350 Mattingley 21M65/B4/2/72
John Goodwin, vicar of Heckfield 1763–7
[Unsigned.]
1 Repair of church Yes.
2 Services Yes.
3 Sacrament Yes.
4 Registers Yes.
5 Terrier No.
6 Churchyard Yes.
7 Alterations No.
8 Impropriation No stipend allowed.
9 Repair of parsonage Repaired by the present vicar.
10 Residence The vicar resides.
11 Dissenters No.
12 Loss of benefactions No.
13 Misbehaviour No.

351 Medstead 21M65/B4/2/11
John Hoadly, rector of Old Alresford 1737–76
John Downes, curate
1 Repair of church The church with its chancel are in good and sufficient repair. And all things necessary for the celebration of divine service and the administration of the holy sacrament are provided.
2 Services Divine service is performed in our church twice on every Sunday.
3 Sacrament The sacrament is administered 4 times in each year.
4 Registers We have a register book for christenings and burials, and also a separate one for marriages.
5 Terrier For an answer to this article, I beg leave to refer Your Lordship to the Revd Mr Chancellor Hoadly, rector of this parish.
6 Churchyard The churchyard is sufficiently fenced etc. And no person has encroached upon it.
7 Alterations The fabrick of the church has not been altered; no pews have been errected, no galleries built, nor vaults dug, nor dead bodies removed.
8 Impropriation This is not a lay impropriation.
9 Repair of parsonage The only buildings belonging to the church in this parish are a house for the curate, and a barn, both in proper repair.
10 Residence This is a chapel of ease to Old Alresford, the usual residence of the rector of these parishes. At Medstead I am his resident curate, but have not been licenced to act as such.

11 Dissenters There are no dissenters of any denomination in this parish.
12 Loss of benefactions I know of no such benefaction, which has been either witheld or misapplied.
13 Misbehaviour The ecclesiastical officers have not, as far as I know, misbehaved themselves. The several officers of this church do perform their respective duties.

352 Micheldever with chapels 21M65/B4/2/185
Abraham Smith, vicar 1765–73
Mr Smith, the vicar of Mitcheldever, has been so lately presented that he has not been able yet to remove his family, but is doing it forthwith, and the apparitor sent Your Lordship's citation so few days ago to the curate, that they could not be transmitted to Mr Smith in due time for him to return an answer. Therefore Mr Coleman, the curate, begs His Lordship to accept such answers as he can give to his articles of inquiry.
1 Repair of church The mother church, Northington, and Stratton chapels are in good repair, but Popham chapel is in so ruinous a condition that divine service cannot be performed there.
2 Services When the vicar resides, he proposes serving the mother church twice a day, but at present that is impossible to be done.
3 Sacrament It is.
4 Registers Yes.
5 Terrier Mr Coleman knows of no terrier.
6 Churchyard It is well fenced and not encroached upon.
7 Alterations No alteration for some years past.
8 Impropriation Mr Coleman does not believe Mr Smith has any curacy.
9 Repair of parsonage The vicarage-house with the several buildings thereto belonging are in good repair.
10 Residence No for the reasons assigned above.
11 Dissenters There are no dissenters in the parish.
12 Loss of benefactions There is a charity left by Mr Pincke which is not applied according to the will of the donor. The original gift was £80, it is now reduced to £60, of which the poor have no advantage.
13 Misbehaviour Officers all do their duty.

353 Michelmersh 21M65/B4/2/127
Daniel Mayo, rector 1759–68
1 Repair of church It is; and all things necessary etc. provided.
2 Services It is.
3 Sacrament It is.
4 Registers I have.
5 Terrier I have not.
6 Churchyard A small encroachment has been made (as I am informed) in my predecessor's time.
7 Alterations I know of no alteration in the fabric of the church, nor pews erected, vaults dug, galleries built, or dead bodies removed.

8 Impropriation I have no curacy.
9 Repair of parsonage The parsonage house a little shaky at one corner, and has been so almost from its first building, through the badness of the foundation. A barn wants some thatching.
10 Residence I live at Winchester, and have a curate at Michelmersh who does his duty to the satisfaction of the whole parish. I think he is licenced.
11 Dissenters There may be, but I know of none, nor of any meeting-house for divine worship.
12 Loss of benefactions I know of no benefaction witheld, or any abuse of charity.
13 Misbehaviour I know of no misbehaviour in ecclesiastical officers, churchwardens etc.

354 Milford 21M65/B4/2/115
Bolton Simpson DD, vicar 1759–86
1 Repair of church Yes.
2 Services Divine service is performed at Milford only in the morning and at Hordle in the afternoon.
3 Sacrament Yes.
4 Registers Yes.
5 Terrier I have a terrier of the glebe etc. a copy of which, I believe, was delivered into the Registry by my predecessor.
6 Churchyard It is well fenced and no incroachments.
7 Alterations No.
8 Impropriation I have no curacy.
9 Repair of parsonage Yes.
10 Residence I reside upon my vicarage at Milford.
11 Dissenters Few dissenters. They have no meeting-house and frequently attend the service of the church.
12 Loss of benefactions I know of no benefaction which is withheld or abused.
13 Misbehaviour I dont know that any ecclesiastical officers have misbehaved themselves, and I believe the parish officers have performed their repective duties.

355 Minstead 21M65/B4/2/116
James Willis LLB, rector 1759–70
Colston Carr, curate
1 Repair of church Yes.
2 Services It is served alternately with Lyndhurst.
3 Sacrament Yes.
4 Registers Yes.
5 Terrier [No reply.]
6 Churchyard The churchyard is properly fenced and kept, and no one has incroached on it.
7 Alterations No.

8 Impropriation [No reply.]
9 Repair of parsonage Yes.
10 Residence [No reply.]
11 Dissenters There are several Anabaptists who have no meeting-house.
12 Loss of benefactions I know of none.
13 Misbehaviour All right.

356 Monxton 21M65/B4/2/46
George Bally, rector of 'Munckston' 1759–79
1 Repair of church Church in bad, chancel in good, repair. Things necessary for divine service etc. provided.
2 Services Performed twice a Sunday, except in case of illness, or when a neighbour wants to be assisted.
3 Sacrament Administered 4 times a year.
4 Registers Yes.
5 Terrier A perfect terrier is in my possession. I know of no pensions or dues but what are common. No terrier delivered in my time, but I suppose before.
6 Churchyard No complaint to make on this head.
7 Alterations Nothing of this sort has been done in my time.
8 Impropriation I serve no church but mine own.
9 Repair of parsonage All in proper repair.
10 Residence I have hitherto constantly resided on my parsonage.
11 Dissenters None that I know of.
12 Loss of benefactions No benefaction left to my parish.
13 Misbehaviour I never had any dealings with them; so have no reason for complaint. The churchwardens etc. perform their duty as far as I know.

357 Morestead 21M65/B4/2/151
J. Gough, rector 1758–67
1 Repair of church The church with its chancel is in good and sufficient repair, and all things necessary are provided for the celebration of divine service and administration of the holy sacrament.
2 Services Divine service is performed but once by custom.
3 Sacrament The parishioners may receive the sacrament 3 times every year if they be disposed.
4 Registers A register book for each purpose is provided.
5 Terrier The parsonage has no glebe-lands belonging to it.
6 Churchyard The churchyard is sufficiently fenced, and decently kept. No incroachment has been made upon it.
7 Alterations The fabric of the church has not been altered. No pews erected, galleries built, vaults dug or dead bodies removed.
8 Impropriation I have no curacy.
9 Repair of parsonage They are all in good repair.
10 Residence The attendance I give at the cathedral as minor canon prevents my residence upon the parsonage.

11 Dissenters There are no dissenters of any denomination.
12 Loss of benefactions I know of no benefaction lost, either to the church or the poor.
13 Misbehaviour I know of no misbehaviour in any ecclesiastical officer, and have no cause of complaint against any officer of our church.

358 Mottisfont with chapels 21M65/B4/2/128
Edward Jones, rector before 1734–75
1 Repair of church My church and two chapels (Lockerly and East Dean) are in very good repair.
2 Services Divine service is performed in my church twice every Sunday.
3 Sacrament The sacrament is administered in my church 3 times in every year.
4 Registers I have all the register books here named.
5 Terrier I have not by me a terrier of the glebe-lands etc. but believe that there was some years since delivered to the Registry a copy of the same.
6 Churchyard My church and chapel yards are sufficiently fenced and decently kept, and no person has incroached upon them.
7 Alterations There have been galleries built at Mottisfont and Lockerly, but I dont think there has been any faculty for building them. No vaults have been dug in them or dead bodies removed. There has been lately a pew built in my chancel at Mottisfont.
8 Impropriation [No reply.]
9 Repair of parsonage My parsonage-house etc. are all in good repair.
10 Residence I have not resided at Mottisfont for some years, the roads having been so exceeding bad that for the sake of my family I removed about 10 miles off, but constantly did the Sunday's duty there till within these 3 years, but kept a resident curate. My son who was my last curate left me but last week and he was so short a time there that he had no licence.
11 Dissenters There are a few dissenters but no Roman Catholick in my parish, and there is a meeting-house belonging to the former.
12 Loss of benefactions I know of no benefaction that has been witheld, or any abuse of the charitys.
13 Misbehaviour I know of no abuse of any of the ecclesiastical officers. The churchwardens etc. perform their duties.

359 Nether Wallop 21M65/B4/2/47
Edward Hill, vicar 1762–85
[Unsigned.]
1 Repair of church Yes.
2 Services Yes.
3 Sacrament Yes.
4 Registers Yes.
5 Terrier Yes.
6 Churchyard Yes.
7 Alterations No.

8 Impropriation [No reply; not applicable.]
9 Repair of parsonage Yes.
10 Residence Yes.
11 Dissenters There are many Anabaptists and they have a meeting-house in the parish.
12 Loss of benefactions No.
13 Misbehaviour [No reply.]

360 New Alresford 21M65/B4/2/12
John Hoadly, rector of Old Alresford 1737–76
Robert Thomas, curate
1 Repair of church Yes. It is.
2 Services Yes. It is.
3 Sacrament Yes. It is.
4 Registers Yes.
5 Terrier The rector, the Revd Dr Hoadly, hath a measurement of the glebe of Old and New Alresford, and will take care that a copy thereof, well attested, be forthwith lodged in the Bishop's Registry.
6 Churchyard It is. No person hath encroached upon it.
7 Alterations Nothing of this sort hath been done irregularly.
8 Impropriation This respecting lay-impropriators, I apprehend does not concern the curacy of New Alresford, which is a chapelry of the rectory of Old Alresford, the mother church.
9 Repair of parsonage The parsonage house is at Old Alresford, and with the barns, outhouses and other buildings is in proper repair.
10 Residence The rector resides at Old Alresford, the mother church, and at his other rector[y] of St Maries near Southampton, every other year alternately. The curate of New Alresford is constantly resident, and in the absence of the rector serves the church at Old Alresford also twice every Sunday. He never was licensed to the cure of either church.
11 Dissenters There are no dissenters in the parish except 2 families of reputed papists, and 2 other persons. There are several small children in one of the families. There are the ruins of a fabrick left by will to serve for a Quakers' meeting house, but none have assembled there for some years.
12 Loss of benefactions I know of none.
13 Misbehaviour I know of none. The church officers do their duties.

361 Newnham 21M65/B4/2/73
Joseph Richmond DD, rector 1762–1816
[Unsigned.]
1 Repair of church Yes.
2 Services Divine service is performed in the morning at Newnham, and in the evening at Maplederwell according to custom.
3 Sacrament Yes.
4 Registers Yes.
5 Terrier No.

6 Churchyard Yes; no incroachment upon it.
7 Alterations No.
8 Impropriation I am not possessed of a curacy.
9 Repair of parsonage Yes.
10 Residence Yes.
11 Dissenters No.
12 Loss of benefactions No.
13 Misbehaviour No; yes.

362 Newton Valence 21M65/B4/2/28
Richard Yalden, vicar 1761–85
1 Repair of church It is.
2 Services It is.
3 Sacrament It is.
4 Registers We have.
5 Terrier I have.
6 Churchyard It is.
7 Alterations No.
8 Impropriation Hawkly cure £30 p.a.; impropriation £100.
9 Repair of parsonage They are.
10 Residence I do.
11 Dissenters No.
12 Loss of benefactions No.
13 Misbehaviour None that I know of.

363 Newtown (Burghclere) 21M65/B4/2/187
Thomas Lisle DD, rector of Burghclere 1737–67
Michael Philipps, curate
1 Repair of church No cause of complaint to my knowledge.
2 Services Yes.
3 Sacrament Yes.
4 Registers Yes.
5 Terrier This is a chapelry appended to the rectory of Burghclere.
6 Churchyard No cause of complaint.
7 Alterations No.
8 Impropriation For serving the chapel the rector allows the profits, about £30, curate paying Land Tax for the same.
9 Repair of parsonage There is neither, nor has been [one], in the memory of man.
10 Residence No house to be lived in in the parish or chapelry.
11 Dissenters Only William Hawkins, gardener, and his wife, Catholics, who have not brought their two last children to be baptized, the youngest about half a year old — and one other Catholic, a servant maid, who all go to mass in Lord Fingal's family, as I am informed.
12 Loss of benefactions No.
13 Misbehaviour No cause of complaint.

364 North Stoneham 21M65/B4/2/137
Edward Beadon, rector 1762–1811
1 Repair of church Yes.
2 Services Yes.
3 Sacrament On the first Sunday of every month, and on the three great festivals.
4 Registers Yes.
5 Terrier I have no true and perfect terrier of the glebe-lands etc. or note in writing of the pensions and other dues etc.
6 Churchyard My churchyard is sufficiently fenced and in good repair, and no incroachments have been made upon it.
7 Alterations The fabric of the church has not been altered and I know of no pews erected, galleries built, vaults dug, or dead bodies removed without a licence or faculty from the ordinary.
8 Impropriation I am possessed of no curacy.
9 Repair of parsonage Yes.
10 Residence Yes. I serve my own church.
11 Dissenters 2 or 3 Roman Catholicks, but no place for divine worship.
12 Loss of benefactions I know of no benefaction witheld from those for whom it was designed; or of the abuse of any charity.
13 Misbehaviour No; yes.

365 North Waltham 21M65/B4/2/74
Robert Flint, rector 1759–66
1 Repair of church Yes.
2 Services It is performed twice.
3 Sacrament Yes.
4 Registers There is a register book, but not a register for marriages.
5 Terrier There are 80 computed acres of glebe-land; but they do not measure quite so much.
6 Churchyard The churchyard hath been very much incroached on, the graves trod in, and digged by hogs, owing to the neglect of Thomas Archer, or else of John Savage.
7 Alterations No.
8 Impropriation Mr Flint is possessed of none.
9 Repair of parsonage Yes.
10 Residence The cause of Mr Flint's non-residence is, that he hath a vicarage in Sussex.
11 Dissenters None.
12 Loss of benefactions I know of none.
13 Misbehaviour They all do their duty as far as I know.

366 Northington 21M65/B4/2/129
Abraham Smith, vicar 1765–73
William Sealy, curate
1 Repair of church Yes.

2 Services Northington is a chapel of ease to the v[icarage] of Micheldever, and once a day is the customary duty.
3 Sacrament Yes.
4 Registers Yes.
5 Terrier There is no terrier at present, but one shall be made out and delivered to the Register.
6 Churchyard The pails are at present out of repair, the fence toward the street is good, and the whole is intended I believe to be walled in, or otherwise repaired as soon as possible.
7 Alterations [No reply.]
8 Impropriation The church is served for the tythes belonging to the chapelry.
9 Repair of parsonage There is neither house nor barn.
10 Residence [No reply; answer implied in reply to 9.]
11 Dissenters Not that I know of.
12 Loss of benefactions None, I believe.
13 Misbehaviour Not that I know of.

367 Old Alresford 21M65/B4/2/188
John Hoadly, rector 1737–76 5 September 1765
1 Repair of church It is. They are.
2 Services It is.
3 Sacrament It is.
4 Registers We have.
5 Terrier There is a terrier in the office dated November 13, 1695. I have a new measurement of the glebe-lands etc., and an extract of a survey of the manor of Alresford as far as relates to the same, taken 6 Ed. VI, an authentic copy of which shall be lodged in the Bishop's Registry.
6 Churchyard Yes; no.
7 Alterations The church was rebuilt AD1753, and everything executed according to the faculty then had.
8 Impropriation This referring to a curacy under an impropriator, does not concern me.
9 Repair of parsonage They are.
10 Residence I am resident every other summer; in my absence my curate of N[ew] Al[resfor]d serves both churches, being constantly resident there, within half a mile of Old Al[resfor]d. He is not licenced.
11 Dissenters There are no dissenters.
12 Loss of benefactions We have some benefactions, of which I know of no abuse.
13 Misbehaviour They have not; they do.

368 Old Basing 21M65/B4/2/59
Curacy.
[Unsigned.]
[No replies.]

369 Over Wallop 21M65/B4/2/48
Benjamin Woodroffe, rector 1729/30–70 2 September 1765
1 Repair of church All well repaired; and all things requisite to the celebration of divine service duely provided.
2 Services Performed twice.
3 Sacrament It is.
4 Registers We have.
5 Terrier The terrier of Over Wallop was lost before my coming in to the rectory, nor have I with the utmost pains taken, been able to recover it.
6 Churchyard Sufficiently fenced, and no incroachment thereupon.
7 Alterations No contravention to this article.
8 Impropriation The rectorial tithe of Over Wallop is under no other impropriation but that of the tithe of Townsend Farm to the Wallop family; it belonged at the Reformation to a suppressed chantry in Yorkshire and was then granted by H[enry the] 8th to them.
9 Repair of parsonage In the fullest repair.
10 Residence Mr Barry, my curate for 11 years, to whom I allowed £40 p.a. salary, surpless fees, and other emoluments to near £20 p.a., leaving me to go to his own living at Lady Day last, it has been served by myself ever since; but propose putting in another curate on the same terms, at Michaelmas.
11 Dissenters Some Anabaptists, but [they] have no meeting-house.
12 Loss of benefactions Several summs of money given to the poor of Over Wallop have been lodged in the hands of the Swanton family — Mrs Swanton, widow of Francis Swanton, by her tenant farmer Joliffe. Sent from a vestry meeting in the church to enquire what poor's money she might have in her hands, [she] returned by message, that she would be answerable for £70. On her death, her estate devolved to the late Mr William Swanton, who at a parish meeting, met upon the subject of enquiring after legacys to the poor, at the parsonage house, about 12 years since, promised to give the parish officers a bond for £50. He dyed without any such bond given, which is all the respondent can to this article reply.
13 Misbehaviour To the last article the respondent answers he knows nothing referring thereto blamable.

370 Ovington 21M65/B4/2/13
Jacob Freer, rector 1760–73
1 Repair of church Yes.
2 Services Service is performed twice every Sunday.
3 Sacrament Yes.
4 Registers Yes.
5 Terrier Yes.
6 Churchyard The churchyard is sufficiently fenced and no incroachment made upon it.
7 Alterations No.
8 Impropriation I have no curacy.
9 Repair of parsonage All in good repair except an old brewhouse which was left in a decayed condition by my predecessor.

10 Residence I reside upon my living of St Thomas in Winchester. I have a curate who serves Ovington and Itchen Stoke, and lives at Itchen Stoke, which is not more than half a mile from Ovington.
11 Dissenters There are dissenters but no place of divine worship that I can bear testimony to.
12 Loss of benefactions No.
13 Misbehaviour Not that I know of; they do.

371 Penton Mewsey 21M65/B4/2/49
George Woodward, rector 1764–90
[Unsigned.]
[No replies]

372 Portchester 21M65/B4/2/98
William Powell, vicar 1750–92
[Unsigned.]
[No replies.]

373 Portsea 21M65/B4/2/99
Vicarage vacant
1 Repair of church Yes.
2 Services Yes.
3 Sacrament Monthly.
4 Registers Yes.
5 Terrier No.
6 Churchyard It is well fenced and no incroachments made upon it.
7 Alterations No.
8 Impropriation The vicarage of Portsea is an appropriation in the gift of the college of Winchester.
9 Repair of parsonage Yes.
10 Residence The living of Portsea at present is vacant. There is a resident curate, and [he] is licensed.
11 Dissenters Yes, and there is one Anabaptist meeting-house in the parish.
12 Loss of benefactions No.
13 Misbehaviour No. The churchwardens and the clerk perform their respective duties very well.

374 Portsmouth 21M65/B4/2/100
Henry Taylor MA, vicar 1745–85
Benjamin Forester, curate
1 Repair of church Yes.
2 Services It is.
3 Sacrament Yes.

4 Registers Yes.
5 Terrier As I am the curate, I know nothing about it.
6 Churchyard Yes, it is sufficiently fenced, and *tolerably* decently kept, and has not, I believe, been incroached upon.
7 Alterations I cant say.
8 Impropriation The stipend allowed is £50 p.a., as much I believe as hath been usually allowed, and I am satisfied with it. As to the yearly value of the impropriation, I am a stranger to it.
9 Repair of parsonage Now repairing.
10 Residence I reside upon my curacy, but have not been licenced.
11 Dissenters There are dissenters of most denominations. The Presbyterians and Quakers have each a meeting-house for divine worship.
12 Loss of benefactions No.
13 Misbehaviour No undue fees have been taken by any of the present ecclesiastical officers that I know of; and they all perform their respective duties.

375 Portsmouth, St George's Chapel 21M65/B4/2/101
Henry Swann, curate 1764–89
1 Repair of church Yes; and all things necessary are provided.
2 Services It is.
3 Sacrament Monthly.
4 Registers By the Act of Parliament for building St George's Chapel, the minister is restrained from marrying, christening, or burying.
5 Terrier No glebe-lands etc. belonging to St George's Chapel.
6 Churchyard The chapel-yard is walled in.
7 Alterations [No reply.]
8 Impropriation The stipend arising by subscription, paid to the minister, is £40 p.a., as settled by Act of Parliament.
9 Repair of parsonage None belonging to St George's Chapel.
10 Residence Yes.
11 Dissenters [No reply.]
12 Loss of benefactions [No reply.]
13 Misbehaviour No. By the Act of Parliament aforesaid two collectors are chosen annually instead of chapel-wardens, who, with the clerk, perform their respective duties regularly.

376 Priors Dean 21M65/B4/2/29
Thomas Harrison, rector of Colemore 1758–67
1 Repair of church Yes.
2 Services Once a day alternately, morning and evening with Colmer, this being only a chapelry annexed.
3 Sacrament Yes.
4 Registers Yes.
5 Terrier Yes.
6 Churchyard The churchyard is well fenced and no incroachments have been made.

7 Alterations No.
8 Impropriation I have no curacy.
9 Repair of parsonage This article is answered under Colmer R[ectory].
10 Residence Yes.
11 Dissenters No.
12 Loss of benefactions No.
13 Misbehaviour Not that I know of. Every officer, I believe, performs his respective duty.

377 Quarley 21M65/B4/2/50
Thomas Sheppard, rector 1762–1814
1 Repair of church The church is in good repair and everything necessary is provided for the celebration of divine service and the administration of the sacrament.
2 Services Yes.
3 Sacrament Yes.
4 Registers Yes; yes.
5 Terrier The terrier of the house and glebe was, I presume, delivered into the Registry of the Archdeacon some time ago, agreeable to an injunction from Archdeacon Lowth.
6 Churchyard It is well fenced, and no person hath incroached upon it to the best of my knowledge.
7 Alterations No.
8 Impropriation [No reply; not applicable.]
9 Repair of parsonage Yes.
10 Residence Yes.
11 Dissenters No.
12 Loss of benefactions No.
13 Misbehaviour No; yes.

378 Ringwood 21M65/B4/2/117
John Maule MA, vicar 1750–78
[Unsigned.]
1 Repair of church The west window of the the church and north wall out of repair. They are provided.
2 Services It is performed twice.
3 Sacrament At the festivals and the first Sunday in every month.
4 Registers Proper registers are provided.
5 Terrier Upon enquiry no terrier to be found in the bishop's office. The composition for the vicarage of Ringwood at large in Ecton.
6 Churchyard All is well.
7 Alterations No alteration. Pews are erected and vaults dug, as I believe without a faculty from the court.
8 Impropriation [No reply; not applicable.]
9 Repair of parsonage They are.
10 Residence The vicar resides.

11 Dissenters There are dissenters of several denominations, and 4 meeting-houses in the parish.
12 Loss of benefactions I know of none but what is disposed of according to the intent of the donor.
13 Misbehaviour None.

379 Romsey 21M65/B4/2/130
John Peverall MA, vicar 1742–80
James Burch, curate
1 Repair of church Yes.
2 Services It is performed twice every S[unday].
3 Sacrament Administered monthly.
4 Registers Both.
5 Terrier [No reply.]
6 Churchyard It is; nor hath been incroached upon.
7 Alterations Not to my knowledge.
8 Impropriation No stipend. The surplice fees and Easter offerings are given up to the curate; which amount to £60.
9 Repair of parsonage There are *none* to be repaired.
10 Residence A curate is constantly resident.
11 Dissenters Yes.
12 Loss of benefactions No.
13 Misbehaviour No; yes.

380 Rotherwick 21M65/B4/2/75
Frederick Toll, vicar 1756–66
[Unsigned.]
[No replies.] Every article of this enquiry cant be fully answered by a curate. He, with all humility and duty, declares his belief of matters being in the accustomed [last word lacking]

381 Rowner 21M65/B4/2/189
Philip Henville, rector 1730–57
1 Repair of church The church with its chancel repaired last summer, inside and out. All things necessary for the administration of the holy sacrament very good. The communion table has no covering and looks indecent, which I present.[39]
2 Services Morning and evening service is regularly <and> constantly performed throughout the year.
3 Sacrament The sacrament is without exception administered 4 times every year.
4 Registers We have both register books for christenings and burials, and also for marriages.
5 Terrier An authentic copy of the terrier hath been delivered into the Registry.

6 Churchyard The churchyard is fenced and kept in order. No one incroaches upon it.
7 Alterations The fabrick of the church hath not been altered; no pews nor galleries erected; no vaults dug, or dead bodies removed.
8 Impropriation I serve no other church but my own.
9 Repair of parsonage The parsonage-house with all the appendages are in very good repair.
10 Residence I do not live in my parish, but in an adjoining one. My non-residence occasions no neglect of duty. I am frequently in the parish, tho' I have but little or no weekly duty to perform.
11 Dissenters There are no dissenters in my parish. No meeting-house or place for divine worship, but the church only.
12 Loss of benefactions We have no benefaction left; no charity either to the church or poor.
13 Misbehaviour I do not know that the ecclesiastical officers have taken undue fees, or misbehaved themselves. The churchwarden and clerk perform, their respective duties extremely well.

382 St Mary Bourne 21M65/B4/2/190
John Blair, prebend 1745–
[Unsigned.]
1 Repair of church Yes.
2 Services The customary service is once a Sunday, the income to the minister being very small.
3 Sacrament It is.
4 Registers Yes.
5 Terrier There is no terrier.
6 Churchyard Yes.
7 Alterations No.
8 Impropriation The full income is £27 p.a., and Mr Blair gives it *all* to the curate.
9 Repair of parsonage In pretty good repair.
10 Residence There has been a resident curate and will be again, but at present the curacy is vacant.
11 Dissenters There are some Anabaptists, and they have a meeting.
12 Loss of benefactions Not to my knowledge.
13 Misbehaviour I think not. The churchwardens etc. perform their respective duties.

383 Selborne 21M65/B4/2/30
Andrew Etty, vicar 1758–84
1 Repair of church There is no chapel. All necessary things for celebration of the sacrament etc. provided.
2 Services Divine service is performed twice on every Sunday.
3 Sacrament The sacrament is administered so often in each year, that every parishioner may recieve at least 3 times.

4 Registers We have the registers as required.
5 Terrier A <terrier> has been del<ivered> etc.
6 Churchyard Some part of the churchyard fenced with an indifferent hedge only.
7 Alterations No alteration made in the church, nor pews erected etc. of late.
8 Impropriation The vicar has no other cure.
9 Repair of parsonage All in good repair.
10 Residence The vicar <resides con>stantly.
11 Dissenters No dissenters in the parish.
12 Loss of benefactions No benefaction witheld, nor abuse of charity.
13 Misbehaviour No complaint of ecclesiastical offices. Churchwardens and other officers, as far as appears to the vicar, perform their respective duties.

384 Sherborne St John (and Sutton chapel) 21M65/B4/2/191
Dr Jonathan Shipley, rector 1746–69
1 Repair of church The church of Sherborne St John is in good repair; and all things necessary for the celebration of divine service etc. are provided.
2 Services Divine service is performed twice in this church on every Sunday.
3 Sacrament The sacrament is administered 5 times in the year, 2 of which are at Easter.
4 Registers We have both, and they are regularly kept.
<Ge>neral answer <to> the queries in page[s] 2 and 3 [i.e. numbers 5–13] Dr Jonathan Shipley is rector of Sherborne St John, but he performs no parochial duty, neither does he pay for any being done. Mr Benj[ami]n Huffum Pepper is vicar, who lives at Downham, Wilts., but is about to remove from thence with his family to the vicarage at Sherborn St John. We know of no such place as *Sutton chapel*, yet tradition informs us that there was formerly here another place of public worship called Sherborne Cowderoy church or chapel. But whether it was annexed to, or distinct from Sherborne St John we have not been able to learn. Neither is it known where it stood. The church of Sherborn St John is kept in decent repair, the service duly performed, and there is not a dissenting family, of any denomination, in the parish. Signed by the present officiating minister, September 2, 1765, Samuel Loggon.

385 Sherfield English 21M65/B4/2/131
Richard Budden, rector 1737–69
[Unsigned.]
1 Repair of church Yes.
2 Services Only once, the parish of Whiteparish, Wilts., in the diocese of Sarum being held together with Sherfield by the archbishop's dispensation.
3 Sacrament Yes.
4 Registers Yes.

5 Terrier Yes.
6 Churchyard Yes; no.
7 Alterations No.
8 Impropriation I do part of the duty of the parish of Whiteparish, Wilts., in the diocese of Sarum, for the holding which living together [with] Sherfield I have the archbishop's dispensation.
9 Repair of parsonage Yes.
10 Residence I reside at my vicarige-house at Whiteparish, which is contiguous to Sherfield, and do the duty myself at Sherfield, and the weekly duty of both parishes.
11 Dissenters Yes. They have a meeting-house at Lockerly.
12 Loss of benefactions No.
13 Misbehaviour No; yes.

386 Sherfield on Loddon 21M65/B4/2/192
Knight Burroughs, rector 1748–72 2 September 1765
1 Repair of church Everything relative to this article is in due order.
2 Services Divine service is regularly performed.
3 Sacrament The sacrament is administered 4 times in each year, according to the antient usage of this parish.
4 Registers Proper books of each kind are provided, and kept at the parsonage-house.
5 Terrier A perfect terrier of the glebe-lands, and of all the farms in this parish, is now preparing; and when finished, will be deposited in the Registry at Winchester.
6 Churchyard The churchyard is sufficiently fenced, and free from any incroachment.
7 Alterations No alterations have been made in any respect since the year 1748, nor any irregularities committed.
8 Impropriation There is no curate in this parish, the rector being always resident.
9 Repair of parsonage Everything is in good repair, and greatly <im>proved.
10 Residence See article the 8th.
11 Dissenters No dissenter in this parish, one Quaker excepted.
12 Loss of benefactions No abuses of any kind of charity.
13 Misbehaviour No complaint against any ecclesiastical officers. It is greatly to be wished that the churchwardens were directed to hav<e> the church thoroughly cleaned once a year, especially as such a necessary as well as decent work may be done effectually <at> the small expence of ten shillings.

387 Soberton 21M65/B4/2/102
David Lewis, curate of 'Subberton'
[No replies other than:] All things well.

388 Sopley 21M65/B4/2/118
James Willis LLB, vicar 1760–70
1 Repair of church Yes.

2 Services Yes.
3 Sacrament Yes.
4 Registers Yes.
5 Terrier No.
6 Churchyard In good repair and no one has incroached upon it.
7 Alterations No.
8 Impropriation [No reply; not applicable.]
9 Repair of parsonage Lately built.
10 Residence I reside.
11 Dissenters Many.
12 Loss of benefactions No.
13 Misbehaviour Yes.

389 Southampton, All Saints 21M65/B4/2/138
William Scott, rector 1739/40–1767
[No replies except] All well.

390 Southampton, Holy Rood 21M65/B4/2/139
Daniel Perkins, vicar 1750/1–1772 9 September 1765
1 Repair of church Yes.
2 Services Divine service is performed twice every Sunday.
3 Sacrament The sacrament is administered the first Sunday in every other month, and on all the festivals of Easter, Whitsuntide and Christmas,
4 Registers Yes.
5 Terrier There is no glebe belonging to the living. And the dues from the houses are so vague and uncertain, that no note of them can be delivered into the Registry.
6 Churchyard I have no churchyard.
7 Alterations No alteration in the fabrick of the church. No pews or galleries erected or bodies removed. Mr Robert Ballard has dug a vault. And had my leave.
8 Impropriation I have no curacy.
9 Repair of parsonage The vicarage-house is in good repair, as are also the out-houses belonging to it.
10 Residence I reside upon my vicarage.
11 Dissenters I know of no dissenters in my parish but 4, a widow and her daughter who are leaving the parish, and one Mr Meceanon and his wife.
12 Loss of benefactions I know of none.
13 Misbehaviour All is well.

391 Southampton, St John 21M65/B4/2/140
[Held jointly with St Laurence]
[Unsigned.]
[No replies.]

392 Southampton, St Laurence 21M65/B4/2/141
James Scott BA, rector 1751–94
[Unsigned.]
1 Repair of church Yes.

2 Services Only evening prayers, according to custom; as the income of the church is too small for the support of a minister, it has ever been held with some other church.
3 Sacrament Sacrament is administered once a month.
4 Registers Yes.
5 Terrier The income arises from rates on houses, an account of which is duly kept.
6 Churchyard In good repair without incroachments.
7 Alterations No.
[No replies to questions 8–13.]

393 Southampton, St Mary 21M65/B4//2/142
John Hoadly, rector 1743–76 9 September 1765
1 Repair of church It is; they are.
2 Services It is.
3 Sacrament It is.
4 Registers We have.
5 Terrier There is no such terrier in the office; but a new measurement shall be made, and a proper attested copy delivered.
6 Churchyard Yes; no.
7 Alterations No.
8 Impropriation This article does not concern me.
9 Repair of parsonage It is.
10 Residence I am resident every other summer, and constantly so on one or other of my preferments. I have a constant resident curate not licenced (the Revd Mr Owen Davies, rector of Exton).
11 Dissenters A small meeting-house for a small congregation of *Anabaptists*, as I am informed, is lately erected on some ground given by will to their preacher; of which a proper certificate is delivered into the office, according to the Act of Toleration.
12 Loss of benefactions No.
13 Misbehaviour No; yes.

394 South Tidworth 21M65/B4/2/51
John Goddard BA, rector 1733–85
[Unsigned.]
[No replies.]

395 South Warnborough 21M65/B4/2/76
John Duncan DD, rector 1762–1809
[Unsigned.]
1 Repair of church Yes.
2 Services It is.
3 Sacrament It is.
4 Registers I have both.

5 Terrier No.
6 Churchyard Very well fenced. No encroachment.
7 Alterations No.
8 Impropriation I have no curacy.
9 Repair of parsonage Yes.
10 Residence I reside constantly myself.
11 Dissenters Two families only, who of late frequently come to church.
12 Loss of benefactions There is a small benefaction withheld from the parish which I think it entitled to, and am taking the proper method to recover.
13 Misbehaviour No misbehaviour or neglect.

396 Steventon 21M65/B4/2/77
George Austen, rector 1761–1805
1 Repair of church The church and chancel are in good repair, and everything necessary for the celebration of divine service, and the administration of the holy sacrament are provided.
2 Services Yes.
3 Sacrament Yes.
4 Registers Yes.
5 Terrier I know of no terrier.
6 Churchyard Yes, nor hath any person encroached on it.
7 Alterations No.
8 Impropriation I am possessed of no curacy.
9 Repair of parsonage <Ye>s.
10 Residence Yes.
11 Dissenters There are no dissenters.
12 Loss of benefactions I know of no benefactions.
13 Misbehaviour No ecclesiastical officers have misbehaved in any manner. The churchwarden and clerk do their respective duties.

397 Stoke Charity 21M65/B4/2/194
Gilbert Jackson DD, rector 1744–79
Stephen Kinchin, curate
1 Repair of church Yes.
2 Services Yes.
3 Sacrament Yes.
4 Registers Yes.
5 Terrier [No reply; probably not applicable.]
6 Churchyard Yes, and no incroachments.
7 Alterations No.
8 Impropriation £32 p.a. and the house etc.
9 Repair of parsonage Yes.
10 Residence A constant resident curate.
11 Dissenters No.

12 Loss of benefactions No.
13 Misbehaviour All behave well.

398 Stratfield Saye 21M65/B4/2/78
Joseph Trapp MA, rector 1751–68 2 September 1765
1 Repair of church The church lately rebuilt. They are.
2 Services It is.
3 Sacrament It is.
4 Registers I have.
5 Terrier They are settled by an Act of Parliament.
6 Churchyard The same.
7 Alterations *Vide* art[icle] 1.
8 Impropriation A curate regularly attends.
9 Repair of parsonage Lately rebuilt by the <p>resent incumbent at his own expence.
10 Residence I do.
11 Dissenters No.
12 Loss of benefactions No.
13 Misbehaviour No; yes.

399 Stratfield Turgis 21M65/B4/2/79
Joseph Trapp MA, rector 1748–69 2 September 1765
1 Repair of church They are.
2 Services It is.
3 Sacrament It is.
4 Registers There is.
5 Terrier They are settled without a possibility of mistake.
6 Churchyard It is.
7 Alterations No.
8 Impropriation A regular curate.
9 Repair of parsonage They are.
10 Residence I do at the parish adjoining.
11 Dissenters No.
12 Loss of benefactions No.
13 Misbehaviour No; yes.

400 Swarraton 21M65/B4/2/14
William Sealy, rector 1759–68
1 Repair of church The church and chancel are in good repair except a few tiles lately blown off, which shall be mended as soon as possible, and as to the other part of the quaere everything is as it ought to be.
2 Services As Northington is so near, once each Sunday is the customary duty.
3 Sacrament Yes.
4 Registers Yes.

5 Terrier There is none at present, but one shall be made out and delivered to the Register.
6 Churchyard It is well fenced and there hath been no incroachment.
7 Alterations Not that I know of.
8 Impropriation Swarraton is a rectory and at present supplied by the rector.
9 Repair of parsonage Yes.
10 Residence The rector at present resides; when he does not there is a constant resident curate.
11 Dissenters Not that I know of.
12 Loss of benefactions None.
13 Misbehaviour As to the first part of the quaere, there has been no misbehaviour as far as I know, as to the second, they have all I believe performed their respective duties.

401 Sydmonton 21M65/B4/2/193
[Unsigned.]
1 Repair of church The chancel is repairing, all besides in good order.
2 Services It is performed every other Sunday according to antient custom.
3 Sacrament As often as antient custom requires.
4 Registers Yea.
5 Terrier No such [glebe-] lands etc. belong to the chapel.
6 Churchyard Yea.
7 Alterations No.
8 Impropriation The chapel is annexed to the vicarage of Kingsclere and part of that cure.
9 Repair of parsonage No house.
10 Residence [No reply; answer implied in reply to 9.]
11 Dissenters None.
12 Loss of benefactions No.
13 Misbehaviour In no fault.

402 Thruxton 21M65/B4/2/52
Joshua Barnes MA LLD, rector 1747/8–1772
1 Repair of church All is well as to the articles.
2 Services Duty is regularly performed.
3 Sacrament Sacrament is administered 4 times in the year constantly.
4 Registers Proper books are provided and carefully preserved.
5 Terrier There is a terrier.
6 Churchyard Churchyard is decent and well kept in fences.
7 Alterations Nothing has been done out of order.
8 Impropriation I have no curacy.
9 Repair of parsonage The parsonage house etc. is in good condition.
10 Residence I reside constantly.
11 Dissenters One family of dissenters; no meeting-house in the parish.

12 Loss of benefactions [No reply.]
13 Misbehaviour [No reply.]

403 Timsbury 21M65/B4/2/195
William Bartholomew after 1736–1770
John Evans, curate
1 Repair of church Yes.
2 Services Once every Sunday, being the duty accustomed.
3 Sacrament Yes.
4 Registers Yes; both.
5 Terrier Not that I know of.
6 Churchyard Yes; no.
7 Alterations No.
8 Impropriation The stipend to me as curate is as much as can be expected from so small a parish, viz. £16 p.a..
9 Repair of parsonage There is no house upon it etc., nor glebe that I know of.
10 Residence Being but 2 miles from Romsey, it is served from thence, where a school requires me to reside.
11 Dissenters No.
12 Loss of benefactions I know of none; no.
13 Misbehaviour No; yes

404 Titchfield 21M65/B4/2/103
Gilbert Jackson BD, vicar 1734–79
1 Repair of church The church is in good repair and all things necessary for the celebration of divine service are duly provided.
2 Services Divine service is performed twice on every Sunday.
3 Sacrament It is.
4 Registers We have.
5 Terrier I do not know that there is any terrier of the glebe-lands.
6 Churchyard The churchyard is sufficiently fenced, nor do I know that any person hath incroached upon it.
7 Alterations No.
8 Impropriation [No reply; not applicable.]
9 Repair of parsonage They are.
10 Residence I do reside.
11 Dissenters There are very few dissenters in the parish and no meeting-house.
12 Loss of benefactions I do not.
13 Misbehaviour I do not know that any ecclesiastical officers have misbehaved themselves, and the churchwardens etc. perform their respective duties.

405 Tufton 21M65/B4/2/53

Richard [Ring], vicar of Wherwell 1763–91 and 'curate of Tufton and Bullington annexed'

1 Repair of church The churchwardens will take a view of the chancel and church and report accordingly. Everything necessary for divine service and the sacrament is provided.
2 Services Once a fortnight only, it being a chapel belonging to the mother church of Wherwell.
3 Sacrament Yes.
4 Registers Yes.
5 Terrier There is no house nor any land belonging to the vicar of Wherwell in this parish.
6 Churchyard Well fenced.
7 Alterations No.
8 Impropriation The curate hath the small tithes, but the value of the impropriation I do not know as yet.
9 Repair of parsonage No house nor barn etc.
10 Residence I reside at Wherwell in the vicarage-house.
11 Dissenters No
12 Loss of benefactions No.
13 Misbehaviour I know no officer who has taken undue fees, nor any one who has neglected his duty.

406 Tunworth 21M65/B4/2/80

Joseph Warton, rector 1755–79 2 September 1765
Samuel Loggon, curate

1 Repair of church Tunworth church and chancel are in good repair. And all things necessary for the celebration of divine service and sacraments are provided.
2 Services Divine service is performed in Tunworth church twice in every Sunday.
3 Sacrament The sacrament is administered four times in every year.
4 Registers We have a register book for christenings and burials, and one for marriages pursuant to the directions of the late Marriage Act.
5–13. Mr Joseph Warton of Winchester is rector of Tunworth, who keeps the parsonage house and other buildings in good repair. The church service is duly performed, and there are no dissenters in the parish. [Signed] Samuel Loggon.

407 Twyford and Owslebury 21M65/B4/2/152

Edward Eddowes, vicar 1756–67
Francis Leathes, curate

1 Repair of church They are.
2 Services As there are 2 churches, divine service is performed in each of them every Sunday.
3 Sacrament Yes.

4 Registers I have.
5 Terrier Not that I know of.
6 Churchyard Yes; no.
7 Alterations Not that I know.
8 Impropriation I am not possessed of a curacy.
9 Repair of parsonage They are.
10 Residence I do not reside in my parish, but have a constant resident curate.
11 Dissenters There are some and they have a licenced place for worship.
12 Loss of benefactions I know of none.
13 Misbehaviour They have not; they do.

408 Upham 21M65/B4/2/104
William Tomlins, rector of 'Upham and Durley' 1756–88
1 Repair of church Yes.
2 Services Yes, except in cases of sickness or accident.
3 Sacrament Yes.
4 Registers Marriages have been hitherto registered in the same parchment book at Upham with christenings and burials, but separately and according to the directions of the act of parliament.
5 Terrier There is no glebe-land belonging to the rectory, only tithes.
6 Churchyard The churchyards are sufficiently fenced etc. and no person hath incroached upon them.
7 Alterations No.
8 Impropriation [No reply; not applicable.]
9 Repair of parsonage The parsonage-house and other buildings are all in good repair; and what little may be wanting, shall be done.
10 Residence I have another living in the diocese of Salisbury where I chiefly reside. My curate will answer the rest.
11 Dissenters I know of none.
12 Loss of benefactions No.
13 Misbehaviour I have heard no complaint of misbehaviour in any ecclesiastical officer, or of neglect of duty in the churchwardens, etc.

409 Up Nately 21M65/B4/2/81
[Unsigned.]
[No replies.]

410 Upper Clatford 21M65/B4/2/54
William Roman, rector 'of Upclatford' 1747/8–1782
1 Repair of church They are.
2 Services Yes, unless omitted on some necessary account.
3 Sacrament Yes.
4 Registers Yes.
5 Terrier I have a true and perfect terrier of the glebe-lands etc., and suppose there is also one in the Registry.

6 Churchyard Yes, and I dont know of any incroachment.
7 Alterations No.
8 Impropriation [No reply; not applicable.]
9 Repair of vicarage Yes.
10 Residence I reside about half the year, and always keep a curate who lives at Andover.
11 Dissenters 2 dissenters but no meeting-house.
12 Loss of benefactions No.
13 Misbehaviour None of the officers have misbehaved, and the churchwardens etc. do their duty.

411 Warblington 21M65/B4/2/105
Samuel Torrent MA, rector 1764–89
1 Repair of church They are.
2 Services It is.
3 Sacrament It is.
4 Registers We have.
5 Terrier I have not.
6 Churchyard It is.
7 Alterations Not to my knowledge.
8 Impropriation I am not.
9 Repair of parsonage The dilapidations due from the last incumbent are not yet settled; as soon as they are the parsonage-house etc. will be repaired.
10 Residence I reside at Havant, within a quarter of a mile of my parish, by the bishop's leave. I have no fixed curate, doing the duty myself.
11 Dissenters There are Roman Catholicks in the parish and they have a chapel in the neighbourhood.
12 Loss of benefactions I do not.
13 Misbehaviour There has been no misbehaviour by any ecclesiastical officer to my knowledge. The churchwardens etc. perform their respective duties very punctually.

412 Weeke 21M65/B4/2/156
John Bailley, rector 1759–69
1 Repair of church Yes.
2 Services Divine service is performed regularly on every Sunday, excepting the months December and January.
3 Sacrament The sacrament is administered 4 times in the year.
4 Registers We have.
5 Terrier I have no true and perfect terrier, neither did I ever receive any.
6 Churchyard The churchyard fence is ordered to be repaired, and no encroachments have been made.
7 Alterations No alterations have been made.
8 Impropriation I am not possessed of such a curacy.
9 Repair of parsonage No parsonage-house, barn or outhouse.

10 Residence I cannot reside because there is no house, but I serve the church myself.
11 Dissenters Not one dissenter.
12 Loss of benefactions No.
13 Misbehaviour I do not know that any undue fees have been taken. And the churchwarden and clerk perform their duty.

413 West Tytherley 21M65/B4/2/196
Joshua Harrison MA, rector 'of West Titherly' 1737–7 4 September 1765
1 Repair of church The parish church of We<st Tytherley and its> chancel are in good and suffi<cient repair and all> things necessary are provi<ded for the performance> of divine service, and th<e administration> of the holy sacrament.
2 Services Divine service is perfor<med> twice on every Sun<day unless> some other ex<igency pre>vents it.
3 Sacrament The sacrament is administ<ered ? times> each year, that every pari<shioner may> receive the communion oft[e]ner if he pleases; but a<las for> it! Some of our parishion<ers cannot be> persuaded to receive th<e sacrament.>
4 Registers There is a register book belong<in>g to this pa<rish for christe>nings and burials; and als<o a re>gister book for marriages pursu<an>t to the directions contained in the Act of Parliament 'for the better preventing of clandestine marriages'.
5 Terrier <When the re>ctor came first to this par<ish there was n>either terrier of the glebe-<lands nor any> writing of the pensions <bel>onging to the parsonage. <So> the rector with assist<ance of> sensible parishioners <drew up> a state of the parsonage <and> of terrier, and deliver<ed it to the regi>stry of the archdeacon <for safe> custody; a copy of which <is kept in the pa>rish chest.
6 Churchyard <The church>yard is sufficiently <fenced and decen>tly kept, and no incroachments <have b>een made upon it.
7 Alterations <The fabric o>f the church hath not <been altered in a>ny respect. The pews and <galleries are> ancient, but strong and <. . .> on. There is an ancient <family> vault, and the family <monument and a>ll over the church<yard are grave>stones with inscriptions.
8 Impropriation <The rector possesses no c>uracy, and he <. . .> and he hopes carefully serves <the chur>ch.
9 Repair of parsonage <The parso>nage-house with the <barns, outho>uses and other build<ings there> to belonging are all in very <good> repair.
10 Residence The present rector resi<des in> his parsonage.
11 Dissenters There are 2 familie<s of dissenters> in this parish, who call <themselves> Anabaptists, and resor<t> to a meeting-house o<r chapel> at Broughton.
12 Loss of benefactions There was a benefaction <of £200 made by> John Webb to the poor of <this parish> who departed this life in th<e course> of the year 1736. By his wi<ll he appointed John Mersh and> John Jeans of

Broughton to <take> over the said money, and <with> him to buy land or an ann<uity with> the same, but instead the ro<gue> entered into <a> combination with his two sons (John and Thomas) to rob the poor, delivered up his estates to them (his sons) in his lifetime, and became insolvent; by which means this parish hath lost the greatest part of this benefaction. John Jeans, the eldest son of the said trustee, is an attor<ney>-at-law, and lives at Alton in this county.
13 Misbehaviour The ecclesiastical of<fi>cers have not misbehaved in any manner. The churchwardens perform their duties indifferently well. We have no sexton, but an excellent parish clerk.
[Appended:] The clause in John Webb's will by which he gives a legacy of £200 to the parish of West Titherly.

Item, I give and bequeath unto my kinsman John Mersh of Stockbridge and unto my loving friend John Jeans of Broughton, gentleman, the sum of £200 current money in trust and confidence that they or one of them shall and will lay it out on land and [at] the first opportunity purchase as much land as they can for the sa<m>e or purchase an annuity with the same out of som<e> freehold estate to be conveyed and assured unto the m<ini>ster churchwardens and overseers of the poor of West Titherly fo<r> the <ti>me being to and for the only use and behoof of such <poor> inhabitants of <W>est Titherly aforesaid as shall not or <d>o n<ot> receive alms o<r> are not any way chargeable to the par<i>sh. An<d> my will and desire farther is that the minister, churchwardens and overseers of the poor shall and will for the time being take care of the same, let, set, receive, take and pay or give the yearly rents issues and <p>rofites of all such lands, issues and profits out of such lands or annuities arising at Christmas yearly to the poor abovesaid fo<r eve>r.

414 Weyhill 21M65/B4/2/55

Joseph Simpson, rector 1756–97
1 Repair of church Yes.
2 Services Yes.
3 Sacrament The sacrament is regularly administered 4 times every year.
4 Registers Yes.
5 Terrier I have many; and some of them a hundred years old; and by the papers of Mr Bowerbank, my predecessor, in the year 1735, it appears that authentic copies of the said terriers were delivered into the Registry; because as he was going to law for half an acre, which it seems is now lost, I believe, he consulted the said terriers in the said Registry.
6 Churchyard The church yard is pretty well-fenced in. Different parts of it are repaired by different tenants, and therefore the fence is not regular, or equally good; but no encroachments are made upon it.
7 Alterations No alteration hath been made in any respect.
8 Impropriation Mine is a rectory; I have no curacy.
9 Repair of parsonage The parsonage-house and all other buildings thereunto belonging are in very good repair.
10 Residence I reside constantly upon my parsonage, and perform all the duty myself twice every Sunday.

11 Dissenters I have not one dissenter in my parish.
12 Loss of benefactions I do not. Richard Taunton Esq. left the interest of £200 for bread for the poor, and — Read Esq. 20*s*. p.a. for the use of the poor, which are applyed accordingly.
13 Misbehaviour The ecclesiastical officers have not misbehaved in any respect that I know of, and my parish officers perform their respective duties as they ought to do.

415 Wherwell (alias Horell) Prebend 21M65/B4/2/57
Richard Ring, vicar 1763–91
[Sole reply is to]
5 Terrier There is no terrier of the prebend, one would have been taken against the visitation had not a principal person concerned been so ill, that he could not attend, and who has kept his room for the last six weeks. One shall be taken as soon as can conveniently be done and a copy delivered into the office. The other articles are answered by me as vicar.

416 Wherwell (alias Horell) 21M65/B4/2/56
Richard Ring, vicar of Wherwell 1763–91 and 'curate of Tufton and Bullington'
1 Repair of church Yes.
2 Services Once every Sunday, there being two chapels annexed, viz. Bullington and Tufton, which are served alternately once a fortnight by the vicar of Wherwell.
3 Sacrament Yes.
4 Registers Yes.
5 Terrier A terrier of the vicarage was delivered in about 7 years ago.
6 Churchyard A small part of the churchyard on the north side was inclosed some years ago in the vicarage garden with a general consent and seen and approved of at a local visitation. The churchyard is well fenced.
7 Alterations No.
8 Impropriation I know not the value of the impropriation as yet.
9 Repair of parsonage Yes.
10 Residence I reside.
11 Dissenters About 4 or 5 who almost constantly attend the service of the church. No meeting-house.
12 Loss of benefactions No.
13 Misbehaviour I know of no officer who has taken undue fees nor anyone who has neglected his duty.

417 Whitchurch 21M65/B4/2/58
John Blair, vicar 1745/6–1783
1 Repair of church The chancel and the north wall of the church are not in good repair.
2 Services Yes.

3 Sacrament Yes.
4 Registers Yes.
5 Terrier No tythes of any kind are paid to the vicar.
6 Churchyard Churchyard is well fenced.
7 Alterations A small gallery or seat has been erected between two pillars on the north side of the church without a licence for so doing.
8 Impropriation [No reply; not applicable.]
9 Repair of parsonage The vicarage-house is a poor cottage, and it is in proper repair.
10 Residence Yes I do.
11 Dissenters There are very many dissenters, and 4 meeting-houses in the parish.
12 Loss of benefactions Some legacies have been left to the poor which are embezzled, and are not applied according to the wills of the donors.
13 Misbehaviour The church officers perform their respective duties.

418 Whitsbury 21M65/B4/2/119
Richard Tomkyn BA, 1747–77
[Unsigned.]
1 Repair of church The church and chancel in very good order, with all apurtenances of both.
2 Services Supplyed but once a Sunday as customarily. Rockborn twice a day, which is very contiguous.
3 Sacrament Yes.
4 Registers Yes.
5 Terrier I dont know whether the terrier is laid up in Your Lordship's Registry.
6 Churchyard The churchyard well fenced and decently kept. No incroachment made upon it.
7 Alterations Late Mr Delafaye erected the spire, and built the vestib[u]le and vestry room at his own expence. No dead bodys removed, nor any pews erected.
8 Impropriation Mr Morgan is allowed between 40 and 50£ p.a. for serving the curacys of Witsby and Rockbourn.
9 Repair of parsonage All in good repair.
10 Residence Mr Tompkins begs His Lordship's indulgence being prevented coming to Witsbury this summer. Mr Morgan — not licenced from the ordinary but will if required.
11 Dissenters No.
12 Loss of benefactions No.
13 Misbehaviour The churchwardens and clerk, faithfully perform their respective dutys.

419 Wickham 21M65/B4/2/106
John Sandford BA, rector 1753–66
[Unsigned.]
1 Repair of church Yes.

2 Services Yes, in general.
3 Sacrament The sacrament is administered 4 times in each year.
4 Registers Yes.
5 Terrier No. The parsonage is indowed with a glebe and the predial tithe of the said parish. The glebe consists of 34 acres of good ground in 7 pieces lying contiguous to the house.
6 Churchyard The churchyard is fenced and no incroachment has been made upon it.
7 Alterations No.
8 Impropriation [No reply; not applicable.]
9 Repair of parsonage Yes.
10 Residence No. My patron, the late Mr Rashleigh, wanted the parsonage for himself and family, till he had repaired his own house.
11 Dissenters There are in this parish a few papists, but there is no place for divine worship.
12 Loss of benefactions No.
13 Misbehaviour I dont know that they have. Yes to the best of my knowledge.

420 Widley and Wymering 21M65/B4/2/197
Richard Harris, rector 1748/9–1768
1 Repair of church Both in as good repair as the generality of churches are, and going to be made better.
2 Services Only once a day at each, being united.
3 Sacrament Four times constantly at each.
4 Registers Both.
5 Terrier I cannot say there is a regular terrier, but I believe everything is right.
6 Churchyard Both of them.
7 Alterations There have been seats built, whether lycensed by the ordinary [I] am not certain.
8 Impropriation [No reply; not applicable.]
9 Repair of parsonage At Widley, though a rectory, I have neither house, out-house, or any other building whatever, or place even to putt a horse in, though where and what they were is sufficiently plain, and swallowed up by the squire, [I] should be glad to know by what means, power or authority. At Wimering there is a house in good repair, chiefly built by myself.
10 Residence I reside upon the vicarage, there being no house upon the rectory.
11 Dissenters [I] am not certain of any.
12 Loss of benefactions I believe everything is done in the best manner it can.
13 Misbehaviour The first I know not; the other, to the best of my knowledge they do.

421 Wield 21M65/B4/2/15

John Hoadly, rector 'of Weild' 1737–76
John Downes, curate

1 Repair of church The church with its chancel are <in> good and sufficient repair. And all <things> necessary for the celebration of divin<e> service, and the administration of the <holy> sacrament are provided.
2 Services Divine service is performed in our c<hurch> twice on every Sunday.
3 Sacrament The sacrament is administered fou<r times> in each year.
4 Registers We have a register book for christe<nings> and burials; and a separate one for <marria>ges.
5 Terrier The parish of Weild is a lay impropriation.
6 Churchyard The churchyard is sufficiently fenced, and decently kept. And no person, as far as I know, hath incroached upon it.
7 Alterations The fabrick of the church has not been altered; no pews have been erected; no galleries built, nor vaults dug, nor dead bodies removed.
8 Impropriation The stipend allowed to me by the impropriator is £26, the same which has been usually allowed. The yearly value of the impropriation is computed at £90 or thereabouts.
9 Repair of parsonage <T>here is neither house, nor any other <bui>lding, belonging to the church in this <pari>sh.
10 Residence I do not reside in this parish, but at Medstead contiguous to it, the usual residence of the curate of Weild and Medstead. I have not b<een> licenced to this curacy.
11 Dissenters There are no dissenters of any denomination in this parish.
12 Loss of benefactions I know of no such benefact<ion> which has either been withheld or <mis>applied.
13 Misbehaviour I know nothing of the misbeha<vi>our of the ecclesiastical officers. The churchwardens, clerk, and the other officers of our church do perform their respective duties.

422 Winchester, St Bartholomew Hyde 21M65/B4/2/153

Daniel Mayo, vicar 1759[?]–1768

1 Repair of church It is, and all things necessary etc. provided.
2 Services Service every Sunday in the afternoon. The reason — the income small, about £27 a year.
3 Sacrament It is.
4 Registers I have.
5 Terrier There are no glebe-lands, gardens etc. belonging to the vicarage.
6 Churchyard I know nothing to the contrary.
7 Alterations I know of no alteration in the fabric, no pews erected, galleries built, vaults dug without licence, or dead body removed.
8 Impropriation I have no curacy.
9 Repair of parsonage The vicarage-house is in proper repair. No other building.
10 Residence I live in the city of Winchester.

11 Dissenters There are a few, but no meeting-place for worship.
12 Loss of benefactions I know of no benefaction witheld or charity abuses.
13 Misbehaviour I know of no misbehaviour in ecclesiastical officers, churchwardens etc.

423 Winchester, St Lawrence 21M65/B4/2/154
Reynell Cotton, rector 1742–68
[Unsigned.]
1 Repair of church The church of St Lawrence and all its furniture is neat and decent.
2 Services Service is performed twice every Sunday.
3 Sacrament The sacrament is administered 3 times every year.
4 Registers There are 2 register books.
5 Terrier I have no lands. The profits of the rectory are by modus.
6 Churchyard I have no churchyard.
7 Alterations The fabrick of the church hath not been altered.
8 Impropriation I allow my curate the whole income of the rectory, and we both reside in Winchester.
9 Repair of parsonage The parsonage-house is in good repair.
10 Residence This is answered in the 8th article.
11 Dissenters I have only one family of dissenters.
12 Loss of benefactions I know of none.
13 Misbehaviour I have no complaint under this article.

424 Winchester, St Maurice, with SS. George, Vade, Mary Kalendar and Peter Colebrook 21M65/B4/2/198
Richard Wavell, rector of St. Maurice etc. 1741–79
1 Repair of church My church with its chancel is in good repair, and all things necessary for the celebration of divine service etc. are provided.
2 Services Divine service is performed in my church twice on every Sunday.
3 Sacrament The sacrament is administered so often in each year that every parishioner may receive the communion three times.
4 Registers I have a register book for christenings and burials, and also a register book for marriages etc.
5 Terrier I have an account in writing of the lands etc. belonging to my parsonage; but I have no terrier.
6 Churchyard We bury in the cathedral churchyard.
7 Alterations [No reply.]
8 Impropriation [No reply.]
9 Repair of parsonage All the buildings belonging to my parsonage are in good repair.
10 Residence I reside on my parsonage.
11 Dissenters There are some protestant dissenters, and some reputed Papists, in my parishes. The former have a meeting-house in the parish of S. M[ary] Calendre.

12 Loss of benefactions I do not know etc.
13 Misbehaviour There is no reason to complain of any person mentioned in this article.

425 Winchester, St Michael (in the Soke) 21M65/B4/2/199
William Mence BA, rector 1756–89
John Bailley, curate
1 Repair of church All in good order.
2 Services Twice every Sunday.
3 Sacrament The sacrament is administered upon the festivals, and upon the first Sunday of every month in the year.
4 Registers We have.
5 Terrier No glebe or tythe belonging to the rectory.
6 Churchyard Well fenced, and no encroachments.
7 Alterations No alterations.
8 Impropriation [No reply.]
9 Repair of parsonage No parsonage-house, barn or out-house.
10 Residence The rector is in Minorca and I serve the church in his absence.
11 Dissenters Few dissenters of any denomination; but no house or place of divine worship.
12 Loss of benefactions No.
13 Misbehaviour I do not know that any undue fees have been taken. And the churchwardens and the clerk perform their respective duties.

426 Winchester, St Peter and St John (in the Soke) 21M65/B4/2/200
Thomas Rees, rector 1765–69
1 Repair of church Yes.
2 Services Service is performed but once by custom.
3 Sacrament Yes.
4 Register Both.
5 Terrier We have no glebe-land.
6 Churchyard It is; nor hath it been incroached upon.
7 Alterations Not to my knowledge.
8 Impropriation The stipend of my curacy is £20 p.a. The same as usually allowed.
9 Repair of parsonage There is no house.
10 Residence I live in the neighbourhood of the parish.
11 Dissenters There are dissenters of various denominations, and there is a licenced meeting-house for Methodists.
12 Loss of benefactions I know of no abuse of any benefaction or charity relating to either.
13 Misbehaviour I know of no misbehaviour, nor have I cause of complaint against any ecclesiastical officer.

427 Winchester, St. Swithin (alias Kingsgate) 21M65/B4/2/201
William Jourd, curate
1 Repair of church Yes.

2 Services Divine service is only performed once on a Sunday; twice on all sacrament days.
3 Sacrament Yes.
4 Registers Yes.
5 Terrier There is no house, no garden, etc. There is a pension paid yearly (by His Majesty) of £3 5*s*. clear.
6 Churchyard No churchyard.
7 Alterations The church is in good repair.
8 Impropriation The value of the living is no more than 11 guineas p.a., and very few surplice fees.
9 Repair of parsonage No house etc.
10 Residence The curate lives near the place, and constantly serves it.
11 Dissenters No dissenters.
12 Loss of benefactions I find no abuse of any benefaction or charity.
13 Misbehaviour The churchwardens and officers, clerk etc., do their duties.

428 Winchester, St Thomas (with St Clement and St Peter in Macellis)
Jacob Freer, rector 1756–73 21M65/B4/2/155
1 Repair of church Yes.
2 Services Service is performed every Sunday.
3 Sacrament Yes.
4 Registers Yes.
5 Terrier Yes.
6 Churchyard The churchyard is sufficiently fenced, and no person hath incroached upon it in my time.
7 Alterations No.
8 Impropriation I have no curacy.
9 Repair of parsonage There is no parsonage-house.
10 Residence I do.
11 Dissenters There are dissenters, but no place for divine worship that I can bear testimony to.
12 Loss of benefactions No.
13 *Misbehaviour* Not that I know of; they do.

429 Winnall 21M65/B4/2/202
John Derby BA, rector 1753–65
John Monk Newbolt, curate
1 Repair of church Yes.
2 Services Service is performed but once by custom.
3 Sacrament Yes.
4 Registers Both.
5 Terrier No glebe-land belonging to the living.
6 Churchyard It is, nor hath been incroached upon.
7 Alterations Not to my knowledge.
Impropriation The stipend of my curacy is £25 p.a., the same as usually allowed.

9 Repair of parsonage There is no house belonging to the living, to my knowledge.
10 Residence A curate is constantly resident.
11 Dissenters Yes.
12 Loss of benefactions No.
13 Misbehaviour No; yes.

430 Wolverton 21M65/B4/2/82
John Craven, rector 1759–1804
1 Repair of church Yea.
2 Services Yea.
3 Sacrament There are 5 sacraments in a year, viz., the 3 festivals, Trinity Sunday and the Sunday before St Michael.
4 Registers Yea.
5 Terrier No.
6 Churchyard Yea; no.
7 Alterations No.
8 Impropriation The living is 6 score £ p.a., and the curate is allowed £35 p.a. and very little duty to perform.
9 Repair of parsonage Yea.
10 Residence Yea. No; the curate resides in the parish of Hannington, and is only as an assistant to the rector of Woolverton.
11 Dissenters No.
12 Loss of benefactions There has been an abuse for 19 years, but is now, I hope, properly applied.
13 Misbehaviour No; yea.

431 Wootton St Lawrence 21M65/B4/2/83
Philip Eyre LLB, vicar 1743–71
John Raisbeck, curate
[No replies.] I am only curate of Lawrence Wooton.

432 Worting 21M65/B4/2/84
Walter Bigg LLB, rector 1745–72
1 Repair of church The church and chancell in good repair, and necessary things decently provided.
2. Services Yes.
3 Sacrament Yes.
4 Registers Yes.
5 Terrier A very small and indisputable glebe; and no pension belonging to the parsonage.
6 Churchyard Beautifully fenced and decently kept and not encroached upon.
7 Alterations The fabric of the church has not been altered for many years. The chancell rebuilt on the old foundation, and the pews repaired.

8 Impropriation I am possessed of no curacy.
9 Repair of parsonage All in good repair, being rebuilt not long since.
10 Residence I reside.
11 Dissenters No.
12 Loss of benefactions No.
13 Misbehaviour Not as I know of; very well.

433 Yateley 21M65/B4/2/85

John Price Jones, curate 1760–76
[No replies.] *Omnia bene.*

The Visitation of 1788
Hampshire and Isle of Wight

Brownlow North (1741–1820), Bishop of Winchester 1781–1820. Engraving by W. Bond from a painting by H. Howard.
(Hampshire Record Office, Winchester City Archives, W/K2/4/31)

Episcopal Visitation, 1788

Printed Articles of Inquiry

Reverend Brother,

It is my purpose, God willing, in the course of the present year to visit the diocese of Winchester, and at the same time to hold a confirmation therein; but, wishing to be particularly informed of the state of my diocese, and to be provided with such materials as may enable me to act according to the variety of occasions which may at that, or at any other time, arise, I desire that you will answer distinctly in writing to the several questions which I have thought it necessary to put to you: directing your returns to me at Farnham Castle, Surry, on or before the last day of March next: subscribing the said return with your name and title, together with that of your parish. I am,

Reverend Sir,
Your loving brother,
B[rownlow North] Winchester

Farnham Castle,
January 1, 1788

1 What compass of ground do you suppose to be in your parish?
2 What number of souls, according to the best information you can get, do you suppose to be in your parish?
3 What number of marriages, births and burials, may you have at a medium, one year with another?
4 Who is the patron of your living?
5 Have you any chapel, or chapels within your parish? By what name are they called? By whom are they served? How maintained or supported? And who hath the right of nomination to them?
6 Have you any lecturer or curate within your parish? Who are they? By whom are they nominated to their respective lectureship or curacy? Are they licensed to the same?
7 What number of Papists are supposed to be in your parish? What meetings are held therein of Protestant Dissenters? Of what denomination are they? And about what number of each sect respectively may there be?
8 What schools are there in your parish? How are they endowed? Who are the masters or mistresses of such schools, and by whom nominated? What is the number of scholars?

9 Are there any hospitals or endowed charitable instiututions, or any fixed annual donations for the benefit of the poor in your parish? In order that I and my successors may be particularly informed herein, I must desire that you will send to me, together with your answer to these questions, a copy of the return which you made to the late parliamentary enquiry on this subject.

434 Abbotts Ann 21M65/B4/3/1

Thomas Burrough MA, rector 1774–1831

1 Area I cannot ascertain the exact number of acres of land there are in this parish, but suppose there are about 2,800.

2 Population 417.

3 Marriages &c. On a medium for the last 4 years there have been 4 marriages; 18 births; 11 burials.

4 Patron The Revd J. Willis Burrough, rector of St Mary Blandford, Dorset, and the Revd Thomas Burrough, the present rector, are patrons of the living of Ab<bots Ann>.

5 Chapels Non<e>.

6 Lecturer None.

7 Dissenters We have no reputed Papist or dissenters' meeting in this parish.

8 Schools Thomas Criswick in the year 1727 left £3 a year to be paid out of his freehold estate in Little Anne, for educating the <p>oor children of this parish. The present <mas>ter's name is Charles Brown.

9 Charities None.

435 Aldershot 21M65/B4/3/2

James Jackson, perpetual curate

1 Area The parish of Aldershott is about 11 miles in circumference.

2 Population About 350.

3 Marriages &c. There have been for 5 years last past, at a medium, marriages 3; births 10; burials 6.

4 Patron The living of Aldershott is a perpetual curacy; the tythes are held by the Dean of Chichester of the Master of St Cross.

5 Chapels Not any.

6 Lecturer The curate is the Revd James Jackson.

7 Dissenters Papists none; meetings none; and very few dissenters.

8 Schools None.

9 Charities There are no hospitals. Only one donation of 30*s.* p.a. left by Mr Viner for the benefit of the poor of the parish.

436 Alverstoke 21M65/B4/3/3

John Sturges, rector 1774–1807? 31 March 1788

1 Area It is about 4 miles long and 1½ at a medium wide.

2 Population There are in Gosport about 1,000 houses, which at 5½ inhabitan<ts> a house would make the number of inhabitants 550<0>. In the other parts of the parish 263 houses which at 5<½> to a house would make the number <1,446.>

3 Marriages &c. Average of the 4 years 1780, 81, 82, 83 in war:

	Marriages	<Births>	<Burials>
Alverstoke	156	4<4>	< >
Gosport	115	197	< >
The whole parish	261	24<1>	< >
Do. of 4 years 1784, 85, 86, 87 in peace:			
Alverstoke	115	51	< >
Gosport	36	144	< >
The whole parish	151	195	< >
Average of whole parish, taking peace and war together:	206	218	< >

4 Patron The Bishop of Winchester.

5 Chapels There is a chapel in Gosport, called Gosport chapel. <It is> served by a perpetual curate or minister of its own, <nominated> by the rector. The present minister is Isaac Moody <Bingham>. A farm or glebe belongs to it, purchased by several benefactions of Queen Anne's Bounty. The minister also receives voluntary contributions.

6 Lecturer There is no lecturer or curate of any <sort> within my parish, except the aforesaid c<urate> who is licensed.

7 Dissenters Papists are supposed not to exceed 25 or 30. <There is a> meeting of protestant dissenters, chiefly Independents, <seating about> 700 persons.

8 Schools There is no endowed school.

9 Charities *1660* Ltnt John Man gave by his will £5 yearly <paid> to the churchwardens and overseers out of some <houses in ... > Alley in St George's parish, Southwark, now < ... > of St Thomas's Hospital and paid by their...

1671 Newham Hewlett by will gave 20*s.* to the poor payable to the collectors every Lady Day in rents of his dwelling house now belonging to <Mr> Grist.

Jane Holmes widow, by her will gave 40*s.* to be distributed <to poor> widows on every Christmas Eve by the minister and churchwardens, chargeable on her <estate> near the church, now belonging to Mr James Ayling. The said Jane Holmes also gave her cottage and garden <at the> west end of the said messuages to the churchwardens and <overseers> and their successors for ever, and ordered the rent <thereof> to be distributed annually among poor widows.

1719 William Allen gent. by his will g<ave to be> paid quarterly to the churchwardens to be <distributed> to the poor at their discretion out of the rents of <houses in> Gosport and Alverstoke.

1749 Charles Childe, merchant, by his will gave to wit £5 on every Christmas Eve and £5 on every< ... > payable to the minister and church-wardens out of the <rent of> a house in Middle Street, Gosport <to be by>

them distributed <to> poor persons residing in Gosport and not receiving alms.
1773 Mr William Clowe by will charged his house in Gosport with £5 yearly for ever free of all taxes and <rates> to the churchwarden of the Liberty part of the church to be given by him after every Sunday morning service therein. Widows in preference, not receiving alms.

For some remaining charities in the town of Gosport I refer to the return made to Your Lordship <by the minister of Gosport> chapel.

437 Amport 21M65/B4/3/4
Charles Harwood MA, rector 1784–1802
Henry White, curate
1 Area About 3,500 acres.
2 Population About 380.
3 Marriages &c. Baptisms about 8 yearly; burials about 5; marriages scarcely 2.
4 Patron The Dean and Chapter of Chichester.
5 Chapels Appleshaw is a chapel of ease, but maintains its own poor etc., the curate appointed and paid £30 p.a. by the rector of Amport.
6 Lecturer No lecturer of any kind.
7 Dissenters None of any kind.
8 Schools None of any kind.
9 Charities No charitable donations of any kind.

438 Appleshaw 21M65/B4/3/5
Charles Harwood MA, rector of Amport 1784–1802
Henry White, curate
1 Area Nearly 600 acres.
2 Population Upwards of 200.
3 Marriages &c. Baptisms about 5 yearly; burials about 3; marriages 42 in 32 years.
4 Patron Appleshaw is a chapel of ease to the rectory of Amport.
5 Chapels Served by the curate of Amport generally; and the curate always appointed by the rector of Amport.
6 Lecturer None.
7 Dissenters None.
8 Schools No endowed school.
9 Charities £50 legacy left by Mrs Offlay, the interest of which is applied to the teaching poor children to read. No copy of the return made to the parliamentary enquiry can be found.

439 Arreton [IoW] 21M65/B4/3/161
Tovey Jolliffe, vicar 1784–91 25 March 1788
Henry Worsley, curate –1791
1 Area Understanding that your Lordship has signified that you would be pleased to accept the estimate of the quantity of land of the whole island as

given in Sir Richard Worsley's *History*, I suspended my enquiry with respect to the quantum of my particular parish. The whole island is computed at 100,000 acres.
2 Population I suppose from the best information I can get the number of souls to be about 1,160.
3 Marriages &c. I have at a medium yearly marriages 5, births 32, burials 14.
4 Patron The patron, John Fleming Esq.
5 Chapels There is no chapel within my parish.
6 Lecturer There is no lectureship or curacy within my parish.
7 Dissenters There is no Papist, no meeting of protestant dissenters of any denomination whatever within my parish.
8 Schools There is no endowed school in the parish, but the minister, churchwardens and overseers employ a person resident in the village to educate the poor children and allow him £15 p.a. out of their annual donations for that purpose; at present he has about 30 children under his care.
9 Charities There is no hospital, or endowed charitable institution in my parish.
Copy of the return to the late parliamentary enquiry
John Mann, by will bearing date 1687/8, gave the sum of £46 p.a. for the education and setting up in the world poor children of this parish and after that to the maintenance of poor and impotent persons of the parish.
John Serle by will bearing date 1592 gave the sum of £100 to the use of the poor of the parish, to be laid out in the purchase of lands or otherwise.
Richard Gard gave by will bearing date 1617 10*s*. p.a. for the use of the poor of the parish.
Mr Mann's donation was in land being the fee farm rents issuing out of pastures called Nobb's, and meadows called Northings, Sidings, and Marshallings in the county of York, received annually by the minister, churchwardens and overseers, who apply it agreeably to the instruction of the will. The amount is £46; annual produce after deducting land tax and other expenses £40.
Mr Gard's donation was in money payable out of lands and tenements in the parish of Newchurch in the Isle of Wight and received by the minister, churchwardens and overseers and applied as directed, amount £10 a year.
Mr Serle's donation of £100 was laid out in land the rent of which is received by the minister, churchwardens and overseers and applied to the use of the poor as the will directs, amount £11 a year.
There are 30*s*. more paid yearly from certain lands in the parish, but by whom left I have not been able to learn.

440 Ashe 21M65/B4/3/6
Isaac Peter George Lefroy, rector 1783–1806 20 March 1788
1 Area By the perambulation and measurement made last May, it appears the circumference is rather more than 15 miles. But the quantity of acres given in seems to fall far short, amounting to only 1,859, exclusive of roads, fences, houses and gardens.

2 Population About 184.
3 Marriages &c. Only 7 marriages from June 30, 1757 to [the] present date; births 19 from 1767 to December 1787; burials 26 from do. to do.
4 Patron Wither Bramston Esq. of Hall Place, Hants.
5 Chapels Neither chapels nor chapel in my parish.
6 Lecturer No lecturer or curate.
7 Dissenters I know of no Papists <nor> dissenter of any description in the parish.
8 Schools There is one privat<e school> where children learn to <read> but not any endowed scho<ol in> the parish.
9 Charities There are no hospitals, o<r> charitable institutions <with> fixed annual donations for the poor in this par<ish.> The parish had formerly a right, with the adjoining pa<rish> of Dean, to send one pauper each to the almshouse <at> Basingstoke, founded <by> Sir James Dean, but tha<t> right has long since <been> lost to this parish a<s Dean> now sends 2 paup<ers yearly.> The average of the po<or rate> from Easter 1738 to do. <1787> has been about £16 p.a. amounting to abo<ut> £57 9*s*. 4*d*. But for the few years of that period from < ... > 20 rates have been coll<ected> amounting at 20 rates to £71 16*s*. 8*d*. Not having preserved any copy of the return made to the late parliamentary enquiry, this is the fullest answer that can be made to the last question.

441 Ashley 21M65/B4/3/7
John Speed BCL, rector 1777–93
Henry Taylor, curate
1 Area 1,700 acres.
2 Population 86 souls.
3 Marriages &c. Medium for the last 8 years beginning with 1780 births 3; marriages not quite 1; burials 2. In the last 8 years, marriages 7; births 26; burials 16.
4 Patron Revd Dr Taunton and Miss Ballard.
5 Chapels None.
6 Lecturer No lecturer or lectureship. No curate but the substitute of the rector Henry <Taylor> nominated by the rector. Not licensed. Curate Henry Taylor.
7 Dissenters None.
8 Schools None.
9 Charities None. No hospital, no endowed charitable institution, or fixed donation for the benefit of the poor, so far as I can find by the best enquiry I can. Such was the tenor of the return made to Parliament of which I have preserved no copy.

442 Ashmansworth 21M65/B4/3/8
Thomas Shephard, curate
1 Area About 7 miles in circumference.
2 Population About 150.

3 Marriages &c. Marriages 2; burials 2; births 5.
4 Patron The Bishop of Winchester.
5 Chapels None.
6 Lecturer None.
7 Dissenters None.
8 Schools None.
9 Charities None.

443 Barton Stacey 21M65/B4/3/9
John Dennis MA, vicar 1778–89
Bradnam Tawney, curate
1 Area About 8,136 acres.
2 Population About 462.
3 Marriages &c. Marriages about 5; births 12; burials 9.
4 Patron The Dean and Chapter of Winchester.
5 Chapels None.
6 Lecturer Bradnam Tawney, curate, not lic<ensed>, appointed by Revd John Dennis AM.
7 Dissenters No Papists or dissenters, nor any meetings held in the parish.
8 Schools One school for 12 poor children nominated to and supported by Miss Wright, daughter of the late Sir Martin Wright. The name of the mistress, Elizabeth Price. This is only <a> voluntary subscription of 5 guineas p.a., < ... > will help with the ladies.
9 Charities No hospital, but an annual donation of £1 10*s*. to be distributed in bread, which money is paid from the rent of a piece of land, appropriated for that purpose, by the will of the late Mr Jacob Hinxman of the parish of Barton Stacey.
NB A copy of the return made to Mr Gilbert's inquiry could not be procured, the farmer who made the same being removed at some distance from the parish and he himself having no other copy than that delivered in to the Justices.

444 Basingstoke 21M65/B4/3/10/1–2
Thomas Sheppard DD, vicar 1768–1814
1 Area 3,300 acres.
2 Population 1,740.
3 Marriages &c. Marriages 19; births 62; burials 49.
4 Patron Magdalen College, Oxford.
5 Chapels Holy Ghost Chapel, endowed with lands, the minister the Revd Mr Evans, the chapel in ruins. The right of nomination [in] the king. Basing and Nately chapels, served by the Revd Mr Evans.
6 Lecturer One lecturer, the Revd Thomas Sheppard DD; one curat<e,> Revd Isaac Williamson. The lecturer nominated by <the> corporation of Basingstoke, is licensed. The <curate is> not licensed to his present curacy, but licensed in <another> diocese.
7 Dissenters No Papists. Methodists 190, with a chapel. Presbyterians 163, with a meeting. Quakers 16, with a meeting.

8 Schools The blue coat school, endowed with lands, the number of scholars, 8. Holy Ghost School, indowed with lands, the number of scholars that may be received unlimited, the number at present about 10. Another charity school endowed with land, the number of scholars that may be taught unlimited, the present number between 10 and 20.
9 Charities No hospitals. What donations there are may be seen in the copy of the return.
A [condensed] copy of the return made by the vicar and churchwardens of Basingstoke of all the charitable donations for the benefit of the poor
Robert Holloway in 1578 left 10*s*. p.a. each for the use of the poor, for the master of the Holy Ghost School, and for repairing the highways, from tenements in Chapel Street, Basingstoke.
John Green in 1582 left 10*s*. p.a. each for the use of the poor, for the master of the Holy Ghost School, and for repairing the said school, deriving from sources unknown and still yielding £1 10*s*. p.a.
Mr Brown, vicar, in 1586 left £20 in money for the use of the poor; yield unknown.
Mr Thomas Henry in 1598 left £10 in money for the use of the poor; yield unknown.
Mr Richard Deane in 1600 left an annuity for the use of the poor yielding £5 4*s*. p.a. from lands vested in the corporation of Basingstoke.
Sir James Deane in 1607 left an annuity of £72 18*s*. p.a. from lands vested in the corporation of Basingstoke to be divided as follows:- for the maintenance of 6 poor persons in his almshouses in Basingstoke at £6 1*s*. 8*d*. p.a. each, £36 10*s*.; for a gown each of the price of 13*s*. 4*d*. annually, £4; for repairing the almshouses p.a. £1; for bread to be distributed to the poor weekly, £10 8*s*.; for the lecturer, £10; for the master of the Holy Ghost School, £10; for repairing a footway, £1.
Mr John Wigg in 1607 left £20 in money for the use of the poor; yield unknown.
Mr John Petty in 1613 left £20 in money for the use of the poor; yield unknown.
Sir James Lancaster in 1618 left by will the sum of £118 6*s*. 8*d*. p.a. from lands vested in the corporation of Basingtoke to be divided as follows:- to be distributed in money weekly to the poor, £45; for the lecturer, £40; for the master and usher of the Holy Ghost School, £20; for the petty school master, £13 6*s*. 8*d*.
Mr Matthew Stocker in 1621 left £5 in money for the use of the poor; yield unknown.
Mrs Ursula Stocker in 1622 left £10 for the use of the poor, vested in the corporation of Basingstoke and yielding 10*s*. p.a.
Mr Robert Pain in 1622 left by will £100 in money vested in the corporation of Basingstoke and yielding £1 p.a. to be distributed among 20 poor people.
Mr Henry Plumpton in 1623 left £25 in money to produce £2 p.a. for the use of the poor; yield unknown.
Mr John Hall in 1632 left by will £5 4*s*. p.a. issuing out of a cow meadow in Basingstoke and vested in the corporation, to be distributed in bread weekly to 24 poor people; and 1*s*. p.a. vested in Mary Cooke, spinster, for the master of the Holy Ghost School.

Mr George Pemberton in 1634 left by deed £100 in money vested in the corporation of Basingstoke and yielding £5 p.a. for the use of the poor.
Mr John Smith in 1638 left by will £4 p.a. from lands vested in the churchwardens of Basingstoke, to be distributed in linen and woollens to 8 poor persons; augmented in 1674 by £52 in money vested in the corporation of Basingstoke, yielding £2 p.a.
Richard Aldworth in 1646 left by will £105 4*s*. p.a. issuing from lands vested in the corporation of Basingstoke, to be divided as follows:- for the lecturer, £10; for dieting and clothing 10 poor boys in the blue coat school in Basingstoke, £6 13*s*. 4*d*. each, £66 13*s*. 4*d*.; for a master educating the said boys, £10; for apprenticing one of such boys annually, £6 13*s*. 4*d*.; for a gown each to 5 poor old men and 5 women, £6 13*s*. 4*d*.; for 12 penny loaves every Sabbath day for the same, £2 1*s*.; for the same every lecture day, £2 12*s*.
Charles, Duke of Bolton, in 1694 gave by will £42 p.a. in lands vested in the mayor of Basingstoke for the use of the poor.
William Blunden Esq. in 1732 gave £10 p.a. in an annuity from lands vested in trustees for the use of the poor.

445 Baughurst 21M65/B4/3/11

William Dee Best, rector 'of Baghurst' 1769–96

1 Area I suppose the compass of ground in my parish to be about 1,300 acres.

2 Population According to the best information I can get, the number of souls in my parish are about 250.

3 Marriages &c. The number of marriages at a medium one year with another are about 3; the number of births about 12; the number of burials about 6.

4 Patron The bishop of the diocese.

5 Chapels There is no chapel within my parish.

6 Lecturer There is no lecturer nor curate within my parish.

7 Dissenters There is only one Papist. There is a Quakers' meeting-house seldom attended except by the male part of only one family. There are no other dissenters in my parish.

8 Schools There is only one school in my parish, lately opened by my permission, and kept for day scholars who are taught reading, writing, arithmetic, plain-work, knitting and spinning, by John Miles and his wife. The number of scholars [is] about 40.

9 Charities There is neither hospital nor any endowed charitable institution. But there is a fixed annual donation amounting in the whole to the sum of £3 15*s*. 3*d*., which is distributed about Christmas to such poor who do not receive constant relief. By the return delivered to the House of Commons, it appeared that a person by the name of Simpson left a rent charge of £2 10*s*. p.a. out of his estate in the parish of Baghurst, and 10*s*. was a rent charge left by a person called Carter, and 15*s*. 3*d*. was the interest of £19, £10 of which sum wa<s le>ft by a person of the name of Dollery and £9 was left by a person of the name of Smart.[Total £3 15*s*. 3*d*.]

446 Beaulieu 21M65/B4/3/31/1–2

Richard Burleigh, minister of Beaulieu

[This imperfect document contains no attribution of place, but appears to relate to Beaulieu. It is accompanied by a fragment, 21M65/B4/3/31/2, signed '<>d Burleigh, rector' mentioning an endowment for the poor of Chilton Candover.]

1 Area The compass of ground in my parish is about 7000 acres.

2 Population The number of souls in my parish according to the best information I can get, I suppose to be about 1,400.

3 Marriages &c. The number of marriages, births and burials, at a medium, one year with another, is as follows: 12 marriages; 44 births; 23 burials.

4 Patrons <The> patrons of the living are His Grace the Duke of Montagu <and the> Earl of Beaulieu.

5 Chapels <There is> no chapel within my parish.

6 Lecturer <There> is neither lecturer nor curate within my parish.

7 Dissenters <There> are no Papists, nor more than 2 protestant dissenters in my parish.

8 Schools There is one school in my parish, which is entirely supported by a subscription of the inhabitants. The name of the master is Charles Read. The subscribers nominate the master. The number of scholars is about 70.

9 Charities There is no hospital, or endowed charitable institution in my parish. The substance of the return made to the late parliamentary enquiry is this. There is about £70 in the hands of the parish officers, the interest of which is appropriated to the relief of the poor. Whe<n> or by whom bequeathed is not known.

[The fragment, signed < > Burleigh, rector, gives the following answers only:]

7 Dissenters None.

8 Schools None.

9 Charities None.

[A surviving portion of the respondent's summary of his reply to the inquiry under the Gilbert Act refers to the poor of Chilton Candover. Richard Burleigh MA was rector of Chilton Candover from 1766 to 1798, but is not thought to be same man as the minister of Beaulieu.]

447 Bedhampton 21M65/B4/3/12

Edward Tew MA, rector 1780–1818

Griffith Richards, curate

1 Area There are about 1,700 acres of land, including arable, pasture, coppice, forrest and waste lands.

2 Population About 270.

3 Marriages &c. Marriages 1; births 10; burials 3.

4 Patron Lord Stowel.

5 Chapels None.

6 Lecturer There is no curate besides myself, not licensed. No lecturer.

7 Dissenters About 20 Papists, including children and servants; about 6 protestant dissenters.

8 Schools There is a woman's school supported by voluntary subscription; about 20 scholars.
9 Charities None.

448 Bentley 21M65/B4/3/13
Gabriel Tahourdin, curate 1771–1814 31 March 1788
1 Area About 2,000 acres.
2 Population About 400.
3 Marriages &c. Marriages 3; births 15; burials 8.
4 Patron William Bendysh Esq.
[Questions 5–8 no reply.]
9 Charities Smith's money about £5 p.a.; lands let £4 18*s*. p.a.

449 Bentworth 21M65/B4/3/14
Edward Acton, rector 1777–91
1 Area About 3,000 acres.
2 Population About 450.
3 Marriages &c. 2 marriages; 17 births; 10 burials.
4 Patron Edward Acton, rector.
5 Chapels No chapel.
6 Lecturer No lecturer or curate.
7 Dissenters No Papists or dissenters.
8 Schools No schools.
9 Charities No hospitals. 20*s*. p.a. left by Sarah Greaves out of lands situate in Alton. 20*s*. p.a. payable out of an estate now in possession of Stephen Hockley, situate in Bentworth, not known by whom given.

450 Binstead [IoW] 21M65/B4/3/162
William Dickonson, rector 1758–94 25 March 1788
1 Area The superficial content of the whole island (according to Sir Richard Worsley's *History*) amounts to about 100,000 acres.
2 Population The number of souls 154 according to Sir Richard Worsley's *History* taken in the year 1777.
3 Marriages &c. Baptisms 5; marriages 2; burials 6.
4 Patron Lord Bishop of Winchester.
5 Chapels No chapel.
6 Lecturer No lecturer or curate.
7 Dissenters No Papists or meetings of dissenters of any sect.
8 Schools No schools.
9 Charities No hospitals or any endowed charitable institutions or fixed annual donations for the benefit of the poor. No copy was kept of the return made to the late parliamentary enquiry on this subject.

451 Binsted 21M65/B4/3/15/1–2
Thomas Balguy DD, vicar 1771–95
John Mill, curate
1 Area The compass of ground in the parish of Binsted [is] about 25 miles.

2 Population The number of souls in the parish of Binsted [is] about 350.
3 Marriages &c. Marriages from 5 to 7; births from 15 to 17; burials from 8 to 10.
4 Patron The living of Binsted is in the gift of the Dean and Chapter of Winchester; the vicar, the Revd Dr Balguy.
5 Chapels Kingsley.
6 Lecturer Not any.
7 Dissenters Not any.
8 Schools Not any.
9 Charities A donation to the parish of Binsted of 40*s*. p.a., given by the Revd Samuel Woodford. Also 16*s*. p.a. paid by Mr John Knight of Headly, out of an estate in the parish of Steadham in Sussex.
[Appended]
Get from Chelsea curate of Binsted's return to visitation queries in 1788. Alton Deanery, Hants.
As also Frensham in Stoke Deanery, Surrey.
Also John Bap's ordination papers in February 1763.
Also Richard Cheese lic<en>s<e>d to Bentley on 20 May 1760.
Also 29 Aug, 1740 James Phipps lic<en>s<e>d to Frensham.

452 Bishopstoke 21M65/B4/3/16
Creed Turner, rector 1774–1803
William Dyer, curate
1 Area About 3½ miles long and about 10 broad.
2 Population 746.
3 Marriages &c. Marriages 7; births 24; buri<als ... >
4 Patron The Bishop of Winchester.
5 Chapels [No reply.]
6 Lecturer A curate nominated by the re<ctor.>
7 Dissenters 10 Papists. No meeting of protestant dissenters.
8 Schools No school that is endowed.
9 Charities < ... of t>his parish in the 10th year of James I did surrender a cottage <and> land to Stephen Dummer, his son and his heirs with condition <o>nly to the use of the poor and needy inhabitants of the said parish < ... > by equal parts. Present possessor, Thomas Holt.
< ... in the> seventh year of King Charles I did surrender a close < ... > to Stephen Dummer his brother and his heirs with condition < ... o>nly for the use of the poor needy inhabitants of this parish to <be divided at Michae>lmas and Lady Day in equal parts. Present possessor, Robert Lavington.
< ... >parishioner in the year 1630 by her last will gave the sum < ... on>ly to be distributed amongst the poor inhabitants at Easter yearly < ... > Worldridge.

453 Blendworth 21M65/B4/3/17
John Aiskew, rector 1741–89 Fareham, 25 March 1788
1 Area The compass of ground is about 6 miles.

2 Population Number of souls about 188.
3 Marriages &c. Number ... for 7 years from January 1st 1780 to January 1st 1788: burials 28; births 39; marriages 8.
4 Patron Jervoise Clarke Jervoise Esq.
5 Chapels None.
6 Lecturer No lecturer or curate.
7 Dissenters No meetings; no Papists.
8 Schools There are 2 schools. One no endowment, Hannah Heather, about 16 scholars. The endowed school has £8 10*s*. p.a. in estate and £80 in money at 4% by timber and saving; Thomas Heather, master, churchwardens and overseers nominate, about 16 scholars.
9 Charities None. The return I made and sent to Mr Gilbert being a parliamentary enquiry, I kept no copy, as I looked upon that as conclusive. The endowment was left to the school for educating poor children by William Appleford of Winton College, August 1695.

454 Boldre 21M65/B4/3/18

William Gilpin MA, vicar 1777–1804
1 Area <The parish of> Boldre is very extensive; containing Boldre, <Lyming>ton and Bro[c]k<en>hurst; which two last have now < ... r>ight, paying certain considerations to the <mother paris>h. Lymington is supplyed by a curate of <B>ro[c]kenhurst, which is not able to support a <curate> supplyed by the minister of Boldre. The <compass of the three> (Boldre, Lymington, Bro[c]kenhurst) may <be a d>istrict of about 6 miles by 10.
2 Population In Boldre about 1,000. In B<rockenhurst> about 300.
3 Marriages &c. Of marriages in Boldre and Bro[c]kenhurst <about> 15; of births about 50; and of b<urials a>bout 30.
4 Patron William Mitford Esq. of Gilbury near < ... >shire; MP for Newtown, Cornwa<ll>.[40]
5 Chapels There is one chappel, built by the W<idow> Pilewell; which was never consecrated; and <held> by the representative of that family. It is <served by Mr> Burleigh, curate of Beaulieu, and is supported b<y ... >
6 Lecturer There is no lecturer nor <cu>rate within <the parish> except my own curate <Mr W>m. Dixon; and <at> Lymington, Ellis Jones, who is maintained <by an> endowment of £16 a year, <and> a subscription. He is nominated by the vi<car.>
7 Dissenters <There> are no Papists, nor sectaries of any kind, that <I know> of, except a few Presbyterians and Anabaptists <who have> each a meeting-house at Lymington.
8 Schools <There is a> small school at Bro[c]kenhurst for 12 boys <which is> kept by one Davis, and the clerk's wife; <there is an endowment whic>h is about £21 yearly, vested in the funds, <and managed by trus>tees. The income is rather increased; <but I cannot> ascertain the exact sum, as the treasurer <is away in> the country.
9 Charities <There is> no <h>ospital, nor endowed institution, except <the s>chool in o<ur> parish. <In re>gard to the <parlia>mentary return, I

gave <the s>chool £<21> p.a. settled on Boldre by <on>e of the Worsley family; and <outg>oings paid by Mrs. Gilbert, near Lyndhurst.

455 Bonchurch [IoW] 21M65/B4/3/163
Joseph Hewson, rector 1766–1809
1 Area Number of acres, more or less 500.
2 Population Number of souls 77.
3 Marriages &c. Marriages, at a medium, one year with another 1; births 6; burials 1.
4 Patron Patrons, William Hill Esq. and Sarah Popham, gentlewoman.
5 Chapels No chapel within the parish.
6 Lecturer No lecturer or curate within the parish.
7 Dissenters No Papist or protestant dissenter of any denomination, to the best of my knowledge or belief, in the parish.
8 Schools No endowed school in the parish.
9 Charities No hospital or endowed charitable institution or any fixed annual donation for the benefit of the poor in the parish.

456 Bossington 21M65/B4/3/19
[Signature illegible but cf. Broughton, no. 462]
Alexander Thistlethwayte LLB, rector 1781–1827
Alexander Gatehouse, curate
1 Area [Reply lost.]
2 Population 30 and upwards.
3 Marriages &c. Marriages not more than 1 in 7 years; births about 1 in a year; burials 1 in <a year.>
4 Patron Robert Thistlethwayte Esq.
5 Chapels No.
6 Lecturer No.
7 Dissenters None.
8 Schools None.
9 Charities None.

457 Botley 21M65/B4/3/20
Joseph Wallace, rector 1780–1803
1 Area 1,345 acres, *more or less.*
2 Population 550.
3 Marriages &c. Marriages 5; births 30; burials 13.
4 Patron His Grace the Duke of Portland.
5 Chapels We have no place of public worship of any denomination, or description in the parish, except the parish church.
6 Lecturer We have no lecturer or curate within the parish.
7 Dissenters There is one family of Papists, consisting of 5 persons. No protestant dissenters of any denomination.
8 Schools Here are no public endowed schools in the parish.

9 Charities Here are no hospitals, or endowed charitable institutions. £10 left by a person unknown, to be put out to interest, and the monies arising therefrom to be divided amongst the industrious poor people, have been lost by being entrusted to improper hands.
Copy of a return made to the late parliamentary enquiry
Juliana Cassons left 10*s*. p.a. from land, vested in trustees unknown.

458 Brading [IoW] 21M65/B4/3/164
Thomas Waterworth, vicar 1763–90 17 March 1788
My Lord, in obedience to your commands I have sent the following answers to the questions proposed in your Lordship's letter omitting the two first as I am informed your Lordship is pleased to accept the calculation with regard to the size of the whole island and the number of inhabitants as published by Sir Richard Worsley in his *History of the Isle of Wight*. I am, My Lord, your Lordship's most dutiful humble servant, Waterworth, vicar of Brading.
1 Area [No reply.]
2 Population [No reply.]
3 Marriages &c. The marriages in Brading parish at a medium for the last 7 years are one year with another 10 4/7; baptisms 46 2/7; burials including those from Yaverland and Shankling whose inhabitants bury their dead at the mother church of Brading 32 5/7.
4 Patron The Patron Trinity College Cambridge.
5 Chapels No chapel within the parish.
6 Lecturer No lecturer or curate.
7 Dissenters No Papist or protestant dissenter to the best of my knowledge.
8 Schools No endowed school.
9 Charities I kept no copy of the return made to the late parliamentary enquiry but the fixed annual donations for the poor of this parish are as follow:
In the year 1608 Sir William Oglander Knight ancestor to the present Sir William Oglander Bart. gave to the poor of this parish by deed and will £6 yearly for ever payable out of the farm of Smallbrook of which £5 4*s*. distributed in bread and the remaining 16*s*. in meat.
In the year 1617 Mr Richard Gard gave to the poor of this parish by will 10*s*. yearly for ever payable out of the farm of Blackpan and Yleyards.
In the year [left blank] Richard Knight Esq. bequeathed by will unto 6 aged poor men of this parish one great coat and a pair of breeches apiece yearly for ever, each coat and breeches not to exceed £1 5*s*. to be delivered to them respectively in the month of October.
Also to 6 aged poor widow women of the said parish one twelve penny loaf apiece yearly for ever on every first Sunday in every month the said donations payable out of his farm called Lee Farm.
In the year [left blank] Mr Edward How left by will £30 the yearly produce of it to be laid out at Easter in fresh meat for the poor of this parish. The late Sir John Oglander his executor bought yearly with the interest veal for the poor and the present Sir William Oglander his executor continues it.

459 Bramshott 21M65/B4/3/21

Jonathan Dennis MA, rector 1758–91

1 Area About 12 miles.

2 Population AD1746 number of souls 631; AD1776 646; AD1787 683.

3 Marriages &c. Marriages from 1780 to 1786 inclusive 36

Births	do.	170
Burials	do.	125

4 Patron Queen's College, Oxford.

5 Chapels None.

6 Lecturer My son Whitehead Dennis is my assistant.

7 Dissenters None.

8 Schools No schoolmaster. 2 mistresses who teach 36 children.

9 Charities No hospitals or endowed charitable institutions, or any fixed annual donations etc., consequently no return made to the parliamentary inquiry.

460 Brighstone [IoW] 21M65/B4/3/165

Noel Digby, rector of 'Brixton' 1780– 24 March 1788

1 Area About 2,500 acres.

2 Population About 550.

3 Marriages &c. On an average of the last 7 years marriages 4; births 17; burials 8.

4 Patron The Bishop of Winchester.

5 Chapels None.

6 Lecturer None.

7 Dissenters None.

8 Schools None.

9 Charities None.

461 Brook [IoW] 21M65/B4/3/166

Robert Gibbs, rector 1766–95 15 March 1788

1 Area Acres — 628.

2 Population 114 souls.

3 Marriages &c. I have examin'd my register for the last 4 years and find there are 1 marriage, 2 baptisms, 2 burials, 1 year with another.

4 Patron William Bowreman Esq.

5 Chapels One church, Brooke. I serve it myself. The parish maintain the church; the rector, the chancel. William Bowreman Esq.

6 Lecturer No curate.

7 Dissenters No dissenters of any sect.

8 Schools No school, but *one* in the neighbouring parish.

9 Charities No hospital. No charitable institutions. No annual donations. The expences for maintaining the poor of the parish of Brooke amount annually to £38 10*s*. 10*d*. No copy of the return which was made to the late parliamentary enquiry to be found.

462 Broughton 21M65/B4/3/22

Alexander Thistlethwayte LLB, rector 1781–1827

Alexander Gatehouse, curate

1 Area Suppose 1,500 acres and upwards.

2 Population Suppose about 700.
3 Marriages &c. Marriages on an average of eight or ten years, about 2 every year; births 12; burials about 9.
4 Patron Robert Thistlethwayte of Norman Court, Esq.
5 Chapels A chapel at Pottle in this parish which is in ruins; also a chapel at Bossington which is a hamlet of this pa<rish>. They maintain their own poor and there are the same [several words faded illegibly] as for the parish of Broughton.
6 Lecturer No.
7 Dissenters Suppose about 6 Papists. There is in the parish a meeting held of Anabaptists. Suppose about 100 in number. <The>re are also about <t>wenty (as I am informed) who call themselves Sandymanians, who assemble regularly.[41]
8 Schools There is a school for the children of this parish which is supported by the rent of lands in the parish. The master's name, John Bailey; appointed by the trustees. No fixed number of scholars.
9. Charities. The fixed annual donations are as follows:

From an estate at Longstock	£7 13*s*. 1*d*.
Dean etc.	4 0*s*. 0*d*.
Mr Edward's estate	2 0*s*. 0*d*.
From a coppice at East Tuderly	1 0*s*. 0*d*.

Also [interest] of 100[£] in the rector's hands.
No copy of the return which was made to the parliamentary enquiry was kept.

463 Bullington 21M65/B4/3/23
Richard Ring, vicar 1763–91 28 March 1788
Lloyd Williams, curate
1 Area The circuit of the parish of about six miles.
2 Population 150.
3 Marriages &c. Taken at a medium, for the last 10 years there were 1 marriage in 2 years, 4 christenings and 2 burials yearly.
4 Patron The prebendary of Wherwell.
5 Chapels Bullington is a chapel to Wherwell.
6 Lecturer Lloyd Williams, vicar of Whitchurch, is curate nominated by the Revd Richard Ring, vicar of Wherwell. No licence.
7 Dissenters There are no Papists nor dissenters of any denomination.
8 Schools There are no endowed schools.
9 Charities 10*s*. p.a. left by a Mr Mills for the use of the poor.

464 Burghclere 21M65/B4/3/24
William Nevill, rector 1767–1810
1 Area I know of no estimate of the parishe.
2 Population 618.
3 Marriages &c. The number of marriages in the last 10 years was 52; the number of baptisms was 152; and that of burials 117.

4 Patron The Right Hon. Lord Porchester.
5 Chapels Newtown is supposed to be a chapel of ease to Burghclere; the Revd Mr Best, curate.
6 Lecturer An unlicensed curate, the Revd David Middleton, nominated by the rector.
7 Dissenters None.
8 Schools There is one school, endowed by Mrs Elizabeth Cornwallis; the present mistress, Hobson, nominated by the rector of Burghclere.
9 Charities The only charitable institution is the above-mentioned school, endowed by Mrs Elizabeth Cornwallis, the 2d. of August 1721, by will (for the purpose of 'teaching to read such of the poor children of the said parish as' the heirs of Mrs Eliza<be>th Blagrove and the rector shall appoint) with £10 p.a., arising out of the lands of Earlstone in the said parish, which at present are supposed to belong to Lord Porchester and Robert Kingsmill Esq. jointly. The annual produce is £8 p.a. because the Land Tax at 4*s*. per pound is deducted. This is the substance of the answer to parliament.

465 Buriton 21M65/B4/3/26
Philip Barton MA, rector 1751–96 24 March 1788
William Ralfe AB, curate
1 Area By a gross computation in the parish of Buriton with the chapelr<y of> Petersfield annexed there may be 6,000 statute acres, of which at least <...>0 are sheep-down or common pasture or woodlands. The turnpike <ro>ad from London to Portsmouth passes 7 miles through the parish. <It>s greatest breadth is 2 miles.
2 Population It is believed there may be 500 souls in the parish of Buriton, including the hamlets of Upper Weston and Upper Nursted.
3 Marriages &c. Marriages at a medium, 4; births 15; burials 8.
4 Patron The Bishop of Winchester.
5 Chapels Tradition says there were formerly two chapels, one at Nursted, and one called St Andrew's at Petersfield. No traces of either have existed within the memory of man. There is now only one chapel, viz. the parish church of Petersfield. The rector nominates a curate who hath a stip<end> from the rector and an allowance of the Easter offerings and surplice <fees.> The curate is the Revd Thomas Trodd, late of Trinity College, Oxford.
6 Lecturer No lecturer. Neither the curate of Petersfield or Buriton are licensed.
7 Dissenters No Papists nor dissenters of any denomination.
8 Schools No endowed schools. The Revd Mr Dusautoy keeps a small academy. 10 scholars. Mary Caplin keeps a day school for teaching poor children to read.
9 Charities There is a charity in Upper Weston endowed by Mr John Goodyer in the last century with an house and lands which now produce £45 p.a. for the purpose of apprenticing boys of the tithing of Weston. The present trustees are Lord Stawell, Francis Hugonin Esq., Henry Bonham Esq., John Sainsbury Esq., Mr Henry Binsted, Mr Yalden.

Bishop Laney, Bishop of Ely, gave a sum for purchasing lands, the annual rent to be employed in apprenticing a child from Buriton and Petersfield alternately. The rent is £7 p.a. and the trustees are Lord Stawell and the rector of Buriton for the time being.
No hospitals, nor any fixed annual donations for the benefit of the poor. An exact verbal copy of the return made to Parliament cannot be procured at present. If any such exists, it must be in the rector's custody, who is absent at Exeter.

466 Bursledon 21M65/B4/3/27
Joseph Scott, vicar 1761–1811 31 March 1788
William Kent, curate
1 Area Arable 350 acres. Waste and common not ascertained.
2 Population 475.
3 Marriages &c. Burials 9; births 12. Of late years all marriages have been celebrated at Hound, the mother church.
4 Patron Winchester College.
5 Chapels Bursledon is a chapelry, within the parish of Hound, is served by the curate of the mother church, maintained and supported by the small tithes of the parish, and is nominated to by Winchester College.
6 Lecturer A curate; his name is *Kent*, a Master of Arts; appointed by the vicar, the Revd Joseph Scott — not licensed to this particular cure.
7 Dissenters None.
8 Schools None that are endowed.
9 Charities None.

467 Calbourne [IoW] 21M65/B4/3/167
Edmund Poulter, rector 1787–95
J. P. Fisher, curate
1 Area [No reply.]
2 Population [No reply.]
3 Marriages &c. The number of marriages is about 3, of births 21, and of burials 12.
4 Patron The Bishop of Winchester.
5 Chapels There was a chapel formerly belonging to this parish but it has been for many years destroyed.
6 Lecturer There is no lecturer in the parish, but there is a curate nominated by the rector. [In different ink] The Revd J. P. Fisher, not licensed because only temporary.
7 Dissenters There are no papists nor meetings of protestant dissenters in the parish.
8 Schools No schools.
9 Charities No hospitals nor endowed charitable institutions.

468 Carisbrooke and Northwood [IoW] 21M65/B4/3/169
Thomas Dalton, vicar 1782–1822 12 April 1788
My Lord, I have been prevented by a complaint in my eyes from transmitting the following answers to your Lordship's questions previous to your

visitation, so soon as I ought, in conformity to your printed requisition, to have done. This circumstance I mentioned to your secretary Mr Harrison, who, I hope, has reported it to your Lordship as an apology for my unintentional delay. I am, my Lord, your most dutiful and obedient servant, Thomas Dalton.

Carisbrooke

1 Area By computation the land contained in this parish is rated at 8,000 acres including the King's forest or waste ground.

2 Population The number of souls, by Sir Richard Worsley's *History of the Island*, is computed at 1,245.

3 Marriages &c. The number of births are at a medium 27, marriages 8, burials 28.

4 Patron The Provost and Fellows of Queen's College in Oxford are patrons of the living.

5 Chapels The church of Newport is considered as a chapel (to which I was instituted) but by custom is separately provided with a minister elected and supported liberally by the inhabitants.

6 Lecturer The Reverend John Davies is my curate, and lecturer of Newport, and duly licensed.

7 Dissenters I have never heard of any Papists in the parish, but Mr Davies will report to your Lordship the numbers and denominations of dissenters in his district.

8 Schools There is no endowed school in the parish but there is a good private school kept by a Mr Willington at Carisbrook.

9 Charities The House of Industry is in my parish which contains the poor of the whole island.

Northwood

1 Area By computation 4,080 acres of land.

2 Population About 2,030 souls.

3 Marriages &c. Marriages 16, births 22, burials 10.

4 Patron The Provost and Fellows of Queen's College.

5 Chapels There is one chapel at West Cowes which is served by the Revd James Hyde Gill who is supported by the annual donations of £20 left by Bishop Morley and £5 by R. Stephens together with the voluntary contribution of the inhabitants who have the right of nomination.

6 Lecturer The Revd Mr Gill chosen as above mentioned is licensed.

7 Dissenters No Papists known in the parish. Mr Gill will make a report of the dissenters who all live in the district.

8–9 Schools, charities No endowed schools in the parish and no hospitals.

Return of charities

Northwood

Richard Smith, citizen of London, gave by will on 15 July 1699, £2 arising out of certain lands in the parish, to be given annually in bread to the poor of Northwood parish, the money vested in the rector for the time being.

Richard Smith, citizen of London, gave by will on 15 July 1699, £10 arising out of certain lands in the parish, for placing a poor child as an apprentice in London, the money vested in the rector for the time-being.

Carisbrooke
John Serle gave by will dated 1620, for the relief of the poor of Carisbrook, £50 laid out in land situate in the Common Field, vested in the churchwardens of Carisbrook, with an annual produce of £1 18*s*.
Lord Hunsdown in about the 26th year of the reign of James 1 gave by will for the use of the poor of Carisbrook 100 marks laid out in land now part of the manor of Alvington belonging to Sir John Carter, vested in the churchwardens and overseers of the parish, with an annual produce of £3.
NB What regards the district of Newport will be sent by the Revd Mr Davies, and also what relates to Cowes will be sent by the Revd Mr Gill, the curates.

469 Carisbrooke within the Castle [IoW] 21M65/B4/3/168
William Dickonson, 'vicar of the Castle' –1794 25 March 1788
1 Area The superficial content of the whole island (according to Sir Richard Worsley's *History*) amounts to about 100,000 acres.
2 Population According to Sir Richard Worsley's *History* the number of souls taken in the year 1777 were: parish at large 52; in Castle Hold, Newp[ort] 124; total 176.
3 Marriages &c. Baptisms 2. No marriages or burials.
4 Patron The Governor of the Isle of Wight.
5 Chapels No chapel.
6 Lecturer No lecturer or curate.
7 Dissenters No papists or meetings of dissenters of any sect.
8 Schools No schools.
9 Charities No hospitals or any endowed charitable institutions or fixed annual donations for the benefit of the poor. No copy was kept of the return made to the late parliamentary enquiry on this subject.

470 Catherington 21M65/B4/3/28
John Aiskew, vicar 1778–89 Fareham, 25 March 1788
1 Area The compass of ground about 14 miles.
2 Population About 600.
3 Marriages &c. Number of marriages, births and burials for 7 years from January 1st, 1780 to January 1st 1788: marriages 31; births 142; burials 69.
4 Patron Jervoise Clarke Jervoise Esq.
5 Chapels None.
6 Lecturer No lecturer or curate.
7 Dissenters No meetings; about 7 Papists.
8 Schools There are two schools endowed by William Appleford, both appointed by the churchwardens and overseers. Richard Horrad Apr[il] 10 1787, scholars 18, other inhabitants 10. Mary Bolton 1777, scholars 12, other inhabitants 6.
There is one other school in the parish approved of. Thomas Bettesworth, the man and wife, very decent kind of persons, are of service in the parish and if any licence should be required of them I imagine they would give it up.

9 Charities None. The return I made and sent to Mr Gilbert being a parliamentary enquiry, I kept no copy, as I looked upon that as conclusive. The endowment left to the school for educating poor children by William Appleford of Winton College, 1695, the estate is £10 p.a. in the parish of Barton Stacy.

471 Chale [IoW] 21M65/B4/3/170
Francis Worsley, rector 1753–1808 24 March 1788
1 Area The best computations make the superficial content of the Isle of Wight amount to about 100,000 acres contained in 30 parishes. See Worsley's *History of the Isle of Wight*, page 2.
2 Population In the 30 parishes into which the Isle of Wight is divided it was found by a return made by the respective clergy to Sir Richard Worsley in the year 1777 that there were 18,024 inhabitants. See Worsley's *History* Appendix No. VI.
3 Marriages &c. From Jan. 1 1781 to Dec. 31 1787 the numbers are, marriages 17, births 91, burials, 31.
4 Patron The Right Honorable Sir Richard Worsley Bart.
5 Chapels No chapel in this parish.
6 Lecturer No lecturer. No curate.
7 Dissenters No Papist in this parish. No meeting of protestant dissenters in this parish.
8 Schools No school in this parish.
9 Charities There are no hospitals or endowed charitable institutions or any fixed annual donations for the benefit of the poor in this parish, and this was the purport of the answer which was made to the late parliamentary enquiry on this subject.

472 Chalton 21M65/B4/3/29
Edward Bayly, rector 1787–94
Henry Hall, curate
1 Area The number of acres in this parish I cannot really ascertain. Its extent from north to south 3 miles or thereabouts, and from east to west about 2 miles.
2 Population 380.
3 Marriages &c. Marriages at a medium 3; baptisms 16; burials 9.
4 Patron Jervoise Clarke Jervoise Esq.
5 Chapels There is a chapel of ease, called Idsworth, annexed to this rectory and under the same patronage.
6 Lecturer There is a curate, nominated by the Revd Edward Bayley, rector.
7 Dissenters There are in this parish about 12 Papists.
8 Schools No endowed school.
9 Charities None.

473 Chawton 21M65/B4/3/30/1–2
John Hinton, rector 1744–1802
1 Area The compass of ground supposed to be in the parish of Chawton is between 9 and 10 miles.

2 Population The number of souls in this parish is about 250.
3 Marriages &c. There have been in this parish within the last 10 years, taking one year with another, 5 marriages, 13 births, and 5 burials.
4 Patron The patron of the rectory of Chawton is Thomas Knight Esq.
5 Chapels There is no chapel belonging to this parish.
6 Lecturer The Revd Mr Peter Dusautoy is the present curate of this parish. He had a licence from Your Lordship to the curacy of East Meon, but is not licenced to this parish.
7 Dissenters There is neither Papist nor dissenter, nor sectary of any denomination in this parish.
8 Schools There is a school in this parish in which the children of the poor are taught to read and work. It is not endowed; but is supported chiefly by the annual bounty of Thomas Knight Esq. The name of the mistress is Ann Stacey.
9 Charities There is no hospital nor endowed charitable institution in this parish. The fixed annual donations for the benefit of the poor are particularized in the copy (herewith sent according to Your Lordship's requisition) of the return that was made to the late parliamentary enquiry on that subject.
Copy of answers returned under the Act of 26 Geo. III for procuring returns of charitable donations
Sir Richard Knight Kt. gave by will *c.*1650 40*s.* p.a. charged upon Amery Farm in the parish of Alton, vested in the rector and churchwardens, for the use of the poor.
— Sexton at date unknown gave £1 13*s.* 8*d.* p.a. charged upon Spencers Farm, at Vivilrode in the parish of Bentworth, for the use of the poor.
Revd Colwel Brickendon and others at a date uncertain gave £23 in cash, now vested in the rector and churchwardens on the bond of the late Thomas Knight Esq. and yielding 18*s.* 4*d.* p.a. for the use of the poor.
Ann Harford in 1773 gave by will £110 7*s.* 2*d.* placed in the reduced 3% annuities, vested in John Hinton the present rector and yielding £3 6*s.* 2*d.* p.a. for the use of one or more poor persons of the parish as the rector for the time being shall think proper.

474 Chilcomb 21M65/B4/3/149

John Monk Newbolt, rector 1770–1803
1 Area The parish of Chilcomb is about 10 miles round, and 2 miles across.
2 Population 50 parishioners according to the most exact calculation.
3 Marriages &c. There have been 9 marriages in the last 10 years. On an average of 7 years 2 births in a year; and the burials on a like average have been between 2 and 3 in a year.
4 Patron The Lord Bishop of Winchester.
5 Chapels None.
6 Lecturer The Revd Mr Timothy Gabell is curate. Nominated by the rector, but not licensed.
7 Dissenters There is no Papist and only one protestant dissenter, who attends the Presbyterian place of worship.

8 Schools None.
9 Charities None.

475 Chilworth 21M65/B4/3/32
[Unsigned.] Daniel Williams, curate 1788–1823
1 Area Chilworth is supposed to contain 1,000 acres which are not all cultivated.
2 Population The number of souls is about 100.
3 Marriages &c. The births and burials amount, *communibus annis*, to 3 each. A marriage takes place perhaps once in 5 years.
4 Patron Peter Serle Esq. of Testwood, Hants., is patron of the living. It is a donative[1], in train to receive a benefit from Queen Ann's Bounty.[14] The present income is £12 p.a. paid by Mr Serle.
5 Chapels There is no chapel in the parish.
6 Lecturer The curate and incumbent is Daniel Williams, nominated by Mr Serle, above-named. But he is not licenced. He has in his hands a presentation to the living, directed to the bishop of the diocese whenever it shall be entitled to Queen Ann's Bounty.
7 Dissenters There is neither Papist or dissenter in the parish.
8 Schools There is no school in the parish.
9 Charities There is no hospital or charitable institution in the parish for the benefit of the poor.

476 Church Oakley 21M65/B4/3/33/1–2
Miles Halton, rector 1773–92
William Bainbridge, curate
1 Area 2500 [acres.]
2 Population 320.
3 Marriages &c. Births 10; burials 4; marriages 4.
4 Patron Queen's College, Oxford.
5 Chapels None.
6 Lecturer None.
7 Dissenters None I believe.
8 Schools A free school for 4 boys nominated by the patron, Wither Bramston Esq. of Hall-Place. William Marchant, master. Salary, 1 dwelling-house and garden; 1 field, 4 acres, and £8 in cash, annually.
9 Charities No hospitals; no donations.
[The copy of the return under the Gilbert Act simply repeats the information given in No.8, with the additions that the donor is named as '— Wither', the school intended to educate 4 boys from Oakley and 4 from Dean[e], the charity is vested in William Marchant, and the perquisites valued at £6 p.a.]

477 Clanfield 21M65/B4/3/34
Peter Taylor BD, rector 1787–91
Henry Hall, curate
1 Area The arable with the meadow and pasture land of this parish is estimated at 1,600 acres or thereabouts.

2 Population About 150.
3 Marriages &c. At a medium marriages 1; baptisms 7; burials 3.
4 Patron Jervoise Clarke Jervoise Esq.
5 Chapels No chapel.
6 Lecturer There is a curate nominated by the Revd Peter Taylor, rector of this parish. But not licensed.
7 Dissenters In this parish there are 13 Papists.
8 Schools No endowed school.
9 Charities There is an annual donation of 15*s*. to be distributed to the poor who receive no relief from the parish, by the overseers. The name of the person who gave the charity, when given or whether by will or deed, I cannot learn, though I have made every enquiry. The money left was £20, and vested in the hands of the overseers for the time being. But by the failure of one of them this charity was reduced to £15, with which sum the parish afterwards purchased a tenement, and the overseers yearly distribute the 15*s*. to the poor who do not receive any relief.

478 Cliddesden 21M65/B4/3/35
Christopher Fox, rector of 'Cliddesden cum Farleigh' 1782–1803
1 Area 3,000 acres.
2 Population 310.
3 Marriages &c. Marriages not more than 2; births 12; burials 5.
4 Patron The Earl of Portsmouth.
5 Chapels None.
6 Lecturer None.
7 Dissenters None.
8 Schools One school endowed with £10 p.a., James Clarke master, nominated by the Earl of Portsmouth. Scholars 30.
9 Charities Annual fixed donation £4. The same answer returned to the late parliamentary enquiry on this subject.

479 Colemore 21M65/B4/3/36
James Cookson AM, rector of 'Colemore and Priors Deane' 1775–1835
1 Area 1,200 acres or thereabouts.
2 Population 100 or thereabouts.
3 Marriages &c. 1 marriage in about 3 years for the last 20 years; births 2; burials rather more than 1 each year.
4 Patron Myself.
5 Chapels Priors Deane is a chapel annexed to Colemore and served by myself and together [they] constitute one living.
6 Lecturer None.
7 Dissenters There are no Papists or protestant dissenters of any denomination.
8 Schools There are no schools in the parish.
9 Charities There are no hospitals etc. in the parish.

480 Combe 21M65/B4/3/37
Thomas Baker AM, vicar 1772–89
1 Area [No reply.]

2 Population Males 83; females 78; Total 161.
3 Marriages &c. Marriages 13 in the last 10 years; births about 7 [p.a.]; burials 4[p.a.]
4 Patron The Dean and Chapter of Windsor.
5 Chapels No chapel.
6 Lecturer No lecturer or curate.
7 Dissenters No Papist or dissenters.
8 Schools No school endowed.
9 Charities No hospital or endowed charitable institution. No annual donation for the benefit of the poor.

481 Compton 21M65/B4/3/38
Philip Williams AM, rector 1781–1810 29 March 1788
1 Area The parish is in circumference between 7 and 8 miles.
2 Population 210.
3 Marriages &c. 2 m[arriages]; 6 bi[rths]; 5 b<urials.>
4 Patron A peculiar of the Bishop of Winchester.
5 Chapels None.
6 Lecturer None.
7 Dissenters None; none.
8 School There is one private writing and reading school.
9 Charities A fixed donation of £5 10*s*. from Winchester College and £3 from the corporation.

482 Corhampton 21M65/B4/3/39
William Davis, perpetual curate 1779–88
John Upton to Brownlow North, Bishop of Winchester, 26 March, 1788
Corhampton parish is supposed to be about 8 miles in circumference. The number of souls 94, including men, women and children. It is an impropriation, Henry Penruddock Wyndham Esq. and the Revd William Richards, the patrons. The licensed curate and schoolmaster at present is the Revd William Davis, who has for his support as curate and schoolmaster £49 p.a., [including] £22 p.a. rent charge upon the estate of Francis Hugonin Esq., £21 p.a. from a little farm at Clanfield in this county, and £6 p.a., the interest of £300 in the hands of the Governors of Queen Anne's Bounty Money. There is neither Roman Catholic nor dissenter of any denomination in the parish. The marriages, christenings and burials from January 1, 1781 to January 1, 1788 are as follow: marriages 5; christenings 16; burials 7.

When the return was made to the House of Commons respecting the poor, I was in Ireland, and when I am not residing upon my living in Ireland I have taken upon me the care of Corhampton parish.
[PS] The charity school at Corhampton requires the master to instruct 8 day boys free, in reading, writing and arithmetick.

483 Crawley 21M65/B4/3/40
Edmund Poulter, rector 1785–91
Livingstone Booth, curate
1 Area By a very lax computation it is said to contain about 3,150 acres. <It is said> to be 4 miles long and 3 broad and about 15 in <cir>cumference.

2 Population About 260.
3 Marriages &c. The medium of births p.a. is $7\frac{2}{5}$; burials $3\frac{3}{5}$; marriages $2\frac{1}{6}$.
4 Patron The Lord Bishop of Winchester.
5 Chapels There is a chapel annexed at Hunton, which is a separate parish served by the curate of Crawley, supported by the tithes of the parish of Hunton.
6 Lecturer The Revd Liv. Booth is curate nominated by the rector, the Revd Mr Poulter, not licensed.
7 Dissenters There is no Papist nor protestant dissenter.
8 Schools There is a private school kept by a woman with about 40 scholars, without any endowment.
9 Charities No hospital. The interest of about £30 is distributed annually to the poor at Easter. No copy of the return made to the parliamentary enquiry has been kept, and as I was not curate of this parish at that time, I cannot send any more particular account of it.

484 Crondall 21M65/B4/3/41
Charles Smith LLB, vicar 1776–1803 20 March 1788
John Washington, curate
1 Area The circumference of the parish is computed to be about 19 miles.
2 Population Allowing 5 persons to each house, the number of souls is nearly 1,410.
3 Marriages &c. Upon an average of 17 years the marriages, births and funerals are as follows: marriages 10; births 48; funerals 34 <p.a.>.
4 Patron The Master and Brethren of the Hospital of St Cross near Winchester.
5 Chapels None.
6 Lecturer No lecturer. Curate, John Washington, appointed by the Revd Mr Bourne, formerly vicar, and licensed.
7 Dissenters No Papists. One meeting-house of the sect called Methodists, in number supposed to be about 60.
8 Schools One school, not endowed. The master not licensed, but approved of by the vicar and curate; also a Sundays school, well attended.
9 Charities About the year 1743, a donation of £100 was given by Mrs Henrietta Walraven by will to be vested by her executors in the public funds and the interest to be applied to the relief of those poor families that did not receive alms from the parish. The heir a few years after the death of Mrs Walraven disputed the validity of the will and refused to pay it. The parish did not think proper to institute a suit for this legacy and it is lost.

485 Crux Easton 21M65/B4/3/42
John Burton Watkin, rector 1774–1822 20 March 1788
Richard Smyth, curate
1 Area 1,200 acres.
2 Population 64.

3 Marriages &c. Within the course of the last 7 years there has been 4 marriages, 9 births, and 7 burials.
4 Patron William Powlett Powlett Esq.
5 Chapels None.
6 Lecturer Richard Smyth is curate, nominated by the rector, John Watkin, who is also rector of Marchfield in Gloucestershire. The curate is not licensed.
7 Dissenters No dissenters of any kind.
8 Schools No school.
9 Charities No hospitals, charitable institutions or annual donations for the benefit of the poor.

486 Dibden 21M65/B4/3/43/1–2
Joshua Jeans, rector 1784–96
1 Area The parish is somewhat more than 2 miles in length and about a mile in breadth, at a medium.
2 Population In September 1784, the number of souls amounted to 198. There has happened no material increase or decrease since that period.
3 Marriages &c. Marriages from 2 to 5; births from 5 to 8; burials from 4 to 6.
4 Patron Sir James Harris KB.
5 Chapels No chapel nor any place of worship except the parish church.
6 Lecturer No lecturer nor curate.
7 Dissenters No Papists, nor any protestant dissenters.
8 Schools No school, except a very small day school for young children, kept by a dame, and unendowed; the number of scholars about a dozen; the name of the mistress Joanna Barnes. The young people of the parish of Dibden are chiefly instructed at Hythe in the parish of Fawley.
9 Charities No hospital. No charitable institution. No fixed annual donation.
Joshua Jeans to Brownlow, Bishop of Winchester, Dibden, March 29, [1788]
The enclosed paper contains the answers to Your Lordship's queries respecting the parish of Dibden.
As the return made by my parish to the late parliamentary enquiry consisted of negatives only (in having no charitable institution or endowment of any kind whatsoever), and as I have preserved no copy of our return, I presume your lordship will not require any further information on that head.

487 East Dean 21M65/B4/3/45
Oliver Goodyer St John, rector 1773–1804
[Sole fragment of this reply states that there are no charitable endowments and that the copy of the reply to the parliamentary enquiry preserved by the churchwardens is enclosed.]

488 East Meon, Froxfield and Steep 21M65/B4/3/44

Andrew Lewis Boisdaune, 'vicar of Eastmeon with the chapels of Froxfield and Steep annexed' 1763–88 25 February 1788

1 Area The parish of Eastmeon <is> supposed to be about 18 miles <in> circumference.

2 Population The number of souls, according to the best information is 963.

3 Marriages &c. Marriages 5; births 30; burials 20.

4 Patron The Hon. and Right Revd the Lord Bishop of Winchester.

5 Chapels The chapels of Froxfield and Steep are annexed to the vicarage of Eastmeon. The duty of Eastmeon and Froxfield is attended to by the resident vicar. The Revd Mr Stephen Street is curate of Steep, nominated by the vicar. An exact terrier for each of these 3 parishes is in your lordship's office.

6 Lecturer The 3 first queries in this article are answered in the above. The Revd Mr Stephen Street, curate of Steep, will reply to the last.

7 Dissenters There is nothing of the kind in any of the parishes.

8 Schools There are no endowed schools in the parishes of Eastmeon and Steep.

9 Charities There are none.

489 East Tisted 21M65/B4/3/46/1–2

George Watkins, rector 1787–98

James Cookson AM, curate

[Lacks answers to questions 1–3.]

4 Patron The Revd Samuel Prince is patron of the living of East Tisted to the best of my knowledge, and the Revd George Watkins incumbent.

5 Chapels There are no chapels in the parish of East Tisted.

6 Lecturer I am curate and nominated by the rector, but not licensed.

7 Dissenters There are no Papists, nor meetings held of protestant dissenters, nor any sectaries in the parish of East Tisted.

8 Schools In the parish there is one endowed school, the number of scholars 14. Mr and Mrs Dyer have the management of it. A circumstantial account accompanies this.

9 Charities I send herewith a copy of the return which I made to the late parliamentary enquiry respecting charitable donations.

Copy of answers returned to the parliamentary enquiry, September 23, 1786
Revd Philip De Valois, late rector of East Tisted, deceased, in 1760 gave by will £350 for learning the children of East Tisted, viz. the boys to read and write, and the girls to read, write and sew; the numbers not limited. £150 was secured on mortgages on turnpike tolls in various parts of Hants and Surrey [listed], and £200 in 3% Consols, yielding in all £12 p.a. The management was vested in the incumbents of Farringdon, Chawton, Newton Valence, Colemore, Empshot and East Tisted for the time being and their successors for ever. The present trustees are the Revds — Randolph (Farringdon), John Hinton (Chawton), Edmund White (Newton Valence), James Cookson (Colemore), Griffith Richards (Empshot), and George Watkins (East Tisted).

490 East Woodhay and Ashmansworth 21M65/B4/3/47

Thomas Frome DD, rector of East Woodhay and Ashmansworth 1772–89

1 Area In the parish of East Woodhay there are about 3,500 acres of land, exclusive of common, and the parish of Ashmansworth about 1,660 acres. Total about 5,160 acres.

2 Population In the parish of East Woodhay about 900; in the parish of Ashmansworth about 200; total 1,100.

3 Marriages &c. [Annual averages] Marriages in the parish of Woodhay about 7, ditto Ashmansworth 2; baptisms in Woodhay about 15, ditto Ashmansworth 4; burials in Woodhay about 25, ditto Ashmansworth 5.

4 Patron The Right Reverend the Lord Bishop of Winchester.

5 Chapels The chapel of Ashmansworth, served by the rector of East Woodhay or his curate. The occupiers of land pay tythe to the rector of East Woodhay. There is no institution or induction to the chapelry distinct from East Woodhay.

6 Lecturer There is no lecturer in the parish of East Woodhay or any curate, but one who is engaged by the present rector as his assistant in performing the duties of the parish.

7 Dissenters Not one Papist. No meeting held of protestant dissenters or any meeting whatever. Not one dissenter of any denomination whatever in either parish.

8 Schools One school endowed by a late rector with an estate which used to produce about 50*s*. p.a. The rector and churchwardens for the time being who were trustees under the will of the donor granted the land to Francis Page Esq. of Newbury whose executor now regularly and annually pays the schoolmaster who is the present clark of the parish, and nominated by the rector and churchwardens upon a vacancy £7 4*s*. The numbers of scholars are 20.

9 Charities The return made to the late parliamentary inquiry was a parcel of land situate in the parish of Ashmansworth, let at £4 10*s*. p.a. The rent of which land after deducting tythes and taxes (amounting generally to a net produce of about £4) was laid out in the purchase of linen cloth and distributed at the discretion of the rectors and churchwardens of East Woodhay to the poor who do not receive alms from their parish. No hospitals for the benefit of the poor.

491 East Worldham 21M65/B4/3/48

Richard Chandler DD, rector 1779–1810

John Mill, curate

1 Area The compass of the parish of East Worldham <is> 7 miles.

2 Population The number of souls in the parish of East Worldham is about 170.

3 Marriages &c. Marriages about 4 or 6; births about 6 or 8; burials about 7 or 8.

4 Patron The living of East Worldham is in the gift of the President and Fellows of Magdalen College, Oxford. The rector of East Worldham [is] the Revd Dr Chandler.

5 Chapels Not any.
6 Lecturer Not any.
7 Dissenters Not any.
8 Schools Not any.
9 Charities A donation of 20*s*. p.a. to the parish of East Worldham, given by Mr Dunce.

492 Eling 21M65/B4/3/49
John Mylles Speed, vicar 1775–92
1 Area About 5,000 acres of arable and meadow land. A large tract of forrest and common land.
2 Population About 2,000 souls.
3 Marriages &c. Taking 7 years together, about 20 marriages, from 40–50 burials, from 90–100 births.
4 Patron The perpetuity is in myself.
5 Chapels None.
6 Lecturer None.
7 Dissenters No Papists that can be heard of. About 60 families of Presbyterians. A meeting of Methodists.
8 Schools No[t] one endowed school.
9 Charities No copy can be found in my parish of the late parliamentary enquiry, having at that time the Revd Mr Willis as my curate. 4 almshouses with the sum of £1 16*s*. paid yearly out of a small farm in this parish, left by the will of a Mrs Moody of Southampton.

493 Empshott 21M65/B4/3/50
Griffith Richards, vicar 1786–1801 26 March 1788
John Richards, curate
1 Area I cannot ascertain with accuracy what compass of ground is contained in the parish of Empshott, but I suppose it to extend about 1 mile from east to west, and about 1½ miles from north to south.
2 Population The number of souls in the parish amounts to 139.
3 Marriages &c. There is at a medium 1 marriage 3 births, and 2 burials one year with another in the parish.
4 Patron The patron of this living is John Butler Esq. of Bramshott.
5 Chapels There is no chapel or any other place of public worship in the parish than the parish church.
6 Lecturer I officiate as minister in the absence of my brother who is incumbent, and am not licensed to this curacy.
7 Dissenters There are no Papists, nor any meetings of protestant dissenters held in this parish.
8 Schools There are no endowed schools in the parish.
9 Charities There is no hospital nor endowed charitable institution nor fixed annual donation for the benefit of poor persons in this parish. As I did not expect to be called on for any copy of my return to the late parliamentary enquiry on this subject, I kept none; but it was to the same purport with what I have above stated.

494 Ewhurst 21M65/B4/3/51

Thomas Obourn, rector 1762–99

1 Area About 400 acres.

2 Population There are only 2 houses in the parish; the manor in which there are 2 servants when the family is not there; and the farmhouse in which is the bailiff, <his> wife, one servant and three children.

3 Marriages &c. There have not been any burials since the year 17<...>; but 4 marriages, and 7 births of which 2 only in the parish.

4 Patron Robert Mackreth Esq. The next presentation is in Dr Durnford or his assignee.

5 Chapels No chapel.

6 Lecturer No lecturer or curate.

7 Dissenters None.

8 Schools None.

9 Charities No hospital or charitable institution of any description.

495 Exton 21M65/B4/3/52

John V. Walters, curate 1785–1802

1 Area About 10 miles in circumference.

2 Population 221.

3 Marriages &c. 2 marriages; 6 births<;...>

4 Patron The Lord Bishop of Winch<ester.>

5 Chapels No chapel.

6 Lecturer No lecturer or curate.

7 Dissenters No Papists. No dissenter of any denomination.

8 Schools <No sch>ool.

9 Charities No hospital, charitable institution or donation whatever.

496 Faccombe and Tangley 21M65/B4/3/53

Thomas White LLB, rector of 'Faccombe cum Tangley' 1769–89

17 March 1788

1 Area By supposition it contains 2,000 acres.

2 Population Nearly 250.

3 Marriages &c. Burials at a medium 3 or 4; marriages 2 or 3; births 6 or 7.

4 Patron Sylvanus Bevan Esq. of Swallowfield in the county of Berkshire.

5 Chapels Tangley is a chapel of ease annexed to the parish of Faccombe. The church of Tangley is served by the Revd John Gillespie, curate, nominated by the rector of Faccombe.

6 Lecturer Answered above.

7 Dissenters Papists none. Dissenters none.

8 Schools Not any.

9 Charities Not any. The return made to the late parliamentary enquiry cannot be ascertained as no copy was taken.

497 Farley Chamberlayne 21M65/B4/3/54

Thomas Peter Dod Salmon, rector 1786–1802

Anthony Freston, curate

1 Area About 1,439 acres.

2 Population 140.
3 Marriages &c. Marriage 1; burials 2; births 4.
4 Patron Sir Henry Paulett St John, Bt.
5 Chapels No.
6 Lecturer Rector, Revd Thomas Salmon; curate, Revd Anthony Fr<eston...> wishes to be <...>
7 Dissenters No Papists or dissenters to the best of my knowledge.
8 Schools One unendowed school kept by a poor woman of the name of Cook. The curate has procured a subscription of 3 guineas p.a. for the gratis instruction of poor children, but it is hardly sufficient.
9 Charities No hospitals. Annual donation of £5 in bread by the will of farmer Simms. Rate of poor rates £70 p.a. No account of the return sent to Parliament kept by the parish; but if necessary [I] request a printed paper which shall immediately be filled up.

498 Farlington 21M65/B4/3/55
Roger Cole, rector 1781–89
Griffith Richards, curate
1 Area There are about 1,920 acres of land within this parish, including arable, pasture, coppice, forest, and waste lands.
2 Population About 284.
3 Marriages &c. Marriages 2; births 11; burials 3.
4 Patron Charles Taylor Esq. of Purbrook Park.
5 Chapels There is no chapel within the parish.
6 Lecturer There is no curate besides myself. The rector nominates. I am not licensed.
7 Dissenters There are 4 Papists in the parish, but no protestant dissenter of any denomination.
8 Schools There is a woman's school in the parish to teach children the alphabet and to spell. She has about 20 scholars. It is mainly supported by voluntary subscription.
9 Charities There is no charitable institution of any kind in the parish.

499 Farringdon 21M65/B4/4/56
Herbert Randolph, rector 1782–89
James Ventris, curate
1 Area Persons who have gone the circuit of the bounds of this parish suppose it to be about 10 miles in circumference.
2 Population The number of souls in this parish is about 355, reckoning at an average 5 persons in each family.
3 Marriages &c. Of marriages about 2; of births about 9 or 10; of burials 5 or 6.
4 Patron Lewis Gage Esq., near Maidstone, Kent.
5 Chapels There are no chapels in this parish.
6 Lecturer This church is at present served by a curate, James Ventris, nominated by the Revd Mr Randolph of Dinton near Sarum. He is not licensed.

7 Dissenters There are no Papists or protestant dissenters of any denomination in this parish.
8 Schools There are no endowed schools in this parish.
9 Charities There are no hospitals or endowed charitable institutions in this parish, but some small fixed annual donations for the benefit of the poor. No exact copy of the return made to Parliament has been preserved, but it was to the following effect:- that about the year of our Lord 1594 a Mrs Alice Fielder of this parish left by deed 20*s*. p.a. to the poor for ever, to be paid out of a messuage and lands called Crouch-Ouse in the parish of Stedham in Sussex, and from other lands known by the name of Lamborne in Iping in the said county. There are also 16*s*. paid annually to the overseers for the use of the poor out of the land called Post lying in this parish, at present in the occupation of Thomas Fielder. The name of the donor is not known. There was also a sum of money (how much is not known) left to the poor of this parish, but by whom is not now known. Having been lent out without sufficient security it is now reduced to £10 for the use of which 8*s*. is annually paid to the overseers and churchwardens.

500 Fawley 21M65/B4/3/57
Henry Roger Drummond, rector 1786–1806
1 Area The parish extends about 8 miles in length, and about 3 in breadth, including Exbury.
2 Population About 1,000.
3 Marriages &c. Births at a medium 39; burials 26; marriages 9.
4 Patron The Bishop of Winchester.
5 Chapels One chapel at Exbury annexed to the living of Fawley and served by the rector.
6 Lecturer No lecturer nor curate.
7 Dissenters I know not of any protestant dissenters; there are 4 or 5 Papists.
8 Schools There are 2 day schools in the parish, but not endowed.
9 Charities No hospital. No charitable institution. No fixed annual donation. There is a small parcel of land now in dispute, an ancient bequest to the poor of the parish, not exceeding the value of 15*s*. p.a.

501 Fordingbridge 21M65/B4/3/58
John Howes, vicar 1773–1815
1 Area About 4,000 acres.
2 Population About 2,500.
3 Marriages &c. About 70 births; 20 marriages; and 50 burials.
4 Patron King's College in Cambridge.
5 Chapels No chapel within the parish.
6 Lecturer No lecturer or curate.
7 Dissenters <... P>apists. 1 Presbyterian meeting of <abou>t 120 persons. One <Quak>ers' meeting a<bou>t 30 persons.
8 Schools One common school for reading and writing. No endowed school at all.

9 Charities
Return to Parliament
A charitable donation for ever from John Dodington Esq. of £5 every fourth year to apprentice out some parish child, paid out of the rent issuing from certain land called Sandy Balls within this parish. An annual donation from King's College of 1*s*. 4*d*. to be given among the poor about Candlemas time, <as appear>s by the deed of the appropriation of this rectory <to> that College enrolled in the Bishop's Office at Winchester.

502 Freshwater [IoW] 21M65/B4/3/172
Samuel Johnston, rector 1775–91 27 March 1788
John Price, curate
My Lord, I received the favor of your letter, containing several questions to be answered — in consequence of which, I shall endeavour to give your Lordship satisfaction. I understand you intend to visit the diocese of Winchester this year, and at the same time to hold a confirmation therein. I will prepare (God willing) that part of my flock, who shall be objects to receive it. Previous to my answering the questions I shall give a short sketch relating to the rector of this parish and myself, which perhaps will not be unacceptable. Doctor Johnston, rector of this parish, who is an old infirm gentleman, chiefly resides in Yorkshire. I am by his appointment, his resident curate and live in the parsonage house. I have taken care of the parish duty here these seven years for the doctor, and the duty has sometimes been performed jointly by us. I am puzzled to return your Lordship any tolerable answer, respecting the number of acres contained in this parish; therefore will beg leave to give a general description of its extent. I shall be happy to give you any further information concerning this parish, should it be required. My return will be made on this paper by your Lordship's permission; and I desire you will be pleased to take one of these printed papers in your hand when you peruse my answers.
1 Area The parish of Freshwater comprehends an extensive tract of ground, and consists of 4 divisions, hamlets, or villages called East Town, West Town, Middle Town and North Town. The diameter of it may be reconed 3 miles, but I cannot ascertain the circumference of it.
2 Population About 550 souls.
3 Marriages &c. About 42 at a medium.
4 Patron The Master and Fellows of St John's College at Cambridge.
5 Chapels There is no chappel within the parish.
6 Lecturer There is no lecturer, but a curate, as mentioned in my letter, and nominated by the Revd Dr Johnston, and not licensed.
7 Dissenters There is no Papist in the parish, and no meetings of protestant dissenters held therein.
8 Schools There is 1 school in the parish endowed with a salary of £20 p.a. for teaching 16 boys reading, writing and arithmetick: the present master's name is Norris, and is nominated to his office by Captain Urry.
9 Charities There is no hospital, or endowed charitable institution in the parish, but a few fixed donations for apprenticing the poor children of the

parish to some useful trades. A copy of our return to Parliament is inclosed and signed by me.

A copy of the return made to the late parliamentary enquiry on donations
Edward Atkins in 1691 by will gave a donation of £50 in trust that the rector and churchwardens for the time being should apply the interest thereof in putting out apprentice the children of such poor people living in the parish as did not receive alms of the parish, and yet were not able to put out their children themselves.

Collonel David Urry in 1714 by will gave a donation of a messuage and land in the parish of Shalfleet, and a house at Freshwater, for a schoolmaster to teach 16 poor children belonging to the parish to read, write and cypher, and appointed Collonel Holmes, Mr Hayles and Mr Urry of Afton, and the survivors of them and their heirs, trustees for the same, which trustees are now all dead. The present schoolmaster was appointed by Mr Urry of Afton the surviving trustee who hath been dead about 7 years, and the gentleman that enjoys Mr Urry's estate at present nominates the children that are to be taught as above.

The Revd Benjamin Calm in 1768 by will gave a donation of £50 in trust that the rector and churchwardens for the time being should apply the interest thereof in puting out apprentice the children of such poor people belonging to the said parish as did not receive relief from the parish in the same manner as the interest of Mr Atkins's money was directed to be applied.

The above is a true copy of the answers given on oath to the justices Oct 5th 1786 by the minister and churchwardens, in complyance with an act of Parliment passd for that purpose the same year. [Added in different ink] This is a true copy made to Parliament by the curate and churchwardens of Freshwater as witness my hand J. Price, curate.

503 Froyle 21M65/B4/3/59

Richard Pollen, vicar 1773–99
George Robinson Child AB, curate
1 Area 11 miles in circumference.
2 Population 500.
3 Marriages &c. Marriages 9; births 20; burials 18; upon an average.
4 Patron Sir Thomas Miller, Bt.
5 Chapels No chapel.
6 Lecturer George R. Child AB nominated by the vicar and licensed to preach in Your Lordship's diocese.
7 Dissenters 18 of those called Quakers. No meetings held in the parish.
8 Schools One school endowed with £5 p.a. charged upon Highway estate.
9 Charities There are no hospitals nor any fixed annual donations for the benefit of the poor. The curate who preceded me did not reserve a copy of the return which was made to the late parliamentary enquiry.

504 Fyfield 21M65/B4/3/60

Henry White, rector 1762–88
1 Area About 700 acres.

2 Population About 120.
3 Marriages &c. Baptisms about 7 in 2 years; burials about 5 in 2 years; marriages about 1 in each year.
4 Patron The king.
6 Lecturer None.
7 Dissenters None.
8 Schools None.
9 Charities £300 left to the parishes of Fyfield and Thruxton about 100 years since; vested about 50 years since in freehold land situate in the parish of Chute, known by the name of Mancorn, and let at present for £18 p.a., which is annually about Christmas distributed to the ancient poor of each parish by trustees which are occasionally elected for the purpose as lives fail. It was originally intended for building a workhouse for the 2 parishes; but by a decree in Chancery many years since, vested in the lands abovementioned. No copy of the parliamentary enquiry remains or can be procured.

505 Gatcombe [IoW] 21M65/B4/3/173
James Worsley, rector 1773–1801 23 March 1788
1 Area About 1,400 acres.
2 Population 210.
3 Marriages &c. 14 births, 2 marriages, 5 burials.
4 Patron Elizabeth and Jane Worsley.
5 Chapels None.
6 Lecturer None.
7 Dissenters No Papist. 1 Presbyterian.
8 Schools One school endowed with £8 p.a. charged on the estate of Pidfor in the Islewight the property of Thomas Worsley Esq. Elizabeth Barnes mistress, nominated by the rector of Gatcomb. The poor children of Gatcomb parish the scholars.
9 Charities Answered in the 8th question agreeable to the return made to Parliament.

506 Godshill [IoW] 21M65/B4/3/174
John Barwis, vicar 1786–1828 12 March 1788
Daniel Walsh, curate
1 Area I do not know exactly; but, by the poor rates, it appears that at 12*s.* 6*d.* per acre it will amount to 6,872 acres.
2 Population By an account taken 1777 at the request of Sir Richard Worsley the number was 1,083.
3 Marriages &c. At a medium of the last 7 years, marriages 10; christnings 43 1/7; burials 14 3/7.
4 Patron Queen's College, Oxford.
5 Chapels No chapel.
6 Lecturer A curate, nominated by the vicar. Not licensed.
7 Dissenters No Papist. 2 Presbyterians; and several Methodists of the lowest class of the people.

8 Schools A free grammar school, endowed with about £20 a year; Daniel Walsh, master, appointed by Sir Richard Worsley. John Swan, usher, endowed with £10 a year, appointed by the parishioners. The number always varying. All the parishioners are taught gratis.
9 Charities No hospital. There are £10 distributed annually to 8 poor persons of the parish; and 30*s*. which is annually distributed by the officers to the poor, in bread.
Copy of the return to parliament
Sir Richard Worsley in 1612 gave by deed, for the master of a free grammar school at Godshill, £11 6*s*. 8*d*., an annuity out of land, now vested in Sir Richard Worsley, with an annual produce of £11 6*s*. 8*d*.
Sir Richard Worsley gave by deed for the master of the free grammar school at Godshill, an acre of ground, a garden and cottage on the site of which the present school house is built, valued then at £3, now vested in Sir Richard Worsley and worth £20.
The parishioners of Godshill bought of Philip Andrews in 1603 by deed, for the master of the free school at Godshill, an annuity of £5 out of lands (called Marvel), with an annual produce of £5, now vested in Hinton.
Sir Henry Knollys in 1648 gave by deed, for the master of the free school at Godshill, an annuity of 13*s*. 4*d*. out of lands called Bathingbourn, with an annual produce of 13*s*. 4*d*., now vested in Hicks Esq.
The parishioners of Godshill bought of Thomas Rice in 1623 by deed, for the usher of the free grammar school of Godshill, an annuity of £5 out of lands called Bathingbourn, with an annual produce of £5, now vested in Hicks Esq.
Richard Gard in 1617 gave by will for the above usher an annuity of £5 out of several lands, with an annual produce of £5.
Charitable donations:
Richard Gard in 1617 gave by will an annuity of £1 10*s*. out of land, for the poor, distributed by the officers annually in bread, with an annual produce of £1 10*s*.
Sir Richard Worsley gave an annuity of £10 to 8 poor of the parish. The lands out of which the money is payable is the property of Sir Richard Worsley Bart. No deed appears.
All the above are regularly paid annually.
Elisabeth Duncasson in 1728 by will gave lands to the value of £12, with an annual produce of £12, now vested in the wife of Thomas Hollis of Wootton, and the wife of Thomas Young of Newport, for 6 widows and 6 poor childrens' education and other pious uses at the discretion of trustees. This belongs to dissenters, and is applied where the trustees please.

507 Goodworth Clatford 21M65/B4/3/61
Lascelles Iremonger, vicar 1782–1830
1 Area The circumference of the parish is about 16 miles.
2 Population About 250.
3 Marriages &c. Marriages rather less than 2 in a year; births 8 in a year; burials rather less than 6 in a year.

4 Patron Mr Iremonger of Wherwell.
5 Chapels None.
6 Lecturer None.
7 Dissenters None.
8 Schools One weekly school established and supported by the patron and vicar. Elizabeth Wheeler is the mistress. Number of scholars, about 20. Two Sunday schools, one for boys and one for girls, established and supported by the vicar. Thomas Stockell is master of the boys' school, and Sarah Truman mistress of the girls'. Number of scholars nearly 40.
9 Charities No charitable institutions whatever.

508 Gosport 21M65/B4/3/62
Isaac Moody Bingham MA, perpetual curate, 'minister of Gosport chapel' 1778–92 30 March 1788
[No replies to questions 1 and 2.]
3 Marriages &c. The marriages, births and burials in Gosport chapel at <a mean> of the last 8 years stand as follows: baptisms 170; marriages 76; burials 268. It is to be observed that the numbers differ ex<ceedingly> in the different years of war or peace. In <the> years 1780–81–82–83 which may be take<n as> years of war the average stands as so: baptisms 197; marriages 115; burials < ... >. In the years 1784–85–86 and 87 it stands thus: baptisms 144; marriages 36; burials 98.
4 Patron The chapel o<f> Gosport, of which I am the licensed curate perpetual, or augmented curacy, endow<ed by> sundry benefactions. The rector of Alvestoke has the nomination of a minister or curate.
[No replies to questions 5–8.]
9 Charities <In> the town of Gosport [are] 10 small tenements, which <support> 10 widows, and 1 other tenement <yielding ... > pounds p.a. The former are < ... ar> by the rent arising from the latter, and vested in 3 trustees, of which the minister of <the> chapel is at present (but not necessarily) one. <L>ong since the return to the late parliamentary <enquiry> on this subject was made, that, having never <taken a>ny copy or memorandum of it, it is not in my power to subjoin an exact transcript, but I do not know or <think tha>t any other donations or endowed charitable <institutions exist> within this town.

509 Grateley 21M65/B4/3/63
Richard Turner, rector 1787–1819 20 March 1788
Samuel Topping, curate
1 Area The compass of ground is between 1,500 and 1,600 acres, chiefly arable and down land, with 40 acres of coppice.
2 Population The number of souls is 141, including children and servants.
3 Marriages &c. The number of marriages is about 1 in 3 years; of births 3 or 4; and burials not 2, one year with another — about 3 in 2 years.
4 Patron The patron of the living is Thomas Calverly Esq. of Ewel[l] in Surr[e]y.

5 Chapels No chapel.
6 Lecturer The church is served by a curate, nominated by the Revd Richard Turner of Ditchling in Sussex, the present rector, but not licensed to the same.
7 Dissenters No Papists, or dissenter of any denomination in the parish.
8 Schools No endowed school, or master or mistress of any school nominated or appointed by anyone. There is a woman in the parish who occasionally teaches a few children. But there is a Sunday school instituted by William Benson Earle Esq. by the advice and at the request of the curate.
9 Charities The only fixed annual donation is 15*s*. p.a. left by John Pyle (by will) and charged on his estate at Upper Wallop in this county, now in the possession of Joshua Brownjohn, who lays out the said 15*s*. annually in the purchase of a great coat for such poor man as stands most in need of one.

510 Greatham 21M65/B4/3/64
Edmund White, rector 1785–1814 25 March 1788
Stephen Street MA, curate
1 Area It is not in my power to tell you with any exactness what compass of ground there is in this parish. I suppose the widest extent of it may be about 1 mile from west to east. But I have not been able to get any accurate information concerning the eastern boundary of the parish, which on that side makes a part of Wolmer Forest.
2 Population The inhabitants amount to 146 souls.
3 Marriages &c. At a medium there are 2 marriages, 5 births and <3> burials p.a.
4 Patron The patroness of the living is Mrs Beckford.
5 Chapels There is no chapel.
6 Lecturer There is no lecturer. I officiate for the rector, and am not licensed to this curacy.
7 Dissenters There are no Papists, nor any meetings held of protestant dissenters in this parish.
8 Schools There is no school in this parish.
9 Charities There is not any hospital, nor any endowed charitable institution for the benefit of the poor in this parish. The return to the late parliamentary enquiry on this subject was made by my predecessor, and a<s> I am not possest of any copy of it, I cannot send one.

511 Greywell 21M65/B4/3/65
George Watkins, 'vicar of Odiham with the chapel of Grewell' 1773–98
1 Area About 8 miles in circumference.
[No surviving replies to questions 2–6; the document lacks the right-hand margin in which answers may have been entered.]
7 Dissenters None.
8 Schools None.

9 Charities None.

512 Hale 21M65/B4/3/66
Thomas Read, rector –1789
[This return survives only in fragments; what can be inferred of the substance of the replies is given below.]
1 Area [6 miles in circumference.]
2 Population [189 souls.]
3 Marriages &c. [3 marriages; 6 burials.]
4 Patron [The Right Hon. Lady Elizabeth ...]
5 Chapels [None.]
6 Lecturer [None.]
7 Dissenters [No Papists, protestant dissenters, nor dissenters' meetings.]
8 Schools [No endowed school.]
9 Charities [No endowed charitable institution or annual donation. No copy of the return to the parliamentary enquiry survives. It mentioned only one charitable endowment, and its income; this was taken proper care of.]

513 Hamble 21M65/B4/3/67
James Scott, vicar 1761–1812 31 March 1788
William Kent AM, curate
1 Area Arable 206 acres; waste and common 71.
2 Population 325.
3 Marriages &c. Burials 7; births 10; of late years the marriages have been celebrated at *Hound*, the mother church.
4 Patron Winchester College.
5 Chapels Hamble is a chapelry within the parish of Hound; is served by the curate of Hound; maintained by Winchester College, in which is vested the right of nomination.
6 Lecturer A curate; his name is *Kent*, a Master of Arts; appointed by the vicar, the Revd James Scott; not licensed to this particular cure.
7 Dissenters 2 Papists; no dissenters.
8 Schools No schools that are endowed.
9 Charities None.

514 Hannington 21M65/B4/3/68
Gabriel Tahourdin, vicar 1777–1814
William Dee Best MA, curate
1 Area <... According> to the best information I can get [it] is supposed to be about 1,500 acres.
2 Population To the second question I answer that according to the best information I can get, the number of souls in the said parish are about 200.
3 Marriages &c. To the third I answer that the number of marriages at a medium, one year with another are about 3; births about 10; burials about 6.
4 Patron To the fourth question I answer that the patron of the living is the bishop of the diocese.

5 Chapels [Answer wanting.]
6 Lecturer <Neither> lect<urer> nor curat<e wi>thin the par<ish.>
7 Dissenters To the seventh I answer that there is no Papist nor protestant dissenter nor any meeting-house within the parish.
8 Schools To the eight[h] I answer that there is no school within the parish.
9 Charities To the ninth I answer that there is no hospital, no endowed charitable donation, nor any fixed annual donation for the benefit of the poor. Therefore the answer was only in the negative to the return made to the late parliamentary enquiry.

515 Hartley Mauditt 21M65/B4/3/69
John Tuach BA, rector 1783–1816
Bryan Robinson, curate
1 Area The compass of the parish is about 5 miles and contains about 1,000 acres of ground.
2 Population 60.
3 Marriages &c. Marriages about 1 a year; births about 3 a year; burials about 1 in 3 years.
4 Patron The patronage was in the late Sir Simeon Stuart Bt., since whose death the estate etc. has been in Chancery.
5 Chapels None besides the church called Hartley.
6 Lecturer The curate of the parish is Bryan Robinson who makes this return, appointed by the present rector, Mr Tuach, at Stamford near Reading, but not licensed to the same.
7 Dissenters No Papists. No meetings of Protestant dissenters.
8 Schools No schools.
9 Charities No hospitals. A donation did exist in this parish till the death of the late Sir Simeon Stuart Bt. and which was: to such of the poor of the parish of Hartley Maudytt as attended a certain charity sermon preached annually on the Feast of St Michael 10*s*. to be equally divided among them, and 20*s*. to be equally divided among as many of the poor of the parish of Selbourne as attended the same charity sermon, 20*s*. to the preacher of the same sermon, and the further sum of 54*s*. for the relief of the poor in general of the parish of Hartley Maudytt aforesaid. We can find no records, but from the testimony of the oldest inhabitants, it appears that the estate of the late Sir Simeon Stuart Bt. was charged with the payment of this donation.

516 Hartley Wespall 21M65/B4/3/70
Philip Duval DD, rector 1786–92
William Paice, curate
[Unsigned.]
1 Area About 4 miles in length and 1 in breadth.
2 Population 221.
3 Marriages &c. Marriages 2; births 6; burials 4.

4 Patron The Dean and Chapter of Windsor.
5 Chapels None.
6 Lecturer William Paice is the curate, licensed thereto under a title from Dr Lo<ck>ma<n> the late rector.
7 Dissenters None.
8 Schools None.
9 Charities William Paice in the year 1640 left an estate by will to the churchwardens and overseers of the parish (for the time being). At that time the estate let for £3 10*s*. p.a.; one moiety for the repairs of the church, the other for the poor.
Dame Abigail Stawell in the year 1692 left by will £50 to <the> poor, with which sum and £136 arising from timber from the above devised estate of William Paice another estate was <purc>hased (adjoining the former) which two estates now let <to ano>ther at £10 5*s*. p.a. After deducting Land Tax, quit <re>nt and repairs ⅓ is expended in the repairs of the church, <and th>e remainder given to the poor.

517 Havant 21M65/B4/3/71
David Renaud, rector 1776–1807
[Return is a fragment, lacking the first 2 pages entirely.]
7 Dissenters [There are supposed to be upwards of a hundred Papists with a chapel. There is also a meeting of protestant dissenters numbering about 50.]
8 Schools No endowed school.
9 Charities [There is no hospital or endowed charitable institution, nor annual donation for the poor.]

518 Hawkley 21M65/B4/3/72
Edmund White AB, 'impropriator and officiating minister of Hawkley Chapel' 1785–1838
1 Area From the best information that can be obtained, the parish of Hawkley is supposed to be about 4 miles in circumference.
2 Population There are 259 inhabitants of the parish of Hawkley.
3 Marriages &c. In the last 20 years were registered 35 marriages, 153 births, 100 burials. The medium for a year is: 2 marriages nearly; rather more than 7½ births; 5 burials.
4 Patron Vide Newton Valence to which Hawkley is a chapel of ease.
5 Chapels [No reply; see no. 4.]
6 Lecturer There is no lecturer or curate in the parish of Hawkley.
7 Dissenters There is no Papist, or any meeting of protestant dissenters of any denomination in the parish of Hawkley.
8 Schools There is no endowed school in the parish of Hawkley.
9 Charities There is no hospital, endowed charitable institution, or fixed annual donation for the benefit of the poor in the parish of Hawkley. The return made to the parliamentary inquiry was to the following purport:
'No charitable donation for the benefit of the poor hath been given at any time to the parish, to the best of my knowledge and information.'

519 Hayling North 21M65/B4/3/73
John Webster, vicar 1773–96 27 March 1788
Evan Evans, curate
1 Area Between 7 and 8 miles exclusive [of] the mud that surrounds the greatest part of it.
2 Population On the 20th of February ult. it contained 256 souls.
3 Marriages &c. At an average of the last 8 years there have been in it annually 9 births, 3 weddings, and 6 burials.
4 Patron His Grace the Duke of Norfolk.
5 Chapels None.
6 Lecturer No lecturer. The parish is served by Evan Evans clerk, the curate who is nominated and appointed by the Revd Mr Webster, the vicar. Not licensed.
7 Dissenters No protestant dissenters; no sectaries whatever.
8 Schools To the great misfortune of the parish there is no endowed school.
9 Charities None at all.

520 Hayling South 21M65/B4/3/74
John Webster, vicar 1773–96
Evan Evans, curate
1 Area About 11 miles within the compass of [the] high-water mark.
2 Population 280 souls.
3 Marriages &c. At an average taken from the last 8 years there have been annually in it 10 births, 3 marriages and 7 burials.
4 Patron His Grace the Duke of Norfolk.
5 Chapels None.
6 Lecturer No lecturer. The parish is served by Evan Evans, clerk, the curate who is appointed by the Revd Mr Webster, the vicar. Not licensed.
7 Dissenters No protestant dissenters; no sectaries whatever.
8 Schools To the misfortune of the parish there is no endowed school.
9 Charities None at all.

521 Headbourne Worthy 21M65/B4/3/75
Henry Ridley MA, rector 1781–99
F. W. Swanton, curate
1 Area About 1,550 acres.
2 Population About 164.
3 Marriages &c. About 3 births, 3 burials and 1 marria<ge>.
4 Patron University College in Oxford.
5 Chapels None.
6 Lecturer No lecturer. F. W. Swanton, curate.
7 Dissenters None.
8 Schools None.
9 Charities A donation left by the Revd Robert <...>wich and his widow of £80 for which <interest is> paid yearly £4 chargeable on <a hou>se now

the property of Sir Chaloner Ogle. This is a copy of the return sent to Parliament.

522 Headley 21M65/B4/3/76
William Sewell, rector 1765–1800 March 29, 1788
1 Area 14 miles square, or 8,960 acres square, at 640 statute-acres to the mile, of which are 2,434¾ acres arable, 242½ pasture, 285¼ meadow, 85½ woodland, and 5,913 of heathy common.
2 Population In October last past, I took an account of the number of houses and persons in this parish; that of houses was 137, and that of persons, 720.
3 Marriages &c. At a medium for 15 years last past, annually, and for any greater length of time, backward: marriages 6; births 26; burials 15.
4 Patron The Provost and Fellows of Queen's College in Oxford.
5 Chapels No chapel within the parish.
6 Lecturer No lecturer ever in this parish. Thomas Dennis (deacon) licensed curate.
7 Dissenters Neither a Papist, [n]or a dissenter of any denomination in this parish.
8 Schools A school endowed by the late George Holme DD, rector, my predecessor, with £8 p.a., for teaching 6 poor boys and 6 poor girls. William Bayley, schoolmaster, nominated and chosen by the rector of Headley and trustees appointed by the deed of endowment.
9 Charities No hospital here. Only the endowed school or charitable institution aforesaid. There was a legacy in the last century of £20, the interest of which was directed to be distributed annually to the poor of this parish. This £20, some years since, was lent to a farmer here, then supposed to be in good circumstances, but who afterwards failed broke, and is now reduced to a day-labourer with a wife and a large family of small children. I think this money is lost irrecoverably. An account of this was sent in by the return to the late parliamentary enquiry; but I do not learn that parliament ever noticed it, or made any further enquiry about it.

523 Heckfield 21M65/B4/3/77
William Milton MA, vicar 1773–1824
Edward Taylor, curate
1 Area Between 5 and 6,000 acres.
2 Population 1000.
3 Marriages &c. Births 30; burials 25; [marriages wanting].
4 Patron New <College, Oxford.>
[Questions 5 and 6, answers wanting; return damaged.]
7 Dissenters None.
8 Schools One free school for 13 boys <and gir>ls. Master endowed and nominated by Lord Rivers.
9 Charities [No reply.]

524 Herriard 21M65/B4/3/78

Joseph Robertson, vicar 1758–1802
John Ilsley, curate

[Only a fragment of this document survives; what may be transcribed or inferred of its contents is as follows.]

1 Area It is difficult to say what compass of ground <ma>y be in the parish of Herriard, as therein <is> a larg<e ...> and much woodland ground. <It is probable that t>he parish contains at least <... .>

2 Population The number of souls according to <the best> information I can <g>et is 283.

3 Marriages &c. In the space of <...years> there have been 9 <marriages>; 26 bu<rials>; [births wanting].

4 Patron The Duke of Bolton is the patron of Herriard vic<ara>ge.

5 Chapels There is no chapel in the parish.

6 Lecturer John Ilsley i<s curate?> of Herr<iard> and has been cura<te...>.

7 Dissenters I do not kn<ow that> there is one Papist <in> Herriard, or <a single protestant dissente>r.

8 Schools There is no endowed school, and at present <no> school at all <ex>cept for little children to learn to read.

9 Charities <The>re is no hospital, or endowed charita<b>le institu<tion> nor any fixed annual <dona>tion <for the> benefit of the poor. Such <was the return m>ade to the late <parliamentary in>quiry, but no copy thereof ke<pt.>

525 Highclere 21M65/B4/3/79

Richard Davies, rector 1757–97 11 <M>arch 1788

[Lacks first 2 pages.]

7 Dissenters Neither papist nor dissenter of any denomination.

8 Schools This will be answered by the following copy of the return made to the late parliamentary enquiry.

9 Charities No hospital or endowed charitable institution, or any fixed annual donation, except the single one mentioned below, in the answers made to the late parliamentary enquiry.

Copy of the answers to that enquiry

Edward Band, gentleman, on November 3, 1724 gave by surrender to the lord of the manor the cottage and 30 perches of land adjoining more <o>r less near ...[faded illegibly] vested in the churchwardens of Highclere and their successors for ever, producing £1 10*s.* subject to a quitrent of 1*s.* p.a. and charges of repair, to put one or more children of the poor inhabitants of the said parish to school to be taught to read the Bible and to learn the church catechism.

526 Holybourne 21M65/B4/3/80

Thomas Balguy DD, vicar of Alton 1771–95
Lancelot Docker, curate

1 Area The parish is supposed to be 7 or 8 miles in circumference.

2 Population There are 70 families in the parish.
3 Marriages &c. No marriages solemnized here; nearly 5 burials and 9 births.
4 Patron Holybourn is a chapelry under Alton.
5 Chapels The chapel is served by the curate of Alton, nominated by the vicar, and has no other maintenance but the stipend received from him.
6 Lecturer No lecturer or curate but the one already mentioned, who is not licensed.
7 Dissenters No Papist. One family of Quakers.
8 Schools One school, endowed with lands. The number of children admitted free unlimited. The present master, the Revd Bryan Robinson, nominated by trustees.
9 Charities No hospital or endowed charitable institution, or fixed annual donation for benefit of poor.

527 Houghton 21M65/B4/3/81
Samuel Nott MA, rector 1776–93
James Birch, curate
[This return badly faded.]
1 Area About 1½ miles in breadth and the same in length.
2 Population 341.
3 Marriages &c. About 8 births; 2 marriages; and 6 burials.
4 Patron The Bishop of Win<chester.>
5 Chapels No chapel.
6 Lecturer One curate nominated by the rector, but not li<censed.>
7 Dissenters One family of Papists.
8 Schools No school.
9 Charities A fixed annual donation of £2 6*s*. 8*d*. for the poor of the parish.

528 Hound 21M65/B4/3/82
James Scott, vicar 1761–1812 31 March 1788
William Kent MA, curate
1 Area Arable 1,550 acres. Waste and common not ascertained.
2 Population 263.
3 Marriages &c. Burials 5; births 10; marriages 8.
4 Patron Winchester College.
5 Chapels 2 chapelries, Hamble and Bursledon, served by the curate of this parish; maintained, supported and nominated to, as mentioned in the answers to the questions respecting those 2 parishes.
6 Lecturer A curate; his name is Kent, a Master of Arts, appointed by the vicar, the Revd James Scott; not licensed to this particular cure.
7 Dissenters None.
8 Schools None that are endowed.
9 Charities None.

529 Hunton 21M65/B4/3/83

Edmund Poulter of Crawley, rector 1785–91
Livingstone Booth, curate
1 Area About 950 acres.
2 Population About 88.
3 Marriages &c. The medium of births p.a. is 3⅙; of burials 2⅓; of marriages nearly 1.
4 Patron The Lord Bishop of Winchester.
5 Chapels Hunton is a chapel annexed to Crawley, served by the Revd L. Booth, supported by its own tithes and nominated by the Revd Mr Poulter, rector of Crawley.
6 Lecturer The Revd L.Booth is curate as above. Not licensed.
7 Dissenters No Papist nor protestant dissenter.
8 Schools No school.
9 Charities No hospital, endowed charitable institution, nor fixed annual donation. Not being curate of Hunton at the time of the late parliamentary enquiry and no copy of the return being preserved, it is not in my power to send a copy of it.

530 Hurstbourne Priors 21M65/B4/3/84

John Washington, vicar 1787–1803 27 March 1788
John Garnett AM, curate
1 Area The parish of Hurstbourne Priors, including the chapelry of St Mary's Bourne is about 30 miles in circuit, and contains by estimation about 9,000 acres of land. Exclusive of Bourne (which now supports its own poor and is in many other respects an independant parish), Hurtbourne Priors does not measure more than 12 miles in circuit, and contains only about 3,000 acres of land.
2 Population The number of souls in Hurstbourne Priors amounts to about 450.
3 Marriages &c. Taking the medium of the last 10 years there have been in Hurstbourne Priors about 4 marriages, 15 baptisms and 10 burials in a year.
4 Patron The Bishop of Winchester is patron of the vicarage, and the Revd John Washington the present vicar. The rectory is impropriate, belongs to the Master and brethren of St Cross's hospital near Winchester, and is held by the Earl of Portsmouth, their lessee.
5 Chapels The church at Bourne is a chapel of ease to Hurstbourne Priors, is dedicated to St Mary, is served by the vicar of Hurstbourne Priors or his curate, and is supported by the emoluments of his vicarage, which arise in part from certain great and small tythes in the said chapelry as well as in Hurstbourne Priors. It is an appendage to the vicarage of Hurstbourne and of course the right of nomination is vested in the Bishop of Winchester.
6 Lecturer There is no lecturer within the parish Of Hurstbourne Priors. The Revd Mr Washington the vicar, employs 2 curates, the Revd John Garnett for Hurstbourne, and the Revd — Lambe for Bourne, who will return answers to the Bishop of Winchester's several questions for that particular district. Mr Garnett is *not* licensed.

7 Dissenters There are neither Papists nor protestant dissenters of any denomination in Hurstbourne Priors, and consequently no meetings are held there.
8 Schools There is no endowed school in Hurstbourne.
9 Charities There is not any hospital or endowed charitable institution in Hurstbourne Priors, nor any fixed annual foundation for the benefit of the poor, excepting that which is specified in the underwritten return which is a true copy of the answers returned to the late parliamentary enquiry.
[*Copy of Return*]
Robert Oxenbridge about 200 years ago gave by will for the benefit of the industrious poor, not receiving relief, £77 0*s*. 6*d*. in money, now invested in the old South Sea Annuities in the name of the Right Hon. the Earl of Portsmouth and yeilding £2 6*s*. 2*d*. p.a.

531 Hurstbourne Tarrant 21M65/B4/3/85
Peter Debary AM, vicar of 'Hursborn Tarrant and of Burbage, Wilts.' 1755–1814
1 Area About 8,000 acres gross computation, the chapelry of Vernham included.
2 Population About 1,150 including the chapelry of Fernham Dean.
3 Marriages &c. Marriages in church and chapel, about 8; births about 31; burials about 20.
4 Patron The Prebendary of Hursborn Tarrant and Burbage in the church of Sarum.
5 Chapels 1 chapel, portion of the parish, allways possessed by and usually supplied by the vicar; maintained by the tithes etc., as usual, and a glebe of between 40 and 50 acres; named Fernham Dean, commonly written Vernham Dean, but by strange corruption now sometimes stiled Vernon's Dean, and frequently [called] a parish.
6 Lecturer None.
7 Dissenters No dissenters besides 2 Roman Catholicks and 1 young child.
8 Schools 6 children at Hursborn taught to read and work by Mary Smith. 12 children at Ibthrop in Hursborn taught to read and work by Mary Holden or Holdway. 2 children at Upton taught to read and work by Grace Berriman. The copy of the parliamentary return explains all further particulars.
9 Charities
Copy of the Return
Robert Munday, 1706, by deed for widowers and widows charged on land, [vested in] Mr S[amue]l Medhurst, £1.
Peter Dore, 1756, by will for putting 6 children to school, charged on land, [vested in] Dr Alexander senior £2 10*s*.
William Jones 1756 by deed, for putting children to school, charged on land in the heirs of the late Mr Munday, £5.
Richard Bunny, 1775, by deed, for relieving the poor who have no parish relief and putting 2 children to school at Upton in this parish, £300 in consolidated annuities, [vested in] the vicar and Richard Martin, £9.

<L>uke Peace <as i>s supposed, by will for the poor of Ibthrop, charged on land, [vested in] John Godden, 7*s.* 6*d.* irregularly paid. Note, nothing at Vernham Chapel.

532 Kimpton 21M65/B4/3/86

Edward Foyle MA, rector 1785–1832
1 Area About 16 or 1,700 acres.
2 Population 256.
3 Marriages &c. Marriages about 2 in a year; births about 10 or 12; burials 5 or 6.
4 Patron Gorges Foyle Esq.
5 Chapels None.
6 Lecturer None.
7 Dissenters None.
8 Schools None.
9 Charities None.

533 Kingsley 21M65/B4/3/87

Thomas Balguy DD, vicar of Alton 1771–95
John Mill, curate
1 Area The compass of the parish of Kingsley [is] about 9 miles.
2 Population The number of souls in the parish of Kingsley [is] about 220.
3 Marriages &c. Marriages, not any; births from 5 to 7; burials from 7 to 10.
4 Patron Kingsley is annext to Binsted.
5 Chapel Not any.
6 Lecturer Not any.
7 Dissenters Not any.
8 Schools Not any.
9 Charities A donation of 12*s.* p.a. to the parish of Kingsley, paid by Mr Burningham of Kingsley. A donation of 20*s.* p.a. to the parish of Kingsley, paid by Mr Bristow of the parish of Farnham.

534 Kingston [IoW] 21M65/B4/3/175

Henry Worsley, rector 1779–1802
1 Area I believe about 1,000 acres.
2 Population Inhabitants 40.
3 Marriages &c. Burials 4 in seven years, 2 of which were extraparochial; marriage, 1 in seven years; christenings 32, in seven years, 22 of which were extraparochial.
4 Patron Revd James Worsley, Elizabeth Worsley, and Jane Worsley.
5 Chapels No chapel.
6 Lecturer No curate or lecturer.
7 Dissenters None of either sect.
8 Schools No school.

9 Charities None.

535 Knights Enham 21M65/B4/3/88

Arthur Atkinson, rector 1782–1814 28 March 1788

1 Area The rector of Enham receives the tithe of between 7 and 800 acres, including coppices. But there is reason to believe that he ought [also to receive them] of many more, as the parish of Enham is surrounded by Andover, and the lands are intermixed with those of the tithes of King's Enham, which is in the parish of Andover; so that the boundaries between the parishes are not known; which have occasioned many disputes about the tithes so many years ago as 1439 and 40, and have continued ever since at different periods, though there were meetings held and arbitrators chosen. In the year 1634 a law suit was commenced concerning the tithes between th<e> lessee of the great tithes of Andover and the rector of Enham, which should have been tried at Winchester Assizes. But there was only one judge for both benches, so the tryal was put off and never afterwards came to a hearing, owing, it is presumed, to one or both of the parties dying. And it is surprizing the cause should never afterwards be brought to an issue by any of the succeeding rectors. In the year 1784 the people of Andover parish got an Act of Parliament for to inclose Enham Heath and Finchley Down on which the inhabitants of Enham parish (intercommoning with the tithing of King's Enham) time out of mind used to turn their cattle on the above-mentioned heath or down for to feed. In lieu of this feed, the commissioners appointed by the act allotted to each proprietor of land in Enham parish a certain number of acres; the tithe of which the rector thinks belongs to him and intends to have an eminent counsel's opinion whether it does or not, as the lands of both parishes being intermixed and the parish of Enham adjoining to the down and heath.

2 Population There are about 90 souls in this parish, but many of them are included who live in houses which are only part of them, it is said, to be in my parish.

3 Marriages &c.	Marriages	Births	Burials	
1779	0	3	1	
1780	2	1	5	
1781	0	1	1	
1782	1	2	1	
1783	1	3	2	
1784	0	1	4	
1785	0	3	2	
1786	0	2	4	
1787	1	0	1	
1788	0	2	1	([to] March 25th)
In all	4	18	22	

4 Patron Queen's College, Oxford.

5 Chapels None.

6 Lecturer No.

7 Dissenters There are no Papists, nor dissenters of any kind.

8 Schools None.
9 Charities There are no hospitals, nor any charitable institution whatever in my parish. The answers which I made to the parliamentary enquiry were similar to the above, as far as I can recollect, as I unfortunately have not a copy.

536 Lainston 21M65/B4/3/89
Samuel Gauntlett DD, rector 1778–1807
1 Area The parish of Lainston is of very small extent; the clear annual value of all the tithes being only £16. I cannot ascertain the compass of ground contained in it.
2 Population The number of souls in Lainston varies according to the number of Mr Bathurst's family.
3 Marriages &c. During my incumbency from the [beginning?] there have been no marriages, <...> and only 3 funerals, viz. the late Mr and Mrs Bathurst, and their eldest son.
4 Patron Robert Bathurst Esq.
5 Chapels None except the rectorial chapel.
6 Lecturer No lecturer nor curate.
7 Dissenters No Papists nor protestant dissenters.
8 Schools No schools.
9 Charities No hospitals nor endowed charitable institutions.

537 Lasham 21M65/B4/3/90
James Pinnocke, rector 1764–1822
1 Area About 2,000 acres.
2 Population About 140.
3 Marriages &c. About 4 marriages; 6 births; 3 burials.
4 Patron Late William Guidott Esq. Now John Blackburne and — Slade Esqs., purchasers of the estate.
5 Chapels Not any chapel.
6 Lecturer Not any lecturer. The Revd Mr Jeston, master of the free school, Odiham, curate; nominated by the rector.
7 Dissenters Not any Papist [n]or dissenter.
8 Schools Not any endowed school.
9 Charities Not any endowed hospital or charitable institution. 2 fixed annual donations for the benefit of the poor granted upon the inclosure of commons, viz. 40*s*. p.a. from William Guidott's estate, now Blackburne and Slade Esqs.; 10*s*. p.a. from the estate of William Bloos Esq. in the same parish.

538 Leckford 21M65/B4/3/91
Thomas Taylor LLB, rector 1777–1808
Nicholas Westcombe, curate
1 Area About 2,060 acres.

2 Population About 181.
3 Marriages &c. Marriages about 2; births about 6; burials about 4.
4 Patron President and Fellows of St. John's College, <Oxford.>
5 Chapels None.
6 Lecturer Nicholas Westcombe, curate; not licensed. Appointed by the r<ector.>
7 Dissenters 4 Papists; no dissenters nor any meetings held in this parish.
8 Schools None.
9 Charities No hospital or endowed charitable institution, nor any fixed annual donation for the benefit of the poor.

539 Linkenholt 21M65/B4/3/92

Robert Worgan AM, rector 1761–1801
1 Area Somewhat more than 1,000 acres.
2 Population Near 100.
3 Marriages &c. About 2 or 3 annually.
4 Patron Present incumbent.
5 Chapels None.
6 Lecturer None.
7 Dissenters None.
8 Schools A Sunday school and a small day school.
9 Charities None.

540 Liss 21M65/B4/3/93

Thomas Trodd, perpetual curate 1772–92
Stephen Street MA, curate
1 Area Having applied to the only person who is able to tell what number of square acres there are in Lyss, I could not obtain any information. I therefore can only say in answer to your first question that I believe the greatest extent of the parish from east to west is about 4 miles, and from north to south about 3½; but the parish is of a very irregular figure.
2 Population The number of souls according to the best intelligence I can get amounts to 428.
3 Marriages &c. At a medium for the last 10 years there have been 3 marriages, 10 baptisms, and 7 burials yearly.
4 Patron Lyss is a perpetual curacy, the patron of it is Sir James Tilney Long.
5 Chapels There is no other place of public worship in Lyss than the parish church.
6 Lecturer The Revd Thomas Trodd is the licensed curate. I assist him in performing the duty.
7 Dissenters There is but 1 Papist in the parish, and there are no meetings of protestant dissenters.
8 Schools There are 2 schools in the parish; one a reading school for boys endowed with £4 p.a., the master of which is Richard Philp, who was nominated by James Pigott of Crowshole in the county of Sussex; at this

school there are 8 scholars. The other [is] a reading school for girls endowed with £100 principal money, the mistress of which is Mary Parr, who was nominated by Richard Aubrey Esq. of Lyss Place; the number of scholars at this school is 6.
9 Charities There is no hospital in the parish. But there is an annual donation of 10*s*. p.a. to keep the church porch in repair, and, in case no repairs are necessary on the church porch, to be distributed among the poor of the parish. As I kept no copy of the return made to the late parliamentary enquiry on this subject, I cannot send one.

541 Litchfield 21M65/B4/3/94
William Stone, rector of 'Ludshelf alias Litchfield' 1781–8
David Middleton, curate
1 Area I really cannot tell what compass of ground is in the parish.
2 Population 70.
3 Marriages &c. During the last 10 years there have been 25 baptisms, 8 marriages, and 12 burials.
4 Patron Robert Kingsmill Esq. of Sydmonton, Hants.
5 Chapels No.
6 Lecturer An unlicensed curate, the Revd David Middleton.
7 Dissenters None.
8 Schools None.
9 Charities None. The substance of the answer returned to parliament.

542 Littleton 21M65/B4/3/95
Timothy Gabell, curate 1781–92
1 Area About 6 miles.
2 Population 70.
3 Marriages &c. About one birth and one burial. I have had the curacy near 7 years and never read the matrimonial service.
4 Patron The Dean and Chapter of Wi<nch>ester.
5 Chapels None.
6 Lecturer No lecturer. I was ordained priest by <Your> Lordship under this title, and license<d at the same> time.
7 Dissenters None.
8 Schools None.
9 Charities A legacy or donation of £7 10*s*. 0*d*., the interest of which <is pai>d to the poor annually. The name of the testator <or do>nor unknown.

543 Lockerley 21M65/B4/3/96
Oliver Goodyer St John, rector 1773–1804
[Lacks pages 1 and 2.]
8 Schools None.
9 Charities For the education of a certain number of poor children of each parish. No copy taken [of the return to the parliamentary enquiry.]

544 Longparish and St Mary Bourne 21M65/B4/3/97
Edward Woodcock LLB, prebendary 1765–92 19 March 1788
James Lamb AM, curate
I can now make answer with accuracy to the several questions proposed to me. As I have been upwards of 8 years curate of St Mary Bourne, as well as this place, though the first is accounted a chapel to Hurstbourne Prior, I shall send you the information that you wanted concerning it.
1 Area In Long-Parish 5200 acres. In St Mary Bourne 7500 acres.
2 Population In Long-Parish 593. In Bourne 901.
3 Marriages &c. Marriages 3; births 18; burials 10 in Long-Parish. Marriages 5; births 26; burials 15 in Bourne.
4 Patron Mr Woodcock, the prebendary, patron of Long-Parish; Your Lordship is patron of St Mary Bourne.
To questions 5 and 6 I answer in the negative.
7 Dissenters Anabaptists 22 in Long-Parish; 3 in Bourne.
8 Schools No endowed school.
9 Charities Or hospital, and only an annual donation of 10*s*. for the benefit of the poor in Long-Parish.

545 Longstock 21M65/B4/3/98
Sir Charles Mill LLB, vicar 1748/9–92
[Fragmentary.]
1 Area 2,967 acres.
2 Population 278.
3 Marriages &c. 2 marriages; 7 baptisms; 6 burials.
4 Patron Revd Sir Charles Mill, Bt.
5 Chapels None.
6 Lecturer None.
7 Dissenters None.
8 Schools None.
9 Charities A charity farm, but not confined to this parish. Only one pauper is relieved thereby. <The reply to the> parliamentary enquiry was not copied; <the fin>al question was "What did the poor rates amount to in the last three years?" i.e. 1783, 1784, and 1785.
Answer

1783	£141 10*s*. 0½*d*.
1784	132 11*s*. 3*d*.
1785	115 17*s*. 3½*d*.

546 Lymington 21M65/B4/3/99/1–2
William Gilpin MA, vicar of Boldre 1777–1804 31 March 1788
Ellis Jones, curate 1783–1833
1 Area The length of the parish from north to south is about 3 miles. The breadth from east to west is about 1 mile. The circumference is about 14 miles.
2 Population About 2,000.

3 Marriages &c. Marriages about 17; births from 60 to <70>; burials from 40 to 50.
4 Patron Lymington is a chapel of ease to Boldre, the patron of which living is William Mitford Esq.
5 Chapels There are none.
6 Lecturer There are none.
7 Dissenters Only 2 Papists. There are 2 protestant dissenting meeting-houses, one Anabaptist, the other Presbyterian. Of the former there are about 140. Of the latter about 90.
8 Schools There are 2 charity schools. One under the care of Mr Page which has a donation of £12 1*s*. p.a. left by a Mr Fulford to educate 12 boys. The other under the care of Mr Bestlands which has a donation of £15 p.a. left by the late Mrs Burrard to educate a number of boys at the discretion of her executors. There are likewise 2 boarding-schools. One under the care of Mr Davidson, for young gentleman [sic]. And the other under the care of Miss Fry, for young ladies. There are likewise 2 or 3 small day-schools.
9 Charities The endowed charitable institutions and fixed amount donations for the benefit of the poor of this parish are specified in the parliamentary enquiry herewith enclosed.
[*Reply to parliamentary enquiry*]
Thomas Brown gent., on 4 Feb. 1667, gave by will to the use of the poor of Lymington £2 p.a. in land now vested in the heirs or assigns of John Hildersley, William Tulse, Henry Tulse, Edward Hooker, Philip Dore, and Bartholomew Bulkeley Esqs.
George Fulford Esq. on 20 June 1668 gave by deed for the education of youth (NB This school is *at present* under the care of Mr Page.) in land out of the rents of which a saving of £50 has been made now cent [sic] at interest at 5% £12 10*s*. p.a. vested in Thomas Bower the elder, Thomas Bower the younger, Samuel Cleaveland, John Walter and Wadham Wyndham Esqs.
The mayor and burgesses of the borough of Lymington on 25 March 1688 gave by deed a building then standing upon 18 stone pillars on the High St. of Lymington for a school-house, a room to educate the above-mentioned youth, now vested in the heirs or assigns of Thomas Wansey, Mathew Hawkins, Philip Newland and Thomas Hicks Esqs.
George Burrard Esq. on 13 October 1719 gave by will £100 for the use of the poor which has been laid out in the purchase of a piece of ground and towards erecting a poor-house.
Anne Burrard, widow, on 4 July 1777 gave by will £300 in money now yielding £15 p.a. for the education of boys and girls limited to 15 (N.B. this school is under the care of Mr Beesland) now vested in Thomas Rickman, Thomas Missing and Thomas Munday Esqs.

547 Micheldever 21M65/B4/3/100
Peter Smith, vicar 1773–97 26 March 1788
1 Area Though I cannot ascertain the number of ac<res> in my parish of Micheldever, yet that, including the hamlets of Weston, and We<st> Stratton, with the chapelries of East Stra<tton,> Popham and Northington, it may be ab<out> 25 miles in circumference.

2 Population It is, however, so thinly inhabited that I cannot compute it to contain above 700 souls.

3 Marriages &c. The number of baptisms, marriages and burials at Micheldever and the chapels of East Str<atto>n, Popham and Northington may be on an average per annum:

	Baptisms	Marriages	Burials
Micheldever	16	2	12
East Stratton	10	1	have no burying grounds
Popham	1	1 in 3 years	
Northington	8	2	4

4 Patron [Return badly damaged] <...> an impropria<tion...> The chapels of E<ast Stratton,> Popham and Northington are <...> vicar of Micheldever. The<y ...> are supported by the inhabitants and <the> lord of the manor.
5 Chapels [No reply; see 4.]
6 Lecturer I have no curate in my parish, but a son in orders who assists me, sometimes at one chapel, and sometimes at another.
7 Dissenters I have no dissenter, either Papist or protestant in my parish, except one Quaker.
8 Schools There are no schools in my parish.
9 Charities Neither are there any hospitals, or other charitable donations except the interest of £60, the residue of £100 bequeathed to the poor of the parish by — Pink, 15*s*. p.a. issuing from a farm in the possession of His Grace the Duke of Bedford, and 5*s*. p.a. arising from a farm in the parish of Upham in Your Lordship's diocese and county of Southampton. An account of which donations was <given to> the la<te parliamenta>ry en<quiry>. Hoping <this> may afford some satisfaction <to your> Lordship, I remain with all <due> respect, Your Lordship's most faithful and obedient servant.

548 Michelmersh 21M65/B4/3/101
Philip Baker, rector 1772–97
1 Area Supposed 6,000 acres.
2 Population About 700 souls in the hamlets of Michelmersh, Braishfield and Awbridge.
3 Marriages &c. At a medium of 11 years, 6 marriages, 18 persons baptized, 15 funerals.
4 Patron Bishop of Winchester.
5 Chapels None.
6 Lecturer None.
7 Dissenters 2 persons called Presbyterians, both attending divine service in the church.
8 Schools A Sunday and *weekly* school. The master paid the interest of money belonging to the parish, great part of which has always <been app>lyed to the education of poor children, with 40*s*. p.a. now <from> the rector. The master Mr John Beardsley, appointed by the minister; the number of scholars about 25 or 30.
9 Charities No hospitals or *endowed* charitable institutions. £170 belonging to the parish has been collected from <...>t securities and is now in the

hands of Mr Francis Kelsey at Awbridge at 5% applyed with the addition of 40*s*. as a salary to the master of the <Sun>day and weekly school. There has always been a tradition in the parish <th>at the money was left for the education of poor children, but there are no <pa>pers to shew how the parish came possessed of the greatest part, excepting <a> memorandum in the church chest, that Mr Coxe of Braishfield left £40 <to> make a [1 word illegible] use for the poor. This money is supposed to make part of the £<170> in the hands of Mr Kelsey. Mr Sims of Slasted left the value of 30*s*. in bread to be given yearly for 50 years on Candlemas. <It is supp>osed 30 years expired. No copy was taken of the return <to t>he parliamentary enquiry. The answers must have been the same.

549 Millbrook 21M65/B4/3/129

William Harvest, rector 1771–1812

1 Area According to the best information I can get, I suppose there to be in the parish of Millbrook, or that part of the parish so called, about 1,000 acres cultivated, and about 500 acres uncultivated or waste, but there is another part of the parish called Hill and Sipford or Shirley (in which there was formerly a chapel), which contains about 700 acres cultivated and 300 waste. The tithes of this last part are in lay hands, and although I am frequently called out on duty to this part of the parish (it being more populous) the only compensation I receive is £4 p.a. paid by the person who rents these tithes and called proxy tithes. Surely, my Lord, this ought not so to be, more especially as the tithes of Millbrook, all taxes being paid, and *necessary* deductions made, being in clear very little more than £100 p.a., besides the very great inconvenience which every rector of this parish must experience, from the want of glebe land, the whole (including what the house, barn etc. stand on) not exceeding 1 acre. These circumstances I should not have taken the liberty of mentioning to your lordship, had I not imagined, that (the living being in your patronage) you would be pleased to be made acquainted with the condition of it.

2 Population On sending round the parish I find the number of souls to be about 913 (including Shirley).

3 Marriages &c.

	Marriages	Births	Burials
1780	8	32	44.
1781	7	42	19.
1782	15	28	28.
1783	16	27	18.
1784	4	29	15.
1785	12	38	16.
1786	11	31	23.

At a medium: 10 marriages; 23 baptisms; 17 burials.

4 Patron The patron of this living is the Bishop of Winchester.

5 Chapels There is no chapel in this parish.

6 Lecturer Nor any lecturer or curate.

7 Dissenters There is not one Papist in the parish. No meeting of protestant dissenters, nor any dissenters whatever, except 2 small families of Quakers.

8 Schools The only schools in the parish are 2 schools for children not endowed.
9 Charities There are no hospitals or e<ndo>wed charitable institutions, or any fixed annual donations for the benefit of the poor of this parish.
Thus, my Lord, have I endeavoured to answer distinctly the several questions put to me. Your clergy, you may be assured, will all be happy to see you on your visit through the diocese, but not one more sincerely than Your Lordship's most humble and most obedient servant.

550 Monxton 21M65/B4/3/102/1–2
Edward Hawtrey MA, rector 1779–1803 29 March 1788
Thomas Griffith, curate
1 Area 1,050 acres.
2 Population 175.
3 Marriages &c. In the last 3 years the number total of marriages [is] 2; births 16; burials 15.
4 Patron The fellows of King's College, [Cambridge.]
5 Chapels None.
6 Lecturer Thomas Griffith, curate, nominated by Mr Hawtrey.
7 Dissenters None.
8 Schools None endowed.
9 Charities There are no hospitals, or endowed charitable institutions, nor any fixed annual donations. I kept no copy of the return to the late parliamentary enquiry. Annexed is an account of the disbursements as given me by the parishioners, who do not seem disposed to give me correct account of their assessments and quantity of land.
Mony disburst to the poore
1783 £73 1*s*. 7*d*.
1784 63 16*s*.10*d*.
1785 69 19*s*.1*d*.

551 Morestead 21M65/B4/3/103
Henry Norman AB, rector 1767–88[42] Winchester, 15 March 1788
1 Area I suppose my parish to measure about 2 miles two different ways, but if reduced to a perfect square, I suppose it would measure about 1½ miles every way. The number of acres of inclosed ground is by computation about 490.
2 Population The present number of souls in my parish is 50.
3 Marriages &c. Marriages are so very rare there, that there has been <no> wedding at all in the parish since June 1783. The bir<ths> and burials for 20 years past have not amounted to 2 of each in a year, one year with another.
4 Patron I suppose it is hardly necessary to say that the patron of my living is the Bishop of Winchester for the time being.
5 Chapels There is no chapel at all in the parish.
6 Lecturer Neither is there lecturer or curate.

7 Dissenters Nor is there any Papist or protestant disssenter.
8 Schools, 9 Charities Nor is there an<y> school, hospital, or endowed charitable institution, or any fixed annual donation for the benefit of the poor in the parish of Morested. As to any copy of my return to the late parliamentary enquiry <on> the subject, I am s<orry> that it is not in my power to give <Your> Lordship any c<copy> thereof. I preserved no copy of it ...

552 Mottisfont 21M65/B4/3/104
Oliver Goodyer St John, rector 1775–1804
[Apparently unsigned.]
[Fragments only of this document survive. Answers to questions 1, 7 and 8 are wanting.]
2 Population 375.
3 Marriages &c. Marriages 3; births 12; burials 9.
4 Patron O. G. St John.
5 Chapels None.
6 Lecturer None.
9 Charities No copy [of the reply to the parliamentary enquiry] taken.

553 Mottistone [IoW] 21M65/B4/3/176
Richard Walker, rector 1763–1805 28 March 1788
1 Area In the parish of Mottiston there are about 920 acres.
2 Population 166.
3 Marriages &c. 1 marriage, 6 births and 4 burials.
4 Patron The coheiresses of the late John Leigh Esq. of Northcourt.
5 Chapels None.
6 Lecturer None.
7 Dissenters None.
8 Schools None.
9 Charities None. We had nothing to return in consequence of the late parliamentary inquiry on this subject.

554 Newchurch [IoW] 21M65/B4/3/177
Charles John Gough Seare, vicar 1783–1816
John Gill, curate
1 Area The parish of Newchurch is 9¾ miles long, and upon a medium 1½ mile broad, and about 23 miles in circumference, containing something more than 14½ square miles.
2 Population About 1600.
3 Marriages &c. About 14 marriages, 50 births, and 20 burials.
4 Patron The Right Reverend the Lord Bishop of Bristol.
5 Chapels There is a chapel dedicated to St Thomas at Ryde, a large village in the parish, which has always been served by the vicar or his curate, together with the parish church. This chapel was built by Thomas Player

Esq. AD1719, who charged his estate with an annual rent of £10 payable to the said vicar. For this sum of £10 p.a., divine service is expected to be performed once a fortnight; but the present curate with the permission of his vicar, and for a small contribution from the inhabitants of the village and its vicinity, has officiated more than 21 years in the aforesaid chapel once every Sunday.

6 Lecturer No lecturer at all.

7 Dissenters There are no Papists in the parish; nor any meetings of protestant dissenters. There are 2 families however (about 7 persons in all) who call themselves Presbyterians, who sometimes resort to a meeting house of that denomination at Newport, and sometimes attend the service of the parish church.

8 Schools There is an endowed school at Langbridge near the village of Newchurch. The endowment is £4 p.a. with an house to live in. In this 8 poor children are taught reading, writing and accompts. The present master's name is Richard Forward. The nomination to this appointment is vested in the minister and churchwardens. There is a school too at Ryde (but not an endowed one) kept by one Thomas Cheverton, who teaches reading, writing and accompts. And the curate of the parish at Newchurch keeps a boarding school for young gentlemen, where they are instructed in grammar and mathematical learning.

9 Charities There are no hospitals or endowed charitable institutions in the parish for the benefit of the poor, but there are several annual donations, as your Lordship will perceive by the copy of the return which was made to the late parliamentary enquiry.

A copy of the return lately made to Parliament respecting public donations in the parish of Newchurch, Isle of Wight

Mrs Mary Dillington in about the year 1749 gave by will (copy not in the parish's possession) £50 in money, for the relief of the poor of the parish, to have been distributed amongst them, as generally believed, immediately after the testatrix's decease, but judged proper by those in power, to be placed out at interest for their benefit, now vested in the minister and churchwardens, with an annual produce of £2.

Mr Thomas Davis gave by will (copy once in the possession of Mr William Thatcher of Wackland in this parish, but at present not to be found) for the relief of the parish poor payable annually, an annual charity to be paid out of Wackland in this parish, now vested in Mr William Thatcher, with an annual produce of £1.

Mr Richard Gard on 14th August 1617 gave by will, for the relief of the parish poor payable annually at Christmas, an annual charity originally out of Bridgehouse in the parish of St Helens, but now by an exchange of lands out of Blackpan in the parish of Brading, now vested in John White Esq., with an annual produce of £1.

Mr Richard Gard on 14th August 1617 gave by will, for the relief of the parish poor payable annually on the feast of All Saints, an annual charity for many years past paid out of Gard's land adjoining to Princelade in this parish, though not clear by the will, now vested in Mr John White, with an annual produce of £10.

William Bowles Esq., in about the year 1749 (not exactly known but according to the vestry book of accounts about the year 1749), gave by will (copy not in the parish's possession), for the relief of 10 poor families of this parish payable annually, £100 in money, now vested in the minister and churchwardens, with an annual produce of £4.
William Bowles, at the time of the preceding bequest, viz about the year 1749, gave by will (copy as said before not in the parish's possession), £500 in money, towards erecting a schoolhouse and maintaining the schoolmaster for the time being, for his instructing poor children. But to the best of the parish's knowledge, the money was for the most part, if not entirely, spent or lost at law, between the testator's widow and the parish on account of the Mortmain Act. The schoolhouse was nevertheless built, and it is generally believed at the parish's expence. The money was intended to have been invested in the minister and churchwardens (as generally believed) but the present minister and churchwardens are clear in saying, no part of the legacy is now, or ever has been, in their hands. No annual produce.
Maurice Bocland Esq. in about the year 1755, gave by deed, to build a school house on, in land, about ¼ part of an acre, now vested in the minister and churchwardens, with an annual value of £5.
Mrs Elizabeth Bowles, relict of William Bowles Esq. in about the year 1768, gave by will (copy not in the parish's possession) towards maintaining the parish schoolmaster for his instructing poor children, £100 in money, now vested in the minister and churchwardens, with an annual produce of £4.
N.B. The Revd Mr Swinton, late vicar of Newchurch left £100 towards the parish school, but not payable, we hear, till after his widow's decease.

555 Newnham and Mapledurwell 21M65/B4/3/105
Joseph Richmond DD, rector of Newnham '*cum capella* Mapledurwell', 1762–1816
1 Area <The pari>sh of Newnham, about 950 acres; parish of Mapledurwell, about 800 acres.
2 Population In the parish of <Newnham are> 232 souls; in the parish <of Mapledurwell> 170 souls.
3 Marriages &c. [Figures lost by damage to document.]
4 Patron The Provost and <Fellows of Queen's College, Oxfo>rd.
5 Chapels The chapel of Maple<durwell is annexed> to the rectory of Newnham.
6 Lecturer None.
7 Dissenters None.
8 Schools None.
9 Charities [Reply severely damaged.] A donation of His Grace Charles <Duke of Bolton> £94 to the poor of the said parish. £9 <... al>ternately; which donation (4*s*. in the pound <Land Tax deducted i>s clear £7 4*s*. p.a.; and £4 16*s*. p.a. alternately <from the pres>ent duke of Bolton. *Mapledurwell*: a donation of John Smith by deed <for the poor> of the said parish of £5. Annual rest<...>

556 Newport [IoW] 21M65/B4/3/178
John Davies, curate 1786–94? 26 March 1788
1 Area 150 acres.

2 Population 3,000 souls.
3 Marriages &c. 65 baptisms; 19 marriages; 58 burials.
4 Patron Queen's College, Oxford.
5 Chapels Newport is a chapel of ease to Carisbrook; dedicated to Saint Thomas Becket; served by John Davies BA of St Mary Hall Oxford, who is supported by the voluntary subscriptions of the inhabitants. The right of nomination belongs to the vicar of Carisbrook; but as the inhabitants support their own minister, he seldom interferes in their choice.
6 Lecturer One lecturer or curate only, viz: the aforesaid John Davies, nominated by the aforesaid inhabitants of Newport, which nomination is ratified and confirmed under the hand and seal of the vicar of Carisbrook for the time-being. Licensed to the same.
7 Dissenters No Papists are to be found resident in the parish. There are 2 meetings held in the town, one of which is denominated a meeting of dissenters, the other a meeting of Anabaptists. The number of the former sect amounts to about 300, the number of the latter to about 60.
8 Schools There is a free school for 30 boys endowed with land, the rental of which is £55 p.a. There is also a good school-house occupied by the Revd William Dickonson, master. The right of presentation belongs to the Corporation of Newport. There is also a charity school, which admits 14 poor girls. The donations for its support amount to the sum of £1,620 bearing interest 4 per cent. Mistress's name Alice Deacon.
9 Charities There are 6 alms-houses, the endowment of which is £10 annually.
John Mann Esq. bequeathed to the town of Newport, £53 16*s*. 4*d*., for the purpose of apprenticing poor children.
William Bowles Esq. bequeathed the interest of £10 to be distributed among 10 poor families.
Christian Roman Esq. bequeathed the sum of £10 for the benefit of 6 poor widows.
Mary Warland bequeathed the sum of £40, which is applied to the relief of poor widows.
Sarah Ruffin bequeathed the interest of £100 to be distributed in bread and meat.

557 Newton Valence 21M65/B4/3/106
Edmund White AB, vicar 1785–1838
1 Area From the best information I can obtain, the parish of Newton Valence is supposed to be about 10 miles in circumference.
2 Population There are 228 inhabitants in the parish of Newton Valence.
3 Marriages &c. In the last 20 years were registered 30 marriages; 168 births; 73 burials. The medium for a year is 1½ marriages; rather more than 8 births; rather more than 3½ burials.
4 Patron Edmund White, the present incumbent.
5 Chapels There is one chapel belonging to the vicarage of Newton Valence, called Hawkley, which is served by Edmund White, and maintained by the vicar of Newton Valence. E. White has the right of nomination to it.

6 Lecturer There is no lecturer or curate in the parish.
7 Dissenters There is one Papist in the parish, but no meeting held of protestant dissenters.
8 Schools There is no endowed school.
9 Charities There is no hospital etc. in this parish. The return made to the late parliamentary enquiry was to the following purport.
Copy of an inscription on a tombstone in the chancel of Newton Valence church
'Here lies Mistris Christian Campion, daughter to Mr William Stone of London, wife of Mr Henry Campion Esq. buried 18 of February 1594, who had 2 sons, Henry and William, 2 daughters, Anne and Mary, who dyed 5 of July and gave this stone for a remembrance of her mother and £30 to the parish of Newton Valence to be kept in a stock for ever by the feoffees who with the vicar and chiefe parishioners, shall yearly dispense of the increase for the poore's good, not abating the usual collectio'. The above £30 is traditionally said to have been lent on bad security and lost. The oldest inhabitants are unable to give any information concerning it.

Mr Michael Glyd left by will to the churchwardens and overseers of this parish £50 to purchase land, and the income thereof yearly to be distributed on St Thomas's day for ever to the poor inhabitants (not receiving alms) at the direction of the minister. The £50 [above-]mentioned ... was lent to John Albury and John Turner of this parish about 40 years ago, but they not proving responsible men, the money is entirely lost.

558 Newtown (Burghclere) 21M65/B4/3/25

Hon. William Nevill BA, rector of Burghclere 1767–1810
Thomas Best AM, curate Newbury, 3 April 1788
1 Area 230 acres.
2 Population 237.
3 Marriages &c. 1 marriage; 13 baptisms; 3 burials.
4 Patron Hon. and Revd Willam Nevill, rector of Burclere.
5 Chapels Newtown, a chapel in Burclere parish, but considered as a parish of itself and enjoys all parochial rights. The curate nominated by Mr Nevill and supported by the tithes of the chapelry.
6 Lecturer A lectureship founded by Lady Lucy Berkeley. The lecturer nominated by 8 trustees, and £20 p.a. paid to the said lecturer out of an estate at Collingbourne in Wilts. Not licensed to cure or lectureship.
7 Dissenters No dissenter of any denomination.
8 Schools A school founded by Lady Lucy Berkeley with a salary of £10 p.a. Jane Froome, schoolmistress, appointed by the trustees. The number of scholars about 30.
9 Charities 6*s*. 8*d*. paid out of a farm in Burclere parish called Broadlands. The overseer of the poor used to demand of a Mrs Pococke 20*s*. p.a. which is called in the parish book Pococke's legacy, and it is entered in the said book for 50 years. But at the death of Mrs Pococke, which happened in 1774, the house was sold, and the present owner refuses to pay the said legacy, and the parish have nothing to support their claim but custom.

[PS] I beg Your Lordship's pardon for being out of time in making this return. I supposed that Mr Nevill would have done it. Two days ago he signified his intentions to the contrary. This will account for the omission of

Your Lordship's devoted humble servant,
Thomas Best

559 Niton [IoW] 21M65/B4/3/178
John Barwis, rector 1786–1828 12 March 1788
1 Area The parish of Niton contains about 1,100 acres.
2 Population The parish of Niton contains at this time 304 inhabitants.
3 Marriages &c. The average of marriages in a year in the parish of Niton is 5, births 12, burials 4.
4 Patron The rectory of Niton is in the gift of the Provost and Fellows of Queens's College, Oxford.
5 Chapels In the parish of Niton there is no chapel of any denomination.
6 Lecturer The duty of the parish of Niton is done by the rector, Revd John Barwis MA, late fellow of Queen's College, Oxford.
7 Dissenters In the parish of Niton there is no Papist nor dissenting protestant of any denomination; nor any kind of meeting-house.
8 Schools In the parish of Niton there is no endowed school of any sort; the present rector supports a school-master who teaches reading, writing and arithmetic to the children of parishioners gratis.
9 Charities By a person of the name of Pittis (time unknown) was left by will for the use of the poor of Niton £100 the interest of which has sometimes been distributed among the poor and sometimes given to a schoolmaster at the option of the churchwardens. A dispute respecting the abovesaid sum of £100, having arisen between a late rector (Revd William Thornton) and the parish, the money was paid into the hands of a farmer (Abraham Spanner) who after keeping it many years paid it into the hands of a late curate (Mr Price) — who invested it in the funds. About 10 years ago it was resumed by the churchwardens who now have it, but by the falling of the funds it is reduced to £96. The interest will in future be paid for house-rent for the schoolmaster supported by the present rector.

560 North Stoneham 21M65/B4/3/107
Edward Beadon MA, rector 1762–1811
1 Area About 2,000 acres.
2 Population Between 4 and 500.
3 Marriages &c. Marriages 6; births 17; burials 11.
4 Patron John Fleming Esq.
5 Chapels No chapel.
6 Lecturer No lecturer or curate.
7 Dissenters No Papists or dissenters of any denomination.
8 Schools One school endowed with £5 p.a. Master, John Crouch, nominated by John Fleming Esq. 8 scholars.
9 Charities No hospital, or charitable institution. A sum of money left by different persons by will, and amounting to £158 17*s.* 0*d.* produces an

annual interest of £7; which is distributed as the donors have directed to the poor of the parish on Good Fryday. The money is vested in a mortgage on 5 houses in the parish.

561 North Waltham 21M65/B4/3/108/1–2
Charles Jefferies Cottrell, rector 1779–1800
William Bainbridge, curate
1 Area 2,450 [acres.]
2 Population 370.
3 Marriages &c. [Statistics lost owing to damage to document.]
4 Patron The Bishop of Winchester.
5 Chapels None.
6 Lecturer None.
7 Dissenters None, I believe.
8 Schools None.
9 Charities A donation of £100 left by Walter Pincke Esq., the interest of which is applied to the apprenticing of poor children. NB When left only £50 but now accumulated as above, and the interest applyed as above. [This information repeated in copy of return to the parliamentary enquiry.]

562 Nursling 21M65/B4/3/109/1–2
Robert Cranmer, rector 1776–1809 28 March 1788
Samuel Judd Collins, curate
1 Area About 900 acres arable; 200 pasture; 400 common.
2 Population 362.
3 Marriages &c. Births 20; burials 10; marriages 5.
4 Patron Bishop of Winchester.
5 Chapels None.
6 Lecturer S. J. Collins, curate; appointed by the rector, not licensed.
7 Dissenters No Papists nor dissenters.
8 Schools No endowed school. 2 small ones for little children, whose parents pay a trifle for their being taught to read etc.
9 Charities No hospitals or endowed charitable institutions. There is an annual donation to the poor at Christmas of bread, beer and cheese, value about £3, payable by the rector out of the produce of the glebe. A copy of the return made to the late parliamentary enquiry is annexed to these. [This return gives a detailed breakdown of the expenditure of the poor rate, 1783–5, the annual totals of which were: 1783 £177 12*s.* 6*d.*; 1784 £152 11*s.* 0*d.*; 1785 £15 6*s.* 4*d.*]

563 Nutley 21M65/B4/3/110
[Fragments only of this return survive. The only information they contain is that the curate of Nutley was unlicensed, and that there were no Papists, schools or hospitals in the parish.]

564 Odiham 21M65/B4/3/111
George Watkins MA, vicar 1773–98
1 Area <The> parish is about 26 miles in <circu>mference. I cannot get any information as to the number of acres.

2 Population About 1,426 according to the account sent by Mr Howlett.

3 Marriages &c.

	Marriages	Births	Burials
1784	16	32	63
1785	11	25	58
1786	14	44	50
	41 (Av. 13)	101 (Av. 33)	171 (Av.57)

4 Patron The Chancellor of the church of Sarum.

5 Chapels Grewell c<hapel and Odi>ham served by Mr Gunn. The s<econd> Sunday every <mont>h. There is no s<ervice at> Odiham in <the m>orning on those days.

6 Lecturer Mr Gunn <s>erves <G>rewell *every Sunday evening*; a subscription being made by the parishioners of Grewell for that purpose. Mr Gu<nn's> assistant on Sundays, both <at Odi>ham and Grewell [remainder faded illegibly]

7 Dissenters There are no Papists or dissenters. The Methodists now and then hold a meeting, but their number is very trifling.

8 Schools There is only one school indowed. The Revd H. [Humphrey] Jeston is master. Nominated by trustees to the will of Mr May the founder. There are 20 boys. [See **B*** below]

9 Charities There is an almshouse [See **A*** below] for 8 poor people. And several donations as will appear by the list hereunto subjoined. I have also established 5 Sunday schools maintained by the subscription of the parishioners. There are about 160 children in the whole.

An account of donations sent to Parliament, as well as I can remember, having no copy.

Francis Clark in 1600 gave by will £10 p.a. for relief of the poor.

Julian Smith, date unknown, gave by deed land for a poor-house.

Sir Edward More in 1623 gave by will 1*s.* 6*d.* per week to 8 persons in his alms-house [**A***].

John Vause in 1630 gave by will to trustees lands and £10 in money for the poor and to place children in service.

Henry Smith Esq. gave by deed in 1626 £10 to the poor in general.

Robert Ray in 1674 gave by d<eed> the rent of lands to purchase canvas for the poor of Odiham and Hartley.

Robert May in 1694 gave to trustees a school for 20 boys and £800 to apprentice them [**B***].

Edward Gurney in 1638 gave to trustees £27 10*s.* p.a. to clothe 12 poor men and women.

An annuity of 5*s.* charged on a meadow.

565 Old Basing and Up Nately 21M65/B4/3/112

Thomas Sheppard DD, vicar of Basingstoke 1768–1814

John Evans, curate

1 Area Basing is a very extensive tything in the parish of Basingstoke. What compass of land it contains, cannot be ascertained without a survey, as a large quantity of land in the said tything is tythe free.

2 Population Basing about 500, and Nately 87.

3 Marriages &c. *Basing* 7 marriages; 29 births; 18 burials.
Nately 2 marriages; 3 births; 2 burials.
4 Patron President and Scholars of Magdalen College, Oxford.
5 Chapels Basing and Nately are chapels of ease to Basingstoke, and served by J. Evans, curate, maintained and supported by the vicar, who hath also the right of nomination to them.
6 Lecturer J. Evans as above mentioned [is] curate of both chapels nominated to them by Dr Sheppard, vicar, and licensed by the late Bishop of Winchester.
7 Dissenters There are no Papists, no meetings of protestant dissenters of any denomination whatsoever in either of the aforesaid parishes, but the inhabitants are *all* professed members of the established church.
8 Schools At Basing there is one school; the endowment is £1 5*s*. p.a. left by William Barber towards educating 6 poor boys. The mistress's name is Sarah Doho, and the nomination belongs to the minister and parish officers. At Nately there is no school.
9 Charities At Basing there are no hospitals, and the annual donations for the benefit of the poor are the following, viz. £24 p.a. left by Charles, Duke of Bolton. 100 threepenny loaves given away on Good Friday yearly, left by William Barber. 2 bushels of wheat to be made into 24 loaves given away yearly on Good Friday, left by the Uptons. £4 p.a., that is, 40*s*. to be given away on Good Friday, and 40*s*. on St Thomas Day, left by Henry Lamport. At Nately there are no hospitals, no endowed or charitable institutions, nor any fixed annual donation for the benefit of the poor.

566 Otterbourne 21M65/B4/3/113

Samuel Gauntlett, vicar of Hursley 1780–1822
1 Area The greatest length of the parish of Otterbourne is supposed to be near 3 miles, the greatest breadth near 2 miles; in most parts, h<owever,> it seems to be much narrower.
2 Population In the year 1781 the number of inhabitants I found by enumeration to be 357.
3 Marriages &c. The annual average of marriages for 10 years ending with 1780 was more than 3 and less than 4; of baptisms more than 14 and less than 15; of burials more than 8 and less than 9.
4 Patron Sir William Heathcote Bt. is the patron of Hursley vicarage, of which the chapelry of Otterbourne is a member.
5 Chapels The chapel, or church, of Otterbourne may be, and till of late has been, served by the minister of Hursley, the Sunday's duty of each church having been for time immemorial only once a day, and alternately in the morning or afternoon.
6 Lecturer The Revd Mr Richards at present serves the church of Otterbourne as my curate. My predecessor served both the churches of Otterbourne and Hursley himself upwards of 30 years. Mr Richards is not licensed.
7 Dissenters At present the number of Papists is 39. No meetings are held of protestant dissenters.

8 Schools There are no endowed schools in the <parish> of Otterbourne.
9 Charities No charitable institutions exist at present in this parish. The sum of £20 given by one of the Wyndham family that the interest might for ever be applied for the benefit of the poor <wa>s lost some years ago by the insolvency of the person to whom it was intrusted.

567 Over Wallop 21M65/B4/3/114
James Richard Hayes, rector 1781–90
1 Area About 4,000 acres.
2 Population About 330.
3 Marriages &c. Burials about 8 p.a.; births about 9 p.a.; marriages about 2 p.a.
4 Patron The Earl of Portsmouth.
5 Chapels None.
6 Lecturer None.
7 Dissenters No Papists. No licensed meeting-house of any denomination of dissenters.
8 Schools There is one school only for the support of which the interest of £50 is left, to educate 7 children annually; and the rector has been used for many years to give voluntarily 36*s*. p.a. for the education of 6 children. The number of scholars are 20.
9 Charities I did not reserve a copy of my return to the enquiry respecting the charitable donations; but these are all, as I then specified them.
1. £1 15*s*. p.a., which is the moiety of a sum collected by the parish of Tangley among themselves, and left to this parish; the other moiety being left to the parish of Lower Wallop.
2. £5 5*s*. p.a. arising out of an estate belonging to the Revd Mr Richards.
3. 3 greatcoats p.a. given by Mr Brownjohn to 3 poor men as a charge on his freehold estate.
We have no hospital or endowed charitable institution.

568 Owslebury 21M65/B4/3/115
Liscomb Maltbe Stretch, vicar 1767–1813
William Coppard, curate
[This return survives in fragments only.]
1 Area This is a matter I have taken some pains to <inquire> of, but all I can learn in regard to it at present <is that the> parish is almost as extensive as that of <Twyford. When> I am better acquainted with the place I <shall> be able to answer Your Lordship's <questions with the> accuracy they seem to require.
2 Population I can get no information on <this> matter. It may be proper how<ever to inform> your lordship that this parish, a<lthough small> is a very populous one.
3 Marriages &c. 4 marriages; 11 births; <...> burials.
4 Patron The living is ann<exed to Twyford. The information about patronage I> have given your lordship in <the> return for that parish, [it] is in <Emmanuel> College, Cambridge.

5 Chapels There is no chapel of any kin<d.>
6 Lecturer I am curate of this parish as <well as of> Twyford, and was appointed to the c<hurch by the Revd Mr> Stretch, the vicar, without any <license>. There is no lectureship.
7 Dissenters <Of the> first sect [Papists] I find there is only one family in <the parish> and that of no note. And of the other likewise I am <informed the num>ber is very inconsiderable, as well as the class. <I am inf>ormed that there are no meetings.
8 Schools There are no schools at all in the <parish.>
9 Charities <There are> no hospitals , nor any fixed annual <donations> in this parish for the benefit of the poor. <Las>tly had I been here at the time the late <parliamen>tary enquiry was made, a copy of the <return w>ould be useless.

569 Penton Mewsey 21M65/B4/3/116/1–2
George Woodward BD, rector 1764–90
Thomas Griffith, curate
1 Area 837 acres.
2 Population 194.
3 Marriages &c. In the last 3 years the number total of marriages [is] 2; of births 22; of burials 9.
4 Patron Mr Constable.
5 Chapels None.
6 Lecturer Thomas Griffith, curate, nominated by Mr Woodward, the rector.
7 Dissenters None.
8 Schools One school for Penton and Weyhill endowed with £6 p.a. by John Read in 1651 for teaching all the boys and girls of both parishes, paid by the master, wardens and assistants of the Carpenter's Company in London. John Grace, master, nominated by the ministers, churchwardens and overseers of the said parishes. Number of scholars, between 20 and 30.
9 Charities There are no hospitals or endowed charitable institutions. There are 20*s.* p.a. paid agreeable to the will of said John Read for the benefit of the poor of Penton. 13*s.* 4*d.* to the minister for preaching of a sermon on the 5th of November, and reciding an extract of the will. 6*s.* 8*d.* to the clerk for making clean the said church of Penton. Annexed is a copy of the return made to parliament by the overseers.
[This copy reports the breakdown of expenditure on poor rates for the years 1783–5, the annual totals of which were: 1783 £80 17*s.* 6*d.*; 1784 £79 10*s.* 7*d.*; 1785 £95 2*s.* 2*d.*]

570 Petersfield 21M65/B4/3/117
Thomas Trodd AB, curate –1792 26 March 1788
1 Area The parish of Petersfield is an irregular square, being abo<ut> half a mile from north to south, and nearly the same distance from east to west. It is supposed to contain about 300 acres.

2 Population The number of souls about 1,150, including the adjacent hamlets of Sheet, Lower Weston and Lower Nursted, the inhabitants of which attend Petersfield church.
3 Marriages &c. Births 47; burials 36; marriages 10, at a medium for the last 7 years.
4 Patron The Bishop of Winchester.
5 Chapels We learn from tradition that there was formerly a chapel dedicated to St Andrew, but there are now no vestiges thereof remaining, nor have been from time immemorial. A dissenting meeting-house in ruins which has not been used these 50 years.
6 Lecturer No lecturer. The rector nominates the curate, who as such has no other support or maintenance than a stipend from the rector, with an allowance of Easter offerings and surplice fees. He is not licensed to this cure.
7 Dissenters Papists 7. No dissenters of any other denomination.
8 Schools There is one free school, to educate, clothe and apprentice 10 or 12 boys to be taken out of the parish of Petersfield, endowed by Mr Richard Churcher, as will be answered under the next question. The present masters are Mr Robert Steel and the Revd Mr James Cookson AM nominated by the trustees. There are 2 other private grammar schools, one kept by the Revd T. Trodd. Number of scholars between 30 and 40; the other by Mr Henry Wells, number of scholars between 40 and 50. There are several other smaller schools for teaching little children to read and work, but no endowment whatever to any of them.
9 Charities Not having kept an exact copy of my answers to the late parliamentary enquiries, I am obliged to trust to my memory, assisted by notes taken at the time. I believe the following are nearly exact copies.
1st. John Antrobus Esq. late of Heath-house by will, July 16th 1622, gave £100 for the purpose of erecting an almshouse for the relief of as many lone men and lone women as that money would provide to be lodged. The house consists of 4 tenements. The trustees are the owner of Heath-house and the churchwardens of Petersfield.
2d. John Jolliffe Esq. by will 1769 gave £100 since laid out for a house for the benefit of the poor. The trustees are the mayor, churchwardens and overseers of the poor of the parish of Petersfield.
3d. Richard Churcher, East India merchant, by will 16 January, 1722 gave £3,000, since increased to £3,300, Bank stock and £1,000 Old South Sea annuity stock (the annual income of which together is now £228) for the purpose of erecting a free school, now called Churcher's College, for the maintenance of a master and the educating, clothing and apprenticing 10 or 12 boys of the parish of Petersfield, as the trustees should judge most convenient according to the income. The present trustees are the Right Hon. Earl of Clanricarde, Sir Abrah<am> Hume Bt., William Jolliffe, Thomas Samuel Jolliffe, James Tooker and John Missing Esqs.

571 Portchester 21M65/B4/3/118
William Powell, vicar 1750–92 5 March 1788
John Williams, curate and lecturer
1 Area About 1,200 acres.

2 Population About 350 souls.
3 Marriages &c. About 4 marriages; 12 births; and about 6 burials.
4 Patron The Right Hon. Edward Thurlow, Lord High Chancellor of Great Britain.
5 Chapels None.
6 Lecturer John Williams, curate to the Revd William Powell, vicar. Also lecturer to the parish by subscription. Licensed to the curacy by your lordship and ordained priest at Farnham Castle, December 23, 1780.
7 Dissenters One meeting, commonly called Quakers.
8 Schools One boarding school kept by Louisa Boulton for young ladies. About 12 scholars. James Thorpe's school for reading and writing, about 12 scholars.
9 Charities No hospital. No endowed charitable institution. No fixed donations.

572 Portsea 21M65/B4/3/119/1–2
John Ballard LLD, vicar 1783–88 24 March 1788
Joseph Morce, curate
1 Area 12 or 13 miles.
2 Population About 20,000.
3 Marriages &c. About 200 marriages, 600 births, and 400 burials.
4 Patron The Warden and Fellows of St Mary's College, Winchester.
5 Chapels [1.] A chapel in His Majesty's Dockyard, Revd Dr Stevens, chaplain, appointed by the Lords Commissioners of the Admiralty. I know not whether licensed or not. Supported by the artificers employed in the dockyard and by the officers and seamen belonging to the ordnance. 2. St. George's chapel, the Revd Henry Swann, minister appointed by the vicar of Portsea and licensed; the <church> is attended by the Revd Richard Bailey, Mr Swann being incapable of performing the duty. The salary <is> raised by a rate on the seats. 3. St. John chapel now building and to be a perpetual curacy. The [Revd William] Howell is appointed by the Act of Parliament for building the said chapel to be the first minister, the ministers to be appointed by the proprietor. Salary 100 guineas p.a. to be a rate on the seats and a house which is now building.
6 Lecturer There is a lectureship begun this year by a voluntary subscription in St George's chapel. Mr Bailey, the officiating minister is the lecturer, not licensed, I believe. Joseph Morce is curate of the parish church and parish of Portsea, appointed by the vicar of the said parish. He has never had a licence for the <curac>y.
7 Dissenters About 7 families of Roman Catholicks, the whole number about 70. 2 meetings of Anabaptists, in one Joseph Horsey and Daniel Mial teachers, number of subscribers 250. In the other Edward Edwards <teac>her, number about 60. A meeting of no certain sect, David Orange teacher; first in Lady Huntington's Connections , then Mr Westley's, next an Independent, then an Anabaptist, now approaching to the Church of England, about 100 members. An Independent meeting, William Dunn teacher, number about 100. A Methodist meeting under the direction of Mr

Westley, the <te>acher <and congr>egation uncertain. A place of worship lately built to which is given the name of Saint <Pe>ter's, the preacher John Pennington. He uses the services of the Church with such alterations only as enable him to avail himself of the Toleration Act, having taken the oaths prescribed by that act to dissenting teachers. He calls himself a *true*-church of England man. The number of his followers not to be ascertained. And 2 Jewish <synag>ogues, number about 300.
8 Schools Mr Edward Crofts left a certain sum of money to teach a certain number of boys to read and write. But this is left by the will of Mr Crofts to the management and direction of the minister and commissioners of St George's chapel, who are to appoint a master and regulate the number of boys. The present master is William Cox.
9 Charities No endowed hospital or charitable institution, except what is mentioned in the copy of the return which accompanies this.
A copy of the return made to the late parliamentary inquiry.
Thomas Brewer gave in 1666 by will £1 p.a. issuing out of lands and vested in Thomas Ridge Esq. to the poor of the parish of Portsea, to be distributed as the possessors of the land and the churchwardens and overseers of the said parish shall think fit.
Eleanor Brewer in 1667 gave by will £2 p.a. issuing out of land and vested in Thomas Ridge Esq. to be divided among the poor yearly by the churchwardens and overseers.

573 Portsea, St George's Chapel 21M65/B4/3/120
Richard Bailey, 'officiating minister of St. George's chapel, during the indisposition of its minister, the Revd Mr Swann.'
[Questions 1–4, no replies.]
5 Chapels 3 chapels, St George's, the patron the vicar of Portsea; St Peter's, building, patrons the proprietors. St John's, building, patrons the proprietors. All 3 supported by the rents of the respective pews.
6 Lecturer A Sunday's evening lecture in St George's chapel, supported by a voluntary subscription.
7 Dissenters No Roman Catholic meeting that I know of. 2 meetings of the Baptist persuasion, 2 of Mr Whit[e]field's, and one of Mr Westley's. 2 Jews' synagogues.
8 Schools 30 boys educated by voluntary subscription from the members of the Beneficial Society established on Portsmouth Common.
9 Charities £800 3% reduced and £80 upon bond left by will of Mr Edward Crofts to the commissioners of St George's chapel for educating the sons of poor widows who do not receive alms of the parish of Portsea, in reading writing and arithmetic to fit them for trade, and if not widows' children enough offer, then to poor labour[er]s' children in the like circumstances.

574 Portsmouth 21M65/B4/3/121
Henry Oglander, vicar 1785–1805 27 March 1788
William Morgan, curate
1 Area About a mile and a half.

2 Population About 6,000, besides soldiers and marines on duty in the garrison, amounting to 1,500, officers and men.
3 Marriages &c. About 70 marriages; 310 births; and 240 burials annually in time of peace and nearly twice the number of each in time of war.
4 Patron The college of Winchester.
5 Chapels One chapel belonging to the garrison called the Governor's chapel, served by the Revd George Cuthbert, curate to the Revd Mr Herbert who is the chaplain appointed by government.
6 Lecturer Only Mr Cuthbert, curate of the Governor's chapel, and myself who serve the curacy of the parish of Portsmouth, appointed by the Revd Henry Oglander, vicar of the parish. Neither of us licenced. I was ordained on a title to the curacy granted 7 years ago by the late Revd Henry Taylor, vicar.
7 Dissenters The number of Papists at this place is small, about 9 or 10 at most. They have no meeting-house within the parish. There are 2 meetings of protestant dissenters, one belonging to the Presbyterians, about 150 in number, and another belonging to the General Baptists about 40 in number. There is also in building a meeting-house intended for Methodists. Their number in this parish is not more than 100.
8 Schools There is one grammar school in the parish, endowed by the late Dr Smith of Portsmouth. The trustees are the Revd the Dean and Chapter of Christ Church, Oxford. £50 to the head master, the Revd Benjamin Forrester and £30 to the usher, Richard Barton. About 20 scholars in time of peace, but more in time of war. There are some other schools for children for reading, writing and arithmetic.
9 Charities Inclosed Your Lordship has a true copy of the return made to the late parliamentary enquiry upon the subject. In the absence of Mr Oglander, the vicar, I have taken the liberty to answer the above questions according to the best information I could possibly procure.
Copy of the return to the late parliamentary enquiry
Thomas Winter of Fulham Esq. July 28, 1679 gave by will £200 now vested in the corporation of Portsmouth and yielding £10 p.a. to the poor of the parish of Portsmouth. John Mounsher of Portsmouth, gent., 1 August 1702, gave by will £100 now vested in the corporation of Portsmouth and yielding £5 p.a. to poor widows of the parish of Portsmouth. Thomas Longcroft of Portsmouth, gent., 19 September 1740, gave by will £2 p.a. from a house now in the possession of John Grant in Portsmouth to the poor of the parish. This money has not been paid for some years back, the will being made prior to the mortmain act. Charles West of Westerham in Kent, gent., gave by will, 2 December 1765, £100 now vested in John Wardley and Thomas Ellison, gentlemen, of Westerham and yielding £3 p.a. to the poor of the parish. Thomas Timbrell gave by will £<...> to the poor of the parish of Portsmouth, but this bequest could never be got.

575 Priors Dean 21M65/B4/3/122
James Cookson AM, rector of Colemore and Priors Dean 1775–1835
1 Area 1,500 acres or thereabouts.

2 Population 120.
3 Marriages &c. 1 marriage in 2 years; births 3 in a year, nearly; burials 2, all at a medium for the last 10 years.
4 Patron Myself.
5 Chapels Priors Deane is a chapel annexed to Colemore, as described in the statement for Colemore.
6 Lecturer None.
7 Dissenters There are no Papists or protestant dissenters of any denomination.
8 Schools There are no endowed schools.
9 Charities An annual donation of 10*s*. has sometime since been paid for the benefit of the poor by the late owner of a particular farm; but the present owner has refused payment and the parish officers have given it up as not recoverable.

576 Quarley 21M65/B4/3/123
Thomas Sheppard DD, rector 1768–1814
1 Area About 1,600 acres.
2 Population About 100.
3 Marriages &c. About 3 births, 3 burials and 2 marriages.
4 Patron The master, brethren and sisters of St. Catherine's near the Tower, London.
5 Chapels No chapel.
6 Lecturer No lecturer or curate.
7 Dissenters No meeting and only one family of protestant dissenters.
8 Schools No endowed school in the parish.
9 Charities No hospital, or endowed charitable institution, or donation in the parish.

577 Rotherwick 21M65/B4/3/124/1–2
George Watkins MA, vicar 1773–98
Alban Thomas, curate
[Document badly damaged.]
1 Area 1000 acres.
2 Population 314.
3 Marriages &c. At a medium: marriages 3; births 9; burials 6.
4 Patron Sir James Tylney Long, Bt.
5 Chapels Rotherwick is a chapel to Odiham. Alban Thomas who receives annual<y> £35 and also small tithes from <the> parish. The right of nomin<ation is in Sir> James Tylney Long, Bt.
6 Lecturer Answered in the forego<ing.> The curate not licensed.
7 Dissenters <No> dissenter of any denomination <i>n the parish.
8 Schools A free school in the parish endowed with an yearly <sa>lary of £10 together with a house and premises. The master, George Newman nominated by Sir <James Tyl>ney Long Bt. <Number> of scholars 20.
9 Charities <An an>nual donation of £4 for the benefit <of the poor i>n the parish. <1 s>hilling a year is given to 5 poor widows <from> 2 tenements in the parish.
[Severely damaged copy of the return to the parliamentary enquiry enclosed.]

578 Rowner 21M65/B4/3/125

James Henvill BA, rector 1760–1805

1 Area According to the best information I can get the compass of ground is nearly as follows: arable 810 acres; meadow 45; rough 143; woodland 74.

2 Population About 90 souls.

3 Marriages &c. 1 marriage; about 5 bir[t]hs and 3 burials.

4 Patron The Revd Charles Prideaux Brune.

5 Chapels No chapel in the parish.

6 Lecturer No lecturer or curate.

7 Dissenters I have the pleasure to say we have no Papists nor protestant dissenters within the parish.

8 Schools No school of any sort.

9 Charities No hospital. No endowed charitable institution. Nor fixed annual donation within the parish. I must beg leave to say that I received no copy of the return made to the late parliamentary enquiry.

579 St Helens [IoW] 21M65/B4/3/180

Robert Gibbs, perpetual curate –1795

John Gill, officiating curate

1 Area The parish of St Helens is 3¼ miles long, 7 furlongs upon an average broad, and about 8½ miles in circumference, containing something more than 2¾ square miles.

2 Population About 500.

3 Marriages &c. About 4 marriages, 25 births and 13 burials.

4 Patron The living of St Helens is in the patronage of Eton College.

5 Chapels The parish church is by some deemed a chapel. It was dedicated to St Helena. There is in the parish no other chapel.

6 Lecturer No lecturer at all.

7 Dissenters There are neither any Papists in the parish, nor any protestant dissenters.

8 Schools There is in the parish no endowed school at all. But in the village of St Helens there is a poor man whose name is — Collick, who teaches the few children of the neighbourhood to read and write.

9 Charities No hospitals or endowed charitable institutions and only one fixed annual donation of 10*s*. to the poor, payable on the feast of All Saints.

Copy of the return made to Parliament respecting public donations in the parish of St Helens

Mr Richard Gard on 14th August 1617 gave by will, for the relief of the poor of the parish, payable annually on the feast of All Saints (but the distribution has been, for many years past, made at Xmas) an annual charity originally out of Blackpan and Ylyards in the parish of Brading in this island, but now out of lands of late annexed to Westbrook in this parish, now vested in Sir William Oglander Bart., with an annual produce of 10*s*.

580 St Lawrence [IoW] 21M65/B4/3/181
Francis Worsley, rector 1753–1808 24 March 1788
1 Area Answered in the Chale account. NB the livings of Chale and St Lawrence are held by the same person.
2 Population Answered in the Chale account.
3 Marriages &c. From Jan. 1 1781 to Dec. 31 1787 the numbers are: births 13; burials 14, NB 3 of these burials, 3 shipwreck'd mariners; marriages 5.
4 Patron The Right Honorable Sir Richard Worsley Bart.
5 Chapels No chapel in this parish.
6 Lecturer No lecturer in this parish. The Revd Mr Lancaster is engaged to serve the church, but it is supposed he is not licensed. He is now on his journey from Wiltshire to the Isle of Wight.
7 Dissenters No Papist in this parish. No meeting of protestant dissenters in this parish.
8 Schools No school in this parish.
9 Charities There are no hospitals or endowed charitable institutions, or any fixed annual donations for the benefit of the poor in this parish. And this was the purport of the answer made to the late parliamentary enquiry on this subject.

581 Shalfleet [IoW] 21M65/B4/3/182
William Dickonson, vicar 1765–94 March 1788
Andrew Hamilton, curate
1 Area 2,000 acres.
2 Population 640 odd.
3 Marriages &c. On an average of the last 7 years, 6 marriages, 22 births, 10 burials.
4 Patron The King.
5 Chapels None.
6 Lecturer Andrew Hamilton, nominated by the Revd William Dickonson.
7 Dissenters None.
8 Schools None.
9 Charities None.

582 Shipton Bellinger 21M65/B4/3/126
Henry Hawes BA, vicar 1783–9
Basil Cane, curate
1 Area There are about 2,300 acres of land in the parish of Shipton.
2 Population About 150.
3 Marriages &c. Christenings 7; burials 2; marriages 2, per year for 5 years together.
4 Patron Dr Macham has one turn and Mr Gilbert another.
5 Chapels No chapel.
6 Lecturer None.
7 Dissenters No Papist or dissenters of any kind.

8 Schools No school.
9 Charities No hospital or donations of any kind.

583 Shorwell [IoW] 21M65/B4/3/183
Francis Randolph, rector (sinecure) 1752–97 28 March 1788
Richard Walker, vicar 1763–1805
1 Area The parish of Shorwell is 4 miles long, and about 2 miles broad, and contains between 3,000 and 4,000 acres.
2 Population 524.
3 Marriages &c. 5 marriages, 12 births and 8 burials.
4 Patron The coheiresses of the late John Leigh Esq. of Northcourt.
5 Chapels None.
6 Lecturer None.
7 Dissenters None.
8 Schools None.
9 Charities None. We had nothing to return in consequence of the late parliamentary inquiry on this subject.

584 Soberton 21M65/B4/3/127
[Unsigned.]
[Document badly damaged.]
1 Area The occupiers of land (from <un>grounded apprehensions) were unwilling <to grant Your Lordshi>p that satisfactory information on this <head which I en>deavoured to obtain (namely the number <of acres in the> parish). The only intelligence, therefore, <I can with any deg>ree of praecision, procure, makes the compass <of l>and extending from east to west about 1 <mile and> from north-east to southwest, 4 <miles n>early half of which may be considered as <arable> land.
2 Population 500.
3 Marriages &c. The average seems <about the> following proportion: about 3 marriages; 18 b<irths>; 8 <burials.>
4 Patron Your Lordship, as Bis<hop of Winchester>.
5 Chapels There is no chapel within <the parish,> except one belonging to Roman <Catholics.>
6 Lecturer There is no lec<turer. I am the> only curate in the parish.
7 Dissenters <The n>umber of Pap<is>ts is about 39. <Of protestant dissenters t>here are none, of any <denominati>on (as far as I know <for s>ure) in the <parish.>
8 Schools <There is> a schoolmistress appointed and paid by the <subscribers for> the educating of seven poor children; but <payment I app>rehend is optional, and therefore not to be <considere>d strictl<y as> an endowment.
9 Charities <No> hospitals. There were formerly (and ought <to be) annua>l donations to the poor, namely <...>'s Gift of £4. Goodman Arnold's <gift of...>shillings. And the interest of £100 <...>.The two first have been many years <in abeyance, if> not absolutely irrecoverable. The last is <in>

operation. <When the parlia>mentary inquiry was instituted, and the return made <it was done by my pre>decessor to whom I have written for a copy thereof; but <the fact that he unfortu>nately reserved none, deprives me of the means of <fulfilling> that part of your Lordship's directions. I presume, however, <that the above> conveys the purport of it.

585 Southampton, Holy Rood 21M65/B4/3/128/1–2
Miles Halton, vicar 1773–92 (not residing) 27 March 1788
Richard Mant, curate

1 Area No ground but which is built upon; the number of houses is about 200.

2 Population 1,400 and upwards.

3 Marriages &c.	Marriages	Births	Burials
1781	22	26	32
1782	18	41	31
1783	16	37	38
1784	15	37	31
1785	13	44	40
1786	8	54	37
1787	9	43	34

Medium: marriages 14; births 40; burials 34.

4 Patron Queen's College, Oxford.

5 Chapels In the Hospital of St Julian, commonly called God's House, there is a chapel, served by the Revd J. Barnottin, maintained by subscription of French Protestants, who nominate their own minister with the approbation of Queen's College, Oxford.

6 Lecturer Richard Mant MA is the curate, nominated by the Revd Miles Halton, vicar; not licensed.

7 Dissenters No Papists. No meetings held in this parish of protestant dissenters. There are about 7 Presbyterian families, and 1 Jewish.

8 Schools One school for 10 boys, endowed by will of Mr Richard Taunton in the year 1752. The name of the present master is *James Linden* nominated by the trustees of the said Richard Taunton.

9 Charities One hospital called St Julian's or God's House, in which are 4 brothers and 4 sisters, who are paid by Queen's College in Oxford, between them £42 17*s.* 8*d.* annually.

Copy of the return made to the late parliamentary inquiry

Nathaniel Mill on 13 April 1636 gave by will £2 p.a. now vested in the corporation of Southampton and subject to Land Tax to be divided among the poor of Holy Rood parish.

Henry Smith Esq. gave to the corporation at unknown date an annual sum (last year £2 11*s.*) for the poor of Holy Rood Parish.

Katherine Wulfrid on 30 September 1665 gave by will land now vested in the churchwardens of Holy Rood and yielding £5 p.a. for clothing and placing out one poor maid.

Nathaniel Mill on 13 April 1636 gave by will £1 p.a. now vested in the corporation and subject to Land Tax for the poor of the French Church.

Silena Fifield on 8 December 1769 gave by will to the corporation £9 p.a. to clothe the poor of Holy Rood parish. She also on the same date gave £6 16*s.* p.a. to the corporation for fuel for the brethren and sisters in God's House. Edward III on 22 March of the 18th year of his reign gave by letters patent to Queen's College, Oxford, £42 17*s.* 8*d.* to 8 brothers and sisters in St. Julian's hospital.
General Charities.
Robert Thorner on 31 May 1690 gave lands and houses producing £300 p.a. more or less, to build alms-houses, maintain poor widows, and apprentice boys.
William Freeman on 6 April 1780 gave by will £100 now vested in the corporation and producing £5 p.a. for the poor not receiving alms.
Richard Taunton on 15 September 1752 gave £6,139. 0*s.* 2*d.* now vested in trustees and yielding £190 13*s.* 4*d.* to educate and apprentice 10 poor boys, to assist 6 decayed housekeepers, to provide marriage portions for maid servants and other occasional charities.
John Steptoe on 20 February 1667 gave by will land now vested in the corporation and yielding £11 6*s.* 8*d.* p.a. to be divided among the poor of the town in general.
George Pem[b]erton at date unknown gave monies now vested in the corporation and yielding £2 10*s.* p.a. for the poor of the town in general.
Bridget Parkinson gave £20 in money, now vested in the corporation and yielding £1 p.a. for the poor of the town in general.
Mr Jacomin at date unknown left £50 now vested in the corporation and yielding £2 10*s.* p.a. to be divided among 100 poor of the town.
Katherine Reynolds at date unknown gave £50 now vested in the corporation and yielding £2 10*s.* p.a. to be divided among 80 poor of the town.
Paul Mercer at date unknown gave sums now vested in the corporation and yielding £5 p.a. for the poor in general.
George Gallop at date unknown gave £200 now vested in the corporation and yielding £10 p.a. for 8 gowns to the poor.
John Cornish at date unknown gave monies now vested in the corporation and yielding £7 10*s.* p.a. for 7 cloth gowns to the poor.
Nathaniel Mill on 13 April 1636 gave by will monies now vested in the corporation and yielding £3 4*s.* p.a. for 4 gowns for the poor.
Mrs Anne Delamott at date unknown gave monies now vested in the corporation and yielding £1 10*s.* for 15 poor widows.

586 Southampton, St Laurence and St John 21M65/B4/3/130/1–2
James Scott, rector 'of the united parishes of St Laurence *cum* St John' 1751–94
1 Area No other ground but what houses are built upon in the streets of both parishes, whose length multiplied by the breadth make 10,000 yards.
2 Population In St John's 467; in St Laurence's 287; independent boarders at the school 47; total 801.

3 Marriages &c.	Marriages	9; in 7 years 1781–8	65
	Births	23; do.	164
	Burials	25; do.	175

4 Patron The king.
5 Chapel None.
6 Lecturer A curate to assist occasionally, who is an usher to a school in the town; his name Kirkbride, not licensed. Appointed by the rector *ad libitum*.
7 Dissenters None.
8 Schools One free school for Greek and Latin, endowed by King Edward VI, vested in the corporation at £265*s.* p.a. Revd Richard Mant, master, nominated by the mayor and corporation; the number of scholars from the town 20. Independent boarders, 47 at this present.
9 Charities No hospitals. Paid by the corporation and churchwardens to the poor of both parishes, annually £20 15*s.* 2¾*d.* This is particularly specified in the enclosed copy of the return.
[Enclosing printed precept to minister and churchwardens to make their return to the parliamentary inquiry; completed in MS. as in Holy Rood parish above.]

587 Southampton, St Mary 21M65/B4/3/131–2
Newton Ogle, rector 1776–97 27 March 1788
1 Area Difficult to say with any precision, the parish being much intersected by neighbouring parishes. But by the rector's own computation from his own tythe book there cannot be much less than 1,000 acres in St Marie's infra and St Marie's extra (i.e.) on both sides of the river.
2 Population The most probable computation the rector can make is that there are about 600. NB The number of souls is of late much increased in consequence of the increase of buildings.
3 Marriages &c. In the last 7 years at a medium: marriages 14; christenings 51; burials 43.
4 Patron The Lord Bishop of Winchester.
5 Chapels One chapel (called Jesus chapel) situated on the east side of the river, consecrated September 17th, by Bishop Andrewes 1620. Now served by the Revd James Scott who was nominated to it by the late Mr Mylles of Peartree, whose predecessors built the chapel, and whose successors nominate to it. The answer to the other part of this query is hereunto annexed.
6 Lecturer The curate of Jesus Chapel above-mentioned who is licensed by the bishop of Winchester. No other except such assistance as the rector of St Marie's may have at his own church.
7 Dissenters Not more than 5 or 6 papists. No meetings except one small meeting-house belonging to Anabaptists at Romsey; who twice a year meet in it. But there are none of that persuasion resident in the parrish.
8 Schools There is no endowed school in the parish. But there have of late been 2 Sunday schools, maintained by subscription.
9 Charities There are no hospitals nor endowed charitable institutions for the benefit of the poor. But there are some annual charitable donations, an

exact account of which is contained in the copy of the return lately made to Parliament on this subject, which copy in obedience to the Bishop's order is herewith transmitted to His Lordship.

Account of the endowment of Jesus Chapel

[Addendum to answer no. 5 above]

1st. A yearly payment from Woolster Farm £1 16*s*. 3*d*.

2d. Interest of £300 Queen Anne's Bounty 4 0*s*. 0*d*.

3d. Interest of £100 given formerly by Mrs Catherine Palmer and Frances, Countess of Exeter, for which the family of the Mylles of Peartree and their successors have from time to time given a hand to the curate, paying interest 5 0*s*. 0*d*.

4th. A very good house and garden. NB part of the garden belongs to the rector of St Marie's glebe at Itchin.

5th. About 10 years ago the Governors of Queen Anne's Bounty granted £200 more on condition of the last mentioned £100 being better secured. The interest has never been received by the curate. NB The circumstances preventing this are deserving the Ordinary's enquiry. But they are points a little too obscure and intricate to be spoken to here with certainty.

[Copy of the return to parliamentary enquiry, as for Holy Rood parish above.]

588 Southampton, St Michael 21M65/B4/3/133/1–2

Robert Rooke, rector 1752–93

[Very infirm signature.]

1 Area That cannot be well ascertained as it is occupied by houses, some in one street, some in another, etc. etc.

2 Population About 1,600 souls.

3 Marriages &c.

1786 marriages 18; baptisms 37; burials 42.

1787 marriages 12; baptisms 61; burials 44.

4 Patron The king.

5 Chapels No.

6 Lecturer Yes a curate, Robert Rooke, nominated by me, licensed.

7 Dissenters No Papists. No meeting-house. Protestant dissenters called Presbyterians about 60 in number.

8 Schools No endowed school.

9 Charities No hospitals or endowed charitable institutions. The answer to the late parliamentary enquiry contains an account of the fixed annual donations to the poor of the parish — now sent.

[Reply to parliamentary inquiry included, as for Holy Rood parish.]

589 South Stoneham 21M65/B4/3/134

John Mulso, vicar 1786–1815

George Willis, curate

[Unsigned.]

1 Area Waste land 1,900 [acres]; arable and coppice 5,400; meadow 600; total 7,900.

2 Population 1,216.
3 Marriages &c. Marriages 8; births 40; burials 23.
4 Patron The Dean of Winchester.
5 Chapels None.
6 Lecturer George Willis, curate, not licensed, nominated by the Revd John Mulso, vicar.
7 Dissenters Dissenters 100. A meeting held over a coach-house belonging to Mr Taylor. Papists none.
8 Schools 2 schools for small children kept by old women, the custom of the parish to allow the sacrament money for the maintenance of them.
9 Charities No hospital. The return made to Parliament. On Hatch Farm £2 p.a. for ever.

590 South Tidworth 21M65/B4/3/135
Scrope Berdmore DD, rector 1785–98
John Selwyn, curate
1 Area About 2,000 acres.
2 Population About 100.
3 Marriages &c. Marriages seldom any; births about 2; burials about 1.
4 Patron Thomas Asheton Smith Esq.
5 Chapels None.
6 Lecturer None.
7 Dissenters None.
8 Schools None.
9 Charities There are none of either as was set forth in the return made to the parliamentary enquiry on this subject.

591 Sparsholt 21M65/B4/3/136
Richard Keats MA, vicar 1775–94
Nicholas Westcombe, curate
1 Area 12 miles in circumference, 3 in width, the same in breadth.
2 Population About 311.
3 Marriages &c. Marriages 2; births 9; burials 5.
4 Patron The king.
5 Chapels None.
6 Lecturer Nicholas Westcombe, curate. N<...[ot licensed?]>. Appointed by the Revd Richa<rd Keats>
7 Dissenters No Papists or dissenters, nor any meetings held in this parish.
8 Schools None.
9 Charities No hospital or endowed charitable institution, but 3 fixed annual donations of 5*s*. each for the use of the poor.

592 Thorley [IoW] 21M65/B4/3/184
Andrew Gother, vicar 1770–1803
1 Area A small parish, it contains about 1,300 acres.

2 Population About 143.
3 Marriages &c. On an average of the last 7 years marriages 1, births 3 and burials 3.
4 Patron Miss Gother.
5 Chapels None.
6 Lecturer None.
7 Dissenters None.
8 Schools None.
9 Charities None.

593 Thruxton 21M65/B4/3/137

John Harrington DD, rector 1772–95
1 Area About 6,000 acres.
2 Population 140.
3 Marriages &c. Marriages 2; births 0; burials 5.
4 Patron George Powlett Esq. of Amport in the county of Hants.
5 Chapels None.
6 Lecturer None.
7 Dissenters None.
8 Schools A Sundays school, kept up by a subscription. The master, John Brown. Scholars about 40.
9 Charities There is a charity belonging to the parish called Mankhorn, originally intended as a fund to build a workhouse, it pays annually £9 which is distributed by the trustees among the poor. It pays a quit rent of 11*s.* 9½*d.*

594 Titchfield 21M65/B4/3/138/1–2

Peter Taylor BD, vicar 1779–91
1 Area The length of the parish of Titchfield is about 8 miles, and its width upon a medium 4½ miles.
2 Population The number of souls, as near as I can gain information, is nearly 3,000.
3 Marriages &c. The medium of births for the last 6 years 102; of burials 61; of marriages 22.
4 Patron Peter Delmé Esq. the patron of the living.
5 Chapels There is one chapel in the parish called Crofton, which is served by myself. It is doubtful whether there is any maintenance or support for the chapel distinct from Titchfield, the mother church.
6 Lecturer There is no lecturer or curate within the parish.
7 Dissenters There are no Papists in the parish. Neither is there any meeting of protestant dissenters of any denomination and not more than 8 or 10 persons supposed to be dissenters.
8 Schools There is one school endowed with £4 p.a. by Richard Godwin for teaching 12 poor children to read the English tongue. The name of the mistress, Mary Petty, nominated by the churchwardens and overseers of the poor, who are the trustees.

9 Charities There is no hospital within the parish. There are 2 charitable institutions: the one left by the Earl of Southampton for establishing a <clothing> factory for the employment of the p<oor, th>e other left by Robert Godfrey for the relief of the poor. I have unfortunately preserved no copy of the return which I made to the late parliamentary enquiry on this subject.
Donations for the benefit of the poor in the parish of Titchfield
Robert Godfrey in 1597 left by will £11 10*s*. p.a. vested in trustees [named] for the relief of the poor of Titchfield.
Earl of Southampton in 1620 gave land now vested in trustees and yielding £31 10*s*. p.a. that trade may be renewed in the said town, for the good of the inhabitants thereof and the poor people set to work, whereby they may be the better enabled to sustain themselves and families and that the lands and tenements may be converted and employed in a stock for setting the poor of the town to work in clothing or some other good and profitable trade, which he, the said earl, conceiveth to be the best way to benefit and enrich the said inhabitants.
Richard Godwin in 1703 left by will in money secured upon land yielding £4 p.a. for teaching 12 poor children of the parish to read the English tongue.
NB The trustees of the Earl of Southampton's charity, having formerly established a manufactory, which afterwards failed; and not having as yet established any other, have in hand a sum of money from the rents of the estate, an account of which is regularly kept, and may be at any time applyed to carry on some good and profitable trade.

595 Tufton 21M65/B4/3/139
Richard Ring, vicar of Wherwell 1763–91 Whitchurch, 28 March 1788
Lloyd Williams, curate
1 Area About 6 miles.
2 Population 160.
3 Marriages &c. 5 marriages in 10 years; 3 christenings yearly; and 1 burial.
4 Patron The prebendary of Wherwell.
5 Chapels Tufton, I believe, has always been considered as a chapel of ease to Wherwell.
6 Lecturer Lloyd Williams, vicar of Whitchurch is curate, nominated by the Revd Richard Ring, vicar of Wherwell, not licensed.
7 Dissenters There are no Papists here, nor any meeting-houses.
8 Schools There is no endowed school.
9 Charities There are neither hospitals nor any donations for the poor.

596 Twyford 21M65/B4/3/140
Liscomb Maltbe Stretch, vicar 1782–1813
William Coppard, curate
[This return has suffered extensive damage.]
1 Area <Upon enq>uiry I am given to understand that the <circumference> of the parish of Twyford is 16 miles. <I do not> pretend to ascertain

this matter from my <own knowledge>, nor indeed can I take upon me to <answer the> other questions with that accuracy which <Your Lordship> may wish and expect, as I am almost <a stranger.> However Your Lordship may <accept> the information I am able to <return and> I shall hope for an opportunity <to do better> after a longer residence.
2 Population In regard to this particul<ar I have no> information whatsoever. It may <be pertinent,> however, to observe that the parish is <reckoned a> populous one.
3 Marriages &c. 3 marriages; 18 births; < > burials, at a medium.
4 Patron It is in the gift of Emm<anuel College, Cambridge.>
5 Chapels There is no chapel in the paris<h except a> popish one that belongs <to> Mr Smith.
6 Lecturer Mr Stretch is the Principal and <I> was appointed by him. Ther<e is no> lectureship, nor am I licensed to the curacy.
7 Dissenters <The family> of — Smith Esq. are the only Papists <of any> consequence, and I have no doubt but Your <L>or<dship will find they> have a priest in the house. There are 20 Papists in this parish. And I am informed there are a few protestantant dissenters, but the exact number I have not yet heard. Probably not more than 12 or 14, and those of the lower class of people. There are no meetings.
8 Schools <There is a schoo>l in this parish, the endowment of which <is a hund>red pounds vested in the funds for <te>aching the children of the poor in the mother <tongue> and arithmetick. The present master is the clerk <w>ho was nominated by the 2 trustees, viz. the <vica>r for the time being and the Revd Mr Mentz. <The number> of scholars is unlimited.
9 Charities <There> are no hospitals in this parish, nor any fixed <donat>ions for the poor, the above charity excepted. <This report> was made to the late parliamentary <enquiry and i>s not for that reason assigned in my answer <to this ques>tion.

597 Upper Clatford 21M65/B4/3/141
Thomas Willis MA, rector 1783–1830 26 February 1788
1 Area There are in this parish of Upper Clatford 2,000 acres.
2 Population It contains about 260 people.
3 Marriages &c. 10 christenings and 5 burials in a year and 2 marriages.
4 Patron My mother is the 'patroness'.
5 Chapels There is no chapel belonging to it.
6 Lecturer Nor any curate as the duty is entirely done by me.
7 Dissenters There are not more than 2 or 3 dissenters who are Presbyterians.
8 Schools [No reply.]
9 Charities There is no charitable foundation of any kind.

598 Warblington 21M65/B4/3/142
Samuel Torrent, rector 1764–89 12 February 1788
John Webster, curate
1 Area The parish of Warblington extends from east to west 2 miles, and from north to south 3 miles; and contains about <... >00acres.

2 Population About 1,200.
3 Marriages &c. Marriages 12; births 30; burials 25.
4 Patron William Nevins of Emsworth, lately purchased of the Revd R. Ramsay.
5 Chapels No chapel in the parish.
6 Lecturer I have been curate of the parish 10 years. Appointed by the Revd Mr Torrent.
7 Dissenters Number of Papists about 18. 1 Presbyterian only.
8 Schools No endowed school in the parish. 2 private schools for boys and 4 for girls. Masters William Matthews and George Barrow. Scholars to the first about 60; to the latter about 20. Mistresses Jane Prowting, Ann P<...>n, Martha Toms and Elizabeth Clewer. Scholars to the 2 first about 30 each; to the 2 last about 20 each.
9 Charities Return made to Parliament was: no charitable donation of any kind.

599 Warnford 21M65/B4/3/143
Philip Griffin LLD, rector 1771–1802 26 March 1788
1 Area According to the best information I can obtain, 12 or 13 miles.
2 Population 257.
3 Marriages &c. I hope the following copy of my parish register <for 10> years will be deemed a satisfactory answer <to> this question.

	Baptisms	Burials	Marriages
1778	7	7	2
1779	8	4	3
1780	7	7	6
1781	6	3	5
1782	7	5	3
1783	7	5	<...>
1784	9	2	3
1785	14	3	9
1786	4	5	2
1787	8	6	9
	77	47	<...>

4 Patron The Earl of Clanricarde.
5 Chapels I have no chapel.
6 Lecturer I have no curate nor lecturer.
7 Dissenters I do not know of any Papist that I have in my parish nor any dissenter of any denomination.
8 Schools I have no endowed school in my parish.
9 Charities I have no hospital nor charitable institution in the parish of Warnford. But the following of which I made a return to the parliame<ntary enquiry> I believe without keeping a copy of the same, donation is of £2 p.a., but the Land Tax being deducted at 4s. in the pound was reduced to £1 12*s*. This is paid out of an estate called Amery and was given or left by one of the family of the Knights of Chawton; but at what time I know not.

600 Weeke 21M65/B4/3/155
Charles Blackstone LLB, rector 1769–1804 13 March 1788
1 Area In down, pasture, hop-ground, and in arable land, about 782 acres.
2 Population 74.
3 Marriages &c. [Figures wanting owing to document damage.]
4 Patron The Lord Bishop of Winch<ester.>
5 Chapels None.
6 Lecturer None.
7 Dissenters None.
8 Schools None.
9 Charities <The reply I> made to the late parliamentary enquiry on the subject <of charitab>le institutions and fixed annual donations was as follows, viz.;
[Document damaged. The substance of what is left reads: — Peter of Winchester, gent. left in 1729 £100 to the minister and churchwardens of Weeke in trust for the interest to be given yearly in alms to the poor. It is now in the hands of Mr James of Weeke. At another date, uncertain, the same man gave £40 for the same purpose which is vested in the same hands]

601 West Cowes [IoW] 21M65/B4/3/171
James Hyde Gill, minister (perpetual curate) 1772– 29 March 1788
My Lord, you will receive an answer to your several questions concerning the parish of Northwood in general from the rector of the parish. The following respects the town and chapel of West Cowes in the said parish in particular.
1 Area, 2 Population The town of West Cowes stands upon a small compass of ground, but the houses are crowded and contain about 1,700 souls.
3 Marriages &c. A table of the births and burials at West Cowes for 7 years.
Births

	Males	Females	Total	Average
1781	40	30	70	
1782	22	38	60	Males 27
1783	32	34	66	
1784	18	24	42	Females 30
1785	21	34	55	
1786	35	22	57	Total average 57
1787	25	28	53	

Burials

	Males	Females	Total	Average
1781	28	16	44	
1782	17	18	35	Males 19
1783	26	25	51	
1784	14	12	26	Females 17
1785	10	19	29	
1786	13	12	25	Total average 36
1787	26	22	48	

No one has been married in the chapel of West Cowes since the Marriage

Act, though previous to the said act, marriages both by license and banns were solemnized in the said chapel to the number of 13 or 14 in a year.
4 Patron [no comment made]
5 Chapels, 6 Lecturer The chapel of West Cowes is maintained, partly by Mr Stephen's benefaction of £5 p.a. for ever; and partly by Bishop Morley's benefaction of £20 p.a. on condition that the inhabitants of West Cowes subscribe to the minister £40 p.a., and in case the inhabitants once fail to subscribe the said £40 then the bishop's benefaction of £20 is to be forfeited for ever. The right of nomination is in the subscribers, and the minister of West Cowes chapel is licensed to the same by the bishop of the diocese.
7 Dissenters There are no Papists in this town, but there are 2 meetings, the one Methodist, and the other Presbyterian, yet the advocates of each almost to a man frequent the established church, of which they were originally members.
8 Schools, 9 Charities Here are 2 Sunday schools, one for boys and the other for girls, but no endowed school or hospital in the town. As to the answers made to the late parliamentary enquiry, the rector of the parish, by whom the return was made, will inform your Lordship.

602 West Worldham 21M65/B4/3/144
Bryan Robinson, curate –1827
1 Area The compass of the parish is about 5 miles.
2 Population 90.
3 Marriages &c. Marriages none; births about 2 a year; burials about 1 a year.
4 Patron The living is held by a lease under the college of Winchester, granted for 7 years and renewed every 4 years, now leased to Edward Fisher Esq. at Compton Greenfield near Bristol.
5 Chapels None besides the church or chapel called Worldham.
6 Lecturer The curate of the parish is Bryan Robinson, who makes this return, appointed by Edward Fisher Esq., but not licensed to the same.
7 Dissenters No Papists. No meetings of protestant dissenters.
8 Schools No schools.
9 Charities No hospitals. No annual donations for the benefit of the poor.

603 Weyhill 21M65/B4/3/145
Joseph Simpson DD, rector 1756–96
[Very infirm hand.]
1 Area The parish, as I am informed, is about 7 miles round, and about 1,600 acres, some down included as I suppose.
2 Population Men 61; women 61; sons 65; daughters 66; men servants 22; maid servants 20; in all 295.

3 Marriages &c.	Births	Burials	Marriages
1781	8	7	3
1782	7	11	0
1783	4	9	2
1784	8	9	3
1785	10	9	0
1786	8	4	1
1787	6	4	2

4 Patron The Provost and Fellows of Queen's College, Oxford.
5 Chapels There is no chapel or chapels or any meeting-house in Weyhill parish.
6 Lecturer I have no lecturer or curate. I am constantly resident and do all the duty myself. A sermon every Sunday in the morning and prayers morning and afternoon, except I am occasionally desired to do duty for any neighbouring clergyman in an afternoon.
7 Dissenters No Papists. 2 Scotchmen who are supposed to be protestant dissenters. One of them is a servant and married and has children who come to church sometimes; the other is a pedlar, unmarried, who constantly attends church, but not the sacrament.
8 Schools An extract of John Read's will, date[d] 1631, so far as it related to Weyhill parish: 'I give to a schoolmaster to be chosen and continued at the will and free choice of the ministers, churchwardens and overseers of the parish of Penton and the parish of Weyhill in the county of South[amp]ton £6 p.a. for teaching all the boys in the said parish to read, write and cypher, and the girls to read, which school I desire may be <k>ept in the parish church aforesaid. I likewise give to the poor of the parish of Weyhill aforesaid 20*s*. yearly.' There is a little penny day school, kept at pleasure by a poor woman.
9 Charities An extract of the will of Richard Taunton Esq. dated 15 February, 1752. 'I give and bequeath unto the minister and churchwardens of the parish of Wey alias Weyhill aforesaid £200 upon trust that they and their successors do and shall for ever place and keep the same out at interest upon securities, and do and shall apply the yearly interest and produce thereof in buying bread to be given on Sundays to poor people of the said parish at the church there, to wit, 5*s*. every Sunday after the last day of October yearly, and so to continue as long as the said interest will hold out, in distributing which I would have the preference given to such poor persons as do not receive relief from the parish officers'. I found this money in a farmer's hand at 3%. He wanted to pay it in and the parish put it out on Andover Turnpike securities at 5%. But the Commissioners pay off that principle occasionally by casting lots and one of the said securities of £50 was drawn and we were obliged to put out the £50 at 3% till we can get more interest.

604 Wherwell 21M65/B4/3/146
Richard Ring, vicar 1763–91
[Unsigned.]
1 Area About 11 miles. [18 seems to have been written and scratched out.]

2 Population Between 4 and 500.
3 Marriages &c. 2 marriages, 14 births and 10 burials in the last 10 years.
4 Patron The prebendary of Wherwell.
5 Chapels Bullington and Tufton; [nomination in] prebendary of Wherwell.
6 Lecturer Mr Williams for Bullington and Tufton, of Whitchurch, where he lives, not a mile from Tufton and not far from Bullington.
7 Dissenters No Papist nor profest Dissenter.
8 Schools No endowed school.
9 Charities 14 christenings for 10 years and 10 burials for the same time. [This entry clearly intended for 3.]
1691 purchased of the Right Hon. John Lord [de] la Warr by Philadelphia Whitehead out of the rent of the White Lion Inn in Wherwell, the sum of 12*s*. p.a. to be paid to 12 old men and old women at Christmas yearly. This is the only memorandum of any donation in the parish of Wherwell, and is the only donation, and such [sic] was made to the parliamentary enquiry on this subject.

605 Whippingham [IoW] 21M65/B4/3/185
John Lewis, rector 1777–1802
Tovey Jolliffe, curate –1802?
1 Area Understanding that your Lordship had signified that you would be pleased to accept the estimate of the quantity of the land of the whole island as given in Sir Richard Worsley's *History*, I suspended my enquiries with respect to the quantum of my particular parish. The whole island is computed at 100,000 acres.
2 Population I undertook to procure a list of the inhabitants of the parish for the compiler of that history, and find from the inquiries that were set on foot in consequence of your Lordship's instructions, that there is no material change one way or the other. The number then amounted to 779.
3 Marriages &c. I have, at a medium, marriages 7, births 24, burials 12.
4 Patron The living is in the patronage of the Crown.
5 Chapels There is no chapel within my parish.
6 Lecturer There is no lectureship or curacy within my parish.
7 Dissenters There is no Papist in my parish. Of protestant dissenters there is one family of the Anabaptist persuasion, and one of the Presbyterian. There are no dissenters of any other denomination. A small wooden building was erected last year at East Cowes about one mile and a half from the parish church, with a view, it was said of accomodating the old and infirm. Service is performed in it by a Presbyterian minister once a day i.e. Sunday, how supported I have not been able to learn. The most part of those who frequent it are poor and unable to contribute anything, and I believe all are of the Church of England and resort thither only from a principle of conveniency.
8 Schools There is no endowed school in the parish. But the minister, churchwardens and overseers pay a part of their annual donations to a schoolmaster resident at East Cowes for the education of 10 poor children. The sum so applied is £10 per annum.

9 Charities There is no hospital or endowed charitable institution in my parish. In the copy of the return to the late parliamentary inquiry, hereunto annexed, is given an account of all the fixed annual donations.
Copy of return to the parliamentary enquiry
John Mann Esq., by will bearing date 1687/8 gave the sum of £23 p.a. to be applied first to the education and setting up of poor orphan children of East Cowes and after that to other poor children of the parish at large, and after that to the maintenance of poor, lame and impotent persons of the parish. Mr Thomas Cole by will bearing date 1725/6 gave the interest of £50 to be applied to the use of the poor children of East Cowes for their education and provision.
Mr Mann's donation was in land payable out of the fee farm rent of Lazonby Grange in the county of York. It is received of a Mr Fouquet, the sole executor of Thomas Urry Esq. who was descended from and heir to one of the trustees to the will, by the ministers, churchwardens and overseers who are charged by the said will with the application of it. The amount is £23; annual produce (after deducting land tax, £4 12*s*. and other expences amounting to £1 15*s*. 8*d*.) is £16 12*s*. 8*d*.
Mr Cole's donation is in money and the produce is paid by a Mr Hicks, executor to the last descendant of Mr Cole, to the minister and churchwardens to be by them applied as directed by his will. The amount is £1 15*s*. p.a. (the interest of £50 at 3 ½%) which is paid in without any deduction.

606 Whitchurch 21M65/B4/3/147
Lloyd Williams, vicar 1787–1819
1 Area The circuit of the parish is about 20 miles.
2 Population About 1,300.
3 Marriages &c. Taken at a medium for the last 10 years, there were 10 marriages, 30 christenings, and 23 burials annually.
4 Patron The Bishop of Winchester.
5 Chapels Freefolk chapel is served by Mr Lamb, curate of Longparish. The Master of St. Cross's Hospital nominates to it, and I believe that Joseph Portal Esq., who is the lessee, pays the curate.
6 Lecturer There is neither a lecturer nor a curate in Whitchurch.
7 Dissenters There are no Papists. About 120 Independents, 80 Anabaptists, 11 Quakers, a few Moravians. The Methodists of Mr John Wesley's persuation are very numerous, yet attend the church constantly and communicate regularly.
8 Schools There are no endowed schools.
9 Charities The underwritten is an authentic copy of the return made to the late parliamentary enquiry.
Richard Brooke in 1607 gave by will £1 to the parish church, At the same time he also gave £20 for the use of the poor.
Elizabeth Warren at date unknown gave £20 for the poor. Richard Pearce in 1610 gave by will £20 for the poor. Richard Pointer at date unknown gave by will £20 for the poor. Susan Pointer gave by will £10 for the use of the poor. NB The above £90 from the best information we have been able to

obtain, have been applied towards new pewing of the church, and building a workhouse for the poor.
Richard Wollaston in 1689 gave for c[l]oathing the poor, land producing £95 p.a. This donation is vested in several trustees, of whom Joseph Portal Esq. of Whitchurch is one.

607 Whitwell [IoW] 21M65/B4/3/186
Daniel Walsh, curate 12 March 1788
1 Area Is of a very irregular figure, and may contain about 2,000 acres.
2 Population By an account taken in 1777 contained 344 souls.
3 Marriages &c. At a medium of 7 years marriages 2 6/7, christenings 15 5/7, burials 6 5/7.
4 Patron Queen's College, Oxford.
5 Chapels No chapel. It is said to have been a chapel itself in the parish of Godshill, but on account of the separate parochial rates, is deemed a distinct parish.
6 Lecturer A curate, engaged by the vicar, not licensed.
7 Dissenters No Papist, no dissenter, a few Methodists.
8 Schools No school or endowment.
9 Charities No hospital or charitable institution.

608 Widley 21M65/B4/3/148
Charles Blackstone LLB, rector 1777–1804
Morgan Price, curate
1 Area About 10 miles.
2 Population 180.
3 Marriages &c. Marriages 2; births 7; burials 6.
4 Patron The Warden and Fellows of Winchester College.
5 Chapels None.
6 Lecturer Morgan Price is the present curate, nominated by the late rector of Widley and licensed by the late bishop. No lecturer.
7 Dissenters None.
8 Schools There is one school (but not endowed) kept by a Mr Knight, who teaches about 20 scholars.
9 Charities There are no hospitals, but Mr Taylor, late rector of Widley, left a part of £3 to buy religious books and tracts for the use of the poor.

609 Winchester, St Mary Kalendar 21M65/B4/3/150
John Monk Newbolt, rector 'of St Mary Calendre' 1779–1803
1 Area [The parish con]tains from north to south 1,335 feet; [from] east to west 450 feet.
2 Population About 315.
3 Marriages &c. The account of the marriages, births and burials <being contained in> the register belonging to St Maurice parish, and those <for ea>ch pa<rish> being particularly distinguished, I must refer your

<l>ordship to my answer of this query in number 3 of the queries respecti<ng> St Maurice.
4 Patron The Lord Bishop of Winchester.
5 Chapels None.
6 Lecturer The Revd Mr Woodburne does the oc<casiona>l d<uty and> reads the weekly prayers. He is app<ointed by the> rector but not licensed.
7 Dissenters <...> Pap<ists.> There is a meeting of protestant dissenters, <Presbyte>rians; about 8 of whom reside in this <parish;> likewise their place of worship is.
8 Schools None.
9 Charities None.

610 Winchester, St Maurice 21M65/B4/3/151
John Monk Newbolt, rector 1779–1803
1 Area <The Parish con>tains from east to west 1,170 feet; from north t<o sou>th 1,365 feet.
2 Population About 690.
3 Marriages &c. On the most exact average that can be m<ade> here, yearly in both parishes of St Maurice and St Mary Calendre: 11 marriages; 49 christenings; and 51 burials.
4 Patron The Lord Bishop of Winchester.
5 Chapels None.
6 Lecturer The Revd Mr Woodburne does <the> occas<ional> duty and reads the weekly prayer. <He was appointed> by the rector, but not licensed.
7 Dissenters 10 Roman Catholics; but no dissenters <excep>t the Methodists, who attend an house <of wo>rship in this parish; but whose numbers in <the> parish the rector has not been able to <ascer>tain.
8 Schools There is no endowed school in the parish, but one for boys and another for girls supported by voluntary contributions.
9 Charities There is a college adjoining to St John's house in this parish, founded and end<ow>ed by William Lamb Esq. in the year 1554 <for> 6 poor <...>ens widows. Each widow has an income of <...a> week, besides some apparel, and other occasional <bene>facti<ons>. There are no fixed annual donations for the <poor of> this <paris>h; but the Dean and Chapter of the church <o>f Winchester usually distribute £6 p.a. on the <... to the poor of> St Mary Calendre and St Maurice; being part of the interest of £1,100, left to them as trustees by Mr Percival, for the relief of the poor of the whole <cit>y to be dispensed according to their discretion.

611 Winchester, St Michael 21M65/B4/3/152
William Mence AM, rector of 'St Michael in the West Soke' 1756–89
31 March 1788

1 Area ¾ mile.
2 Population 335.
3 Marriages &c. 6 marriages; 12 births; 12 funerals.

4 Patron The Lord Chancellor.
5 Chapels No.
6 Lecturer No.
7 Dissenters 16 Papists. No dissenting meetings.
8 Schools 3 kept by elderly women, Mrs Barton, Mrs Hater, Mrs Prudence. No endowment. Schollars between 50 and 60.
9 Charities No hospitals or endowed charitable donation excepting a fixed annual sum of 20 guineas, lately bequeathed to this parish by Mr Samuel Kent, being the produce of £500 purchased in the 3% annuities consols, £8 of which is distributed in gowns and coates to the poor and old, the remainder in bread. The last article was the only return to the late parliamentary enquiry.

612 Winchester, St Peter Chesil 21M65/B4/3/153
Timothy Gabell, rector 'of the united parishes of St Peter and St John' 1769–1804
1 Area About 85 acres.
2 Population About 420.
3 Marriages &c. Marriages on an average of 7 years, not quite 5; births about 15; burials about 12.
4 Patron The king.
5 Chapels None.
6 Lecturer None.
7 Dissenters There are in the parish 9 Papists and 6 protestant dissenters, Presbyterians, but no meeting of any kind. 2 Quakers.
8 Schools No endowed school.
9 Charities There is no hospital, but the following fixed annual donations etc., viz.,

Paid by the town clerk of Winchester	£1 10*s*. 0*d*.
By Mr Pink	13*s*. 4*d*.
Moiety of the Shalden estate	10 0*s*. 0*d*.
By the Dean and Chapter	3 0*s*. 0*d*.

The above is the substance of the return made to Parliament, but there is no copy existing.

613 Winchester, St Thomas 21M65/B4/3/154
Henry Stevens, rector 1773–88 29 March 1788
John Woodburn BA, curate
1 Area About 150,000 square yards.
2 Population 890.
3 Marriages &c. Marriages 9; births 26; burial<s ...>
4 Patron The Lord Bishop of the diocese.
5 Chapels No chapel within the parish.
6 Lecturer I, the Revd John Woodburn, a<m curate> but was never licen<sed>.
7 Dissenters Papists 73. Presbyterians 12, but there is <no> meeting held in the parish of either the <Presbyterian or> any other protestant dissenters. On a survey made in the year 1781 by order of <t>he late lord bishop there were 67 Papists in this parish.

8 Schools No school endowed in the parish.
9 Charities A Mr Peter Simonds founded an hospital for the s<upp>ort of 6 poor men and 4 boys, each of whom <has> an allowance of 3*s*. 6*d*. per week.
Mr Percival left a benefaction to the poor of this city in general, and the sum of £3 3*s*. is usually <a>llowed every year by the Dean and Chapter out of this benefaction for the poor of this parish in particular.

I have no copy of Mr Gilbert's plan nor of the return I made to it, but the above is the substance of it.

614 Winnall 21M65/B4/3/156
John Dennis MA, rector 1769–89 28 March 1788
1 Area About 440 acres according to a calculation delivered in by a farmer who has occupied the <w>hole.
2 Population About 72.
3 Marriages &c. 1 marriage; 2 or 3 births; 2 or 3 burials.
4 Patron The Lord Bishop of Winches<ter.>
5 Chapels None.
6 Lecturer None.
7 Dissenters None.
8 Schools None.
9 Charities None. No copy of the return which was <m>ade to the late parliamentary <enqui>ry has been preserved in <th>e books belonging to the parish, <b>ut I may venture to say the <a>nswer then returned was *None*.

615 Wonston 21M65/B4/3/157
William Buller, rector 'of Wonsington' 1769–89 31 March 1788

1 Area 4820 acres.	Norton Farm	1100 [acres]
	<Cr>anbourn Up Farm	500
	<Mr?> Lowe	300
	<...>	20
	Wonston Farm	740
	Sutton	700
	Sutton Tenantry	440
	Pidgeon H[ouse] Farm	220
	Parkers	40
	Wonston Tenantry	740
	Glebe	20
		4820

2 Population 400.
3 Marriages &c. 4 marriages; 20 christenings; 11 burials.
4 Patron The Lord Bishop of Winchester.
5 Chapels None.
6 Lecturer None excepting the rector's assistant, the Revd John Knight who was ordained priest on that title about <...> years since and licensed at that time.

7 Dissenters Only one family supposed to be Anabaptists.
8 Schools A school endowed with £100 by Mr John Wickham late of Wonston Farm which July 23, 1784 was invested in £166 13*s*. 4*d*. ordinary annuities at 57 ⅜ p<ence by ...> & co. in the names of William Buller, W. and J. Wickham and W. Pern. The mistress is Sarah Twine, nominated by the executors of the said John Wickham.
9 Charities No hospitals. But it is said that Dr Sayer, late rector of Wonston, who died about the year 1718, left £30 which <remained[?]> in the hands of the farmers and the interest by them distribu<ted> once in 4 or 5 years. This sum of £30 was vested August 20, 1743 in £47 12*s*. 5*d*. ordinary annuities in the names of William Buller, W. and J. Wickham, and William Pern.

616 Wootton [IoW] 21M65/B4/3/187
Richard Walton, rector 1767–1804 29 February 1788
1 Area 971 acres.
2 Population 47.
3 Marriages &c. Only 2 marriages in the last 7 years, births 3, burials 2, one year with another.
4 Patron The present incumbent.
5 Chapels None.
6 Lecturer None.
7 Dissenters No Papists, nor meetings of protestant dissenters in the parish of Wootton.
8 Schools None.
9 Charities None. And my return to Parliament was, that we had no charitable donations of any kind in the parish of Wootton.

617 Wootton St Lawrence 21M65/B4/3/158
James Webster BA, vicar 1774–92
D. B. Thain, curate
[This report survives only in a fragment on the parish charities conveying no useful information.]

618 Wymering 21M65/B4/3/159
Charles Blackstone LLB, rector 1777–1804
Morgan Price, curate
1 Area About 12 miles.
2 Population 600 [650 crossed out.]
3 Marriages &c. Marriages 4; births 20; burials 20.
4 Patron The Warden and Fellows of Winchester College.
5 Chapels None.
6 Lecturer Morgan Price is the present curate, nominated by the late vicar of Wimering, and licensed by <the> late bishop. No lecturer.
7 Dissenters Few or none.

8 Schools There are 2 small <schools> (but not endowed) for girls kept by Mrs Alexander and Mrs Mills; the number of children is about 30.
9 Charities There are no hospitals, but there is an almshouse established in the year 1600 <b>y a Mrs Wyatt of Chidham for 4 antient poor widows, and endowed by her with £6 p.a. She also left 6*s*. 8*d*. p.a. for the repairs of the house, together with 20*s*. for the poor of Wimering. There is also a legacy left by Mr Taylor, the late vicar of Wimering of £3 p.a. for the purpose of buying <r>eligious books and tracts for the poor of the parishes of Wimering and Wid<ley> and for repairs of the forementioned almshouse.

619 Yarmouth [IoW] 21M65/B4/3/188
William Dickonson, rector 1769–94
Andrew Hamilton, curate –1796?
1 Area 46 acres.
2 Population 330 souls.
3 Marriages &c. On an average of the last 7 years, 3 marriages, 14 births, 7 burials.
4 Patron The King.
5 Chapels None.
6 Lecturer Andrew Hamilton, nominated by the Revd William Dickonson.
7 Dissenters None.
8 Schools None.
9 Charities The only donations in the parish are £10 a year to the rector, £10 a year to apprentice a parishioner's child, and £10 a year to the poor of the parish bequeathed by the late Lord Holmes.

620 Yateley 21M65/B4/3/160/1–2
John Richards, curate 1776–1802 13 March 1788
[Document severely damaged.]
1 Area <...> round <...>
2 Population <1,>200.
3 Marriages &c. [Reply wanting.]
4 Patron It is a curacy and the impropriator, John Limbrey, of Upton Grey, Esq., has the right of nomination to it.
5 Chapels There is no chapel within this parish.
6 Lecturer [Reply wanting.]
7 Dissenters [Reply wanting.]
8 Schools There is only one school in this parish. A Mrs Barker left £5 p.a. for the purpose of instructing 12 children, viz. 6 boys and 6 girls, the boys to be instructed in reading only, but the girls in reading, knitting and plain work. The present mistress of this school is Elizabeth Searl, <who> was nominated by the trustee to the will of the said Mrs Barker.
9 Charities [Much of reply wanting; list of annual donations returned to the parliamentary enquiry on separate sheet.]

Donations for the benefit of the poor of Yately
Peter Smith gave by will 6 July 1670 £6 15*s*. p.a. chargeable upon an estate at Finchampstead, Berks.
Sir Richard Ryves Kt. Alderman of London left £3 10*s*. charged upon houses and land.
[Mrs Barker in 1706 created the educational charity described in 8.]
Mrs Ann Shorter, widow, left 10*s*. p.a. to be laid out in bread and given to the poor of the out-tything of Cove in this parish. This sum is charged upon a house and garden at Farnham in Surrey. Mrs Shorter's will bears date in 1763.
[Total in charities, £15 15*s*. p.a.]

621 Yaverland [IoW] 21M65/B4/3/189
Heneage Robinson, rector 1772–99 17 March 1788
Thomas Waterworth, curate –1790
1 Area [No reply.]
2 Population [No reply.]
3 Marriages &c. The marriages at a medium for the last 7 years are one with another 1; baptisms 4 4/7; burials at the mother church of Brading.
4 Patron The patron Mrs Mary Wright a maiden lady.
5 Chapels No chapel within the parish.
6 Lecturer The vicar of Brading serves the cure at present to which he was nominated by the Revd Heaneage Robinson the rector. Is not licensed to the same.
7 Dissenters No Papist or protestant dissenter.
8 Schools No endowed school.
9 Charities No charitable donation belonging to the parish.

Notes

1. A donative is a spiritual preferment which is in the free gift or collation of the patron without making any presentation to the bishop, and without admission, institution or induction by any mandate from the bishop.
2. Glebe was land assigned for the maintenance of a parish priest, originally including the parsonage-house, and, at one time, the indispensable condition for the consecration of a church. After his induction the parson had the freehold, but in the eighteenth century might not alienate it.
3. In law a park was an enclosed tract of land held by royal grant or prescription for keeping beasts of the chase. Being 'disparked' this piece of land was no longer enclosed, but had not acquired liability to tithe.
4. A modus, or *modus decimandi*, was a voluntary composition for the payment of tithe, whereby (as here) a fixed sum of money or fixed quantity of titheable produce was taken by the tithe-owner instead of the literal tithe of the produce of the property.
5. Robert Boreman *The Countryman's Catechism: or the Churches' plea for Tithes. Wherein is plainly discovered the duty and dignity of Christ's ministers and the people's duty to them* (London, 1652). The last section pp. 30–32 is 'A catalogue of benefactors and restorers of impropriations to the Church'. Of Sir William Dodington it is said 'The memory of the righteous is blessed for evermore.'
6. A close was simply an enclosed space which might or might not be near a building.
7. There was originally a distinction between 'appropriation', the transfer of some form ecclesiastical benefice to a monastery or other church party, and 'impropriation' where the new holder was a layman. But great numbers of parishes were appropriated to religious houses in the Middle Ages, and many of these endowments fetched up in lay hands after the dissolution. Hence in the eighteenth century Burn remarked that 'the words are generally used promiscuously' (R. Burn *Ecclesiastical Law* (London, 1763) i, p. 614). After impropriation, the lay rector took the great (or corn-) tithes.
8. This was already a somewhat archaic equivalent for a dwelling-house or manse.
9. The yardland was a square measure, varying locally, but commonly equal to 30 acres.
10. A rack-renter paid the full, or almost the full, commercial value of his land, as distinct from the lower annual rents of holders of beneficial leases. He also had less security than a freeholder, copyholder, or holder of a lease for 21 years or 3 lives.
11. 'The right of advowson, tho' appendant to a manor, castle or the like, may be severed from it; and being severed, is become an advowson in gross' (Burn, *Ecclesiastical Law* i, p. 5). William Hughes *The Parson's Law collected out of the whole body of the common law and some late reports* (London, 1641 and 2 later eds.) discusses in ch. 8 the

presentation to benefices with cure, who may be presented, and the conditions under which the bishop may refuse. Page 62 says that the presentation must be to the bishop unless the see is vacant, or the bishop is away on the business of king and state, in which case the presentation must be to the guardian of the spiritualities, commonly the dean and chapter or the vicar-general.

12. Under the act of 30 Charles II st.1 c.3 it was required 'for the encouragement of the woollen manufactures and prevention of the exportation of money for the importing of linen', that no one be buried in a shroud 'other than what is made of sheep's wool only', and the same applied to the coffin lining. Relatives of the deceased must bring an affidavit (sworn before the magistrate) to this effect to the parish priest within 8 days. Where this was not done the minister must give notice to the magistrate to impose a fine of £5. The form of the affidavit is given in Burn *Ecclesiastical Law* i, p. 91.
13. A noble was a gold coin first minted by Edward III which had a current value of 6*s*. 8*d*.
14. In 1704 Queen Anne surrendered the papal revenues annexed by Henry VIII (annates and tenths) to the church, principally to augment small livings by grants of capital. One of the devices used by the governors of the Bounty to promote this work was to promise matching grants to poor parishes where patrons and other benefactors produced standard capital augmentations from private sources.
15. A measure of length varying in different countries. The English ell was 45 inches.
16. A contribution, originally in kind, but after the thirteenth century in money, paid by incumbents to an ordinary in visitation, as an equivalent for providing him and his train with hospitality during the visitation. J.S.Purvis *Dictionary of Ecclesiastical Terms* (Edinburgh, 1962) p. 157.
17. A tithing was originally a company of 10 households in the system of frankpledge; then a tenth part of a hundred; but at this time simply a rural division.
18. Cf. the neighbouring parish of Longparish, below no. 133.
19. On the difference between appropriation and impropriation see n. 7 above.
20. 'Let the just judge'.
21. A clue to the economy of these responses may be afforded by the frailty of the handwriting.
22. But see Greywell, below.
23. Since, even during the civil wars, a full system of presbyterian church government by a hierarchy of committees had been established in few places, the most obvious difference between presbyterianism and the congregational polity favoured by the Independents who came off the same Calvinist stem, had been much obscured. Presbyterians had tended, however, to favour the reconstruction of a comprehensive religious establishment, while the Independents favoured toleration alongside the existing establishment.

24. Church and college property in the eighteenth century was generally let, not at a commercial rack-rent, but on beneficial leases. One of the common forms of these was a lease, the duration of which was determined by the life of three named tenants. In addition to a small annual rent, a fine was due for the renewal of the lease (and the insertion of a new name) at the expiry of each of the named lives. This system (which was not wound up till the third quarter of the nineteenth century) meant that church dignitaries benefited from their revenues at unpredictable intervals, drained the church's wealth by spending in advance what what should have been invested at compound interest till the next fine fell due, and, by continually renewing the leases, forfeited control over the church's property.
25. The best-known peculiars were those which were exempt from the jurisdiction of the ordinary, in the first instance royal free-chapels, and, in the second, the peculiars of archbishops or bishops in which they had the right to exercise jurisdiction in parishes where they had property outside their diocese. (There were several Canterbury peculiars in the archdeaconry of Surrey). In this and a number of other cases, where the ordinary is exercising jurisdiction within his see, the peculiar is of a third kind, in which it is the jurisdiction of the archdeacon which is excluded. These included churches of former religious orders where archdeacons had never had jurisdiction, but also cases where the bishop had reserved jurisdiction to himself. In these cases the bishop not only had, or had formerly had, property in the parish, but also the patronage as well. Burn *Ecclesiastical Law* ii, pp. 139–40.
26. A mark was a denomination of currency, originally representing a mark weight of pure silver. In England this was 13*s*. 4*d*. or two-thirds of the £ sterling.
27. In 1567 a body of Walloons which had fled the Netherlands to escape the Inquisition, petitioned for leave to settle in Southampton, and to have a church assigned to them for their use. Mayor, Queen and bishop concurred, as did Queen's College, Oxford, the patron of St Julian's or God's House. The registers of the congregation thus established have been published to dates far down the eighteenth century (*Registre de l'Eglise Wallonne de Southampton* ed. H.M.Godfroy (Huguenot Society Publications 4; 1890). In 1712, this congregation, or much of it, conformed to the Church of England. Its first baptism 'suivant la Liturgie Anglicane' was on 21 April 1712. *Hampshire VCH* ii, 75.
28. A sequestrator is a person appointed or commissioned by a bishop to manage the affairs, particularly financial, of a parish during a vacancy; he holds the fruits in the interests of the benefice, and after paying necessary expenses during the vacancy, hands over the balance to the next incumbent, thus acting as the agent or bailiff of the bishop. Purvis *Dictionary of Ecclesiastical Terms* p. 177.
29. A union represents the joining together of two parishes each with its own parish church. Nearness, lack of inhabitants and poverty (as here), are common reasons for union. No change is made in the advowsons or the obligation of parishes to maintain their church, but after union they

are so much one that (again as here) another parish may be held in plurality with them, and union is often followed by the demolition of one of the churches, or its conversion to a chapel of ease, or some other purpose. In this union St John's church was demolished, the changes being sanctioned by a special act in the reign of Charles II. *The Southampton Guide* (Southampton, 1805) p. 19.

30. I.e. John Ponet, Bishop of Winchester 1551–6.
31. This was James Craggs the younger (1686–1721), southern secretary of state, 1718–21. By a short margin he predeceased his father (of the same name, postmaster-general) who amassed a great fortune and was deprived of part of it under a special act to compensate the victims of the South Sea Bubble.
32. This word [litten] which does not appear in the *OED*, is defined in Wright's *Dialect Dictionary* as a churchyard, cemetery or burial ground.
33. Fee farm was a tenure in which the land was held in fee-simple (or absolute possession) subject to a perpetual fixed rent.
34. In its modern sense a quit-rent was simply a charge upon an estate for some special purpose.
35. On Queen Anne's Bounty, see note 14 above.
36. The English groat coined in 1351–2 was equal to four pence. It ceased to be issued for circulation in 1662.
37. John Ecton (d.1730), a native of Winchester, was employed in the first-fruits department of Queen Anne's Bounty, and gained an unrivalled knowledge of the old valuations of livings which it was the purpose of the Bounty to augment. The work here referred to is his *Liber Valorum et Decimarum; being an Account of the Valuations and Yearly Tenths of all such Ecclesiastical Benefices in England and Wales as now stand chargeable with the Payment of First-Fruits and Tenths* (London, 1711). This work proved so useful in the eighteenth century that it went through seven further editions, was enlarged by Browne Willis, and pirated by John Bacon. Here an appeal is made to its record of a tithe composition in lieu of a formal record of parish property.
38. Like other local parishes the advowson of Leckford belonged to a prebend which was itself in lay gift. Here a copy of the terrier had been lodged with each of the patrons, cf. no. 128 above.
39. A presentment is the reply given by the incumbent or churchwardens or both to the questions put by a visitor in a visitation, the replies forming the basis of the visitor's injunctions. The legal point of this presentment is thus explained by Burn: 'In all churches within the realm of England, convenient and decent tables are provided and placed for the celebration of the holy communion; we appoint that the same tables shall from time to time be kept and repaired in sufficient and seemly manner, and covered in the time of divine service with a carpet of silk or other decent stuff, thought meet by the ordinary of the place (if any question be made of it), and with a fair linen cloth at the time of ministration, as becometh that table...*And all this to be done at the charge of the parish*' [Editor's emphasis]. Burn, *Ecclesiastical Law* i, 260.

40. William Mitford of Exbury was actually MP for Newport 1785–90, Bere Alston 1796–1806, and New Romney 1812–18. He wrote a *History of Greece* (1785–1810) of some celebrity.
41. Robert Sandeman of Perth (1718–71) early came under the religious influence of John Glas (1695–73) and in 1737 married his daughter. Glas was a minister of the Scottish establishment who turned against the right of the civil authority to interfere in religious matters and against the obligation of national covenants, and was deposed. He introduced various practices such as the kiss of peace and the agape on grounds of apostolic authority. Sandeman brought Glas's ways to London and to New England, and the community normally known as Glassite in Scotland, has been commonly called Sandemanian in England and America.
42. The dramatic circumstances in which Henry Norman parted company from his parish are best narrated in the *ipsissima verba* of his brother's obituary. '27 March 1788 [died] Revd William Norman, rector of Bledon. co. Somerset. As he was sitting at supper (on the 25th) with a friend, he observed his brother, the Revd Henry N., take a large knife from the case, and go out into the kitchen. He immediately called to the servant to take it from him, which, through fear, he omitted to do. Soon after, Henry returned to the parlour, with the knife concealed under his coat, and, unobserved by his brother, came behind him and stabbed him twice. The unfortunate gentleman lay in the greatest agonies of pain till the morning of the 27th when he expired. The wretched perpetrator of this horrid act is rector of Morsted near Winchester; and having been some time since deranged in his intellect, was removed to his brother's at Bledon, for security, and in August last appeared in a more serene state than for some years before. He therefore had greater liberties allowed him, and the tragic event happened as above related. The unhappy maniac, we are told, being asked by his servant when he should return home, gave for answer, "as, soon as he had killed his brother". No notice, however, was taken of this. He has since been confined to a private madhouse.' *Gentleman's Magazine* 1788 ii, 935–6.

Appendix

Hampshire Parishes in the Eighteenth Century (by deanery)

Alresford Deanery
Abbotstone and Itchen Stoke
Avington
Bighton
Bishops Sutton, with Ropley chapel
Bradley
Bramdean
Brown Candover, with Woodmancott chapel
Cheriton, with Kilmeston and Tichborne chapels
Chilton Candover
Easton
Hinton Ampner
Itchen Abbas
Kings Worthy
Martyr Worthy
Old Alresford, with Medstead and New Alresford chapels
Ovington
Preston Candover, with Nutley chapel
Swarraton
West Tisted
Wield

Alton Deanery
Alton, with Binsted, Holybourne and Kingsley chapels
Bentworth
Bentley
Bramshott
Chawton
Colemore, with Priors Dean chapel
East Tisted
East Worldham
Empshott

Farringdon
Froyle
Greatham
Hartley Mauditt
Headley
Lasham
Liss
Newton Valence, with Hawkley chapel
Selborne
Shalden
West Worldham

Andover Deanery
Abbotts Ann
Amport, with Appleshaw chapel
Andover, with Foxcott chapel
Burghclere, with Newtown chapel
Combe
Crux Easton
East Woodhay, with Ashmansworth chapel
Faccombe, with Tangley chapel
Fyfield
Goodworth Clatford
Grateley
Highclere
Hurstbourne Priors, with St Mary Bourne chapel
Hurstbourne Tarrant, with Vernham Dean chapel
Kimpton
Knights Enham (Enham)
Linkenholt
Litchfield *alias* Ludshelf
Longparish *alias* Middleton
Monxton
Nether Wallop
Over Wallop
Penton Mewsey
Quarley
Shipton Bellinger
South Tidworth
Thruxton
Upper Clatford
Weyhill
Wherwell, with Bullington and Tufton chapels
Whitchurch, with Freefolk chapel
Woodcott

Basingstoke Deanery
Aldershot

Ashe
Basingstoke, with Old Basing (Basing) and Up Nately chapels
Baughurst
Bramley
Church Oakley
Cliddesden and Farleigh Wallop
Crondall
Deane
Dogmersfield
Dummer
Eastrop
Ellisfield
Elvetham
Eversley
Ewhurst
Farnborough
Hannington
Hartley Wespall
Hartley Wintney
Heckfield, with Mattingley chapel
Herriard
Kingsclere, with Ecchinswell and Sydmonton chapels
Laverstoke
Long Sutton
Monk Sherborne
Nately Scures
Newnham, with Mapledurwell chapel
North Waltham
Odiham, with Greywell chapel
Overton, with Tadley chapel
Pamber
Rotherwick
Sherborne St John
Sherfield on Loddon
Silchester
South Warnborough
Steventon
Stratfield Saye
Stratfield Turgis
Tunworth
Upton Grey
Weston Patrick
Winchfield
Winslade
Wolverton
Wootton St Lawrence
Worting
Yateley

Droxford Deanery
Alverstoke, with Gosport chapel
Bedhampton
Bishops Waltham
Blendworth
Boarhunt
Buriton, with Petersfield chapel
Catherington
Chalton, with Idsworth chapel
Clanfield
Corhampton
Droxford
East Meon, with Froxfield and Steep chapels
Exton
Fareham
Farlington
Hambledon
Havant
Hayling South, with Hayling North chapel
Meonstoke, with Soberton chapel
Portchester
Portsea
  St George's Chapel
Portsmouth
Rowner
Soberton
Southwick
Titchfield, with Crofton chapel
Upham, with Durley chapel
Warblington
Warnford
West Meon, with Privett chapel
Wickham
Widley and Wymering

Fordingbridge Deanery
Boldre, with Brockenhurst and Lymington chapels
Breamore
Christchurch, with Holdenhurst chapel
Ellingham
Fordingbridge, with Ibsley chapel
Hale
Milford, with Hordle and Milton chapels
Minstead, with Lyndhurst chapel
Ringwood, with Harbridge chapel
Rockbourne
Sopley
South Charford

Whitsbury

Isle Of Wight Deanery
Arreton
Binstead
Bonchurch, with Shanklin chapel
Brading
Brighstone *alias* Brixton
Brook
Calbourne
Carisbrooke and Northwood, with Newport chapel
Chale
Freshwater
Gatcombe
Godshill
Kingston
Mottiston and Shorwell
Newchurch
Niton
St Helens
St Lawrence
Shalfleet
Thorley
West Cowes
Whippingham
Whitwell
Wootton
Yarmouth
Yaverland

Somborne Deanery
Ashley
Barton Stacey
Broughton, with Bossington chapel
Chilbolton
East Tytherley
East Wellow
Eldon
Houghton
Kings Somborne, with Little Somborne and Stockbridge chapels
Leckford
Longstock
Micheldever, with East Stratton, Northington and Popham chapels
Michelmersh
Mottisfont, with East Dean and Lockerley chapels
Romsey
Sherfield English
Stoke Charity

Timsbury
West Tytherley
Wonston

Southampton Deanery
Beaulieu
Botley
Chilworth
Dibden
Eling, with Ower chapel
Fawley, with Exbury chapel
Hound, with Bursledon and Hamble chapels
Millbrook
North Baddesley
North Stoneham
Nursling
Southampton, All Saints
  Holy Rood
  St Laurence with St John
  St Mary, with Jesus chapel
  St Michael
South Stoneham

Winchester Deanery
Bishopstoke
Chilcomb
Compton
Crawley, with Hunton chapel
Farley Chamberlayne
Headbourne Worthy
Hursley, with Otterbourne chapel
Lainston
Littleton
Morestead
Sparsholt
Twyford, with Owslebury chapel
Weeke
Winchester, St Bartholomew Hyde
  St Faith
  St John
  St Lawrence
  St Michael
  St Maurice with St Mary Kalendar
  St Peter Chesil
  St Swithin
  St Thomas with St Clement
Winnall

Index

Small Roman numerals refer to pages of the Introduction; Arabic numerals refer to the sequence of visitation returns.

HAMPSHIRE RECORD SERIES

SUBSCRIBERS

Subscribers to the Hampshire Record Series do not pay a regular subscription but undertake to buy each book, at a reduced price, when it appears. They are also able to buy earlier volumes at reduced prices. Further details of Hampshire Record Series volumes are available from Hampshire Record Office, Sussex Street, Winchester, Hants SO23 8TH (tel. 01962 846154).

Personal subscribers

Mrs B. Acheson, 19 Dell Road, Bitterne Park, Southampton, Hants, SO2 4QT
Mrs E. Albery, PO Box 71, Penguin, Tasmania, 7316
Miss P. M. Andrews, 45 Hillmead Gardens, Bedhampton, Havant, Hants, PO9 3NN
Mr A. E. Baker, Close Court, The Close, Ringwood, Hants, BH24 1LA
Mr D. B. Beckel, 3884 Lewister Road, North Vancouver, BC, Canada, V7R 4C3
Mrs C. Bethune, All Saints Cottage, Queens Road, Alton, Hants, GU34 1HU
Professor M. Biddle, Hertford College, Oxford, OX1 3BW
Mrs S. Bond, 14 Lanark Close, Ealing, London, W5 1SN
Mr J. W. M. Brown, 294 Spring Road, Sholing, Southampton, Hants, SO2 7NX
Mr C. D. Chalmers, 24 Waldens Park Road, Horsell, Woking, Surrey
Mr G. W. Clewer, 5 Mann Close, Whitchurch, Hants, RG28 7LB
Mrs D. K. Coldicott, Mill Pound Cottage, Monxton, Andover, Hants, SP11 8AW
Dr S. J. J. Corcoran, 30 Knowsley Road, Cosham, Portsmouth, Hants, PO6 2PF
Mr C. N. Cornes, 80 Coombe Road, Croydon, Surrey, CR0 5RA
Mr A. L. T. Davies, Albany Cottage, West Street, Odiham, Hants
Mr C. H. Donnithorne, 3 The Avenue, Alverstoke, Gosport, Hants, PO12 2JS
Mr M. Drummond, Cadland House, Fawley, Southampton, Hants
Mr S. R. Dumper, 5 Elder Grove, Crediton, Devon, EX17 1DE
Mr S. Dunford, 140 Crabble Hill, Dover, Kent, CT17 0SA

Mrs J. Hagens, 7 Leybourne Dell, Benenden, Cranbrook, Kent, TN17 4EA
Mr R. H. Hall, Flat 1, Gannet House, 5 Eastern Parade, Southsea, Hants, PO4 9RA
Mr M. R. Hickman, 184 Surrenden Road, Brighton, BN1 6NN
Professor M. Hicks, King Alfred's College, Sparkford Road, Winchester, SO22 4NR
Miss C. J. Humphreys, Flat 7, The Weirs, Chesil Street, Winchester, SO23 8HX
Mr and Mrs J. Ide, Karingal, Stewart Road, Emerald, Victoria, 3782 Australia
Mr J. Isherwood, Chalcot, Penton Mewsey, Andover, Hants, SP11 0RQ
Dr T. B. James, King Alfred's College, Sparkford Road, Winchester, SO22 4NR
Mr J. James, 3 Sylvan Close, Hordle, Lymington, Hants, SO41 0HJ
Mrs I. Jeffreys, 18 Roundwood Gardens, Harpenden, Herts, AL5 3AJ
Dr J. Lane, Heirweg 27, 6243 AC Geulle, The Netherlands
Miss S. J. Lewin, 21 Greenhill Road, Winchester, SO22 5EE
Mr G. J. Linter, 19 Anson Road, Goring By Sea, West Sussex, BN12 6JB
Mrs G. M. Lowe, 26 Frankland Road, Croxley Green, Rickmansworth, Herts, WD3 3AU
Mr D. E. Lowman, 6 Cranford Gardens, Millersdale, Chandlers Ford, Hants, SO5 1PU
Mr J. Lunn, 2 Florence Road, Fleet, Hants
Mr W. J. Marsh, 68 Mulvagh Avenue, Nepean, Ontario, Canada, K2E 6M6
Mr T. M. Matthews, 18 Mandhill Close, Grove, near Wantage, Oxon, OX12 7HY
Mr R. A. Merson, Tanyard House, 13a Bridge Square, Farnham, Surrey, GU9 7QR
Mr M. A. Pinhorn, Norman's Place, Newbridge Road, Calbourne, Newport, Isle of Wight, PO30 4QR
Mrs C. Riddell, 48 Common Lane, Tickhill, Doncaster, DN11 9UN
Mrs M. Riglar, 614 Kenton Lane, Harrow, Middlesex, HA3 7LG
Mr P. Roberts, 110 Woodlands Road, Ashurst, Southampton, Hants
Mrs E. Smith, 5 Hillmead Gardens, Bedhampton, Havant, Hants, PO9 3NL
Mr R. Snudden, 9 Bury Court, Stone Street, Cambridge, CB1 2RX
Mr G. Soffe, 26 Bromsgrove Cottages, Faringdon, Oxon, SN17 7JQ
Mr D. J. Stagg, 6 Alpine Road, Ashurst, Southampton, Hants, SO4 2AN
Mr P. Stevenage, 16 Wychperry Road, Haywards Heath, Sussex
Mr C. P. Stone, 55 Marlborough Road, Exeter, Devon, EX2 4LN
Mr D. J. Swindell, 9 Laurence Court, Ludgershall, Andover, Hants, SP11 9QN
Mrs J. Thorp, Ridgewood Grange, Chilton Road, Upton, Didcot, Oxfordshire, OX11 9JL
Mr J. Townsend, 95 Arbor Lane, Winnersh, Wokingham, Berks, RG11 5JE
Mr A. Webb, 6 Roseberry Street, Taunton, Somerset, TA2 6NF
Miss P. White, 3 St Mary's Road, Liss, Hants, GU33 7AH
Miss J. A. Williamson, 6 Heather Close, Walkford, Christchurch, Dorset, BH23 5RP

Institutional subscribers

Great Britain

Aberystwyth, National Library of Wales (copyright library)
Birmingham Public Libraries
Birmingham University Library
Cambridge University Library (copyright library)
Colchester, Essex University Library
Edinburgh, National Library of Scotland (copyright library)
Leicester University Library
London, British Library (copyright library)
London, Guildhall Library
London, Institute of Historical Research
London, Lambeth Palace Library
London, London Library
London, Public Record Office
London, Royal Historical Society
London, Society of Antiquaries of London
Newport, Isle of Wight County Reference Library
Oxford, Bodleian Library (copyright library)
Portsmouth City Records Office
Southampton, Hartley Library, University of Southampton
Winchester, King Alfred's College Library
Winchester, Hampshire County Library
Winchester, Hampshire Record Office
York, Borthwick Institute

Overseas

Barr Smith Library, University of Adelaide, Australia
Boole Library, University College, Cork, Ireland
Dalhousie University Library, Nova Scotia, Canada
New England Historic Genealogical Society, Boston, United States of America